D0742965

SHORELINE AND SEXTANT

Practical Coastal Navigation

SHORELINE AND SEXTANT

Practical Coastal Navigation

John P. Budlong

VNR VAN NOSTRAND REINHOLD COMPANY
NEW YORK CINCINNATI ATLANTA DALLAS SAN FRANCISCO
LONDON TORONTO MELBOURNE

Van Nostrand Reinhold Company Regional Offices:
New York Cincinnati Atlanta Dallas San Francisco

Van Nostrand Reinhold Company International Offices:
London Toronto Melbourne

Library of Congress Catalog Card Number: 76-52451
ISBN: 0-442-21142-2

Manufactured in the United States of America

Published by Van Nostrand Reinhold Company
450 West 33rd Street, New York, N.Y. 10001

Published simultaneously in Canada by Van Nostrand Reinhold Ltd.

15 14 13 12 11 10 9 8 7 6 5 4 3 2 1

Library of Congress Cataloging in Publication Data

Budlong, John P 1942-
Shoreline and sextant.

1. Navigation. I. Title.
VK559.B854 1977 623.89 76-52451
ISBN 0-442-21142-2

CONTENTS

1: Introduction

There is no part even of the open sea that is entirely foolproof, but the difficulties of navigation are always intensified when there is land.

Alan Villiers, Cruise of the Conrad

Piloting—the art of navigating within sight of land—has a lot in common with screwdrivers and bicycles.

First, about the screwdrivers. A good friend of mine collects screwdrivers, not to look at, like a coin collection, but to use. When he does a job, his first move is to pick the screwdriver that fits. If there isn't one that fits, he files another until it does. Piloting is like that. You have a whole collection of methods and techniques. The trick lies in picking the method that fits the situation.

Most people think that celestial navigation, out of sight of land, is a complicated operation. It's not. It really boils down to an established routine, which you can follow even if you don't understand it. *And there is lots of time.* But when you're picking your way between islands and past reefs, or into an unfamiliar harbor where the buoy lights are lost amongst neon signs, time is short and decisions have immediate consequences.

Accuracy is another matter. The offshore navigator, a thousand miles from land, is content if his calculations come within five miles of the truth. He's resigned if poor conditions lead to ten mile errors, pleased with two mile accuracy, and elated if wibbles cancel wobbles within one mile. The coastal pilot, on the other hand, may need to know his position within a tenth of a mile. And if he spends five minutes working it out, he knows where he was, but not where he is.

There is great range in the degree of sophistication used in piloting. On the one hand, there's the casual, day sailor who figures that as long as he can see the ol' whatchamaycallit lighthouse, he can still make it back to town before the beer store closes. At the other extreme, a skilled pilot in a narrow channel can allow for the number of yards his ship moves forward, while making a 30 degree turn at 6.5 knots.

The aim of this book is to present some of the more practical and useful techniques that can be used by any navigator in any size of craft. Some of these techniques are as old as the art of piloting, which itself is much older than celestial navigation. Others are new. The recent introduction of inexpensive plastic sextants has been a blessing, not only to the offshore navigator, but also to the coastal pilot. A good portion of piloting work depends on measuring angles, and as the title of this book suggests, a sextant is admirably suited to the job. The numerous uses of a sextant are covered in one entire chapter, and in parts of others. Advice on choosing and adjusting a sextant is also included.

All of the methods have been tried and proven, and are included for their practical utility. Most of the explanations and example problems have been used, and hopefully refined, in courses on piloting conducted by the author.

Now, about the bicycles. Watching somebody else ride one won't help you learn to balance. And so with chartwork, which is synonymous with piloting—the only way to learn it is to do it. For the many examples and practice problems in this book, a practice chart is provided as a loose insert. It was laid out with exercise work in mind, and incorporates actual features and names from about a dozen standard navigational charts. The compass rose shows a variation of 23° 30′ E, which is typical of Canada's west coast. The latitude and longitude are entirely fictitious, having been chosen to give a convenient proportion for the grid.

I suggest that you make several dozen photocopies, and use them for working the individual problems. Then you can keep them for reference. It should also be quite a satisfaction to compare your first attempts with later work, and see the improvement in your technique.

Happy plotting and good sailing!

2: *Tools of the Trade*

We measured our longitudinal progress by "dead reckoning," or by estimating how many miles we had moved in a day's time. We clocked Nina's speed by throwing a chip of wood into the water at the bow and timing it until it reached the stern.

Robert Marx, The Voyage of the Nina II

The offshore sailor, using celestial navigation, works with only a few basic instruments. In contrast, the coastal pilot usually has quite an array of tools to work with, because he uses quite an array of techniques. His tools range in importance from the absolutely essential to the optional conveniences, and any given item is usually available in several types or styles. This chapter covers the more commonly used instruments, with some tips and pointers on each.

Basic equipment, which should be found aboard any well equipped craft, would include the following:

Compass
Charts and publications
Chart table
Dividers }
Protractor } or Douglass protractor
Parallel rule }
Stopwatch
Speed log
Hand-bearing compass
Sextant
Lead line or depth sounder
Binoculars
Slide rule
Lights

The compass is such an essential device that a whole chapter is devoted to it. The same is true of charts and publications. The other items are covered in this chapter; if you're surprised to see a sextant on the list, read on.

CHART TABLE

Since piloting and chartwork are inseparable companions, you should provide yourself with a good chart table. On larger boats this is usually no problem, though it's worth taking the trouble to be sure that the table is sturdily built; in a heavy seaway, you will often find yourself hanging onto it for support. It should have a raised edge around it to keep things from sliding off. If you do any night sailing, an overhead light will also be a necessity. Two other very useful features you should include are a drawer located under the table, to hold the various smaller items, and a nearby book rack.

Some means of holding the chart flat and still is also needed, especially if you store your charts rolled up (see below). Chunks of lead are often used, and you can buy fancy brass weights if you don't mind the price. Leather bags filled with lead shot work very well, and can be bought at drafting supply stores for a couple of dollars each. Another favorite standby is masking tape.

In a small boat, where there is no room for installing a permanent table, you should at least provide something temporary. Almost any arrangement is better than none. If you've ever tried to lay off a course with a chart in your lap, while a frisky wind does its best to carry the chart overboard, you'll know what I mean. One possibility is to tape the chart around a piece of plywood, business side out.

Charts have to be stored, and there are two schools of thought about this—the rollers and the folders. Both sides defend their favorite method bitterly. Folded charts can be stored easily, in drawers or under seat cushions. They're also more civil to use, *until* the critical buoy you're looking for gets lost on the fold. Rolled charts can be stored in a rack attached to the cabin top, or under the chart table, or in other cunning spots you may find. Four inch plastic pipe (the lighter weight DWV type) makes a good holder. An advantage of rolling is that the charts aren't marred. Moreover, one roll will hold a great number of charts.

DIVIDERS

These are necessary for measuring distances on the chart. A runaway pair is also unbeatable for skewering your foot, for which reason it's customary to push a cork over the points when they're not in use. Just about any pair you can come by will do, but we might note in passing that there is an "English" type. The advantage is supposed to be that you can use them with one hand, but I can use plain dividers with one hand anyway, and the price is about half.

PROTRACTOR

You should have a fairly large one for measuring courses on the chart. The ordinary plastic ones work well. You can also get fancier versions which are easier to use. The well-known Hoey plotter is one of these. Another version—my favorite—is the Douglass protractor, which rates a separate section.

PARALLEL RULE

It you've ever watched a navigator at work, you'll remember these. The traditional form has two parallel blades which are joined by swinging links, and move crabwise across the chart. Their most frequent use is in the transferring of courses to or from the compass rose. Another type of rule has a single blade, with a central roller built in. This type can be operated with one hand, moving from one place to another with a single push. It really does work, though it may take a certain amount of faith at first.

Figure 2-1 shows standard dividers, protractor, and parallel rule.

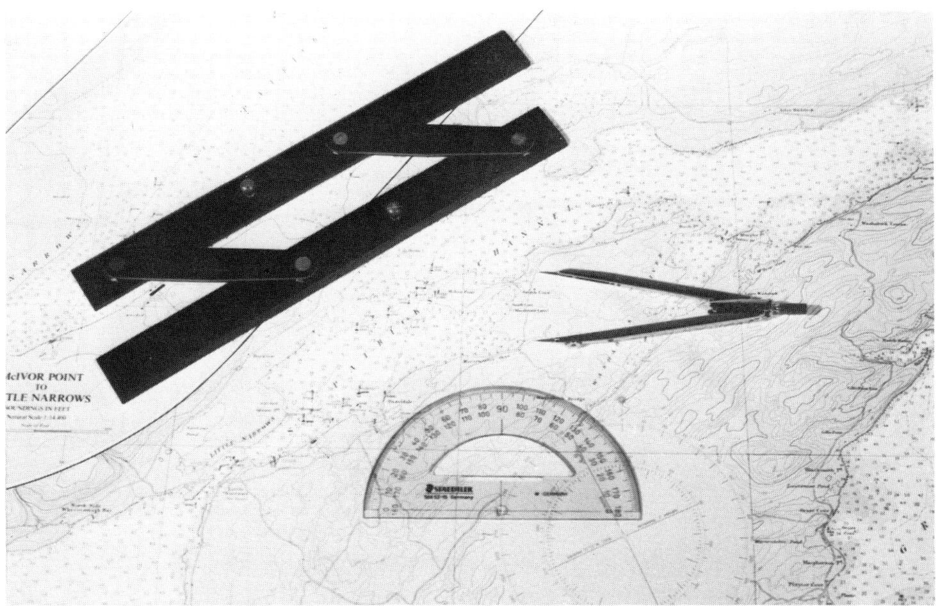

Figure 2-1 Dividers, protractor, and parallel rule are used for chart work.

DOUGLASS PROTRACTOR

This device is so useful that I wouldn't sail without one. It replaces dividers, protractor, and parallel rule with less cost and more convenience. That's a hard combination to beat. It's a square piece of transparent plastic, with a lined grid and degree scales marked around its edge. The surface is slightly frosted, to allow a pencil to write upon it. The degree scales are useful for measuring courses or bearings, often without even drawing the line on the chart. Using the grid, you can do the job of a parallel rule. Finally, with small pencil marks on the surface you can measure distances on the chart in the same manner as dividers, but with no danger from sharp points and no chance of the setting changing.

Douglass protractors are made in two sizes: a 5 inch, intended for aircraft use, and a 10 inch, which I recommend for working with nautical charts. Unfortunately, they aren't easy to find in stores. Drafting supply stores sometimes carry them, and they can often be obtained at air training establishments. Figure 2-2 shows a 10 inch Douglass protractor on the same chart as Figure 2-1 for comparison. Chapter 3 gives illustrations on it use.

STOPWATCH

Worth its weight in gold. Very often, the only practical way of identifying a light or buoy is by timing its flash and referring to the light list. Without

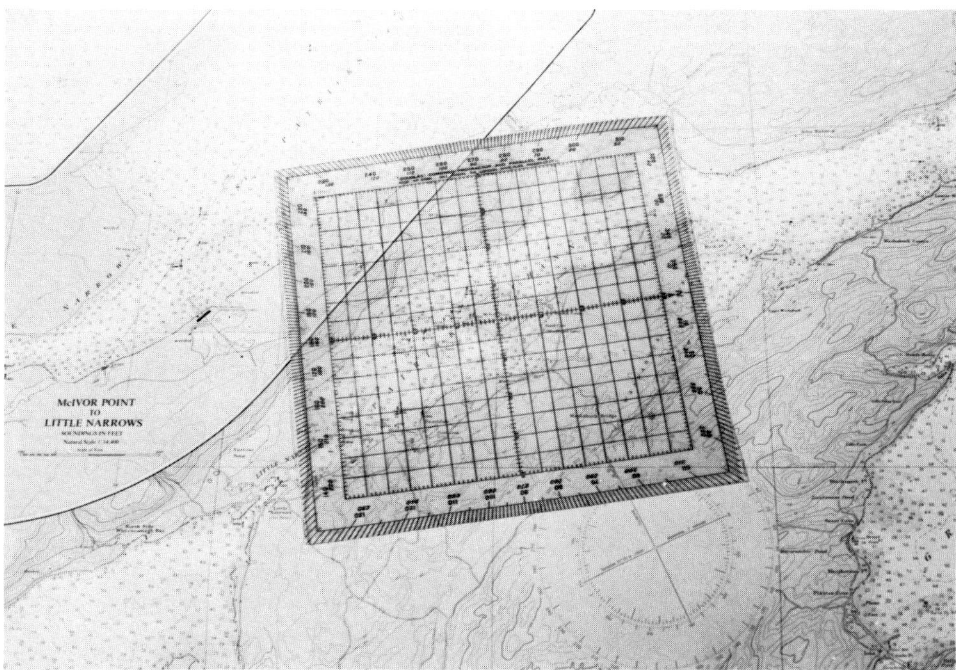

Figure 2-2 The Douglass protractor replaces dividers, protractor, and parallel rule.

a stopwatch this can be difficult or impossible. Other applications will be timing racing starts, timing course legs for dead reckoning, and finding speed by the "Dutchman's Log" method.

Nothing slips out of your shirt pocket faster, or hits the deck harder, than a stopwatch. Fit yours with a lanyard and use it!

SPEED LOG

The ability to measure your speed through the water is vital in piloting work. There are at least four ways to do it.

Oldest of all is the Dutchman's log. It isn't common today, though I must say I've been well pleased to use the method on several occasions, while aboard small boats with minimum equipment. This system involves the timing of a floating object as your boat passes it (a stopwatch earns its keep). Knowing the length of your boat and the time needed to pass the object, you can easily work out your speed. An object, such as a chip of wood, can be thrown over for this purpose, or something that is already floating can be used. Even a bubble will do. For the calculation, remember that a speed of one knot (one nautical mile per hour) means that you move 25 feet in 15 seconds. If your boat's length is 25 feet, and it takes 15 seconds to pass the object, your speed is 1 knot. If it takes 5 seconds, your speed is 3 knots. If you pass it in 4 seconds, your speed is about 4 knots, and the same would be true of a 12 foot boat passing it in 2

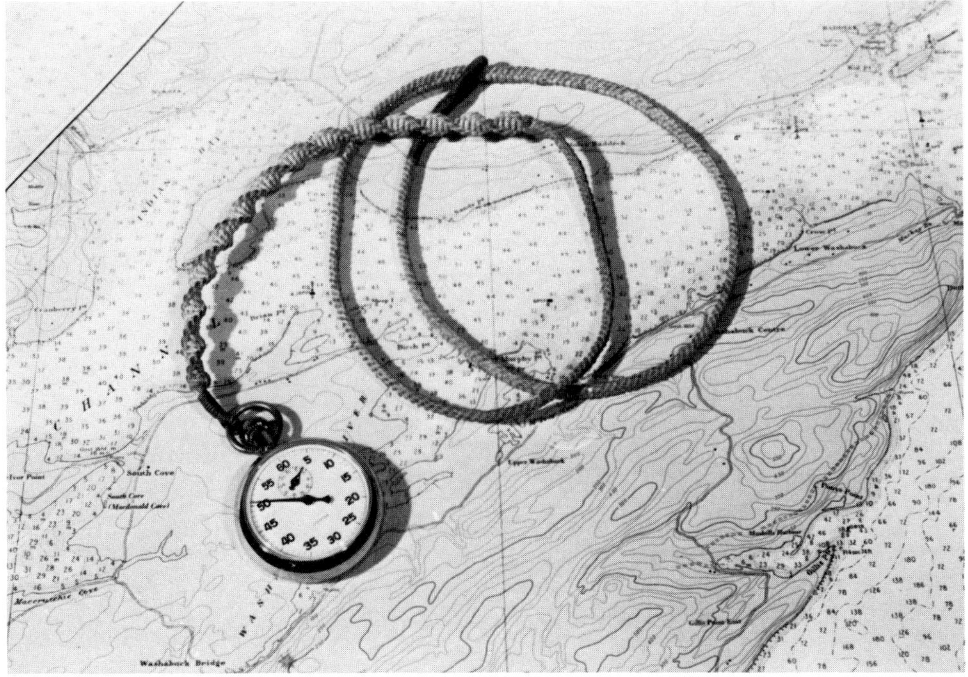

Figure 2-3 You won't drop your stopwatch if it has a lanyard.

seconds. If you want to use this method often, you can make a small table for your boat's length. The formula would be Speed = $15L/25T$ where L is the length in feet and T is the time in seconds.

A person could eventually run out of things to throw overboard. The logical way to beat this problem is to attach a light line to the object, so that it can be recovered and used again. After this, the *next* logical step is to use the length of line run out to measure the ship's forward progress. This was first done in the 1500's, and by the 1700's the method had been quite standardized. The line was marked by knots at intervals of 50 feet. The triangular wooden *chip* was weighted and provided with a three-legged bridle to keep it vertical and stationary in the water. It was thrown over the side, and the line was allowed to pay out for 28 seconds, as measured by a sandglass. The number of knots running out in this time indicated the speed of the ship—hence the term *knots*. For easier recovery of the chip, one leg of the bridle was attached by a loose wooden peg, which was dislodged by a sharp tug on the line.

This is a very practical device, even today, and I always have one on board. My chip is about 4 inches on each side, with a lead ballast weight, as shown in Figure 2-4. The 200 foot line is braided dacron on a small spool. It is knotted every 25 feet, and the timing interval is 15 seconds, indicated by stopwatch. There is a goodly length of line between the chip and the scrap of rag that marks the beginning of timing, to allow everything to start running smoothly. With this rig, the speed can be easily determined to within a quarter of a knot, and to a tenth of a knot if you're feeling fussy. It's simple and foolproof, and interesting to use. Visitors, and children in particular, find it quite fascinating. I can highly recommend it to any sailor!

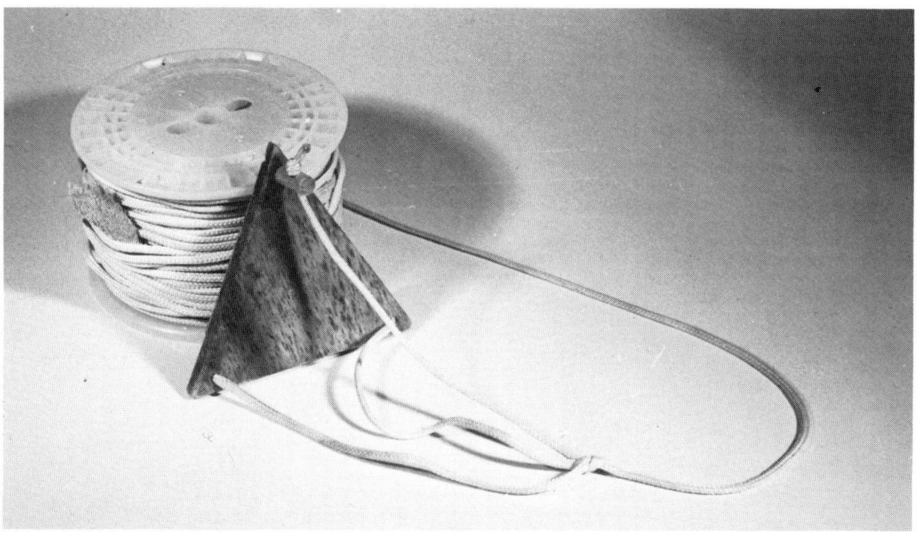

Figure 2-4 The chip log is a practical and accurate way to measure speed through the water.

The next step in evolution was the patent log, which actually measures not speed, but distance travelled through the water. (Some present-day units also indicate speed.) This device uses a metal rotator, shaped like an elongated propeller, which tows continuously at the end of a line. The rotator, via its line, turns the dials of a register unit, which is attached to the rail (hence the name taffrail log) or sometimes hung from a sling. The dials read directly in miles and tenths (see Figure 2-5). Patent logs are still in common use, and can be bought from several suppliers. The cost runs to a couple of hundred dollars. They are quite satisfactory to use, although their accuracy should be checked occasionally against a known run. Because the rotators are sometimes lost to large fish, several spares are usually carried.

Today we have convenient speed logs, which indicate both speed and distance. They use a pickup unit mounted through the bottom, which senses either water pressure against a strut or tube, or the turning of a small rotator. Figure 2-6 shows a representative model that registers only speed. Such logs are convenient and popular. They can, however, be put out of action, or at least become seriously in error if fouled by weed. When installed on a sailboat, another source of error is present. This is

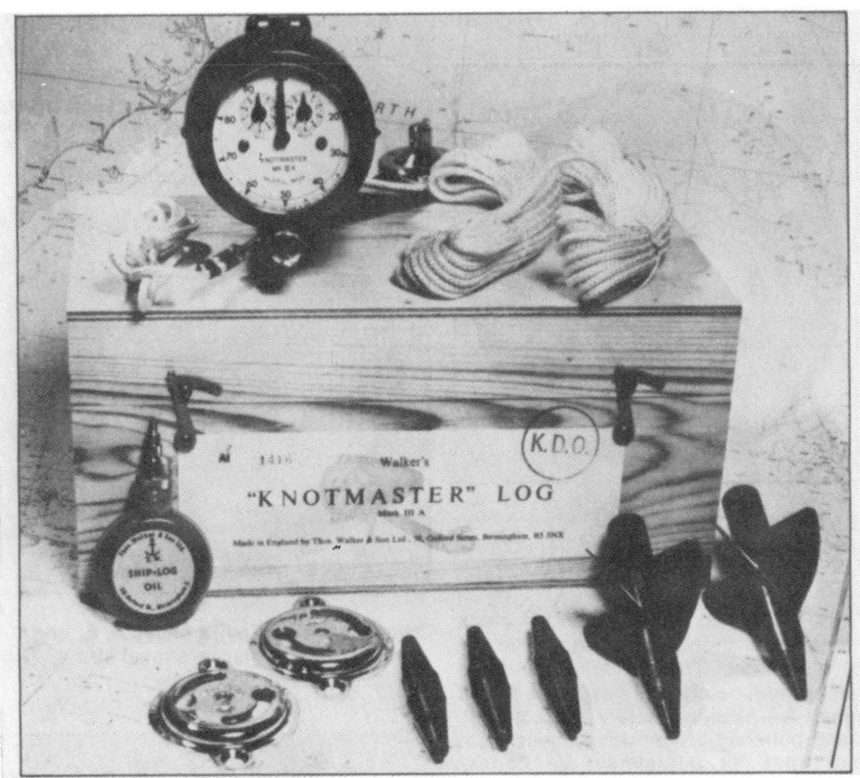

Figure 2-5 A patent log indicates distance by means of a rotator towed at the end of a line.

Figure 2-6 A modern speed log with bottom mounted sensor and cockpit indicator.

heeling error, caused by the different flow of water along the hull on different tacks. This error can be large enough to be considered.

HAND-BEARING COMPASS

One of the ways of finding your position is by taking compass bearings on known objects. This can often be done with the steering compass, but with some installations it's difficult or impossible. The hand-bearing compass is an excellent alternative. There are many styles, but most of them have a pair of sight vanes to line up on the object while reading the compass card (see Figure 2-7). There's another advantage; you can usually carry the hand-bearing compass to a part of the boat where it isn't affected by nearby metal, thereby avoiding deviation corrections. These compasses aren't cheap (prices range from $15 to $75), but are well worth the investment.

SEXTANT

Sextants used to cost an arm and a leg, and sailors usually carried one only for its traditional and indispensable use in celestial navigation at sea. Today, there are several models of plastic sextant available at a fraction of the price of brass instruments. They are compact and light, so stowage is no problem.

Even if you sail a small boat and never intend to cruise out of sight of land, you'll find one of these sextants a very useful device. A good

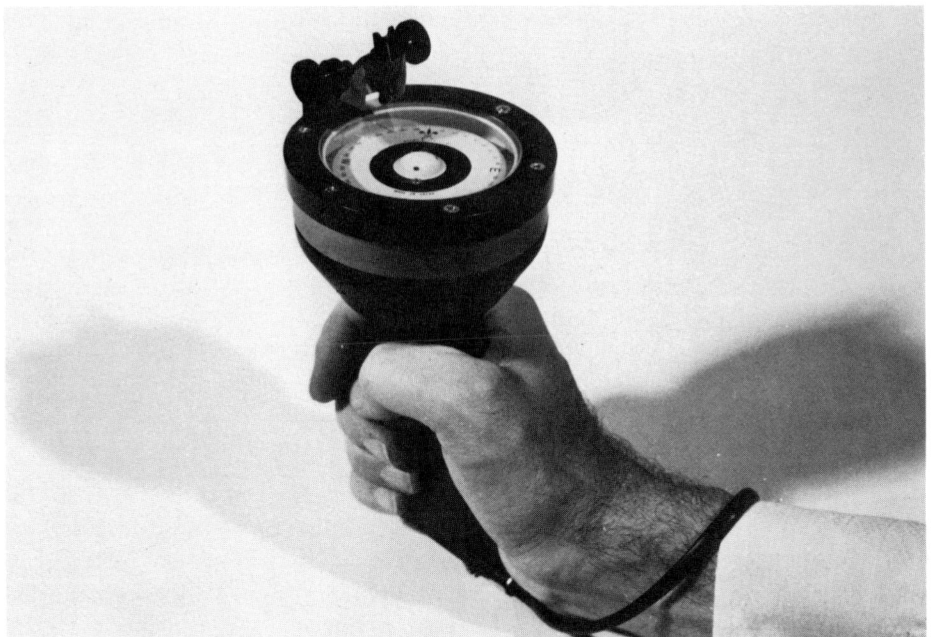

Figure 2-7 The hand-bearing compass gives convenient and accurate bearings for finding position.

part of piloting depends upon measuring angles, and the sextant is a fast and accurate instrument for doing the job. Chapter 10 gives a number of valuable methods for position finding with the sextant, as well as information on some of the models available.

LEAD LINE

Knowing the depth of water beneath you is often important as a precautionary measure, and will sometimes give a clue about your location. The traditional device for measuring depth is the lead line, which basically amounts to a piece of line tied to a weight. If the line is marked every 6 feet, it will measure directly in fathoms. Custom dictates that the line should be hemp, marked with bits of leather and colored rag, and the weight should be lead. Today you'd be hard pressed to find hemp line, but one of the synthetics works just as well—maybe better. Braided (plaited) construction should be used. I can never remember the leather and rag system, so I tie knots instead (three knots at three fathoms and so forth).

Many marine supply catalogs list the sounding leads in 7 and 14 pound sizes, but, failing that, a piece of brass rod works well. The leads come with a hollow on the bottom; in theory you can fill this with grease and obtain a sample of the bottom to compare with the chart. The trick in using a lead line is to swing it ahead as you let it go, so that, as it sinks, the boat sails up to it and when it reaches the bottom the line is straight up and down.

DEPTH SOUNDER

On many boats, technology has replaced the lead line with the depth sounder. Reduced to basic terms, this device sends out a pulse of sound and times its echo from the bottom. From the length of time elapsed, the depth is calculated and displayed. The display is generally on a dial, which may or may not have a recording chart attached. More recently, digital displays have become available (see Figure 2-8).

The convenience of an echo sounder comes at a price. There is the price in dollars—usually in the range of one to three hundred. Just as important, there is the price in complexity. The transducer has to be mounted, one way or another. The display unit has to be connected to the transponder and to electric power. The need for power introduces complications as well. I like to go cruising for simplicity, not for complication. All in all, I still prefer the lead line.

BINOCULARS

A good pair is almost essential. Uses will range from spotting distant buoys to reading sail numbers, and they will be in use constantly. High power is definitely *not* an advantage on a moving boat, but a wide field of view is. Popular models are 6 × 30 (magnification 6 times, size of objective lens 30 millimeters) and 7 × 50; the latter is the famous navy night glass.

Figure 2-8 A depth sounder reflects pulses from the bottom.

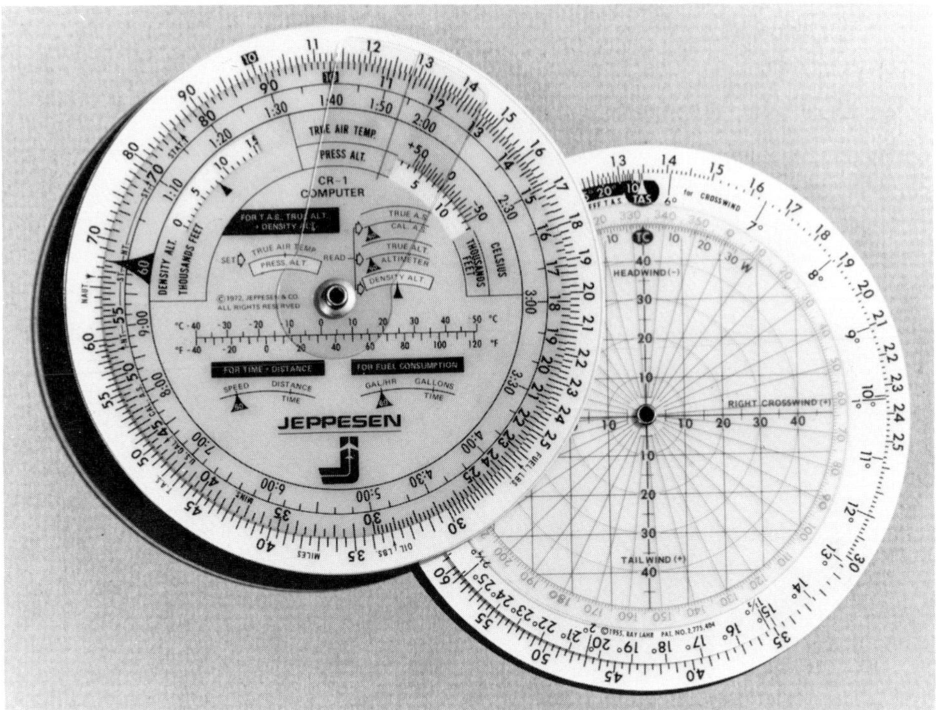

Figure 2-9 The CR slide rule makes short work of many calculations.

SLIDE RULE

In piloting work, you are constantly doing calculations. For example, if the speed is 5.5 knots, how long will it take to travel 32 miles? Or, with 27 gallons of fuel aboard and an engine burning 1.8 gallons per hour, what is the cruising range? For this type of work, some form of slide rule is very convenient. A cheap plastic student type is perfectly adequate, and the price is right—about two dollars. A similar device in round form is called a nautical slide rule, and of course costs more.

One of my real enthusiasms for this line of work is a circular slide rule with scales on several layers. It's made by the Jeppeson Company, and called a CR computer (I refer to it as a slide rule throughout this book because there's nothing electronic about it. See Figure 2-9). It quickly solves a host of problems, such as those mentioned above. Computations of leeway and current allowances can be made as well. Suppliers are listed in the Appendix.

LIGHTS

A light at the chart table has already been mentioned. A small flashlight is also handy for reading lights in the cockpit. Put some red plastic behind the lens so the light won't affect your night vision.

You'll also need a good spotlight for night work, a device most useful for picking up the numbers or colored reflectors on buoys. It should be the sealed beam type. Although deck mounted units are available, I prefer a hand held type. It won't be forever fouling sheets that come within reach, and it can be taken to any part of the boat.

Contrary to some person's beliefs, the idea is *not* to light the whole area with daytime brilliance. Even if you don't mind being blinded by the glare, others certainly do! Dark-adapted eyes are astoundingly acute, and it can be a real pleasure and satisfaction to run a channel at night, using the light of the sky and natural landmarks. Use your spotlight sparingly!

3: Charts

But even as sailors groped along by dead reckoning, gradually accumulating the knowledge that resulted in charts so others following might have some idea of what lay ahead, learned men were working to transform navigation into a science. Of direct interest to medieval navigators, the Toledan Tables of Arzachel appeared in 1080 and the Alfonsine Tables in 1252, while Roger Bacon added his Opus Majus in 1267, first using the term almanac to describe tables giving data on the apparent motions of heavenly bodies.

Carleton Mitchell, Passage East

The nautical chart is to the navigator, what a road map is to a driver. It represents a portion of the earth's curved surface on a flat sheet, and gives a great deal of information about natural and man-made features. There is much more to a chart than meets the casual glance, and a study of its features and uses will be well repaid.

First of all, where do you get charts, and how do you know which ones you should have? In Canada, the government chart source is:

Hydrographic Chart Distribution Office
Department of the Environment
1675 Russell Road
P. O. Box 8080
Ottawa, Ontario, Canada K1G 3H6

In the United States:

Distribution Division (C44)
National Ocean Survey
Riverdale, Maryland 20840

Usually, it's much more convenient to buy charts locally, and they can be found at most marine supply stores. A number of dealers are listed in the Appendix.

One of the first things you should have is called an *Information Bulletin* and a *Nautical Chart Catalog,* in Canada and the U.S., respectively. There are a number of these bulletins, each covering a large area such as the Atlantic Coast. The bulletin lists all of the charts available in that area, giving for each chart the chart number, title, scale, coverage, and price. Charts printed with a Decca or Loran grid are also indicated. Figure 3-1 shows a typical sample. These free bulletins are very handy, and you should have them on hand.

The *scale* of a chart is important. Most nautical charts are printed in so-called natural scale, which is expressed by a ratio, such as 1:50,000. This means that 1 inch on the chart represents 50,000 inches on the earth's surface, so you can see that 1 inch on the chart equals roughly three-quarters of a nautical mile on the earth's surface. The general terms, *large-scale* and *small-scale,* are often used. A large-scale chart, such as 1:20,000, covers a relatively small area, such as a harbor. A small-scale chart covers a large area. For example, Canadian chart #4316 is a large-scale chart, covering Halifax Harbour at a scale of 1:12,000, and giving many details of lights, buoys, and wharfs. Small-scale chart #2200 covers all of Lake Huron at a scale of 1:200,000. The difference between large-scale and small-scale seems to confuse a lot of people. To keep them straight, remember the little ditty "large scale, lots of detail."

The first chart you should have, logically enough, is Chart #1. This is published by both Canada and the U.S., and shows all the symbols and abbreviations used on nautical charts. Figure 3-2 shows a portion of Chart #1.

An important part of any chart is the title block, as shown in Figure 3-3. This shows the date of the survey, the datum for soundings, whether soundings are in feet or fathoms, the type of projection, and the scale. The date of a new edition (if any) is also given, along with the dates of any corrections from *Notices to Mariners.*

NOTICES TO MARINERS

Navigation aids are by no means permanent. Some buoys are shifted periodically, according to changes in the channels they mark. Others are removed in the winter to avoid ice damage. Numbers are changed, colors altered, lights established or removed, foghorns changed, and so on. Along with those changes to navigation aids, bridges are built or removed, pipelines and cables are laid, and shoals are reported or shown to not exist where charted. With this continuous change going on, the information on a chart becomes obsolete very quickly. In order to keep charts up to date, the government issues weekly *Notices to Mariners.* These give full details on any changes in charts and other publications. A sample is shown in Figure 3-4. Some dealers correct their charts up to the date of sale. You should get on the mailing list for "Notices," and keep your charts up to date.

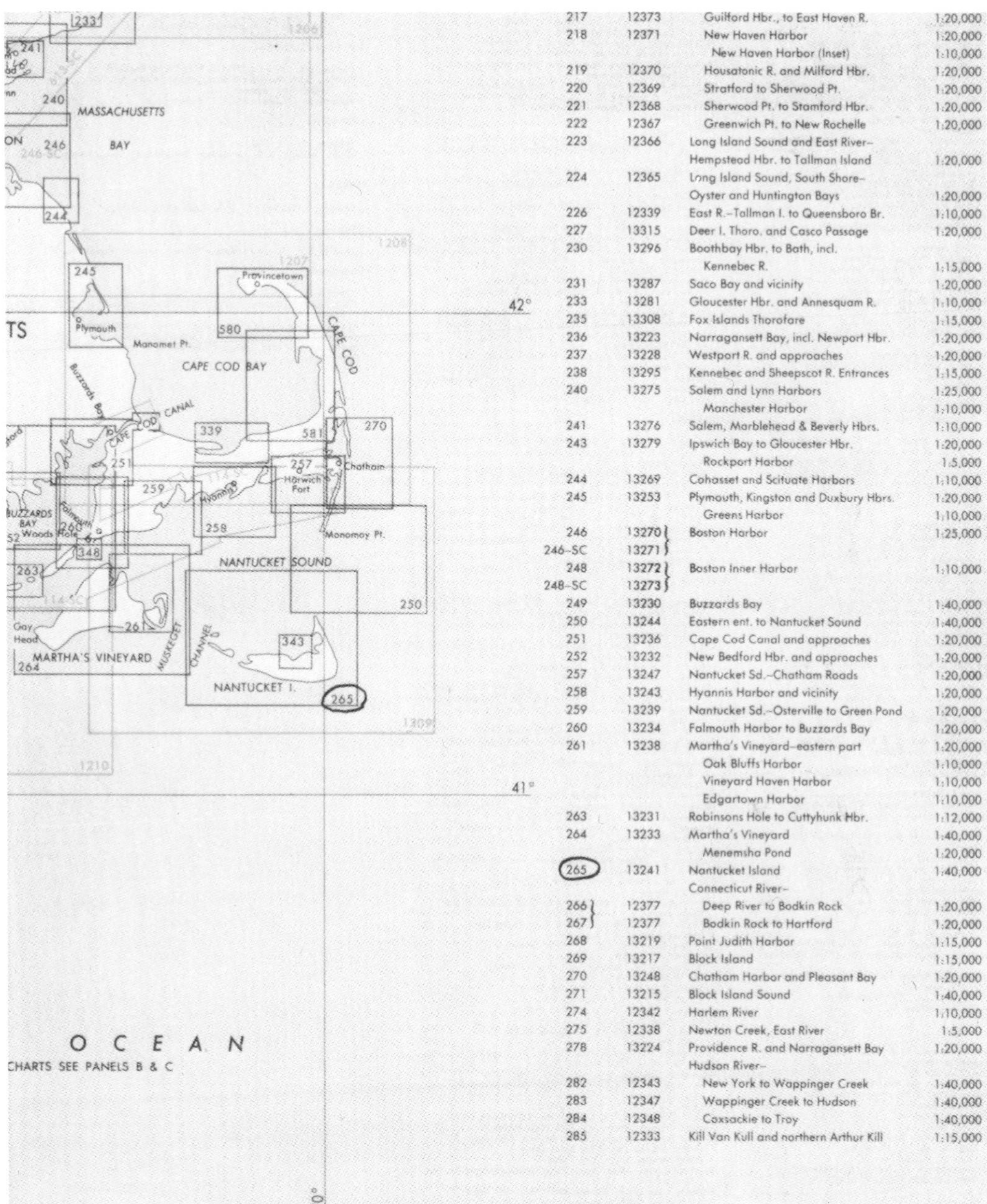

217	12373	Guilford Hbr., to East Haven R.	1:20,000
218	12371	New Haven Harbor	1:20,000
		New Haven Harbor (Inset)	1:10,000
219	12370	Housatonic R. and Milford Hbr.	1:20,000
220	12369	Stratford to Sherwood Pt.	1:20,000
221	12368	Sherwood Pt. to Stamford Hbr.	1:20,000
222	12367	Greenwich Pt. to New Rochelle	1:20,000
223	12366	Long Island Sound and East River–Hempstead Hbr. to Tallman Island	1:20,000
224	12365	Long Island Sound, South Shore–Oyster and Huntington Bays	1:20,000
226	12339	East R.–Tallman I. to Queensboro Br.	1:10,000
227	13315	Deer I. Thoro. and Casco Passage	1:20,000
230	13296	Boothbay Hbr. to Bath, incl. Kennebec R.	1:15,000
231	13287	Saco Bay and vicinity	1:20,000
233	13281	Gloucester Hbr. and Annesquam R.	1:10,000
235	13308	Fox Islands Thorofare	1:15,000
236	13223	Narragansett Bay, incl. Newport Hbr.	1:20,000
237	13228	Westport R. and approaches	1:20,000
238	13295	Kennebec and Sheepscot R. Entrances	1:15,000
240	13275	Salem and Lynn Harbors	1:25,000
		Manchester Harbor	1:10,000
241	13276	Salem, Marblehead & Beverly Hbrs.	1:10,000
243	13279	Ipswich Bay to Gloucester Hbr.	1:20,000
		Rockport Harbor	1:5,000
244	13269	Cohasset and Scituate Harbors	1:10,000
245	13253	Plymouth, Kingston and Duxbury Hbrs.	1:20,000
		Greens Harbor	1:10,000
246	13270	Boston Harbor	1:25,000
246-SC	13271		
248	13272	Boston Inner Harbor	1:10,000
248-SC	13273		
249	13230	Buzzards Bay	1:40,000
250	13244	Eastern ent. to Nantucket Sound	1:40,000
251	13236	Cape Cod Canal and approaches	1:20,000
252	13232	New Bedford Hbr. and approaches	1:20,000
257	13247	Nantucket Sd.–Chatham Roads	1:20,000
258	13243	Hyannis Harbor and vicinity	1:20,000
259	13239	Nantucket Sd.–Osterville to Green Pond	1:20,000
260	13234	Falmouth Harbor to Buzzards Bay	1:20,000
261	13238	Martha's Vineyard–eastern part	1:20,000
		Oak Bluffs Harbor	1:10,000
		Vineyard Haven Harbor	1:10,000
		Edgartown Harbor	1:10,000
263	13231	Robinsons Hole to Cuttyhunk Hbr.	1:12,000
264	13233	Martha's Vineyard	1:40,000
		Menemsha Pond	1:20,000
265	13241	Nantucket Island	1:40,000
		Connecticut River–	
266	12377	Deep River to Bodkin Rock	1:20,000
267	12377	Bodkin Rock to Hartford	1:20,000
268	13219	Point Judith Harbor	1:15,000
269	13217	Block Island	1:15,000
270	13248	Chatham Harbor and Pleasant Bay	1:20,000
271	13215	Block Island Sound	1:40,000
274	12342	Harlem River	1:10,000
275	12338	Newton Creek, East River	1:5,000
278	13224	Providence R. and Narragansett Bay	1:20,000
		Hudson River–	
282	12343	New York to Wappinger Creek	1:40,000
283	12347	Wappinger Creek to Hudson	1:40,000
284	12348	Coxsackie to Troy	1:40,000
285	12333	Kill Van Kull and northern Arthur Kill	1:15,000

Figure 3-1 The Chart Catalog shows the coverage of available charts.

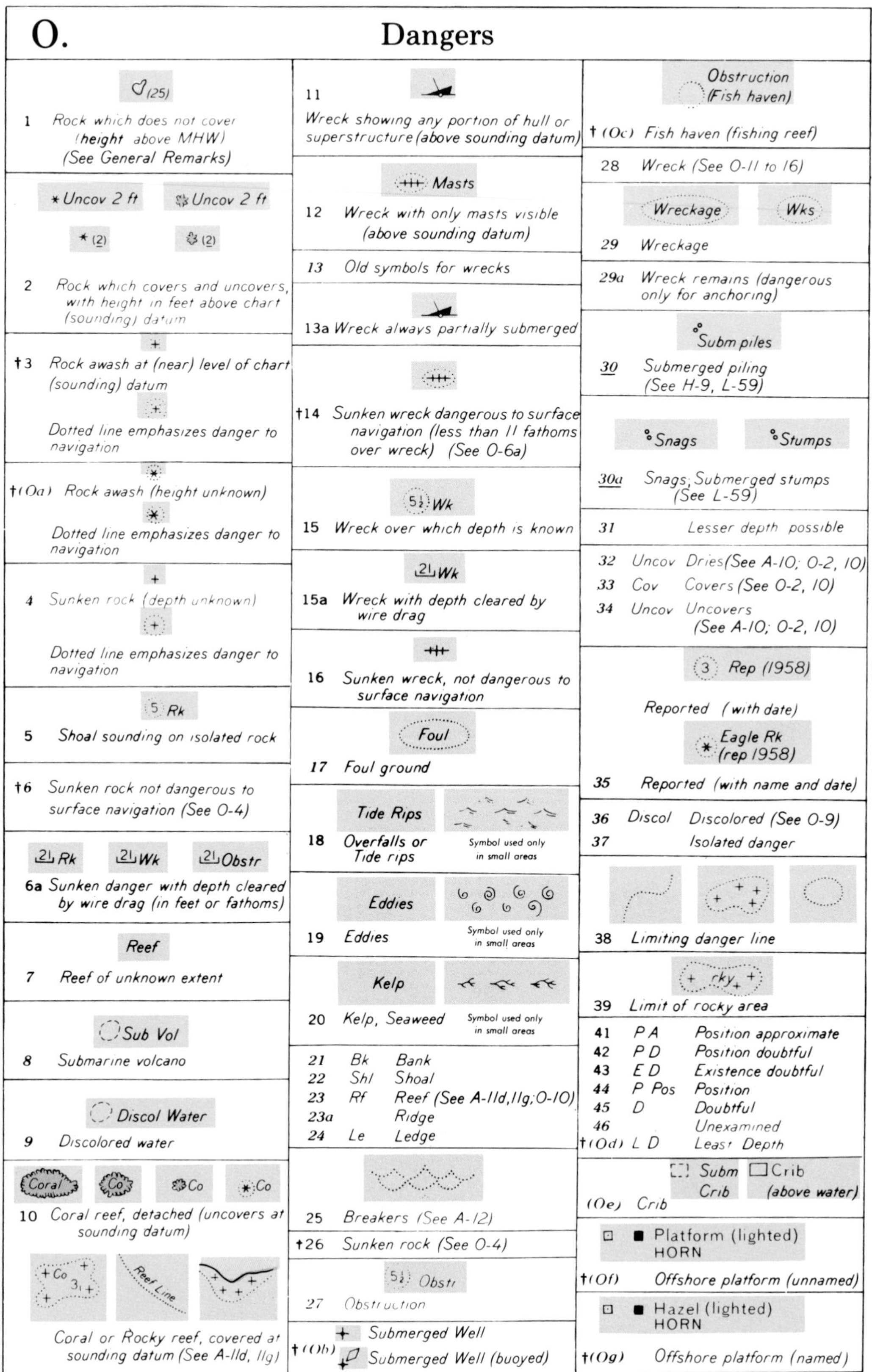

O.
Dangers
1 Rock which does not cover (height above MHW) (See General Remarks)
(25)
Uncov 2 ft
Uncov 2 ft
(2)
(2)
2 Rock which covers and uncovers, with height in feet above chart (sounding) datum
†3 Rock awash at (near) level of chart (sounding) datum
Dotted line emphasizes danger to navigation
†(Oa) Rock awash (height unknown)
Dotted line emphasizes danger to navigation
4 Sunken rock (depth unknown)
Dotted line emphasizes danger to navigation
5 Rk
5 Shoal sounding on isolated rock
†6 Sunken rock not dangerous to surface navigation (See O-4)
21 Rk
21 Wk
21 Obstr
6a Sunken danger with depth cleared by wire drag (in feet or fathoms)
Reef
7 Reef of unknown extent
Sub Vol
8 Submarine volcano
Discol Water
9 Discolored water
Coral
Co
Co
Co
10 Coral reef, detached (uncovers at sounding datum)
Co
Reef Line
Coral or Rocky reef, covered at sounding datum (See A-11d, 11g)
11
Wreck showing any portion of hull or superstructure (above sounding datum)
Masts
12 Wreck with only masts visible (above sounding datum)
13 Old symbols for wrecks
13a Wreck always partially submerged
†14 Sunken wreck dangerous to surface navigation (less than 11 fathoms over wreck) (See O-6a)
5½ Wk
15 Wreck over which depth is known
21 Wk
15a Wreck with depth cleared by wire drag
16 Sunken wreck, not dangerous to surface navigation
Foul
17 Foul ground
Tide Rips
18 Overfalls or Tide rips
Symbol used only in small areas
Eddies
19 Eddies
Symbol used only in small areas
Kelp
20 Kelp, Seaweed
Symbol used only in small areas
21 Bk Bank
22 Shl Shoal
23 Rf Reef (See A-11d, 11g; O-10)
23a Ridge
24 Le Ledge
25 Breakers (See A-12)
†26 Sunken rock (See O-4)
5½ Obstr
27 Obstruction
†(Ob) Submerged Well
Submerged Well (buoyed)
Obstruction
(Fish haven)
†(Oc) Fish haven (fishing reef)
28 Wreck (See O-11 to 16)
Wreckage
Wks
29 Wreckage
29a Wreck remains (dangerous only for anchoring)
Subm piles
30 Submerged piling (See H-9, L-59)
Snags
Stumps
30a Snags; Submerged stumps (See L-59)
31 Lesser depth possible
32 Uncov Dries (See A-10; O-2, 10)
33 Cov Covers (See O-2, 10)
34 Uncov Uncovers (See A-10; O-2, 10)
3 Rep (1958)
Reported (with date)
Eagle Rk (rep 1958)
35 Reported (with name and date)
36 Discol Discolored (See O-9)
37 Isolated danger
38 Limiting danger line
rky
39 Limit of rocky area
41 PA Position approximate
42 PD Position doubtful
43 ED Existence doubtful
44 P Pos Position
45 D Doubtful
46 Unexamined
†(Od) LD Least Depth
Subm Crib
Crib (above water)
(Oe) Crib
Platform (lighted)
HORN
†(Of) Offshore platform (unnamed)
Hazel (lighted)
HORN
†(Og) Offshore platform (named)

Figure 3-2 Chart #1 gives symbols and abbreviations used on charts.

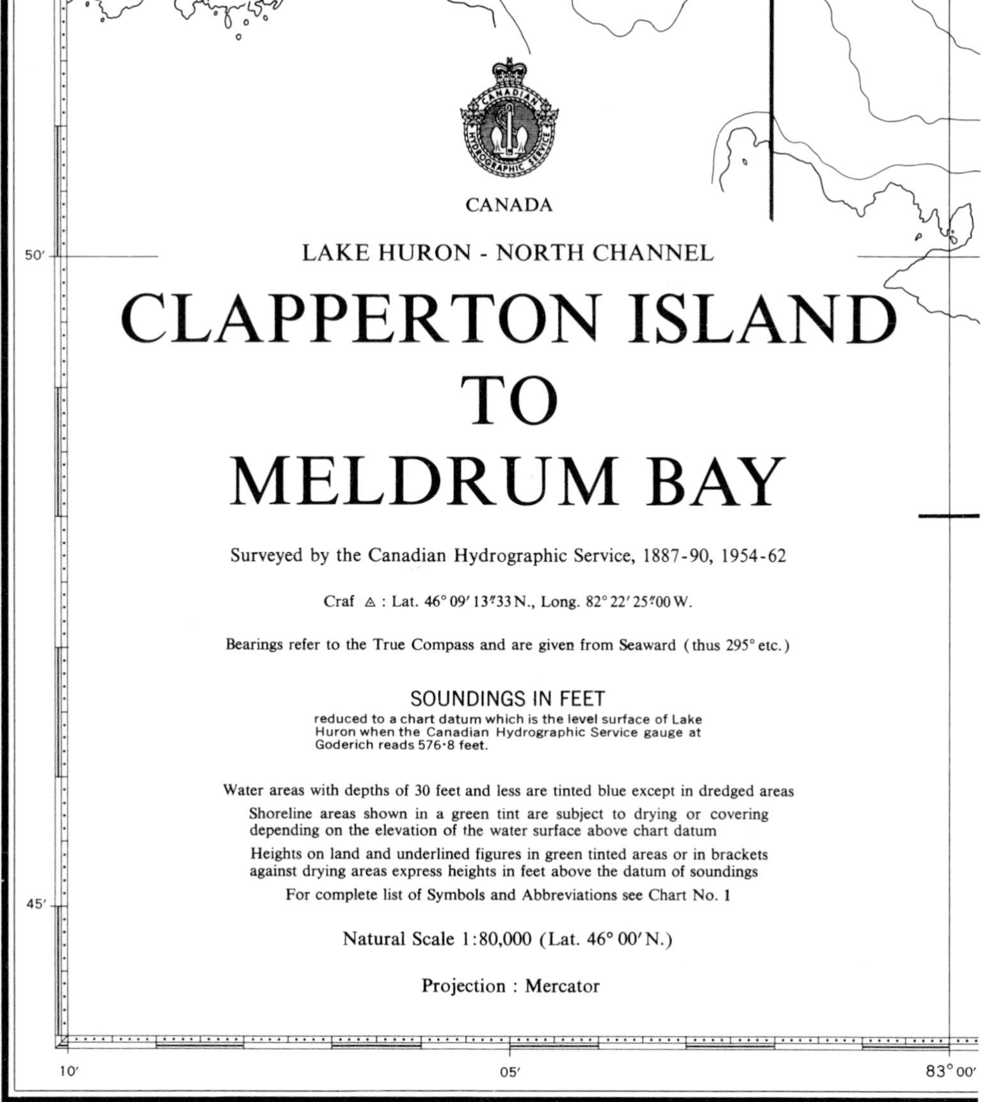

CANADIAN HYDROGRAPHIC SERVICE
CANADA
LAKE HURON - NORTH CHANNEL
CLAPPERTON ISLAND
TO
MELDRUM BAY
Surveyed by the Canadian Hydrographic Service, 1887-90, 1954-62
Craf △ : Lat. 46° 09′ 13″33 N., Long. 82° 22′ 25″00 W.
Bearings refer to the True Compass and are given from Seaward (thus 295° etc.)
SOUNDINGS IN FEET
reduced to a chart datum which is the level surface of Lake Huron when the Canadian Hydrographic Service gauge at Goderich reads 576·8 feet.
Water areas with depths of 30 feet and less are tinted blue except in dredged areas
Shoreline areas shown in a green tint are subject to drying or covering depending on the elevation of the water surface above chart datum
Heights on land and underlined figures in green tinted areas or in brackets against drying areas express heights in feet above the datum of soundings
For complete list of Symbols and Abbreviations see Chart No. 1
Natural Scale 1:80,000 (Lat. 46° 00′ N.)
Projection : Mercator
50′
45′
10′
05′
83° 00′

FIRST EDITION DEC. 16 1966 CORRECTED REPRINT NOV. 23 1973

CORRECTIONS FROM CANADIAN
NOTICES TO MARINERS TO : 1973 *526*

Figure 3-3 The title block of a chart gives important information. Be sure to check whether soundings are given in feet or fathoms.

NEWFOUNDLAND, EAST COAST - TRINITY BAY - HICKMAN HARBOUR -
Information about reported rock.

Chart (Last correction) - 4545(1089/75).

Substitute submerged rock 48°12'33"N 53°34'51"W
(PA) (Repd 1975)
for depth 16 fathoms (DOE)

Figure 3-4 *Notices to Mariners* report changes in charts and other publications.

MEASUREMENTS ON THE CHART

Direction is measured from true north on the chart, which is usually, but not always, at the top. There are two basic ways of doing the job. You can use a protractor, or you can refer to the compass rose printed on the chart (you'll need a parallel rule as well). The methods are illustrated by examples on the practice chart. The problems in this chapter and the rest of the book also use the practice chart. If you have read the Introduction, you'll have provided yourself with copies. If not, you might as well do it now, because you'll be needing them from here on.

What is the direction from the fairway buoy HB to the Brig whistle buoy? To use an ordinary protractor, first draw a line between the buoys. However, don't draw any lines over chart symbols, since repeated erasures can obliterate important details. Center the protractor on buoy HB (the starting point), while lining it up north and south (see Figure 3-5). The direction line is 70° from south on the protractor, but directions are measured clockwise from north, so the actual direction is 180° (south) plus 70°, or 250°. Here you can see the disadvantage of using an ordinary protractor; you very often have to add or subtract figures, and it's surprisingly easy to make a mistake.

Using a Douglass protractor avoids any figuring. Figure 3-6 shows a Douglass protractor centered on the same buoy, with its north pointing to chart north. Reading the outside scale gives the direction : 250°. That's

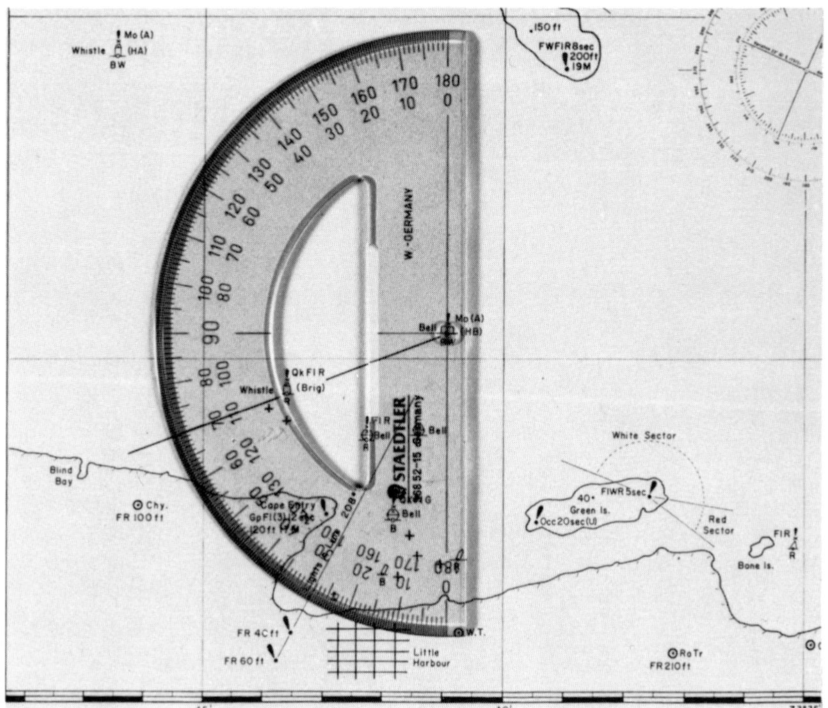

Figure 3-5 Measuring direction with a protractor.

quite an improvement, but the *really* smart way of using a Douglass protractor means that you don't even have to draw the line. Figure 3-7 shows the edge of the protractor lined up on the two buoys, with north pointing in the direction we're measuring. The center is on a meridian (north-south) line, and the same line on the *inside* scale gives the direction : 250°. This method takes a little getting used to, but it works so well that it's worth the practice.

Finally, let's measure the same direction using a parallel rule. Lay the edge of the rule between the buoys, as shown in Figure 3-8. then hold the lower blade fixed, and swing the upper blade until it crosses the center of the compass rose, as in Figure 3-9. Read the outer (true) scale of the rose : 250°. This works quite well, but often you have to "walk" the rule across the chart to reach the rose, with a good chance of slipping.

Reviewing the above methods briefly, you actually have a choice of four ways to measure direction: an ordinary protractor, a Douglass protractor used in two different ways, or a parallel rule. I highly recommend the second way of using the Douglass. A few minutes practice will make you proficient, and the method is extremely fast and accurate.

Distance can be measured on the chart with a pair of dividers, or by pencil marks on the Douglass protractor. Some charts include distance scales, as shown in Figure 3-10. They aren't needed, though. Use the latitude scale on the side of the chart as a distance scale, with one minute

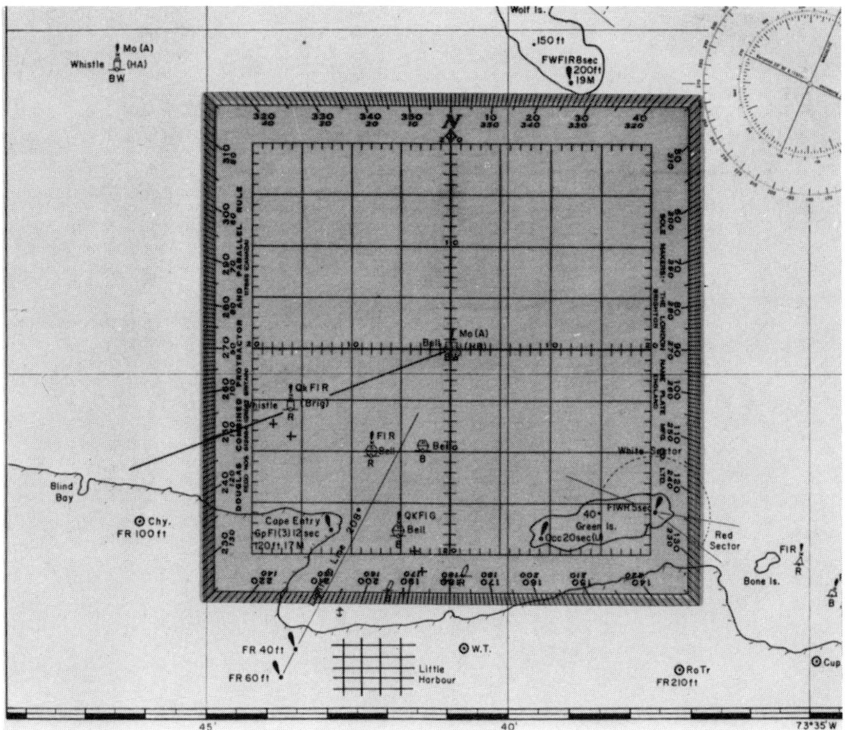

Figure 3-6 One way of measuring direction with a Douglass protractor.

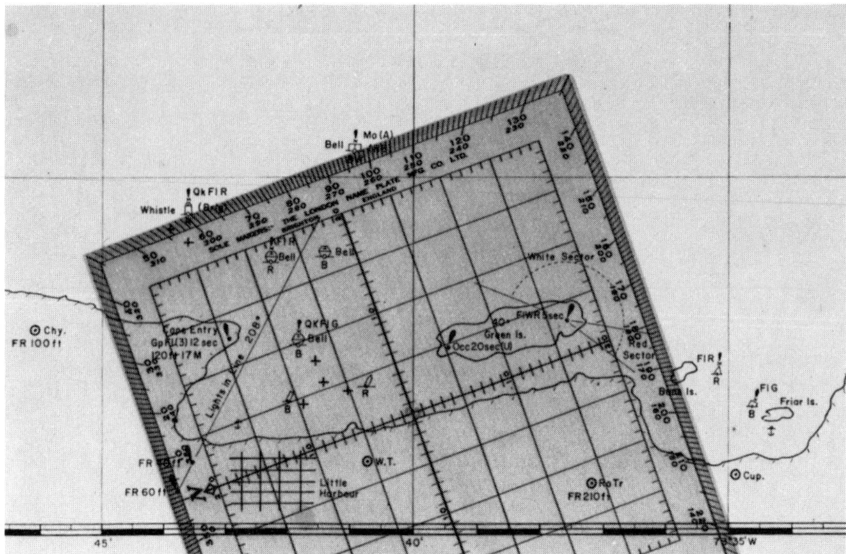

Figure 3-7 You can also use the Douglass protractor without drawing a direction line.

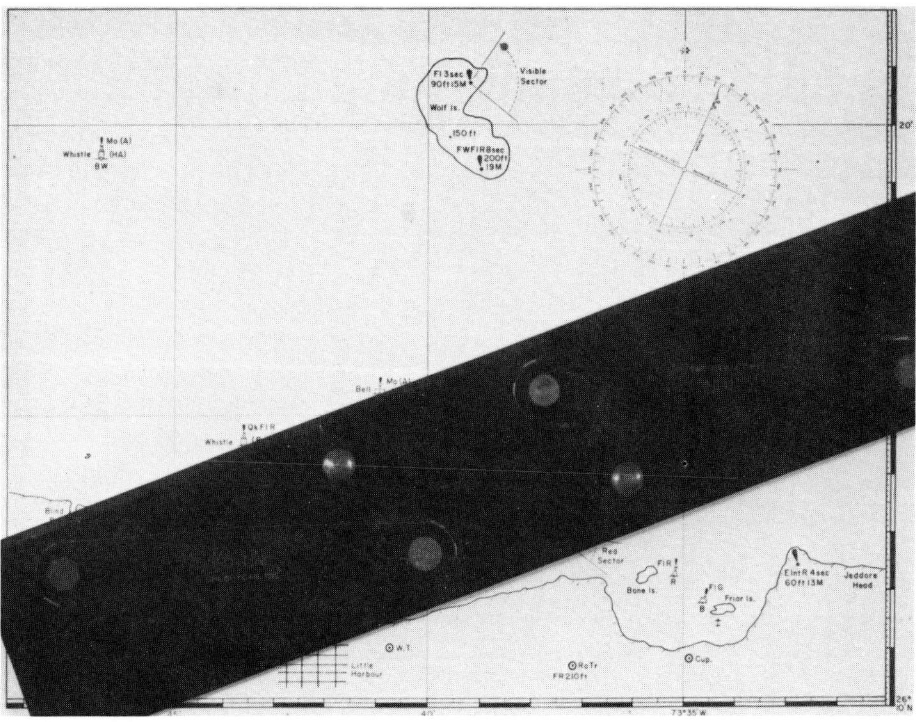

Figure 3-8

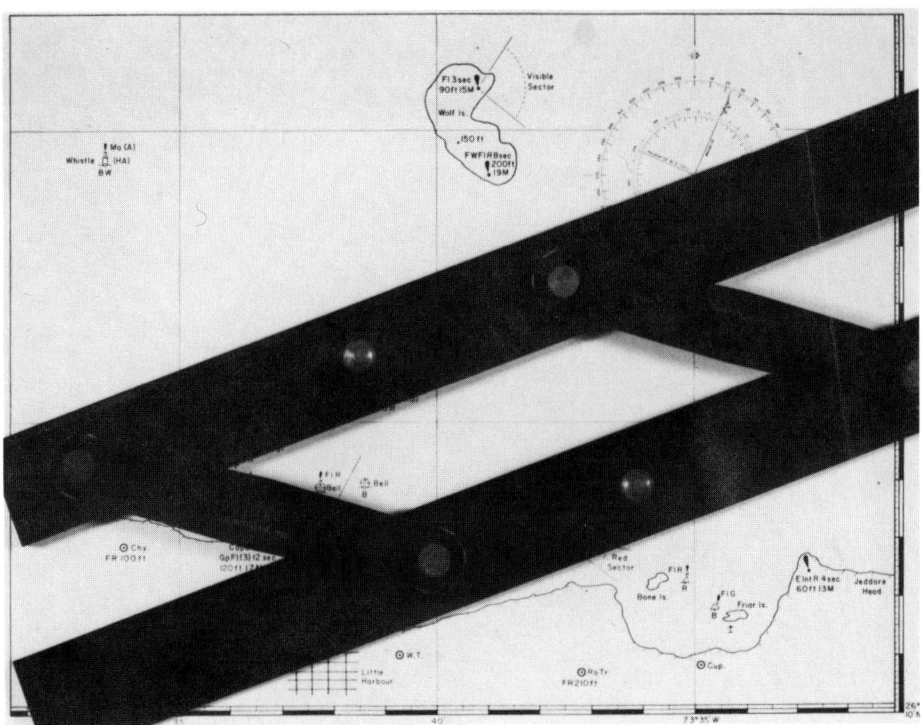

Figure 3-9 Measuring direction with the compass rose and a parallel rule.

of latitude equal to one nautical mile. Charts used for piloting commonly have a black or white band for each minute, divided into tenths, as shown on the practice chart. Harbor charts on very large scale may show black and white bands for half minutes, and be divided into seconds. At the other extreme, small scale ocean charts may show black and white bands for five minutes, or even for degrees. The moral: check your chart and be sure.

Working on this basis, Figure 3-11 and 3-12 show that the distance between buoy HB and the Brig buoy is 2.6 nautical miles. A caution: never use the longitude scale across the bottom for measuring distance. The longitude spacing varies according to the chart's latitude, and "distance" measured on this scale will be too great. One of my favorite yarns concerns the owner of a 14 foot dinghy who claimed speeds of 8 knots for his boat. Someone else realized that about half that speed would be a more reasonable figure and investigated. It turned out that the proud owner was measuring his distance run on the longitude scale!

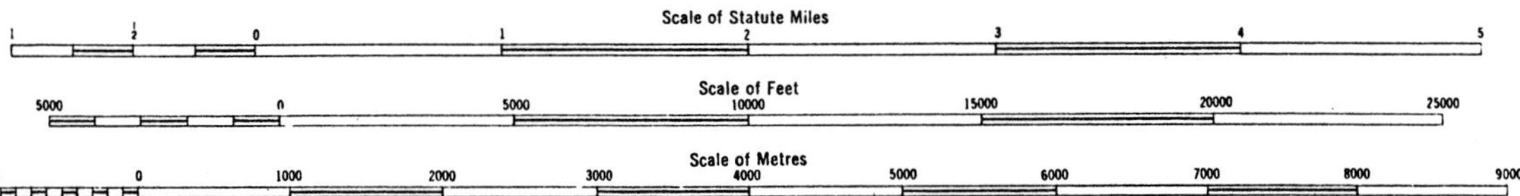

Figure 3-10 Some charts have distance scales.

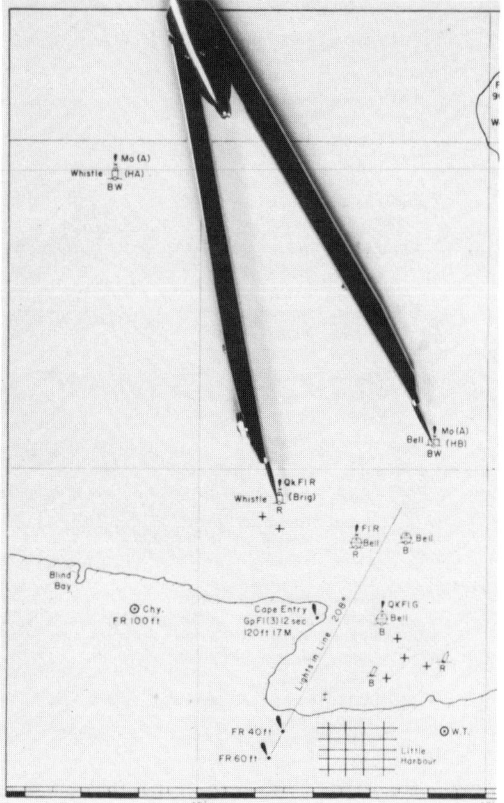

Figure 3-11

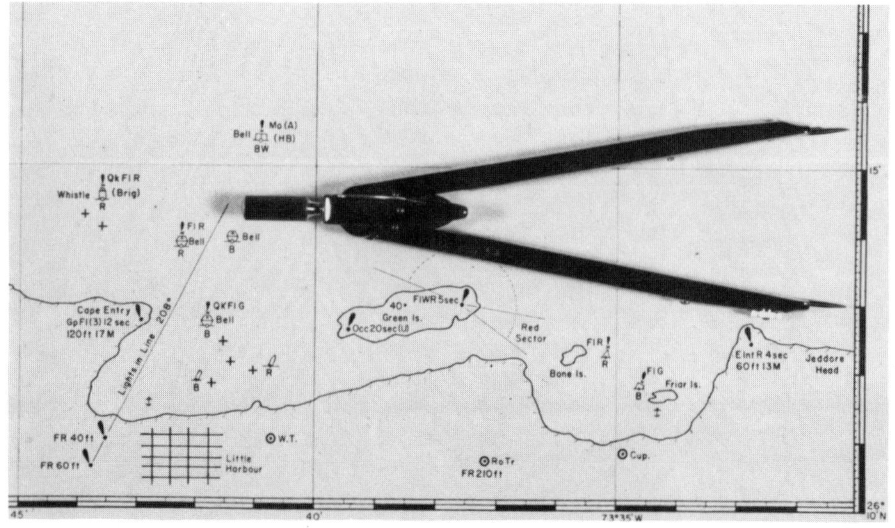

Figure 3-12 Measuring distance on the latitude scale.

Positions on the chart can be specified in terms of latitude (north-south measure) and longitude (east-west measure). For example, the position of the south light on Wolf Island is 26° 19′.2 N, 73° 39′.0 W.

Work these problems on a practice chart.

Problem 3-1:

Find the true direction and the distance between these pairs of points.
(1) Buoy HA and the outer black bell buoy
(2) Brig whistle and the Wolf Island south light
(3) Brig whistle and the mouth of Blind Bay
(4) Jeddore Head light and buoy HB.

Problem 3-2:

Find the latitude and longitude of the following points.
(1) Wolf Island north light
(2) Little Harbor water tank
(3) Fairway buoy HA
(4) Friar Island can buoy

SAILING DIRECTIONS

The limited space on a chart means that a lot of useful information must be left off. For example, a small harbor may be shown, but you have no way of knowing whether the bottom is good holding ground or not. Again, you may want to know whether fuel is available at a certain town, and the chart is no help in that regard. This sort of information, and much more, is given in a series of books known as *Sailing Directions*. A sample is shown in Figure 3-13. It should be remembered that the *Sailing Directions* must be corrected from *Notices to Mariners*.

PILOT CHARTS

The name is a bit deceptive, for these charts are really used more for ocean cruising. Nevertheless, they're very useful aids to have. Published once a month, they show prevailing winds, ocean currents, temperatures, magnetic variation, fog probability, trade wind limits, commercial shipping lanes, and other data. A sample is shown in Figure 3-14. The back of each chart carries an article on some aspect of the marine world. A sampling of 1974 topics includes:

Fisheries Vessels and Gear
Radar Controlled Harbours
Tropical Cyclones
Secondary Uses of HO 229 Sight Reduction Tables
Marine Radiotelephony
Specialized Cargo Ships

These charts are published by the United States Defense Mapping Agency (DMA) Hydrographic Center, and may be obtained from the offices listed in the Appendix, as well as many chart dealers.

Little Island, already alluded to, lies a quarter of a mile southward from Eagle Point, and is a conspicuous feature in approaching the harbour of Bruce Mines from the southeast. With the exception of a narrow spit, extending half a cable from the western side, the island has good water about it. The track to Bruce Mines passes about a third of a mile southwestward of Little Island.

Bruce Mines takes its name from the old Bruce copper mine which was opened in 1846, followed by the Wellington in 1858. They are no longer in operation. The town is supported by a good farming community.

The town, with a population in 1956 of 451, has good stores, schools, churches, and a bank. The local post office acts as a Customs office and the telegraph office is located in the Canadian Pacific Railway station, about 2 miles north of the town. The Government wharf, which extends about 1,000 feet ($304^{m}8$) into the harbour, has a pierhead 90 feet ($27^{m}4$) square. Along the faces of the pierhead there is a depth of 12 to 16 feet ($3^{m}1$ to $4^{m}9$). The remains of the old Bruce Mines Copper Company wharf lie east of the public wharf with the outer end about 200 feet ($61^{m}0$) distant from the pierhead.

Dredged channels. — Leading to the outer corner of the Government wharf is a channel 150 feet ($45^{m}7$) wide and 870 yards ($795^{m}4$) in length with a reported depth of 16 feet ($4^{m}9$). Its approximate direction to the wharf is 327°, and the western edge is marked by four black spar buoys. A turning basin at the wharf is 250 feet ($76^{m}2$) wide.

Jacks Island *(Lat. 46° 18′ N., Long. 83° 47′ W.),* 40 feet ($12^{m}2$) high at its southern end, is situated nearly a mile northwestward from Eagle Point, and half a mile southeastward from the head of the Government wharf.

McKay Island is the outer of two islands sheltering the harbour from the southwest. A boat passage exists between McKay Island and the other called **French Island,** and also between the latter and **McCort Point.** A rocky spit extends a short distance from the east point of McKay Island.

Figure 3-13 *Sailing Directions* give detailed information to supplement the chart.

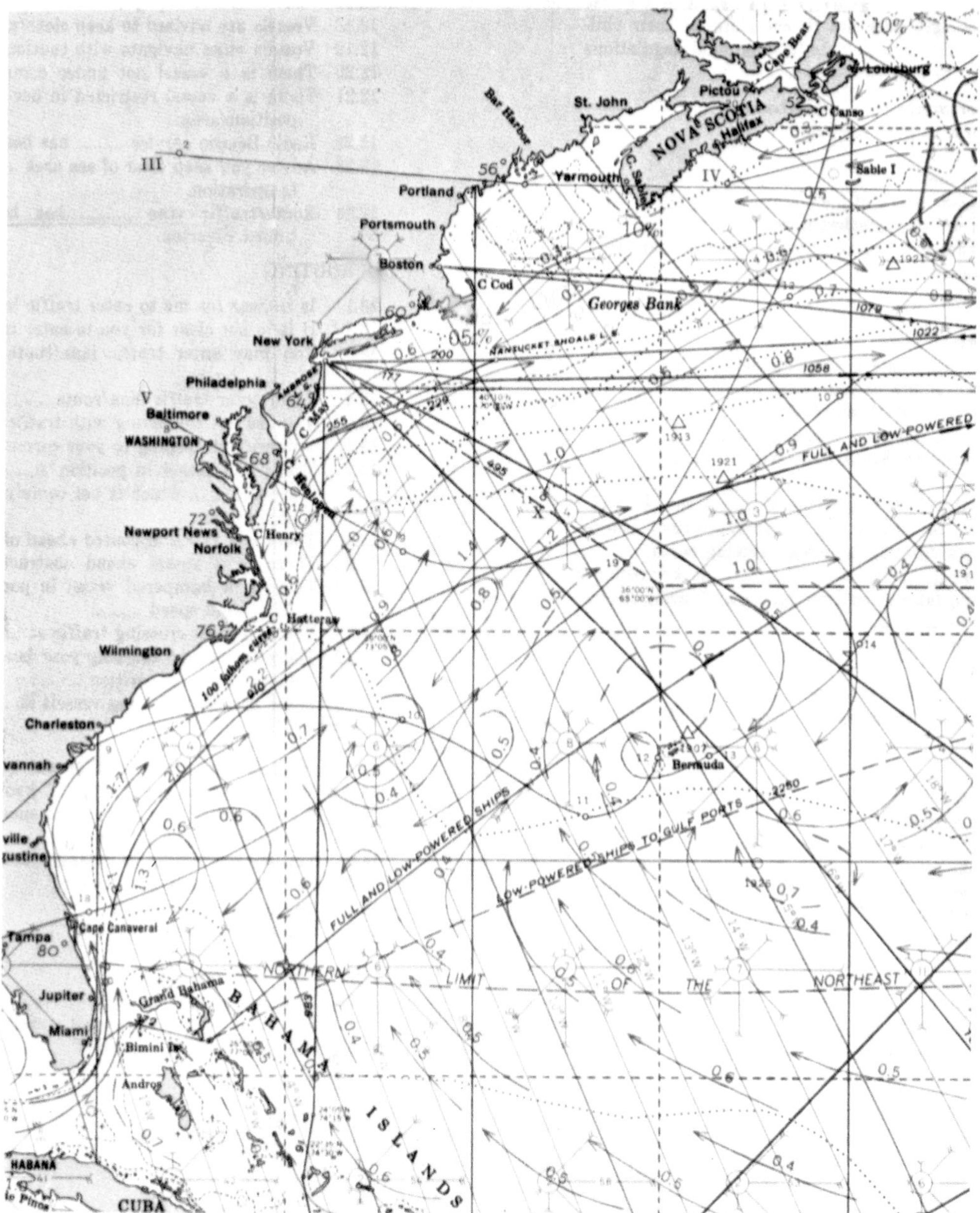

Figure 3-14 Pilot charts contain a wealth of useful information.

4: Lights and Buoys

With a reef rolled in the mainsail we made good but uncomfortable progress, and two hours before dawn sighted the group flash of the 14-mile light on Elbow Cay. But this proved to be on a dangerous bearing, due, no doubt, to the fact that in spite of my allowance for the current we had been set a long way to the west.

Eric Hiscock, *Atlantic Cruise in Wanderer III*

LIGHTS

Lights, popularly called lighthouses, symbolize coastal navigation more than any other aid. Their history is long and honorable, reaching as far back as the Egypt of several hundred years B.C. Light structures are generally built in exposed locations for reasons of visibility. Many of them take severe batterings from bad weather. From the days when all lights were manned by keepers, we have countless stories of water going over the top of the light, or large rocks being hurled through windows at heights of hundreds of feet. It might be supposed that the many electronic aids available today would make the light obsolete, but this is far from true. Not all vessels are fitted with electronic gear, and even those which are, have to consider the possibility of breakdown. Even with electronic aids, many a navigator working along the coast has found that the coming of night actually simplifies his work, for he can be guided by the winking of those familiar signposts of the sea.

Light structures take many forms. The choice of structure for a given location depends primarily on the importance of the light, in terms of the amount of traffic it serves or the danger it marks. Important lights are, generally, rather imposing structures of masonry or steel, with heights often in the two hundred foot range. Along with brilliant lights, they are often equipped with fog signals, radio or radar equipment, and other aids. Many of them are manned the year round. At the other extreme, a minor light, which serves as an aid to primarily local traffic rather than marking a hazard, may be a small skeleton structure, which carries a low power light operating automatically for many months at a time.

CHARACTERISTICS

A light won't be much help to the navigator unless he knows which light he is looking at. By day, the light can usually be easily identified by the type of structure and other features in the area. By night, identification depends on the type of flash the light shows, known as the *characteristic*. There are almost endless combinations of duration and color, so that each light has a unique characteristic and can be positively identified.

Most lights show only one color, which can be either white, red, or green. Depending on the relative duration of light to dark intervals, they are classified as *flashing* (light shorter than dark), *equal interval* (light equal to dark), or *occulting* (light longer than dark). A light can also be *fixed* (on continuously), *fixed and flashing* (on continuously with periodic brighter flashes), or *group flashing* (two or more flashes at intervals). Various combinations are illustrated in Figure 4-1, with chart abbreviations and descriptions.

Similar characteristics can be shown with color variations. Figure 4-2 shows some possible combinations. The chart will often show the period of the light. If it is a simple flashing light, the chart might show Fl. G. 8 sec, meaning that the light shows a green flash every 8 seconds. If the light is group flashing, the time shown is from the *beginning of one group to the beginning of an identical group*, as shown in Figure 4-3.

Light characterisitcs change occasionally, as shown by *Notices to Mariners*. Figure 4-4 shows a sample. Keep your charts up to date.

SECTORS

A light may be obscured from certain directions by natural obstructions. In such cases the chart will indicate a visible sector for the light. In other cases, a light may be arranged to cast different lights in different directions. For example, it may show white if you're navigating in a safe area, and red if you're in a dangerous area. Examples of both types of sectors are shown on the practice chart. The Wolf Island north light is not visible from the west, because the island is higher than the light. The Green Island east light has two colored sectors. North of the island, there are no hazards and the light shows flashing white. To the southeast, however, Bone Island is a hazard. If you're in this area, the light will show flashing red.

HEIGHT AND RANGE

Because of the earth's curvature, there's a limit to the distance from which even a very bright light can be seen, as shown in Figure 4-5. Other

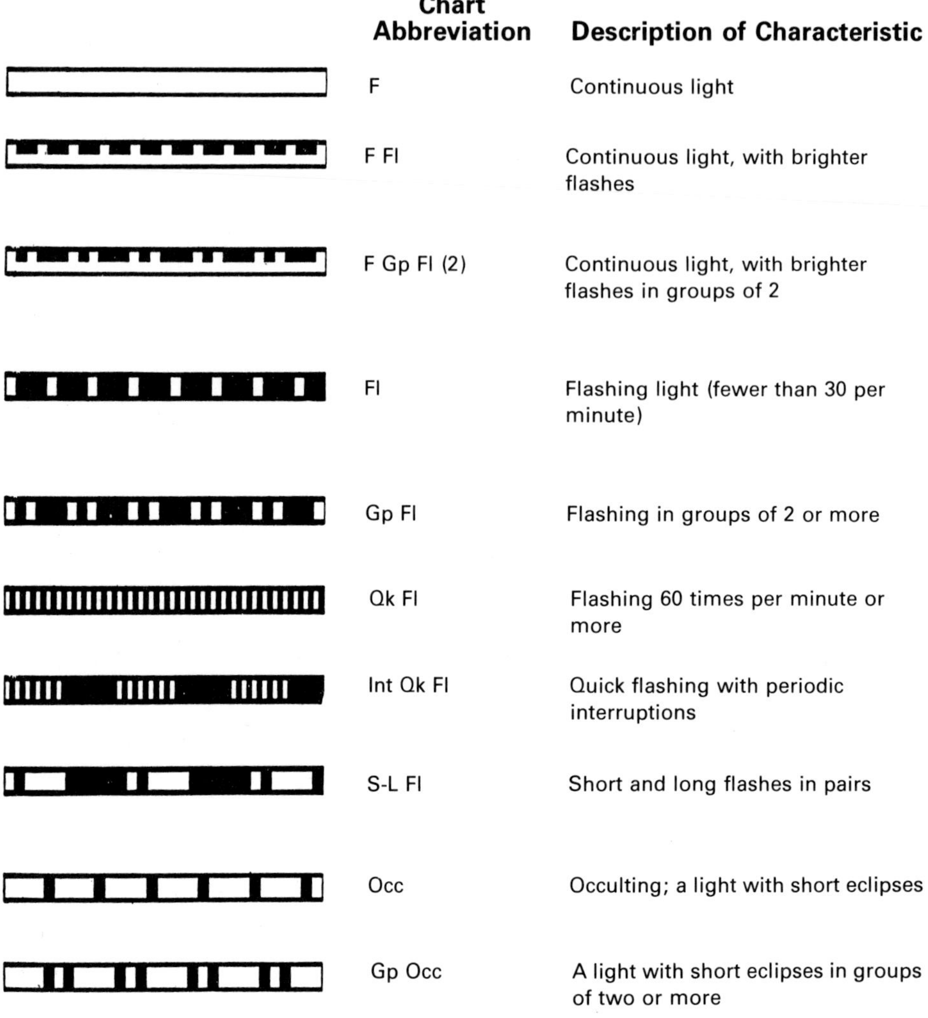

Chart Abbreviation	Description of Characteristic
F	Continuous light
F Fl	Continuous light, with brighter flashes
F Gp Fl (2)	Continuous light, with brighter flashes in groups of 2
Fl	Flashing light (fewer than 30 per minute)
Gp Fl	Flashing in groups of 2 or more
Qk Fl	Flashing 60 times per minute or more
Int Qk Fl	Quick flashing with periodic interruptions
S-L Fl	Short and long flashes in pairs
Occ	Occulting; a light with short eclipses
Gp Occ	A light with short eclipses in groups of two or more

Figure 4-1 Characteristics of single color lights.

things being equal, a high light will be visible from farther away than a low light. Also, increasing the height of the observer will make the light visible from farther away. The table in Figure 4-6 gives the *geographic range* for various heights of the light, and two heights of eye. Because it's very helpful to know the range of a light, charts often give this figure, rounded to the nearest mile and based on a height of eye of 15 feet. In

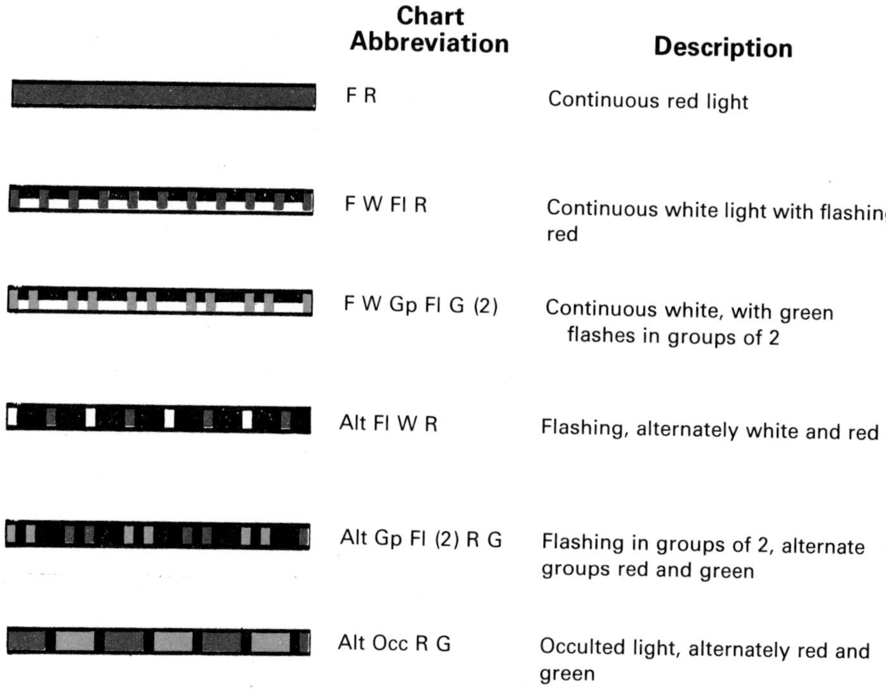

Chart Abbreviation
Description
F R
Continuous red light
F W Fl R
Continuous white light with flashing red
F W Gp Fl G (2)
Continuous white, with green flashes in groups of 2
Alt Fl W R
Flashing, alternately white and red
Alt Gp Fl (2) R G
Flashing in groups of 2, alternate groups red and green
Alt Occ R G
Occulted light, alternately red and green

Figure 4-2 Characteristics of multiple color lights.

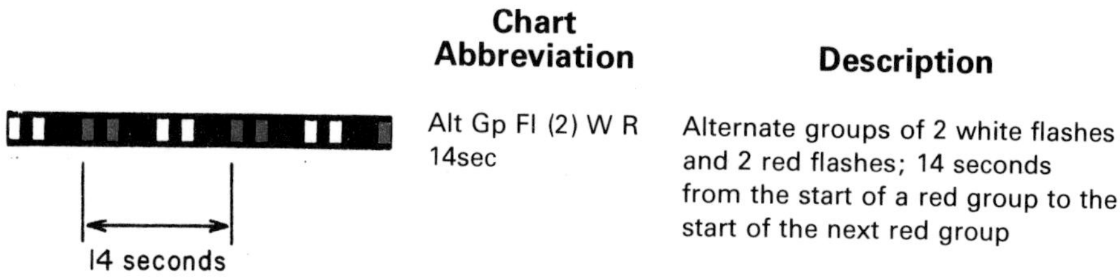

Chart Abbreviation
Description
Alt Gp Fl (2) W R 14sec
Alternate groups of 2 white flashes and 2 red flashes; 14 seconds from the start of a red group to the start of the next red group
14 seconds

Figure 4-3 Time designation for group lights.

*62 GULF OF ST. LAWRENCE, NORTH SHORE - APPROACH TO BRADORE BAY - GREENLY ISLAND - Light characteristic changed.

Charts (Last correction) - 4670(Plan, Blanc Sablon)(669/75) - 4470(669/75) - 4020(794/75) - L-4021(905/75).

Amend *Fl 2.5 sec 111 ft 15 M* 51°22'32"N 57°11'31"W
to *Fl 15 sec 111 ft 15 M*
(8010-816) (DOT)

Figure 4-4 A *Notice to Mariners* showing a light characteristic change.

many small boats, your height of eye is more like 6 feet. You can find the approximate range by subtracting two miles from the charted range.

A few lights are very weak, and are lost from sight long before the geographic range in the table is reached. In those cases, the range shown on the chart will be the actual *luminous range* in average conditions, rather than the geographic range.

The chart symbols for lights have been fairly well standardized. Extracts from the U.S. and Canadian Chart #1 are given below. The amount of information given for the light will depend on the scale of the chart. A very small scale may show only the position of major lights, while a large scale chart will show all the lights, with rather detailed information. For example, the notation for one light on a 1:50,000 chart reads FW F1R 5sec 53ft 12M. This light is fixed white, with red flashes every 5 seconds. The height of the *light* (not the structure) is 53 feet above mean high water, and the range is 12 miles.

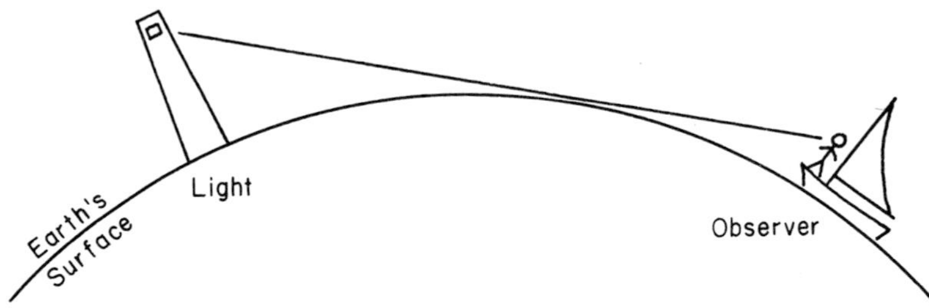

Figure 4-5 The earth's curvature sets a limit to the geographic range of a light.

LIGHT LIST

Because there's limited space for printed information on a chart, only part of the information about a light can be shown. Sometimes a small scale chart doesn't show any. The *List of Lights, Buoys, and Fog Signals* is a useful publication that gives full details on these aids. Figure 4-9 shows a sample. Notice the detail given for the characteristic of the Esteven Point light. The same light might be shown on the chart as Gp Fl (3) 10sec, or simply Gp Fl, depending on the scale. Incidentally, a

Height of Light – feet –	RANGE—NAUTICAL MILES	
	Height of Eye 6 Feet	Height of Eye 15 Feet
20	7.9	9.5
30	9.1	10.7
40	10.0	11.7
50	10.9	12.5
60	11.7	13.3
70	12.4	14.0
80	13.0	14.7
90	13.7	15.3
100	14.2	15.9
120	15.3	17.0
140	16.3	18.0
160	17.3	18.9
180	18.2	19.8
200	19.0	20.6

Figure 4-6 The geographic range of a light depends on its height and the observer's height of eye.

stopwatch will be very useful in timing lights for comparison with the light list.

Like other publications, the light list must be corrected from *Notices to Mariners*.

BUOYS

Floating buoys are certainly the most numerous aids to navigation, numbering several tens of thousands in North America alone. They range from simple wooden spars to massive steel structures with automatic lights, sound apparatus, and radar transponders. All buoys, however, follow a common system of shapes, colors, and numbers. The same system is used in the U.S. and Canada, and is illustrated in Figure 4-10. The system of buoy *lights*, however, differs slightly in the two countries. In Canada, a red buoy carries a red light, and a black buoy carries a green light. In the U.S., a red buoy may carry either a red or white light, and a black buoy may carry either a green or white light. The chart symbols also differ slightly in the two countries. Extracts from Chart #1 are given in Figures 4-11 and 4-12. The system deserves a few comments. Simple spar buoys are either wood or steel, red spars have pointed tops, and black spars have square tops. The shape is a real help in identifying spars by day. By night they may be identified by colored reflectors, red reflectors on red spars, and white or green reflectors on black spars.

Larger steel buoys are called nuns if pointed (red) and cans if square (black). Buoys with superstructures for light and/or sound apparatus are not distinguished by shape, but are colored red or black. Many buoys are numbered; red buoys with even numbers and black buoys with odd numbers.

K. †(new optional symbol) Lights

No.	Symbol/Abbreviation	Description
†1		Position of light
2	Lt	Light
†(Ka)		Riprap surrounding light
3	Lt Ho	Lighthouse
†4	AERO AERO	Aeronautical light (See F-22)
4a		Marine and air navigation light
†5	Bn Bn	Light beacon
†6		Light vessel; Lightship
8		Lantern
9		Street lamp
10	REF	Reflector
†11	Ldg Lt Ldg Lt	Leading light
†12	RED RED	Sector light
†13	RED RED GREEN GREEN	Directional light
14		Harbor light
15		Fishing light
16		Tidal light
†17	Priv maintd	Private light (maintained by private interests; to be used with caution)
21	F	Fixed light
22	Occ	Occulting light
23	Fl	Flashing light
23a	Iso E Int	Isophase light (equal interval)
24	Qk Fl	Quick flashing (scintillating) light
25	Int Qk Fl I Qk Fl	Interrupted quick flashing light
25a	S Fl	Short flashing light
26	Alt	Alternating light
27	Gp Occ	Group occulting light
28	Gp Fl	Group flashing light
28a	S-L Fl	Short-long flashing light
28b		Group short flashing light

No.	Abbreviation	Description
29	F Fl	Fixed and flashing light
30	F Gp Fl	Fixed and group flashing light
30a	Mo	Morse code light
31	Rot	Revolving or Rotating light
41		Period
42		Every
43		With
44		Visible (range)
(Kb)	M	Nautical mile (See E-11)
(Kc)	m; min	Minutes (See E-2)
(Kd)	sec	Seconds (See E-3)
45	Fl	Flash
46	Occ	Occultation
46a		Eclipse
47	Gp	Group
48	Occ	Intermittent light
49	SEC	Sector
50		Color of sector
51	Aux	Auxiliary light
52		Varied
61	Vi	Violet
62		Purple
63	Bu	Blue
64	G	Green
65	Or	Orange
66	R	Red
67	W	White
67a	Am	Amber
67b	Y	Yellow
68	OBSC	Obscured light
68a	Fog Det Lt	Fog detector light (See N-Nb)

Figure 4-7 Symbols for lights on U.S. charts.

K Lights

No.	Symbol	Meaning
1	!	*Position of Light*
2	Lt Lts	*Light, Lights*
3	Lt Ho	*Lighthouse*
4	Aero	*Air Obstruction Light*
(4a)	✲ AERO	*Airway Beacon*
5		*Light Beacon*
6		*Light Vessel*
(7)		*Light Buoys*
12	 Red Sector	*Sector Light*
17	(Private)	*Privately maintained light*
21	F	*Fixed*
22	Occ	*Occulting*
22a	E Int	*Equal Interval*
23	Fl	*Flashing*
24	Qk Fl	*Quick Flashing*
26	Alt	*Alternating*
27	Gp Occ	*Group Occulting*
28	Gp Fl	*Group Flashing*
28a	Fl (S-L)	*Flashing Short-Long*
29	F Fl	*Fixed and Flashing*
30	F Gp Fl	*Fixed and Group Flashing*
31	Rev	*Revolving*

No.	Symbol	Meaning
42	ev	*every*
44	† vis	*visible*
45	† fl	*flash*
47	Gp	*Group*
63	† bl Bl	*Blue*
64	† g G	*Green*
66	† r R	*Red*
67	† w W	*White*
67a	Am	*Amber*
68	Obscd	*Obscured*
69	(U)	*Unwatched*
70	Occasl	*Occasional*
71	Irreg	*Irregular*
72	Provl	*Provisional*
73	Temp	*Temporary*
77	Lr	*Lower*
80	Vert	*Vertical*
81	Hor	*Horizontal*

† *Abbreviation is obsolescent*

Example of description of light Occ Alt W R ev 5 sec 25 ft 10 M

All lights are white unless otherwise stated.

Alt *(Alternating) signifies a light which alters colour.*

The number in brackets after the description of Group Flashing or Group Occulting lights denotes the number of flashes or eclipses in each group.

Occasional Light (or Fog Signal) is one which is given only when a vessel is expected or in answer to vessels signals or at other irregular times.

The elevation given against a light is the height of the focal plane of the light above Mean High Water Spring Tides, or, in the case of non-tidal waters, above the datum of the chart.

The visibility of lights is given in nautical miles, assuming the eye of the observer to be 15 feet above the sea. Bearings of lights are given from Seaward.

Figure 4-8 Symbols for light on Canadian charts.

No.	Name	Position Latitude N. Longitude W.	Colour of lights	Character and period of light	Height in feet above high water	Miles seen in clear weather	Character of apparatus	Description of buildings, vessels and buoys. Height in feet from base to vane.	Year established or last altered	Remarks Fog Signals
113 *G5222*	Gold River	W. side of entrance to Gold River. 49 40 31.5 126 07 34	G	Qk.Fl.	26	.....	D, electric..	White circular tower, black band at top.	1955 1973	Flash 0.3 sec., eclipse 0.7 sec. Unwatched.
114 *G5224*	ESTEVAN POINT Radiobeacon......	SW. extremity of point at Hole-in-the-Wall. 49 23 00 126 32 32	W	Gp. Fl. 10 sec.	125	17	D, 1, electric	White octagonal tower.... White square building, red roof.	1907 1963 1908 1972	Flash 0.3 sec., eclipse 1.4 sec., flash 0.3 sec., eclipse 1.4 sec., flash 0.3 sec., eclipse 6.3 sec. Diaphone–Blast 5 sec., silence 55 sec. Horn points 210°.
115	*Hesquiat Harbour light and whistle buoy ZE*	At entrance to harbour ... 49 23 07 126 25 48	W	Fl. (Mo.A.)	.....	.....	D, electric..	Black and white vertical stripes, marked "ZE".	1907 1972	Radar reflector.

Figure 4-9 An extract from the List of Lights. Buoys, and Fog Signals.

Sound may be produced by bells, gongs (multi-pitched bells), or whistles. In many cases, these are operated by wave action, so the sound is unpredictable, and may not operate at all on calm days. The sound of a bell doesn't carry very far. It seems to depend on the wind, and I've often approached a bell buoy almost within yards before hearing the bell. Whistles carry much better; on a quiet night you may hear one for miles.

"Red right returning" is the most quoted rule for remembering which side you should leave a buoy on. When you're returning from sea (heading upstream), leave red buoys on your right (to starboard) and black buoys on your left (to port). Black-and-white buoys may be passed on either side. To see how this system is applied, refer to the approach to Little Harbour on the practice chart shown in Figure 4-13. The outer fairway buoy has vertical black-and-white stripes, and may be passed on either side. The light flashes a Morse code (A); short-long. Next you encounter a black bell-buoy, which you leave to port, and a red bell-buoy which you leave to starboard (red right returning). The inner black bell-buoy carries a quick-flashing, green light, since it marks a particular hazard, and you leave it to port. The last buoy, a black spar, is also left to port.

In some situations, such as proceding along a coast, the terms "returning" or "upstream" have no meaning. In such cases, buoyage will follow an arbitrary system such as considering north or west to be upstream. These systems are different in various areas, so check on the one used in your area.

Some cautions. Because buoys are occasionally moved by storms or ice, don't depend entirely on the charted position. Also, buoys are frequently changed or moved as part of the continuous process of maintaining and upgrading navigation aids. Changes are listed in *Notices to Mariners*, as shown in Figure 4-14. Keep your charts up to date. It's very embarrassing to be unable to find a white light shown on the chart, only to find later that it was changed to green, as happened to me once. Finally, never use a buoy as a handy place to tie your boat while fishing. There are stiff fines for any such nonsense; the buoy could be moved or damaged, and would certainly be obscured from view by other boats.

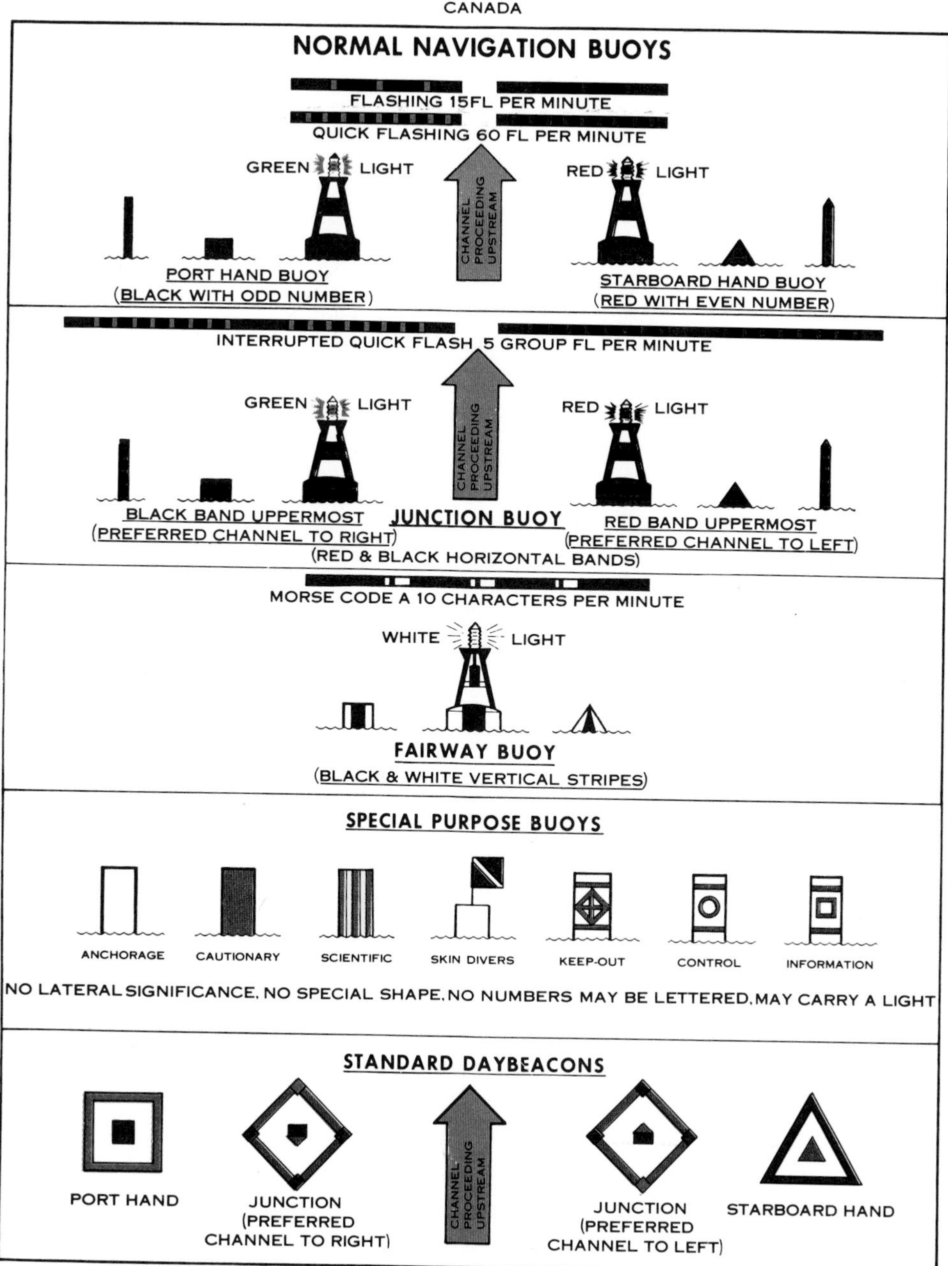

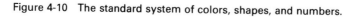

Figure 4-10 The standard system of colors, shapes, and numbers.

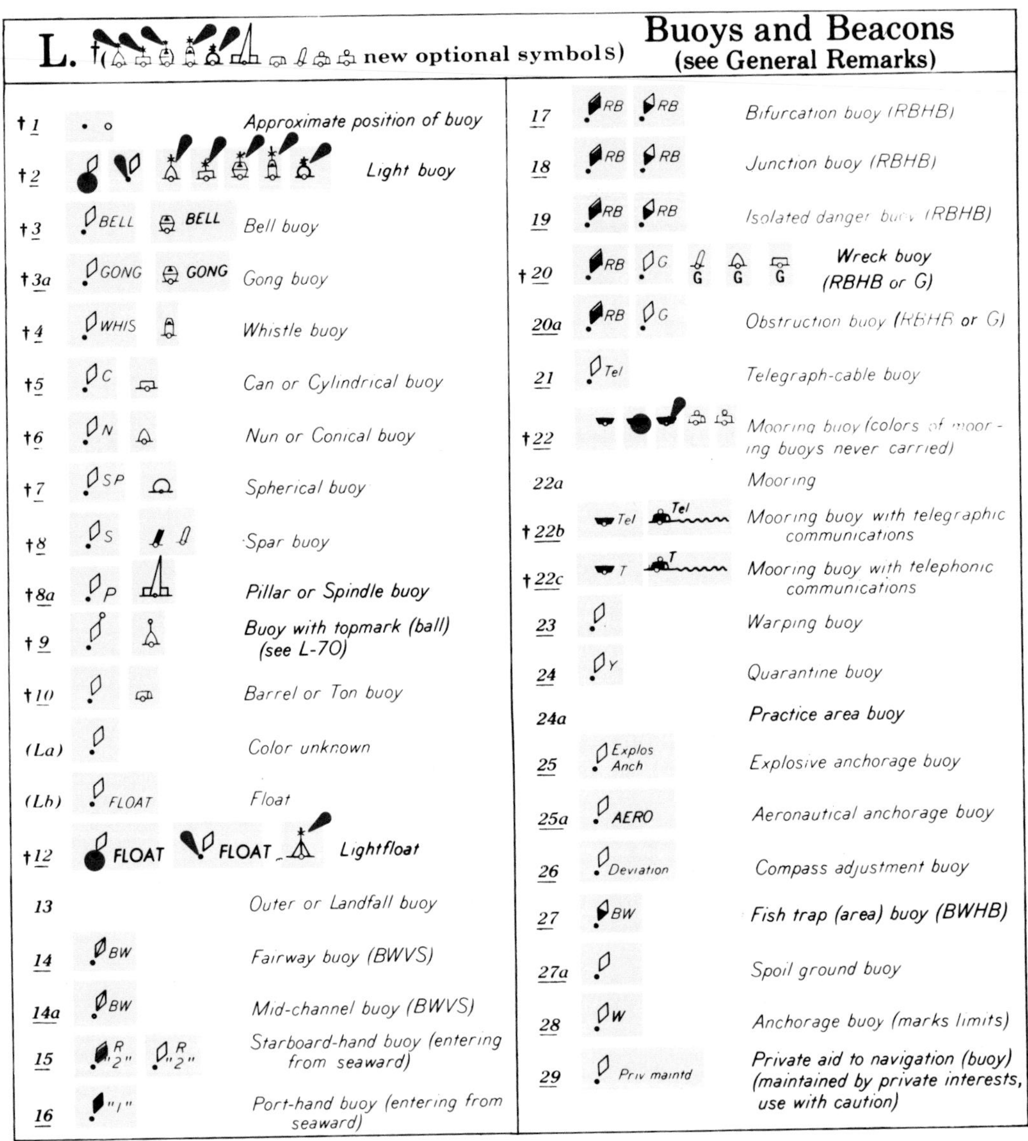

L. (new optional symbols)
Buoys and Beacons
(see General Remarks)
†1 Approximate position of buoy
†2 Light buoy
†3 BELL BELL Bell buoy
†3a GONG GONG Gong buoy
†4 WHIS Whistle buoy
†5 C Can or Cylindrical buoy
†6 N Nun or Conical buoy
†7 SP Spherical buoy
†8 S Spar buoy
†8a P Pillar or Spindle buoy
†9 Buoy with topmark (ball) (see L-70)
†10 Barrel or Ton buoy
(La) Color unknown
(Lb) FLOAT Float
†12 FLOAT FLOAT Lightfloat
13 Outer or Landfall buoy
14 BW Fairway buoy (BWVS)
14a BW Mid-channel buoy (BWVS)
15 R "2" R "2" Starboard-hand buoy (entering from seaward)
16 "1" Port-hand buoy (entering from seaward)
17 RB RB Bifurcation buoy (RBHB)
18 RB RB Junction buoy (RBHB)
19 RB RB Isolated danger buoy (RBHB)
†20 RB G G G G Wreck buoy (RBHB or G)
20a RB G Obstruction buoy (RBHB or G)
21 Tel Telegraph-cable buoy
†22 Mooring buoy (colors of mooring buoys never carried)
22a Mooring
†22b Tel Tel Mooring buoy with telegraphic communications
†22c T T Mooring buoy with telephonic communications
23 Warping buoy
24 Y Quarantine buoy
24a Practice area buoy
25 Explos Anch Explosive anchorage buoy
25a AERO Aeronautical anchorage buoy
26 Deviation Compass adjustment buoy
27 BW Fish trap (area) buoy (BWHB)
27a Spoil ground buoy
28 W Anchorage buoy (marks limits)
29 Priv maintd Private aid to navigation (buoy) (maintained by private interests, use with caution)

Figure 4-11 Buoy symbols on U.S. charts. The position of the buoy is shown by the dot or circle at the base.

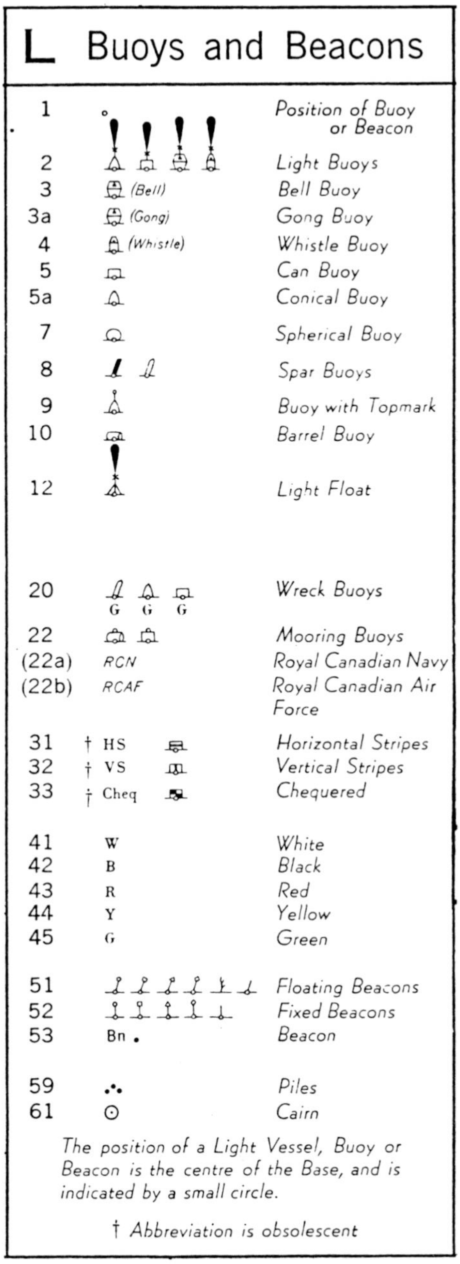

L Buoys and Beacons

No.	Symbol	Meaning
1	°	*Position of Buoy or Beacon*
2		*Light Buoys*
3	*(Bell)*	*Bell Buoy*
3a	*(Gong)*	*Gong Buoy*
4	*(Whistle)*	*Whistle Buoy*
5		*Can Buoy*
5a		*Conical Buoy*
7		*Spherical Buoy*
8		*Spar Buoys*
9		*Buoy with Topmark*
10		*Barrel Buoy*
12		*Light Float*
20	G G G	*Wreck Buoys*
22		*Mooring Buoys*
(22a)	*RCN*	*Royal Canadian Navy*
(22b)	*RCAF*	*Royal Canadian Air Force*
31	† HS	*Horizontal Stripes*
32	† VS	*Vertical Stripes*
33	† Cheq	*Chequered*
41	W	*White*
42	B	*Black*
43	R	*Red*
44	Y	*Yellow*
45	G	*Green*
51		*Floating Beacons*
52		*Fixed Beacons*
53	Bn •	*Beacon*
59	•:•	*Piles*
61	⊙	*Cairn*

The position of a Light Vessel, Buoy or Beacon is the centre of the Base, and is indicated by a small circle.

† *Abbreviation is obsolescent*

Figure 4-12 Buoy symbols on Canadian charts. The position of the buoy is shown by the small circle at the base.

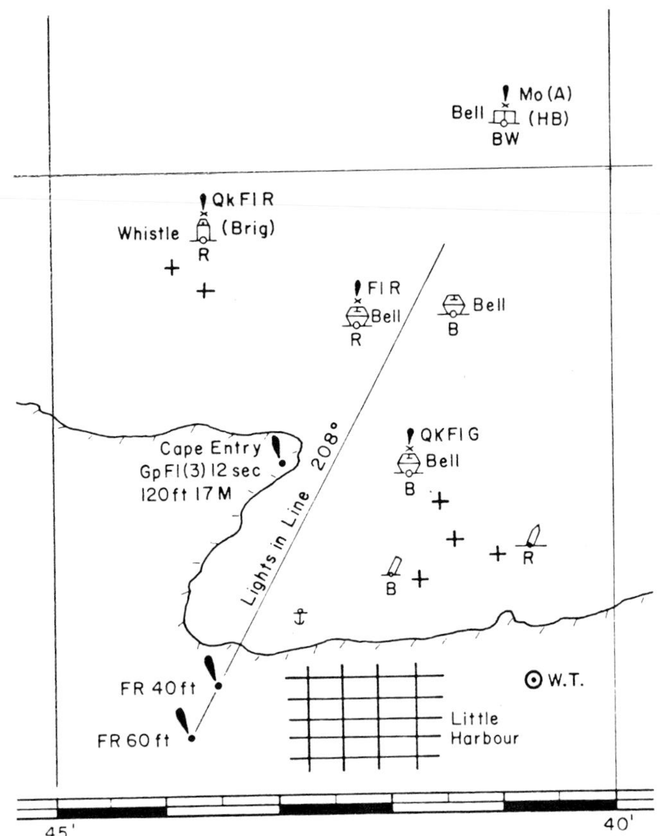

Figure 4-13 The buoyage on the approach to Little Harbour.

*686. CAPE BRETON ISLAND, WEST COAST - OFF PORT HOOD ISLAND - Buoy changed.

The black can buoy in 45°59'06"N., 61°33'22"W. has been replaced by a black light buoy, Fl. G., marked "81U", and equipped with a radar reflector.
(DOT)(8005-32)

Charts (Last correction) - 4448(Plan, Port Hood) (1095/74) - D6-4462(117/75).
List of Lights, Buoys and Fog Signals - Atlantic 1975; Insert No. 879.5.

*685. GULF OF ST. LAWRENCE - PRINCE EDWARD ISLAND, NORTH SIDE - CONWAY INLET ENTRANCE - Buoy relocated - Chart amendment.

Conway Inlet light and bell buoy 79N has been moved southeastward about 1,200 feet to 46°39'42"N., 63°51'00"W.
(DOT)(8005-32)

Charts (Last correcttion) - 4491(613/75) - D6-4023 and D7-4023(640/75).
List of Lights, Buoys and Fog Signals - Atlantic 1975; No. 1071.4.

Figure 4-14 Notices to Mariners advise changes to buoys.

5: The Compass

Said Captain Porgie, on the deck,
To his mate in the mizzen-hatch,
While the boatswain bold in the forward hold
Was winding his larboard watch,

"Oh, how does our good ship head to-night,
How heads our gallant craft?"
"Oh, she heads to the East, Sou'west by North,
And the binnacle lies abaft."

Journal of the American Canoe Association, 1883

There isn't much room for doubt about the most important instrument used in piloting: the magnetic compass. This single device is the basis of almost every aspect of piloting, and no prudent navigator will put to sea for even a short jaunt without one. There are many legends and few facts regarding the invention of the compass, but it has certainly been in use for 10 centuries, and quite probably more. From its early crude form, the compass has evolved into today's refined and accurate instrument.

In concept, the compass is a simple device. It consists of one or more magnets, pivoted to revolve freely and line up with the earth's magnetic field. The magnet has a card attached, which also lines up with the magnetic poles, and the card is marked to indicate directions to other points. In further discussions of the compass, remember this basic idea: *the magnet and card remain stationary, while the boat does the turning.* Next to the card is a mark lined up with the boat's bow, called the *lubber's line,* that shows which direction the boat is pointing.

In order to work freely, the card has to stay horizontal even though the boat heels and pitches, so that the card, pivot, and lubber's line are supported by a free-swinging mechanism called gimbals. Earlier forms of the compass used gimbals outside the card enclosure, and these external gimbals are still found in today's dory compass or box compass, as shown in Figure 5-1. More modern designs place the gimbals inside the enclosure. A typical, present-day, small boat compass is shown in Figure 5-2, and Figure 5-3 shows the arrangement of its internal gimbals. Such compasses aren't cheap, with prices ranging from $50 to $200. However, their accuracy and reliability make them well worth the price.

Compass cards have traditionally been marked off in 32 points, and many still are. In this system, the four cardinal points (north, south, east, and west) are marked with bold diamonds. Between them are the smaller intercardinal points (northeast, southeast, southwest, and northwest). These are divided again, with even smaller marks, into north northeast, east northeast, and so forth. Generally, these cards also carry small degree markings around the edge.

Many modern compass cards are marked only on the degree system. These are usually marked every 5 degrees, and numbered every 30 degrees. The choice is a matter of personal preference. Degree-type cards have a clean and functional look, which might be preferred on a boat of modern design. Traditionalists may well prefer the point markings, and appreciate their good visibility in poor light.

Ideally, the compass card doesn't turn. Occasionally, though, boat motion will turn the card slightly. Then it tends to swing back and forth with an annoying motion called hunting. To reduce this effect, most good compasses include a feature called *damping,* which is a very slight drag on the card. Usually this is provided by putting the pivot and card in a bowl filled with a clear, nonfreezing liquid. Although varsol and alcohol have traditionally been used, I understand that modern compasses are filled with more exotic liquids. If you're buying a compass, check the

Figure 5-1 The traditional box compass with external gimbals is still popular for its moderate price.

Figure 5-2 A modern compass with internal gimbals

damping by giving the case a sudden turn. The card will probably turn a little, but should settle back to correct position quickly, smoothly, and without oscillation.

Many compasses have built-in lighting, which is a very useful feature. Red is the preferred color, because it doesn't affect night vision. One point to watch in the installation of a lighted compass is the wiring. The light bulb is invariably a low voltage bulb operating on DC. The DC

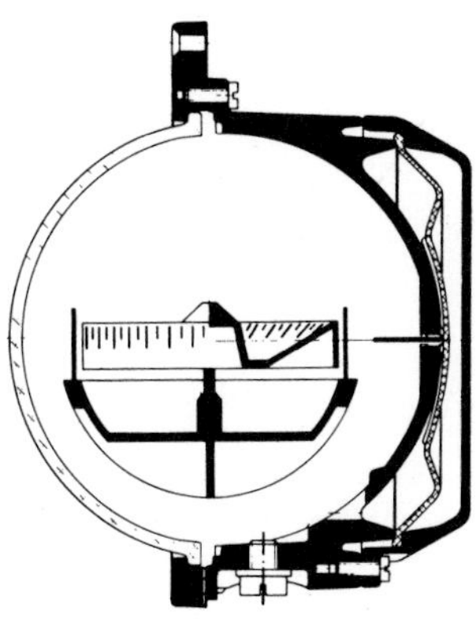

Figure 5-3 Cutaway view of the internal gimbals.

current in the wires produces a magnetic field which can affect the compass. To avoid this, twist the two wires tightly together.

VARIATION

A good compass, properly mounted, is a wonderfully accurate and reliable instrument. But you have to remember that it doesn't point north. Not the north on the chart, that is. The compass points to the magnetic north pole, and charts use the geographic (true) north pole. Since those two are about 900 miles apart, the difference between chart north and compass north, called *variation,* amounts to quite a few degrees.

Variation affects any compass, in any boat or on shore. To correct for it, you have to know the amount of variation that exists in the area where you're sailing. You can get this figure from a special chart, HO 1706, which gives the variation for any point on earth. [Pilot charts, discussed in Chapter 2, also give variation figures.] Refer to Figure 5-4, and you'll see that on the east coast of North America the variation is west, meaning that the compass needle points west of true north. Conversely, on the west coast the variation is east.

In coastal piloting, you're usually working with large-scale charts that cover a small area and give lots of detail. These charts normally have at least one compass rose, which shows the direction of true and magnetic north. A typical compass rose from a Great Lakes chart is shown in Figure 5-5. The outer scale gives true direction, and the next scale gives magnetic directions. The variation figure for the location is also shown −8° west in this case. The variation in this area is "nearly stationary," meaning that it doesn't change from year to year. In other areas there is a small yearly change. For example, the compass rose on the practice chart shows that the variation is decreasing 3′ per year. At that rate, it will be 20 years before the variation has changed one degree, and if your chart is 20 years old, you'll have bigger problems than that.

Now that you know how to find out the variation in a given area, let's see about converting between magnetic and true, or the reverse. A little rhyme is useful: "Variation west, compass best." It means that if the variation is west, the compass reading is "best," or more than the true direction. For a variation of 8° W, a compass reading of 060° will be a true direction of 052°, as you can easily check on the rose in Figure 5-5 by drawing a line through the two scales. For east variation, the rhyme goes, "variation east, compass least," meaning that the compass reading is less than the true direction.

You can do the conversion by adding or subtracting in your head, or you can convert with lines drawn on the compass rose if the chart has one. Just remember that variation can be either east or west, and the figure can be quite large. Variations in the 20's are common on the

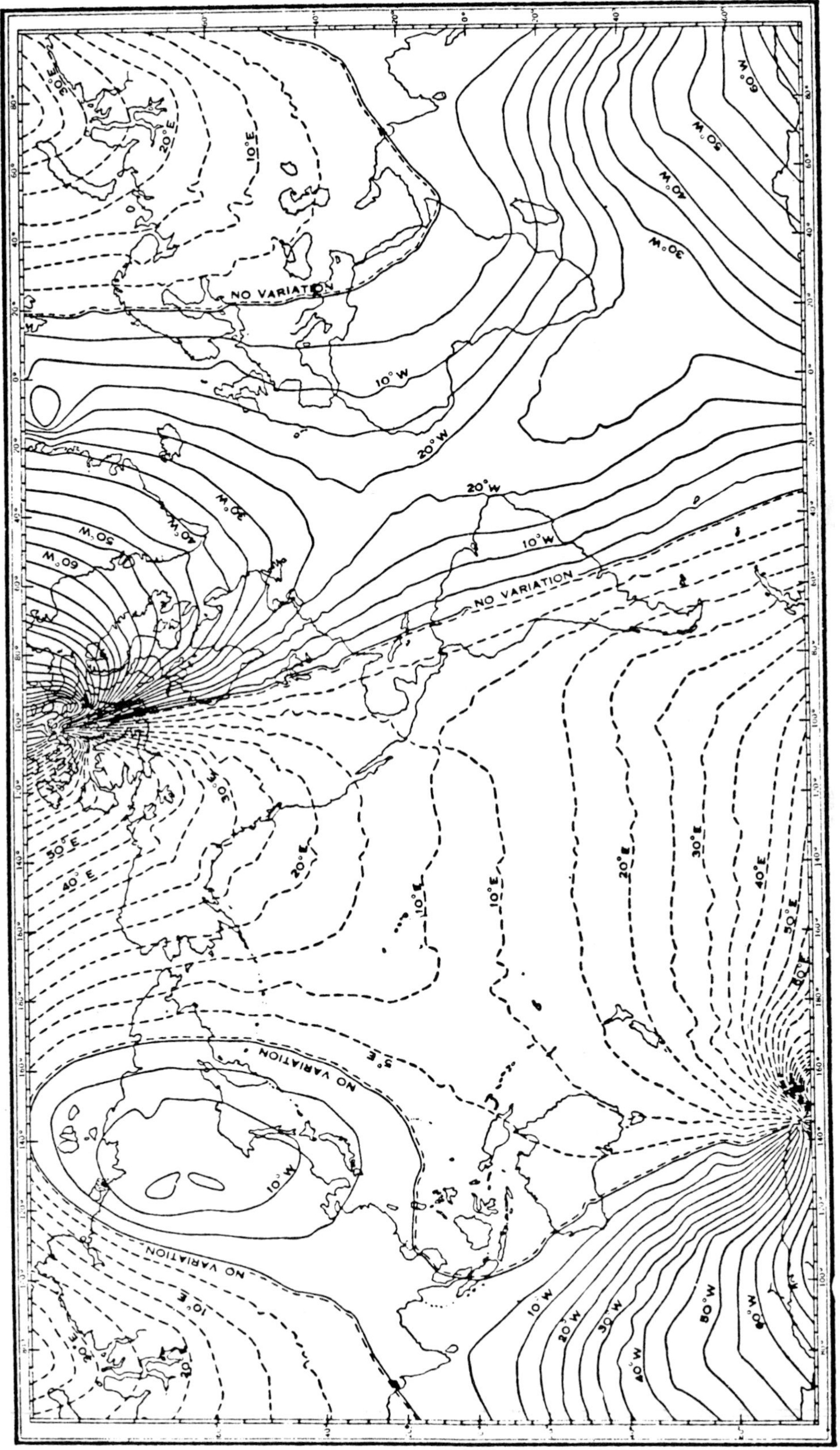

Figure 5-4 Chart HO 1706 shows the variation for any location.

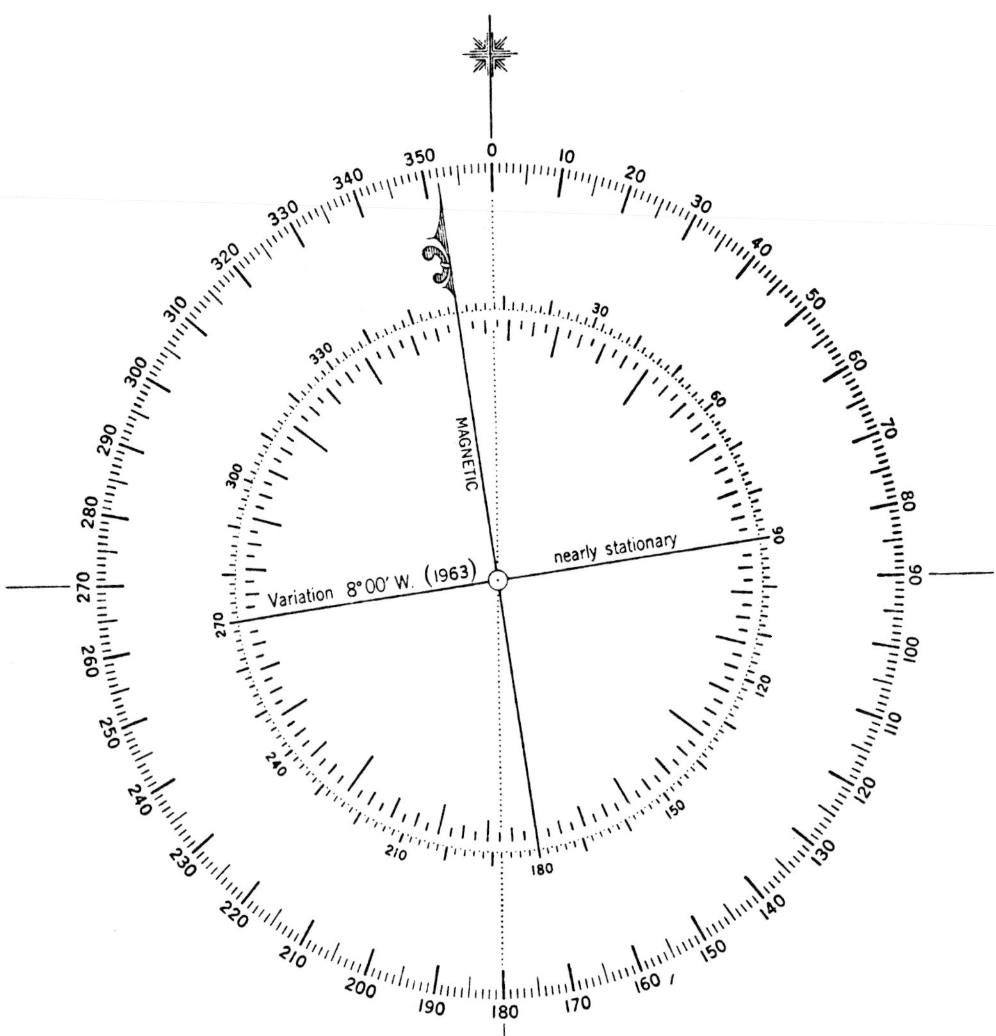

Figure 5-5 A compass rose, showing true and magnetic north.

coasts. Example 5-1 below, illustrates the application of the conversion rule.

Example 5-1: Correction for variation.

Magnetic Direction	Variation	True Direction
230	10 W	220
065	8 E	073
143	22 E	165
335	17 W	318

A word of caution on variation. There are occasional areas, known as *magnetic anomalies*, where the amount of variation changes radically over a small distance. At Pic Island, on the north shore of Lake Superior, the variation changes by 45 degrees, over half a mile. Information on these anomalies is given in the sailing directions, and sometimes the chart has a cautionary notice.

Problem 5-1

Make the conversion between magnetic and true directions.

Magnetic Direction	Variation	True Direction
( )	15 E	148
256	5 W	( )
348	25 E	( )
( )	12 W	040

DEVIATION

As mentioned above, any compass, on any boat, is affected by variation, so a correction for variation must always be made. A second correction may also be needed, if the compass is affected by nearby iron or steel, such as an engine, iron keel, steel hull, or something like an anchor stowed near the compass. In such cases, the compass doesn't point to magnetic north, and the difference is called *deviation*. To illustrate this effect, let's suppose your boat has an iron keel. Ideally, as the boat turns, the compass card should remain still and point to magnetic north. But as the boat turns, so does the magnetized iron keel, and the moving magnet causes the compass card to shift slightly one way or the other. This change in reading from magnetic north is called deviation. Because it results from the turning of the magnetized keel, deviation depends on the heading of the boat.

As early as the 1500's, seamen had noticed that compass readings were not always reliable. A number of theories were given as to the cause. But, it was not until 1804 that Matthew Flinders recognized the real cause of deviation, and suggested a method of correcting it. His important contribution to navigation is still recognized by the name *Flinders Bar*, an important part of a modern compass installation.

Since deviation depends on the heading of the boat, you need a deviation table to correct for it. A sample is shown in Figure 5-6. This table gives the deviation on eight different headings, though many tables have values for more headings. A compass adjuster can provide a table for your boat, or you can work out your own, as shown later in this chapter.

Remember, any compass on any boat is affected by variation. If the boat has large chunks of iron or steel, the compass may also be affected by deviation. The combination of variation and deviation is called compass error. Figure 5-7 shows the relationship.

Let's suppose that you're steering a compass heading of 090°, and the local variation is 24° E. According to the deviation table, the deviation on

Deviation Table

Vessel *Deviant* **Adjuster** *JPB*
Compass *Steering* **Date** *15-8-75*

Ship's Head - Magnetic	Deviation
000	5° W
045	4° W
090	2° W
135	2° E
180	4° E
225	5° E
270	2° E
315	2° W

Figure 5-6 The deviation table.

this heading is 2° W. The compass error is then 24° E plus 2° W, or 22° E. The "east,least-west,best" rule also applies here, so the compass heading must be 22° less than the true heading. Therefore, the true heading is 112°.

Similar reasoning can be used in the reverse direction. Suppose you have a certain destination, and have worked out the heading on the chart as 170° true. Variation is 20° W in the area, and you want to know what heading to steer on the compass. First find the deviation for a heading of 170°, which is 4° E. (This isn't strictly correct procedure, since the table entry is magnetic heading, not true heading. Yet, the error is negligible.) The compass error is then 20° W plus 4° E, or 16° W. Accordingly, the compass heading should be 170° plus 16°, or 186°. Example 5-2 illustrates the application of this method. Known figures are printed in boldface, while figures that are worked out are printed in italics.

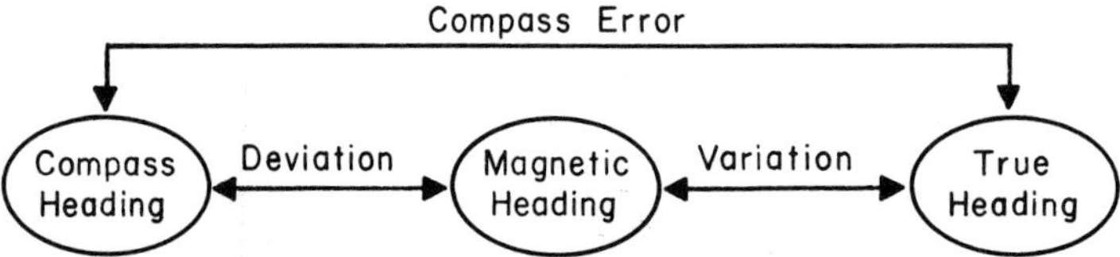

Figure 5-7 Compass error is the combination of variation and deviation.

Example 5-2

Compass Heading	Deviation	Variation	True Heading
125	*2 E*	10 E	*137*
300	*1 W*	24 E	*323*
078	*3 W*	15 W	060
230	*5 E*	5 W	230

Check your understanding wth Problem 5-2.

Problem 5-2

Compass Heading	Deviation	Variation	True Heading
220		25 W	( )
315		8 W	( )
( )		10 E	087
273		14 W	( )
( )		5 E	155
( )		20 E	040
130		12 W	( )
( )		15 E	230
015		22 W	( )
( )		17 W	350

CONSTRUCTING A DEVIATION TABLE

If we can assume that a deviation table is available and correct, the above information is all you need to work out correct headings. The trick is that a deviation table may not be available. Also, deviation can change if the magnetism in the boat changes. This can occur, for example, if you install a new engine. Magnetism in the keel can also be changed by the shock of a hard grounding. In such cases you may need a new deviation table. A compass adjuster can provide this for you, but finding and arranging one can be a nuisance. Moreover, the cost is another factor. It's very nice to be able to do the job yourself, and it's also quite easy.

Remember the basic concept: as the boat turns, the card should remain still. The basic plan of attack is to check whether the card actually does turn, and if so, how much. The process is called "swinging the compass." Now, as the boat turns, the lubber's line turns with it, so that you can't use it to check the card. Instead, you sight across the card at a distant object and check its bearing.

Let's check an example. Suppose you're at anchor in a quiet cove, and can see a distant mountain peak. From the chart the correct bearing to the peak is 109° true, and the variation in the area is 24° E. The magnetic bearing should then be 085°. You swing the boat in a circle, checking the compass bearing to the mountain on a number of different headings. The figures are shown in the first two columns of Example 5-3, below. The deviation is then worked out from the correct bearing and the actual bearing, as given in the third column.

Example 5-3: Constructing a deviation table.

Compass Heading	Compass Bearing	Deviation
000	089	*4 W*
045	091	*6 W*
090	088	*3 W*
135	082	*3 E*
180	077	*8 E*
225	075	*10 E*
270	078	*7 E*
315	083	*2 E*

It's quite possible that you have a convenient object in view, but don't know its correct bearing. For example, you may see a radio mast that makes a fine target but isn't shown on the chart. You can still use it for swinging the compass. Follow the same routine of noting ship's heading and compass bearing. Then, average the bearings and use that figure as the correct bearing. The difference between the individual bearings and the average is taken as the deviation. Consider the headings and bearings in Example 5-4. The average of the bearings is 240°. Using that figure as the correct magnetic bearing, the deviations are worked out as shown in italics.

Example 5-4: Making a deviation table without a known bearing.

Compass Heading	Compass Bearing	Deviation
000	242	*2 W*
045	233	*7 E*
090	228	*12 E*
135	230	*10 E*
180	238	*2 E*
225	247	*7 W*
270	252	*12 W*
315	250	*10 W*
	Avg. 240	

The averaging method is useful, but not entirely foolproof. If the compass has a fixed error—for example, always reading 3° too high—the deviation table will be in error by this amount. For example, suppose the correct bearing on an object is 174° true, and variation in the area is 24° E. Then the magnetic bearing should be 150°. We swing the compass and obtain headings and compass bearings as given in Example 5-5. The deviation figures are then worked out, as shown under "Deviation by correct bearing." But if we didn't know the correct bearing, and instead worked out the average of the compass bearings, we would get a bearing of 148° and obtain results as shown under "Deviation by averaged bearings." The deviation figures are 2° different in every case. Fortunately, this type of compass error is not common, and usually small if it does occur. Still, it's better to use an object of known bearing when you swing your compass.

Example 5-5: Comparison of deviations obtained by averaged bearings and by the correct bearing.

Compass Heading	Compass Bearing	Deviation by correct bearing	Deviation by averaged bearings
000	154	*4 W*	*6 W*
045	156	*6 W*	*8 W*
090	153	*3 W*	*5 W*
135	147	*3 E*	*1 E*
180	142	*8 E*	*6 E*
225	140	*10 E*	*8 E*
270	143	*7 E*	*5 E*
315	148	*2 E*	*0*
Avg.	*148*		

On many boats, it's not possible to sight across the steering compass. In that case, hold the boat on a steady heading and read the compass. At the same time, measure the angle between the bow of the boat and the object. This is called a relative angle, and is best measured with a sextant. The two figures are combined to give an accurate compass bearing. Full details are given in Chapter 9.

Another good method is to sail along a line between two known objects. The heading can then be found from the chart. Occasionally, several objects of known bearing may be available. If so, head the boat for each one in turn, and read the compass heading.

Problem 5-3

The correct bearing to an object is 320° true, and variation in the area is 5° W. Given the compass headings and bearings below, make a deviation table.

Compass Heading	Compass Bearing
000	316
045	322
090	330
135	335
180	334
225	328
270	320
315	315

COMPASS COMPENSATION

I swung the ship in Table Bay and had a shore expert adjust the compass, which had been giving trouble; he was gone in an hour or so and we slipped quietly out to sea under all sail past Sea Point bound first to Ampenan or Boeleleng, 6500 miles away. The compass adjusters charge was £5 5s, but we had not got very far before I was that sure his estimate of the value of his genius was grossly exaggerated. I must add, however, in all fairness to him, that he had not left the compass much worse than he had found it.

Allan Villiers, Cruise of the Conrad

Wouldn't it be nice if your compass had little or no deviation, even though you have an iron keel and an engine. That's the purpose of compensating the compass. The process consists, in effect, of installing small magnets near the compass, in just such a way that they counteract the effect of the ship's magnetism. In practice, many compasses come with the magnets already installed in the case, and it's only a matter of adjusting them.

Remember, if your boat wasn't magnetic, the compass card would remain still even though the boat turns around it, as shown in Figures 5-8 and 5-9.

Now we recognize that the boat is, in fact, magnetic. There may be several sources of magnetism, but they have one net result, as shown in Figure 5-10. As the boat turns, its magnetism will cause the card to swing slightly, as shown in Figure 5-11. This is what we must counteract.

Let's begin by placing the boat on a heading of magnetic north. The card swings slightly to the east, as the boat's red pole repels the card's red pole, as shown in Figure 5-12. We can cure this by installing a thwartships magnet (crosswise to the boat), with its blue pole placed to attract the card's red pole, thereby repelling the card's blue pole. The card swings back to its proper position, as in Figure 5-13.

Now, let's place the boat on a heading of magnetic east. Notice that the thwartships correcting magnet is now lined up with the magnetic north pole. However, the boat's red pole repels the card's red pole, so the card swings slightly to the west, as in Figure 5-14. We correct this by installing a fore-and-aft magnet, with its blue pole placed to attract the card's red pole and repel the card's blue pole. The card again swings into correct position (see Figure 5-15).

This is the compensating procedure:

(1) Head the boat magnetic north, and adjust the thwartships magnet for correct compass reading.

(2) Head the boat magnetic east and adjust the fore-and-aft magnet for correct reading.

(3) Head the boat magnetic south. Some deviation may now be found. Adjust the thwartships magnet to remove half of this deviation.

(4) Head the boat magnetic west. If deviation is found, adjust the fore-and-aft magnet to remove half of it.

(5) That's that!

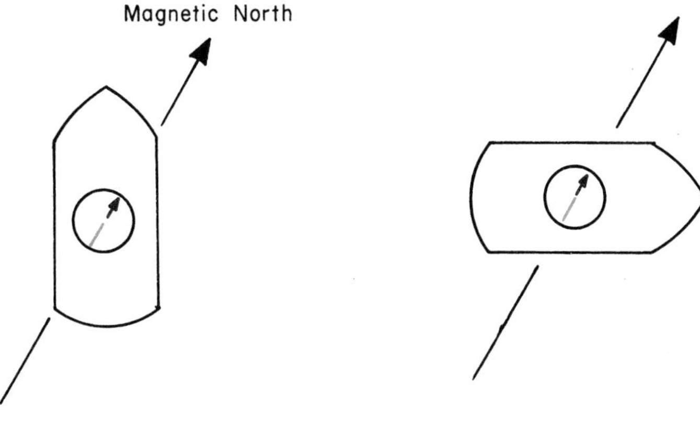

Figure 5-8

Figure 5-9

With a nonmagnetic boat, the card stays still while the boat turns.

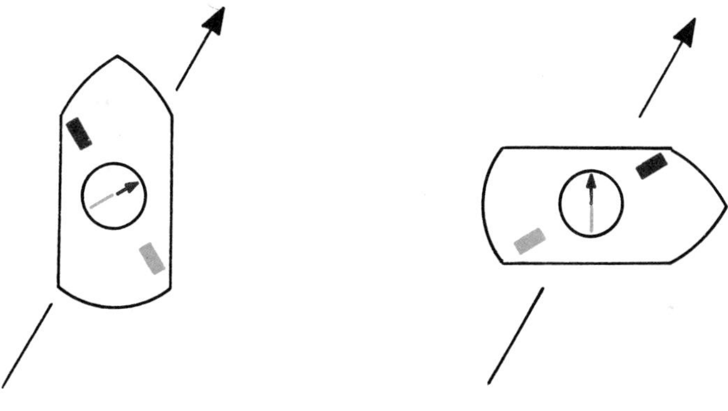

Figure 5-10

Figure 5-11

With a magnetic boat, the card swings slightly as the boat turns.

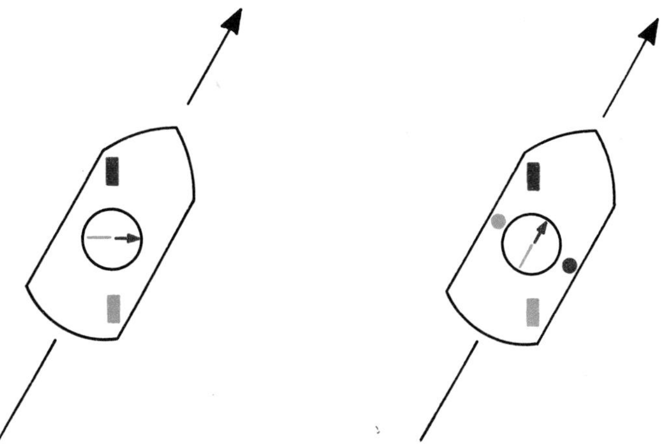

Figure 5-12

Figure 5-13

Adjusting the thwartships magnet with the boat heading magnetic north.

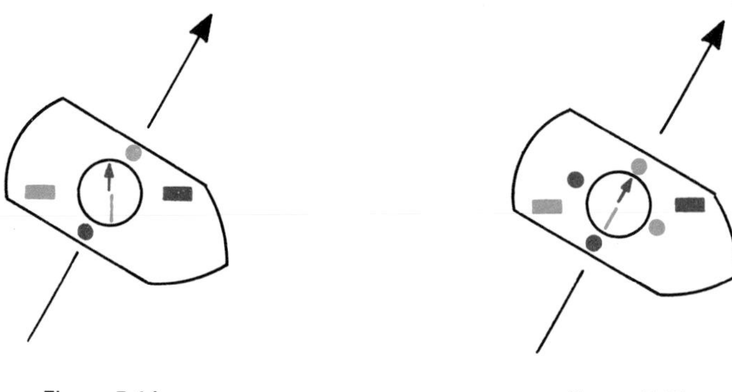

Figure 5-14

Figure 5-15

Adjusting the fore-and-aft magnet with the boat heading magnetic east.

I wouldn't want anyone to think that by learning this procedure he can hang out a shingle as a full-fledged compass compensator. There are other sources of error that must be corrected to make a complete job. For example, we have assumed that the magnetism of the boat is permanent. In fact, as the boat swings, the earth's magnetic field induces a small but changing magnetic field in the boat. This induced magnetism must be separately corrected. Also, when the boat heels, a similar effect causes a change in deviation called heeling error, which again must be corrected. However, these effects are smaller than the boat's permanent magnetism discussed above, and correction for them is not provided in the typical small boat compass. Using the correctors provided for the boat's permanent magnetism, anyone can quickly and easily do a satisfactory job of compensating his own compass.

6: Dead Reckoning

On the night of the day that we passed Cape Horn—June 13—the stars came out and Captain Svensson was able, for the first time in weeks, to establish the ship's position accurately. He discovered that the longitude was four degrees out—not four minutes or four miles, but degrees. *We were four degrees further on than we had thought we were; we had been able only to plot the ship's course by dead reckoning, which is inefficient at the best of times, dependent as it is upon a mechanical log which may or may not be perfect.*

Alan Villiers, By Way of Cape Horn

Let's conduct an imaginary experiment. Climb into your car, and have someone blindfold you. Starting at your house, have him drive through town, announcing each part of the trip. "We're going north. Now we've traveled three blocks and we're turning west. Now we've gone five blocks and we're turning south. Now we've traveled another three blocks, and we're stopping." At this point you can deduce where you are—five blocks west of your house. Keeping track of your whereabouts this way is called dead (deduced) reckoning, and it's an important skill for piloting work.

SPEED-TIME-DISTANCE CALCULATIONS

In the example above, you knew the distance traveled on each leg of your trip. In piloting work, however, you may not have the marine equivalent of an odometer (a log), so you must calculate distance on the basis of speed and time. There are several ways of doing this.

You can often do the calculation by hand or in your head. The equation is $D = S \times T$, meaning that the distance (nautical miles) equals the speed (knots) multiplied by the time (hours). For example, with a speed of 5 knots and a time of 3 hours, you will travel 15 miles. Variations of the equation, $S = D/T$ and $T = D/S$ are useful as well. For example, if your speed is 3.5 knots and you have 7 miles to travel, it will take 3 hours.

The equations will always give the correct answers, but they're not always convenient to use. If you try to mentally calculate the distance traveled in 35 minutes at 5.5 knots, you'll see what I mean. For these problems, a prepared table can be helpful. The old sight reduction tables for celestial navigation, HO 214, gave one such table, but the range of speeds suited warships better than small boats. Another table is given in Figure 6-1, which covers the speeds and times normally used for small boat piloting. Using it is simple. To solve our last problem, find the 5.5 knot column and 35 minute line, and read the distance at their intersection—3.2 miles. At the same 5.5 knot speed, how far would you travel in 4 hours 20 minutes? Find the 4 hour portion (22 miles) and the 20 minute portion (1.8 miles) and add them for the distance—23.8 miles. Of course, the table can also be used in another order. If your speed is 4 knots and you have 3 miles to go, it will take 45 minutes.

	SPEED IN KNOTS												
Minutes	**2.0**	**2.5**	**3.0**	**3.5**	**4.0**	**4.5**	**5.0**	**5.5**	**6.0**	**6.5**	**7.0**	**7.5**	**8.0**
1	.0	.0	.0	.1	.1	.1	.1	.1	.1	.1	.1	.1	.1
2	.1	.1	.1	.1	.1	.2	.2	.2	.2	.2	.2	.3	.3
3	.1	.1	.2	.2	.2	.2	.3	.3	.3	.3	.4	.4	.4
4	.1	.2	.2	.2	.3	.3	.3	.4	.4	.4	.5	.5	.5
5	.2	.2	.3	.3	.3	.4	.4	.5	.5	.5	.6	.6	.7
10	.3	.4	.5	.6	.7	.8	.8	.9	1.0	1.1	1.2	1.3	1.3
15	.5	.6	.8	.9	1.0	1.1	1.3	1.4	1.5	1.6	1.8	1.9	2.0
20	.7	.8	1.0	1.2	1.3	1.5	1.7	1.8	2.0	2.2	2.3	2.5	2.7
25	.8	1.0	1.3	1.5	1.7	1.9	2.1	2.3	2.5	2.7	2.9	3.1	3.3
30	1.0	1.3	1.5	1.8	2.0	2.3	2.5	2.8	3.0	3.3	3.5	3.8	4.0
35	1.2	1.5	1.8	2.0	2.3	2.6	2.9	3.2	3.5	3.8	4.1	4.4	4.7
40	1.3	1.7	2.0	2.3	2.7	3.0	3.3	3.7	4.0	4.3	4.7	5.0	5.3
45	1.5	1.9	2.3	2.6	3.0	3.4	3.8	4.1	4.5	4.9	5.3	5.6	6.0
50	1.7	2.1	2.5	2.9	3.3	3.8	4.2	4.6	5.0	5.4	5.8	6.3	6.7
55	1.8	2.3	2.8	3.2	3.7	4.1	4.6	5.0	5.5	6.0	6.4	6.9	7.3
60	2.0	2.5	3.0	3.5	4.0	4.5	5.0	5.5	6.0	6.5	7.0	7.5	8.0
Hours													
2	4.0	5.0	6.0	7.0	8.0	9.0	10.0	11.0	12.0	13.0	14.0	15.0	16.0
3	6.0	7.5	9.0	10.5	12.0	13.5	15.0	16.5	18.0	19.5	21.0	22.5	24.0
4	8.0	10.0	12.0	14.0	16.0	18.0	20.0	22.0	24.0	26.0	28.0	30.0	32.0
5	10.0	12.5	15.0	17.5	20.0	22.5	25.0	27.5	30.0	32.5	35.0	37.5	40.0
6	12.0	15.0	18.0	21.0	24.0	27.0	30.0	33.0	36.0	39.0	42.0	45.0	48.0
7	14.0	17.5	21.0	24.5	28.0	31.5	35.0	38.5	42.0	45.5	49.0	52.5	56.0
8	16.0	20.0	24.0	28.0	32.0	36.0	40.0	44.0	48.0	52.0	56.0	60.0	64.0

Figure 6-1 A Speed-Time-Distance table.

The table is convenient, but it does have limitations. For one thing, anything paper on a boat is liable to destruction in wet weather. For another, if your speed is 4.8 knots, finding the distance traveled in 66 minutes is going to be something of a problem. This problem, as well as any of the earlier ones, can be solved almost instantly on a slide rule. Now hold on a minute! If you think a slide rule is a fabulous mystery to use, you're in for a nice surprise, because it doesn't have to be. It's all in the way you look at things.

Any kind of slide rule will work. The plastic student type is a good choice; it's cheap—a couple of dollars at most department stores—and you don't have to worry about getting it wet.

To use the slide rule, remember that a speed of 4.5 knots means traveling 4.5 miles in 60 minutes, and think of the problem as a proportion: if I travel 4.5 miles in 60 minutes, how far in 68 minutes? Written in equation form, the problem looks like this:

$$\frac{4.5 \text{ miles}}{60 \text{ minutes}} = \frac{X}{68 \text{ minutes}}$$

On the slide rule, just arrange the numbers on the C and D scales in the same positions, and read the answer (5.1 miles) in its corresponding spot (see Figure 6-2). The slide rule has no decimal point, so supply your own. Common sense says the answer can't be .51 or 51 miles.

Try another problem. If the speed is 4.7 knots, how long will it take to travel 3.3 miles. The problem would be written as 3.3 miles/X = 4.7 miles/60 minutes. Figure 6-3 shows the answer on the slide rule—42 minutes.

You can find your speed just as easily. Suppose you travel 2.9 miles in 37 minutes and want to know your speed. Think of the problem as 2.9 miles/37minutes = X/60 minutes. Setting those numbers on the slide rule, as shown in Figure 6-4, gives an answer of 4.7 knots.

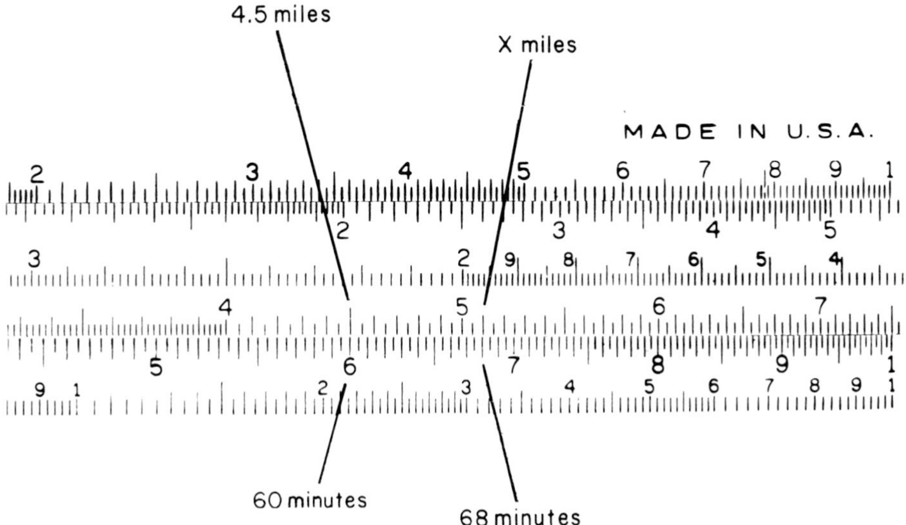

Figure 6-2 How far in 68 minutes at 4.5 knots?

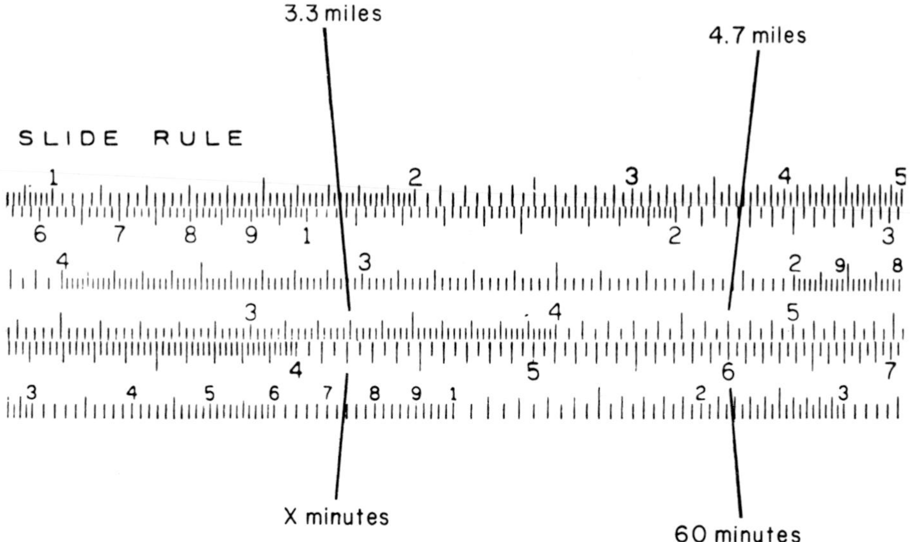

Figure 6-3 How long to travel 3.3 miles at 4.5 knots?

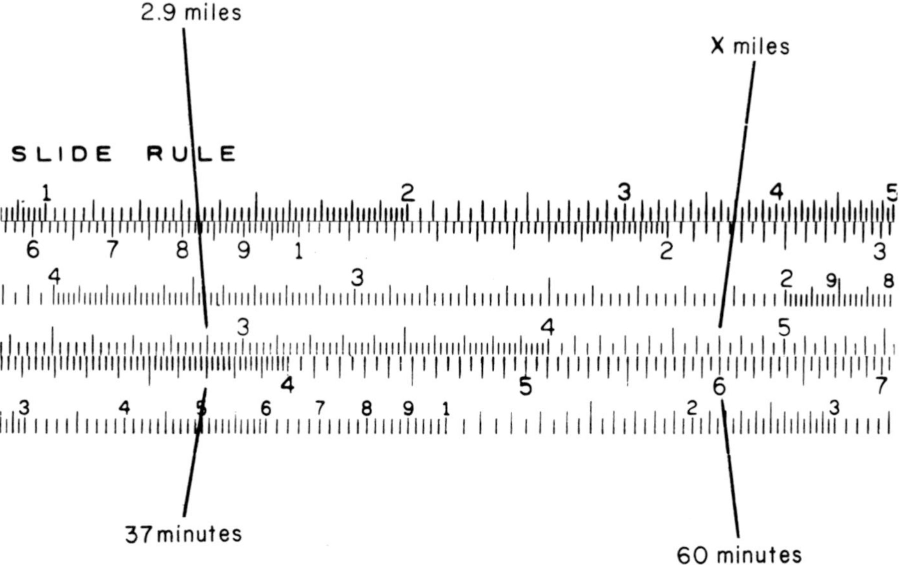

Figure 6-4 What speed gives 2.9 miles in 37 minutes?

The Jeppeson CR slide rule, mentioned in Chapter 2, is a very good way of doing these problems. It's actually a standard slide rule wrapped around until one end meets the other. (I tried this once by dropping my slide rule into the front wheel of my bike while moving at speed, but the product wasn't quite so accurate as Jeppeson's.) They were originally intended for aerial navigation, but they also work extremely well for coastal piloting. Very few boaters seem to know about them, but I hope to spread the word about a good and useful product. Of the various models, I suggest either the CR1, which is small enough (4½ inch diameter) to fit a pocket, or the CR3 (6 inch diameter), which is easier to read and has extra scales. I have one of each, and wouldn't be without them. You can probably find these at an air training school. If not, addresses for mail order are listed in the Appendix.

Figure 6-5 shows a model CR1, with the speed index (arrow on the inner scale) set to 5.3 knots on the outer scale. Again, the decimal is in your head. You can see at a glance that in 51 minutes we will travel 4.5 miles. Conversely, to travel 7.1 miles will require 80 minutes, which can also be read as 1 hour 20 minutes on the third scale.

Speed can also be quickly calculated. If you travel .6 miles in 41 minutes, the speed is 3.8 knots, as shown in Figure 6-6.

Remember the fuel problem in Chapter 2? The engine burns 1.8 gallons per hour at a speed of 6 knots, and there are 27 gallons in the tank. What is the cruising range? Well, we're burning 1.8 gallons for each 6 miles, and we have 27 gallons. The problem could be written (of course you won't bother) as 6 miles/1.8 gallons = *X*/27 gallons. Figure 6-7 shows the CR1 setting, giving a cruising range of 90 miles. Handy gadget, that.

Problem 6-1

Find the missing quantity in each of the following sets of figures.

Speed—Knots	Time	Distance—Nautical Miles
4.0	35 min	( )
2.6	23 min	( )
3.5	( )	2.1
6.4	28 min	( )
6.4	( )	4.8
6.4	1 hr 15 min	( )
5.0	9 min	( )
4.5	( )	15
4.5	2 hr 20 min	( )
( )	35 min	4.2

If you do a lot of work with charts at the same scale, as in the U.S. 1:20,000 series, there's a very handy device you can use. It's a transparent template, with precalculated lines drawn for a range of speeds and times. To use it, just pick the lines corresponding to your speed and time of travel, and the template gives the distance directly on the chart. It can also be used to find the time required to travel a given distance at known speed. Figure 6-8 shows that, at a speed of 6.0 knots, it will take 10 minutes to travel between the two buoys.

Sooner or later it occurs to people—"wouldn't it be a great idea to use an electronic calculator for these problems?" My feeling is that anyone who would take a calculator on a boat would take a sandwich to a banquet. Both are fine things, but only in the right places. This may seem an odd point of view in our calculator age, but I have several reasons.

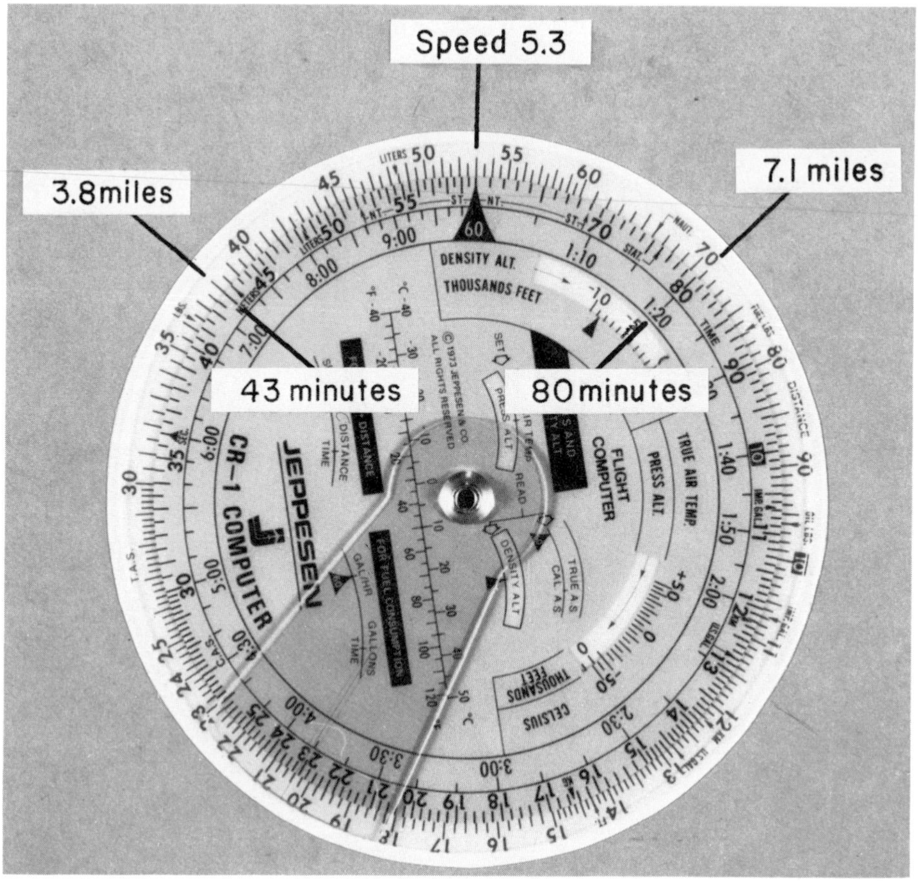

Figure 6-5 Speed-Time-Distance calculations are very fast on the CR slide rule.

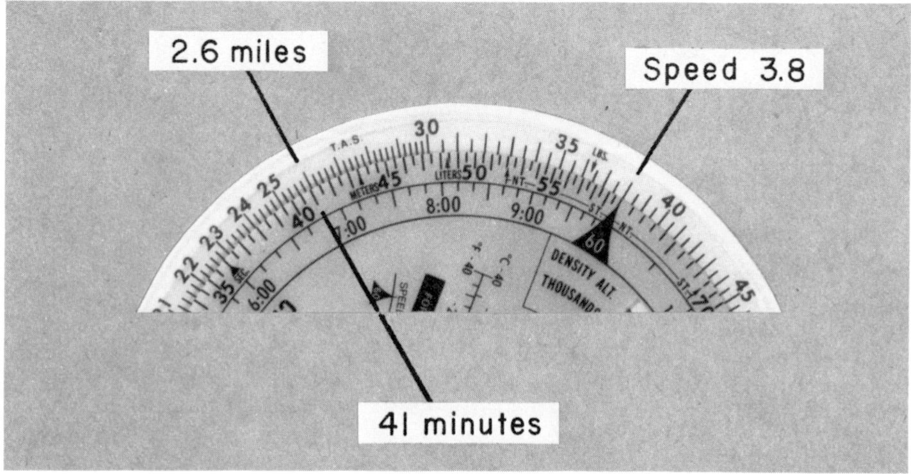

Figure 6-6 Finding the speed on the CR slide rule.

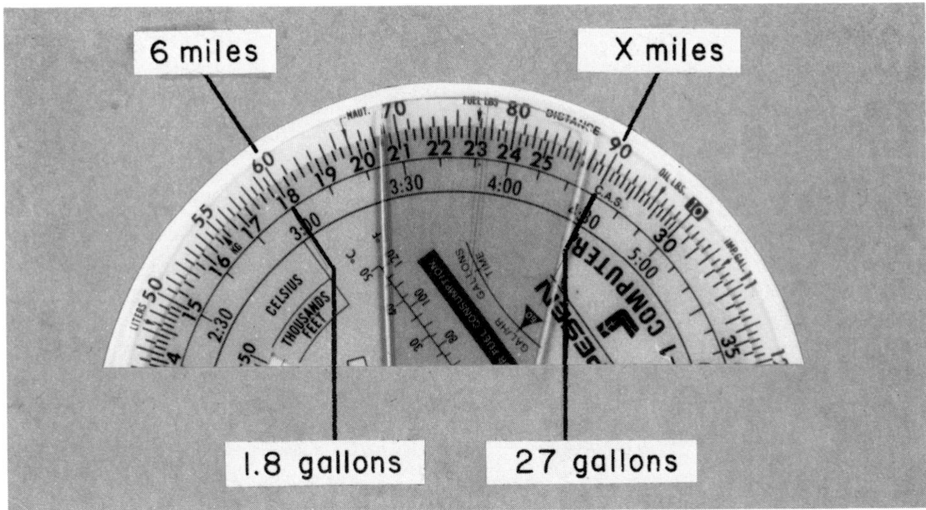

Figure 6-7 Other problems can be worked on the CR slide rule. Here a fuel consumption problem is being solved.

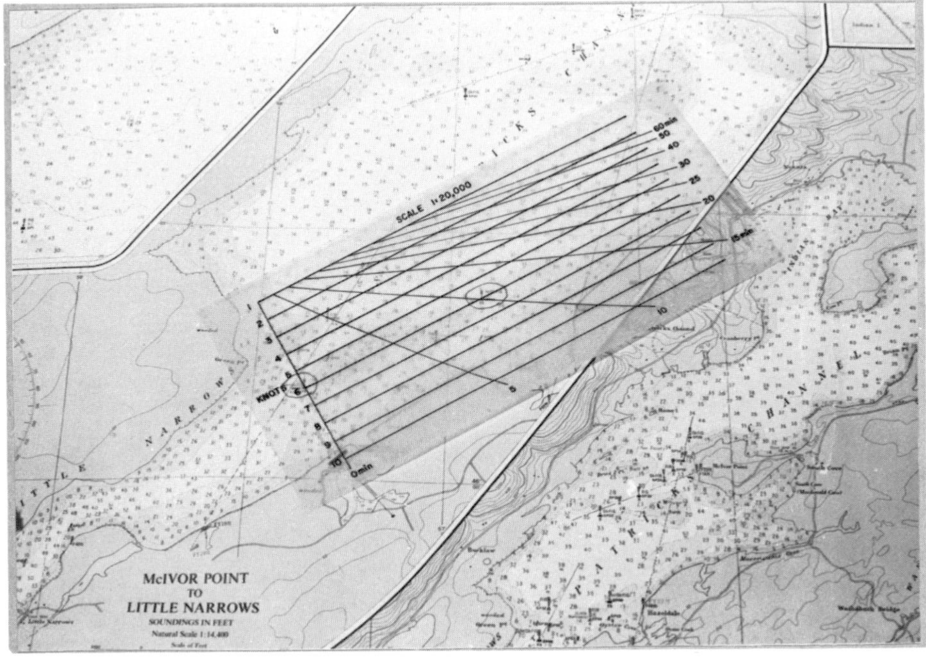

Figure 6-8 A transparent template is useful for speed-time-distance calculations.

For one thing, a slide rule shows all the numbers at one time, so you can visualize the problem very well, whereas with a calculator, you have to key in the numbers in order. Getting the right order isn't always easy when conditions are hectic; in the above fuel problem, would you key 27 × 6 ÷ 1.8, or perhaps 27 ÷ 6 × 1.8? That may seem an easy question, yet you'd be surprised how easily you can calculate wrong answers at great speed. Another problem is the battery operating time on a boat, with no AC to plug an adapter into. Finally, and most serious, salt water and calculators don't agree at all well. Your machine could break down and leave you looking for a pencil at the most untimely moment. I've even had an expensive scientific calculator break down right at the desk. It's a spooky feeling to find it telling the most outrageous lies with a straight face, and nothing to be done about it.

THE DEAD RECKONING PLOT

A major part of the piloting job is keeping a record on the chart of where you have been, and where you expect to be in the near future. When this record is based on dead reckoning, it's called a dead reckoning plot. Now that you can do the speed-time-distance calculations, let's see about the chartwork.

First of all, you need to keep a written record of the important figures in a form that's easy to work with, called a *log*. You can buy printed log books, or you can make up your own. One satisfactory form is shown in Figure 6-9. Obviously, variations are possible. This form has separate columns for compass, magnetic, and true headings. If you have a wooden boat with no engine and a lead keel, you could probably eliminate the deviation column. On the other hand, if all your cruising is done where there are strong currents, you might want a separate column for current data.

The log must be kept up to date. That means filling in the information each time there is a change in heading or speed, or other noteworthy event, such as taking a bearing or running out of beer take place. Even if you're having such an uneventful cruise that nothing is changing, you still note the information at regular intervals. This book uses half hour intervals; shorter or longer intervals might be appropriate to suit the situation. The 24 hour time system is used. All the log entries in this book follow the same format; entries based on known values like time or speed are in boldface type, while entries based on calculation, such as distance, are in italics. Also, the log entries and the chartwork are on the same page or facing pages wherever possible, for easy comparison.

Cruise #1

The first cruise is a very simple one. We depart from the Borgle Shoal buoy at 1000, on a compass heading of 140°, with a speed of 3.0 knots.

Log Book

Vessel ________ **Date** ________

Time	Heading Compass	Heading Magnetic	Heading True	Speed	Distance	Remarks

Figure 6-9 The log book.

There is no deviation and no current, and variation is 18° E. At 1050 the wind picks up and the speed increases to 5.0 knots. Figure 6-10 shows how the log should look for the first hour and a half. At 1000 the magnetic heading is 140°, which equals a true heading of 158°. Because nothing exciting has happened, the next log entry comes at 1030. For the distance calculation, the speed has been 3.0 knots for the first half hour, giving 1.5 miles. At 1050 the speed changes to 5.0 knots, so we make a new log entry. Be careful when calculating the distance; for the 20 minutes between 1030 and 1050 the speed was 3.0 knots, so the distance is 1.0 mile. At 1100 we enter the log again. This time the speed has been 5.0 knots for 10 minutes, for a distance of .8 mile. The rest of the entries follow the same pattern, yet, you always have to be careful to use the right speed (from the *previous* time interval) when calculating distance.

Refer to Figure 6-11. The plot begins at the buoy (not shown), and is labeled 1000 FIX because we are sure of that position, assuming the buoy hasn't moved. Since there is no current, the course is the same as the heading. (The difference between the two is explained in Chapter 7.) The course line is drawn, and the course and speed are labeled. Courses are always written with three figures in degrees true, and speeds are always given in knots, so these units don't have to be written each time. The position drawn at 1030 is labeled 1030 DR, because we don't *know* that it's correct—it's based on dead reckoning. If there is any factor we haven't recognized, such as a current or compass error, the DR position will be in error. The course and speed don't have to be written in after the 1030 DR position because they're the same as before. However, after the 1050 DR position the speed has changed, and we write both values in again.

Cruise 2

This cruise involves only changes in heading. Again, there is no deviation, so the compass heading and magnetic heading are the same, and no current, so the true heading and course are the same. Course changes occur at 1445 and 1510. Notice that the course and speed are both noted against the course line after each change, even though the speed is the same. Also, the last DR position is plotted at 1530, but the course line is extended ahead, to check that the ship is not headed for any dangers.

Cruise 3

This time we again have no current or deviation. However, there are both course and speed changes. The plot in Figure 6-15 shows that both course and speed are written on the course line any time either one changes. From the last DR position at 1510, the course line is extended ahead.

Cruise 4

So far, the examples have not included deviation. However, many compass installations are affected by deviation. The example below shows how deviation is included in the figuring. The deviation table from the good ship Deviant is given in Figure 6-17 for convenience. The log in Figure 6-16 shows the deviation for each heading in the "Remarks" column; something you might not normally bother with. In each case, the heading is very close to a value in the table, so the deviation can be found by inspection.

Time	HEADING Compass	Magnetic	True	Speed	Distance	Remarks
1000	**140**	*140*	*158*	**3.0**	—	Depart Borgle School Current nil Deviation nil Variation 18°E
1030	**140**	*140*	*158*	**3.0**	*1.5*	
1050	**140**	*140*	*158*	**5.0**	*1.0*	
1100	**140**	*140*	*158*	**5.0**	*.8*	
1130	**140**	*140*	*158*	**5.0**	*2.5*	

Figure 6-10 The log for cruise 1.

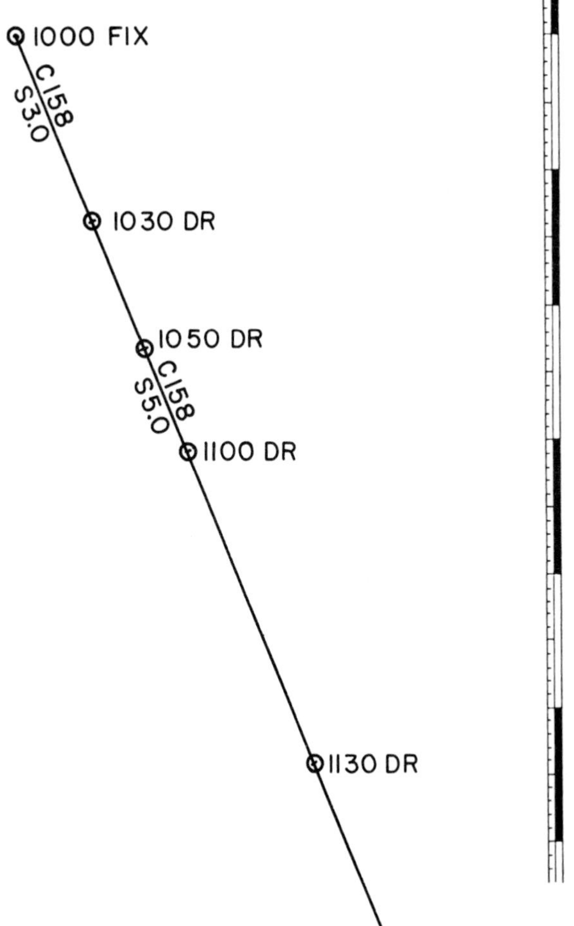

Figure 6-11 The DR plot for cruise 1.

Time	HEADING Compass	Magnetic	True	Speed	Distance	Remarks
1400	**131**	*131*	*120*	**4.0**	—	Depart Red Rock Current nil Deviation nil Variation 11°W
1430	**131**	*131*	*120*	**4.0**	*2.0*	
1445	**236**	*236*	*225*	**4.0**	*1.0*	Port tack
1500	**236**	*236*	*225*	**4.0**	*1.0*	
1510	**111**	*111*	*100*	**4.0**	*.7*	Stb. tack
1530	**111**	*111*	*100*	**4.0**	*1.3*	

Figure 6-12 The log for cruise 2.

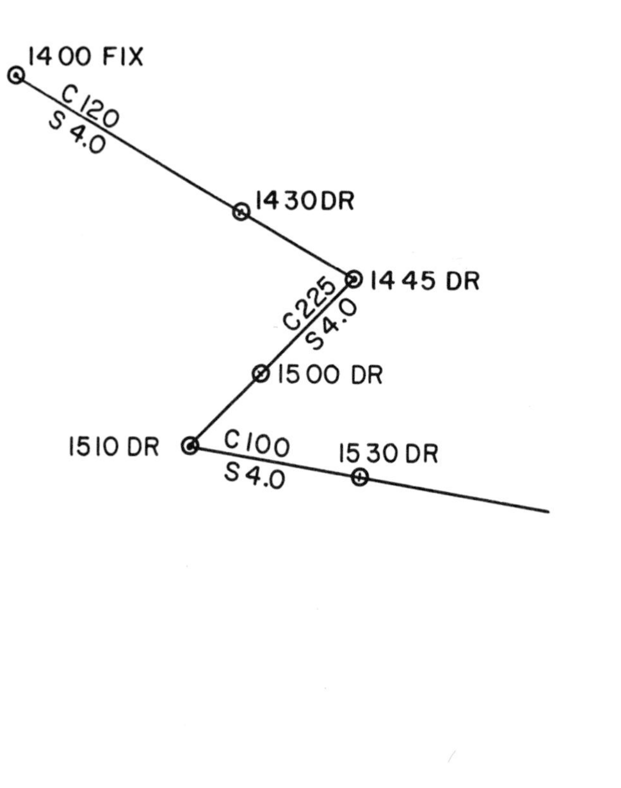

Figure 6-13 The DR plot for cruise 2.

Time	HEADING Compass	Magnetic	True	Speed	Distance	Remarks
1330	040	*040*	*035*	4.0	—	Depart Owl's Head buoy Current nil Deviation nil Variation 5°W
1400	135	*135*	*130*	4.0	*2.0*	
1418	028	*028*	*023*	5.0	*1.2*	
1430	028	*028*	*023*	5.0	*1.0*	
1500	028	*028*	*023*	5.5	*2.5*	
1510	110	*110*	*105*	6.0	*.9*	

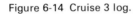

Figure 6-14 Cruise 3 log.

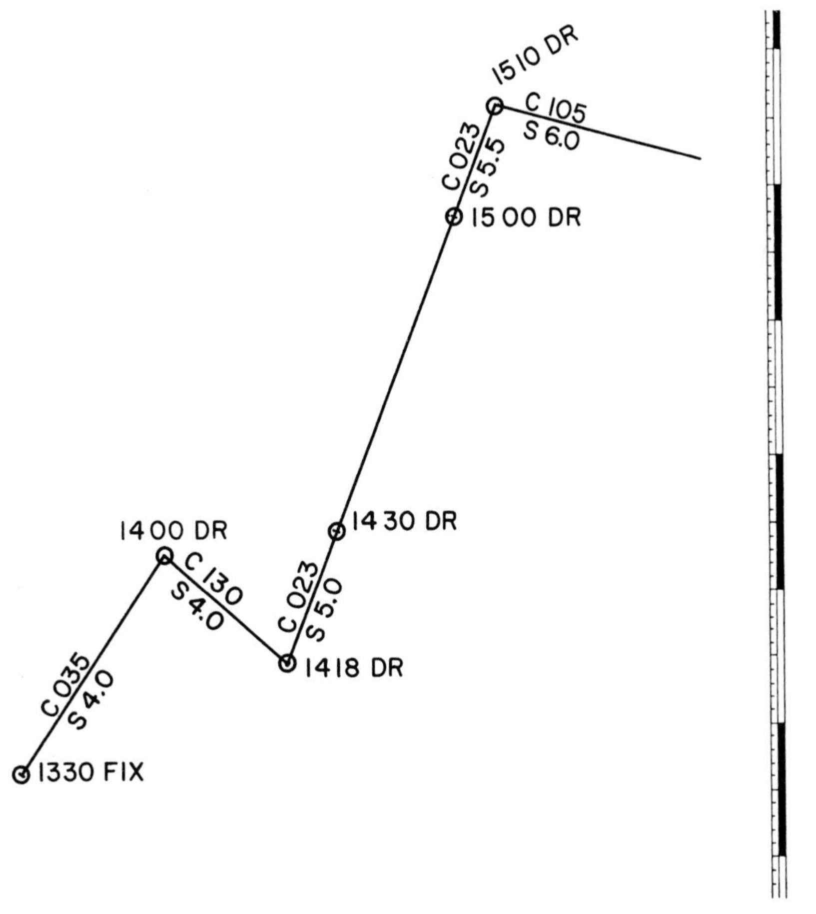

Figure 6-15 Cruise 3 DR plot.

Time	Compass	HEADING Magnetic	True	Speed	Distance	Remarks
0300	320	*318*	*315*	4.0	—	Depart Red Rock buoy Variation 3° W Deviation per table Current nil
0330	087	*085*	*082*	4.0	*2.0*	Dev 2° W
0400	050	*046*	*043*	4.0	*2.0*	Dev 4° W
0430	166	*170*	*167*	4.0	*2.0*	Dev 4° E

Figure 6-16 Cruise 4 log.

Deviation Table

Vessel Deviant Adjuster JPB
Compass Steering Date 15-8-75

Ship's Head - Magnetic	Deviation
000	5° W
045	4° W
090	2° W
135	2° E
180	4° E
225	5° E
270	2° E
315	2° W

Figure 6-17 The deviation table.

Cruise 5

In this cruise, several of the headings fall between entering values in the deviation table of Figure 6-17. That means you must estimate where the actual values would fall between the listed values. For example, the heading of 158° falls almost half way between the listed headings of 135° and 180°, so the deviation would be half way between 2° E and 4° E, or 3° E.

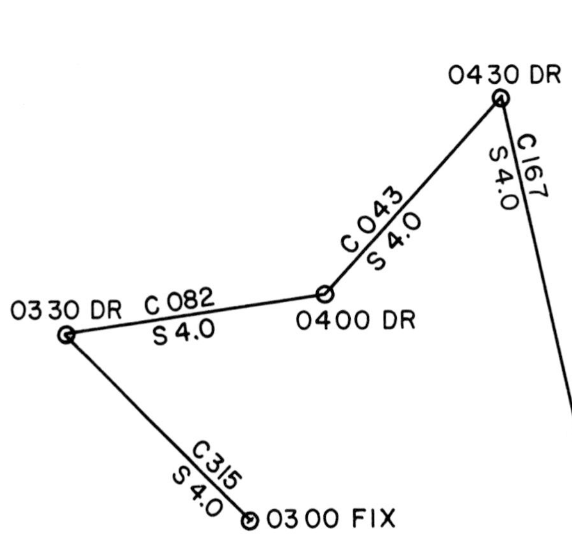

Figure 6-18 Cruise 4 DR plot.

Time	HEADING Compass	Magnetic	True	Speed	Distance	Remarks
1130	**296**	*296*	*310*	**5.6**	—	Depart Foster Bank Variation 14°W Deviation Per Table Current nil.
1200	**042**	*038*	*052*	**6.8**	*2.8*	Dev 4°W
1230	**290**	*290*	*304*	**3.8**	*3.4*	Dev 0°
1300	**158**	*161*	*175*	**6.0**	*1.9*	Dev 3°E

Figure 6-19 Cruise 5 log.

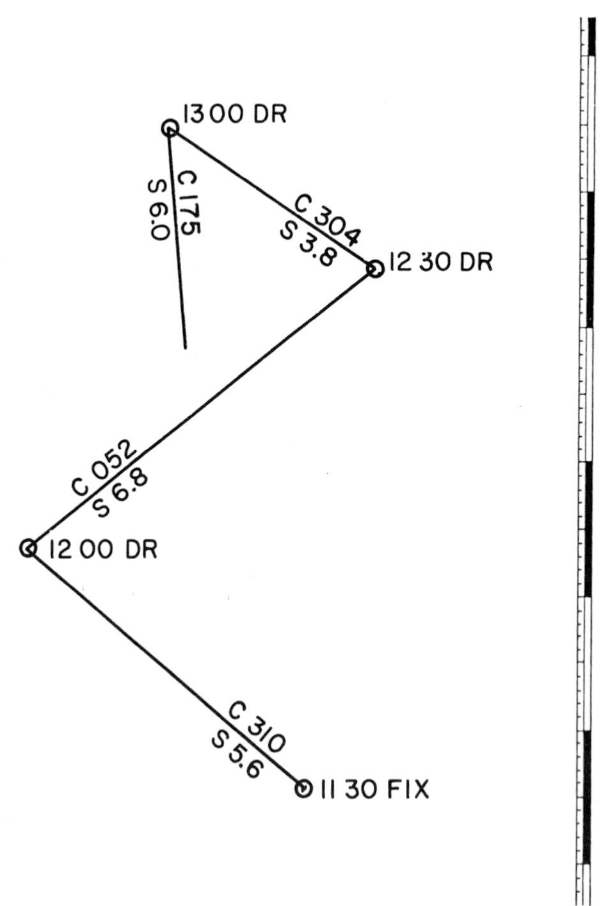

Figure 6-20 Cruise 5 DR plot.

Problem 6-2

Time	HEADING Compass	Magnetic	True	Speed	Distance	Remarks
0930	047			6.0		Depart Little Hbr. inner bell (GK F16) Current nil Deviation nil Variation 23°E
1000	067			4.8		
1030	147			5.5		
						When and where will we run aground?

Problem 6-3

Time	HEADING Compass	Magnetic	True	Speed	Distance	Remarks
1810	307			7.0		Depart Brig buoy Variation 24°E
1830	051			6.0		
1900	051			6.3		
1919	122			7.0		
1930	122			7.0		
2000	122			6.0		When will Green Is. east light change from white to red?

Problem 6-4

Time	HEADING Compass	Magnetic	True	Speed	Distance	Remarks
0900	288			7.5		Depart Little Hbr. inner black bell.
0930	288			7.5		Variation 23°E.
0942	025			6.8		
1000	025			6.8		
1014	025			7.8		
1030	025			7.8		
1037	245			5.1		
1100	152			5.8		
1130	152			5.8		
1200	152			5.8		
1218	152			5.8		
						What is the 1218 DR Position, relative to the 0900 Fix?

Problem 6-5

Time	HEADING Compass	Magnetic	True	Speed	Distance	Remarks
1000	311			4.0		Depart Friar Is. Can.
1030	311			4.0		Variation 23°E.
1039	278			4.5		
1100	278			4.5		
1130	278			4.5		
1143	326			5.2		
1200	326			5.2		
1209	075			4.8		
1230	075			4.8		
1300	308			7.0		
1330	247			6.0		
1400	247			6.0		
1412	199			5.0		
1430	199			5.0		
						What is the 1430 DR Position, relative to Fairway buoy HA?

Problem 6-6

Time	HEADING Compass	Magnetic	True	Speed	Distance	Remarks
0940	344			3.8		Depart Little Hbr. outer black bell. Variation 24°E. Deviation per table. See Fig 6-17
1000	344			3.8		
1030	344			5.4		
1100	106			4.0		
1130	035			6.0		
1145—	We're suddenly fogged in. Find the 1145 DR position. What is the compass heading to return to the starting point? At a speed of 4.0 knots what is the ETA?					

Solutions are in the Appendix.

7: Figuring the Current

By the end of the first week they calculated that they had covered thirty miles, heading south. But when DeLong took his weekly observations, they found that they were farther than ever from the mouth of the Lena. For the ice on which they were traveling had drifted fifty-two miles to the northwest.

Ian Cameron, Lodestone and Evening Star

The previous chapter covered problems which weren't concerned with current, but there are many areas of the oceans where strong currents run. If the speed of your boat is four knots, and there's a six knot current pushing you around, it definitely has to be taken into account.

To illustrate the way current affects your progress, let's consider another imaginary experiment. A river 2 miles wide is flowing to the east at a speed of 1 knot. (Sure, 2 miles *is* a pretty wide river, but this is a pretty imaginary experiment.) There is a town on the north bank, and you are on the south bank with a rowboat, directly across from the town. You're going to row to town, and you decide that instead of craning your neck to check your direction, you'll just keep an eye on a compass at your feet instead. You set off, rowing at a speed of two knots, and carefully watching the compass to keep the boat always pointed north. When you land on the north bank, imagine your surprise to discover that the town is nowhere in sight!

The current is the villain, of course. Figure 7-1 illustrates what has happened. Rowing at a speed of two knots, you spent an hour crossing the river. During that hour, the river has carried you one mile sideways (east), even though you were always pointed north. Your landing point is a mile east of the town, so obviously the *direction of travel* was something quite different from the *direction you pointed*. What's more, even though you rowed exactly two miles through the water, the distance you traveled was quite a bit more than that. It only took an hour, though, so your *speed over the bottom* was different from your *speed through the water*.

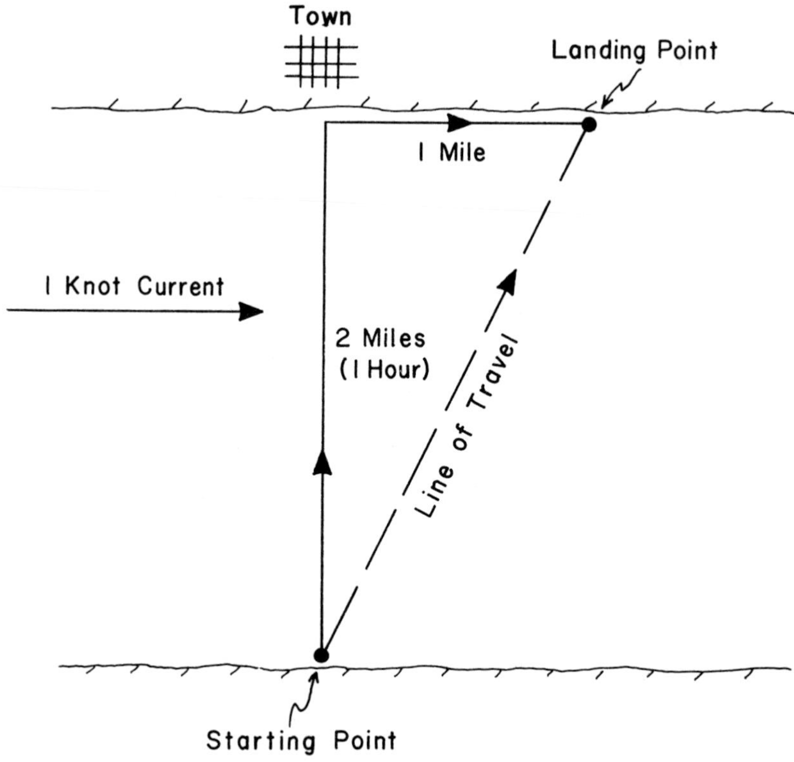

Figure 7-1 The effect of current.

Now let's forget about the town and the riverbanks, and concentrate on the boat, the current, and the result. Figure 7-2 shows these three factors in a diagram called a current triangle. The line for the boat's heading is drawn north, since the boat was always pointing north. The line for the current's direction is drawn east. Connecting the starting point with the finishing point gives the boat's line of travel, called the course. Back on page 64, I commented that with no current, the heading and course were the same. Now there is a current, and we can see the difference. The heading is the direction the boat is pointing, and the course is the direction over the bottom the boat is traveling. The current triangle has another feature. If we make the length of the heading line and current line proportional to the speed, the course line gives not only the direction of travel, but the speed over the bottom as well.

DEFINITIONS

Heading (Hdg)—The direction in which your boat is *pointing*.

Speed (Spd)—The speed of your boat moving *through the water*.

Set—The direction in which the current is flowing.

Drift—The speed of the current.

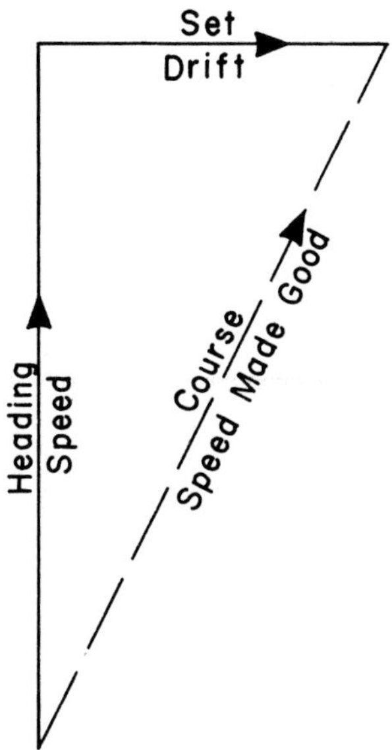

(Heading / Speed) + (Set / Drift) = (Course / Speed Made Good)

Figure 7-2 The Current Triangle.
Each part of the triangle has a direction and a speed. The directions are always given in degrees true, and the speeds are always given in knots.

Course—The intended direction in which the boat is *moving over the bottom.*

Speed Made Good (SMG)—The speed of the boat *moving over the bottom.*

We can note, in passing, another term you may meet. *Track* is the actual direction over the bottom, compared with course, which is the intended direction over the bottom.

CURRENT TABLES

It's no great trick to allow for the current when figuring out your course, Still, you have to know how strong the current is, and what direction it's flowing. This information is found in Tide and Current Tables, shown in Figure 7-3.

At the moment, we are interested in the part of the tables dealing only with currents. Part of a typical page is shown in Figure 7-4. At first glance it looks confusing, so let's work through a few of the numbers.

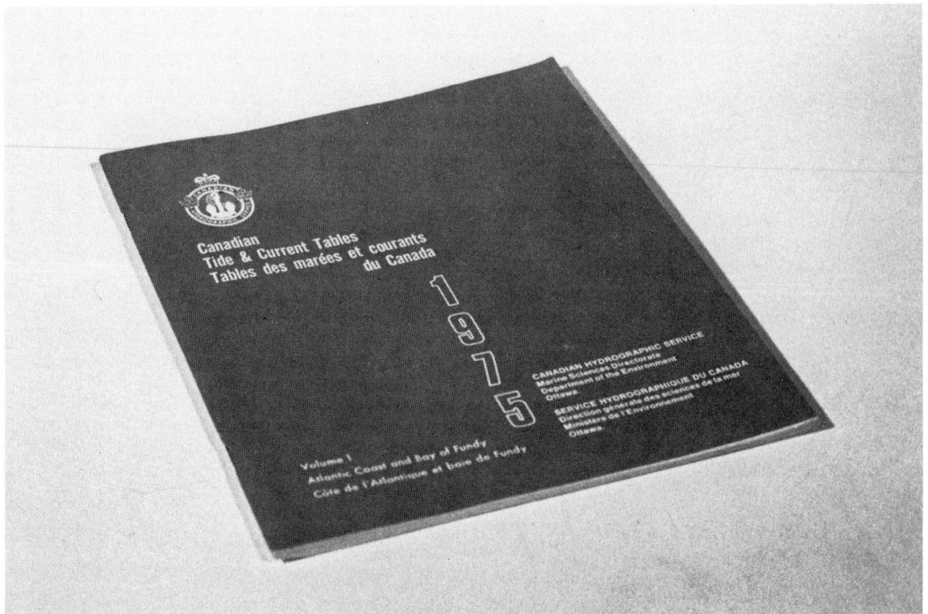

Figure 7-3 Tide and Current Tables

JANUARY 1975

Turns		Maximum	
Day	Time	Time	Rate/kn.
1	0150	**0505**	-3.2
	0805	**1055**	+3.1
WE	1400	**1720**	-3.4
	2025	**2325**	+3.4
2	0235	**0550**	-3.2
	0850	**1145**	+3.0
TH	1445	**1805**	-3.3
	2110		
3		**0005**	+3.3
	0320	**0635**	-3.1
FR	0940	**1230**	+2.8
	1535	**1855**	-3.0
	2155		
4		**0055**	+3.0
	0410	**0725**	-2.9
SA	1030	**1320**	+2.5
	1625	**1945**	-2.6
	2245		

+ FLOOD DIRECTION 100 TRUE

– EBB DIRECTION 280 TRUE

Figure 7-4 Extract from the current tables.

Times are given in standard time, in the 24 hour system. The current first turns (slack water) on January 1 at 0150. For the next few hours it picks up speed, and at 0505 it is flowing at 3.2 knots in the (—), or ebb direction. Referring to the bottom of the table, we find this direction is 280° true. (Please note that, in reproducing the actual table, this figure has been "doctored" in order to use it with the examples and problems in this book). After 0505, the speed begins to drop, and at 0805 it is slack again. Then it picks up speed in the other direction, and at 1055 it's flowing at 3.1 knots in the (+) or flood direction, 100° true. The speed drops again to slack water at 1400. Thus, one complete cycle takes about 12 hours, with about 6 hours from slack to slack. The convention for current direction is different from wind: a west wind blows *from* the west, but a west current flows *to* the west.

In most locations, there are two complete cycles each day, known as a *semidiurnal* characteristic. The length of each cycle may be more or less than 12 hours, and the maximum flood may be quite different from the maximum ebb, but the tables are read in the same way. You should also realize that these figures are *predictions*, and can vary considerably from the actual current. In a channel connecting a harbor with the ocean, a strong onshore wind can delay and weaken the ebb, while strengthening the flood. Also, these predictions are based on current meter recordings. The meters are moored many feet below the surface, for the mutual protection of meters and ships, and surface currents may be quite different. You have to use some judgement.

Well and good. If we want to know the current at 1055 on January 1, we can quickly find the figures: the set is 100° and the drift is 3.1 knots. At 1805 on January 2, the set is 280°, and the drift is 3.3 knots. The only catch is, how do we find the current at 0930 on January 1, or some other time, which isn't listed? The solution is to assume that the speed of the current follows a curve such as shown in Figure 7-5. This curve is drawn with arbitrary time and speed scales, which we modify to suit the circumstances. I suggest you make a dozen copies of this curve for working the practice problems.

Example 7-1

The problem at hand is to find the current at 0930 on January 1. From the tables, we know that slack water occurs at 0805 and at 1400, with a flood of 3.1 knots at 1055. Let's round off these times a bit to 0800, 1100, and 1400, and use them to label the curve. See Figure 7-6. Also label the maximum speed of 3.1 knots. By projecting from the time scale up to the curve, and over to the speed scale, we can read the value for 0930. On the speed scale of 0 to 1.0, the value is .7. Then, the actual current will be 3.1 knots times .7, or 2.2 knots. Therefore, we can say that, at 0930, the set is 100° and the drift is 2.2 knots. Working along the same lines, we can find the current at 1200 (100°, 2.7 knots) or 1330 (100°, .9 knot).

Example 7-2

Figure 7-7 shows that the current speed at 1700 on January 2 is −3.3 knots times .85, or −2.8 knots. Then we can say that at 1700 the set is 280° and the drift is 2.8 knots.

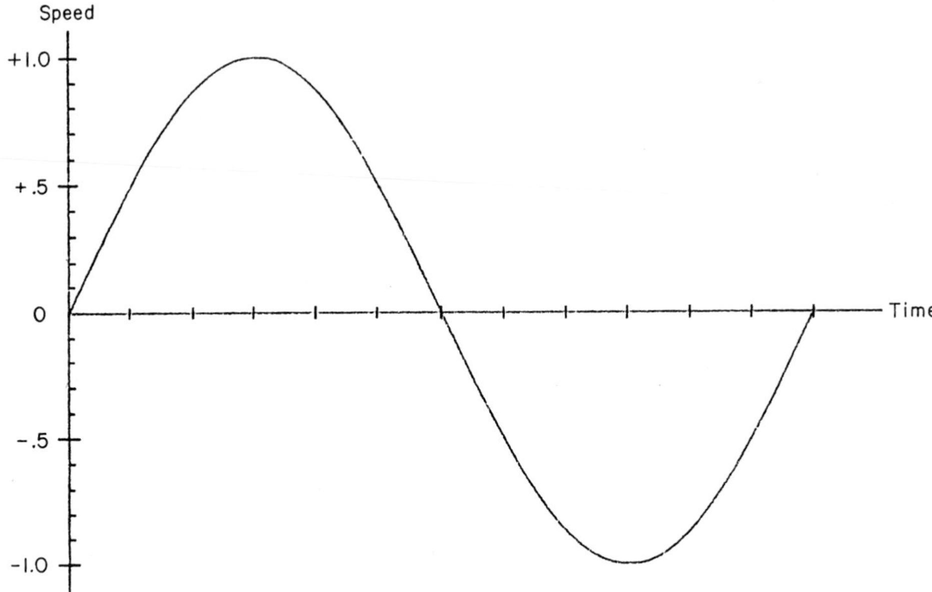

Figure 7-5 A current curve for finding the current's speed between listed times.

Working from the same curve, at 1915 the set is 280° and the drift is 2.6 knots. At 1945 the set is 280°. and the drift is 2.0 knots.

These examples have been picked for times that fit easily on the time scale. While other problems may need a little stretching or squeezing, they can always be worked. The remaining examples and problems illustrate some of the ways the current curve can be used.

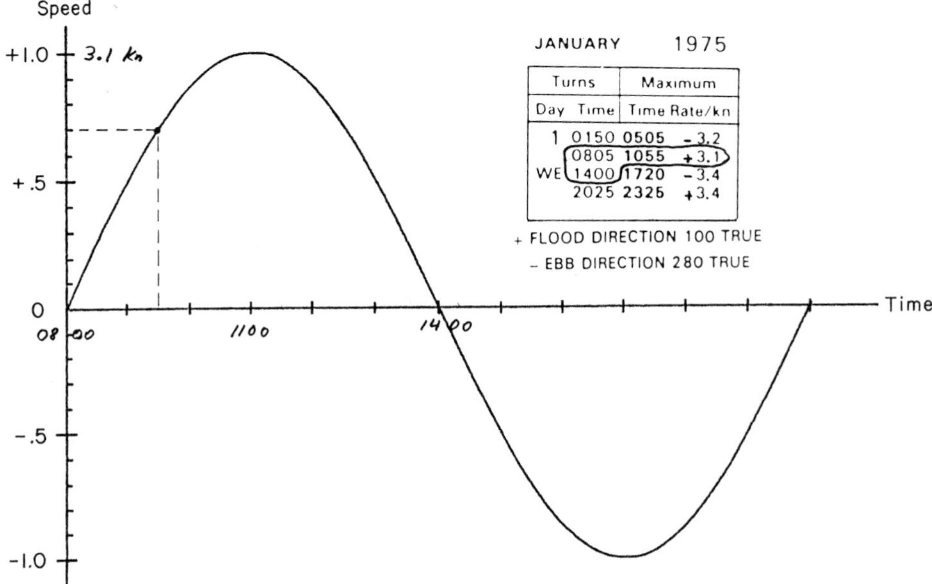

Figure 7-6 The current curve for Example 7-1.

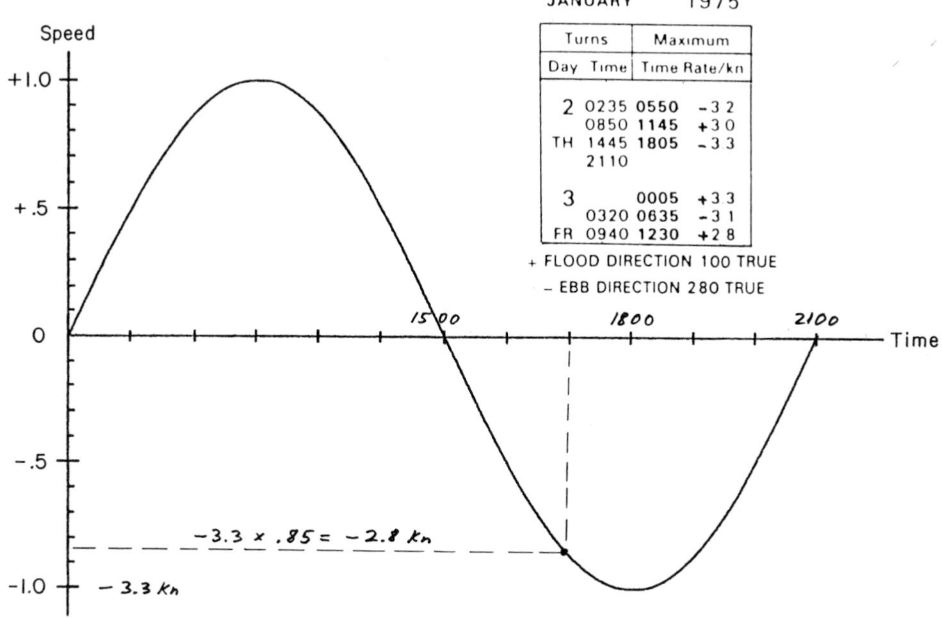

Figure 7-7 The current curve for Example 7-2.

THE CURRENT TRIANGLE

Finding the Course and Speed Made Good

Remember the basic equation involved with current problems.

$$\begin{pmatrix}\text{Heading}\\ \text{Speed}\end{pmatrix} + \begin{pmatrix}\text{Set}\\ \text{Drift}\end{pmatrix} = \begin{pmatrix}\text{Course}\\ \text{Speed Made Good}\end{pmatrix}$$

There are six numbers here. If any four of them are known, the other two can be found by drawing the current triangle. For example, we may know our heading and speed, and the current's set and drift, and want to find the resulting course and speed made good. Graph paper is useful for this work, providing both a distance scale and a reference for directions. A scale of 1 inch to 1 knot is generally suitable. In this chapter, the examples are at a scale of 1 centimeter to 1 knot.

Example 7-3

Suppose we have a heading of 300° and speed of 5.5 knots, and a current set of 240° and drift of 3.0 knots, and want to find the resulting course and SMG. Remember, directions are always given in true degrees for this work. First, draw a line in the direction of the heading, with the length representing the speed (see Figure 7-8(A)). From the point of the heading line, draw another line representing the current, as in Figure 7-8(B). Since the course equals the heading plus the current, draw the course line *from* the tail of the heading line *to* to the point of the current line (see Figure 7-8 (C)). Now measure the course line to find the course (280°) and the SMG (7.5 knots).

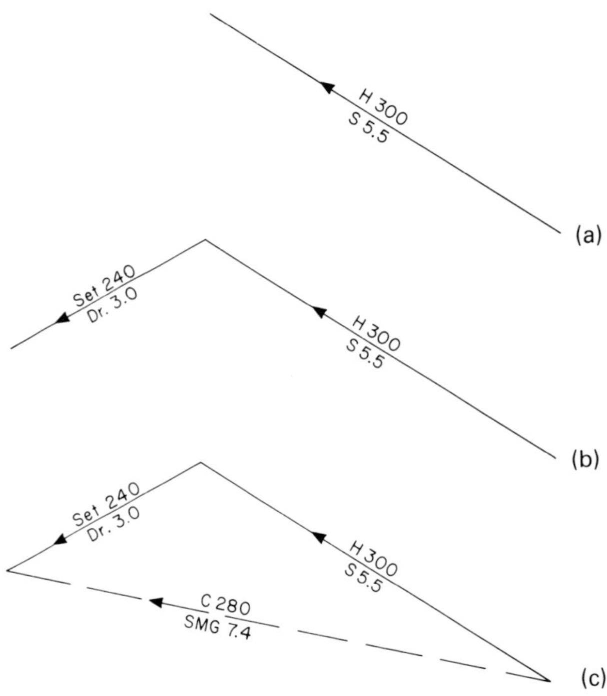

Figure 7-8 Current triangle construction to find the course and SMG.

Example 7-4

With a heading of 030° and speed of 5.0 knots, and a set of 150° and drift of 2.0 knots, find the course and SMG. Solution: the triangle in Figure 7-9 shows that the course is 053°, and SMG is 4.4 knots.

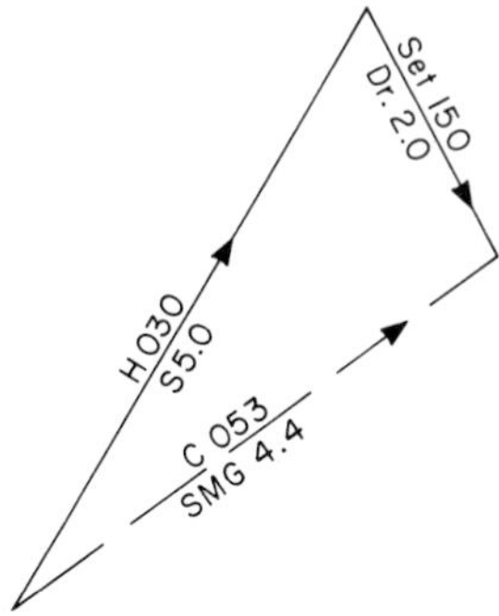

Figure 7-9 The current triangle for Example 7-4.

Example 7-5

Given a heading of 110° and speed of 6.2 knots, with set of 230° and drift of 2.6 knots, find the course and SMG. Solution: the course is 135° and the SMG is 5.4 knots, as shown in Figure 7-10.

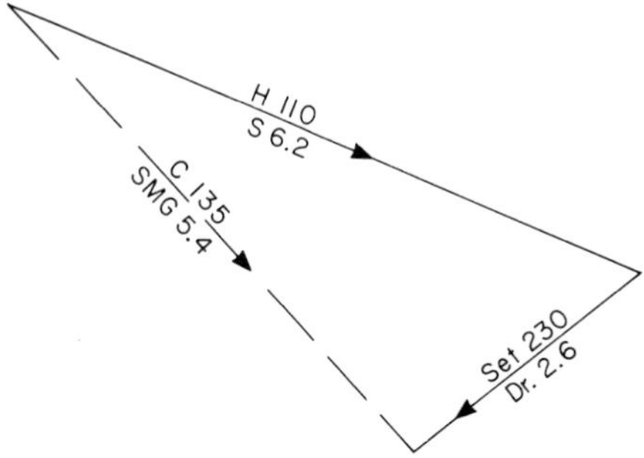

Figure 7-10 The current triangle for Example 7-5.

Finding the Heading for a Given Course

The previous examples illustrated the easiest type of problem; with a given heading and speed, and known current, where will we arrive? That's all right, but usually we have a certain destination in mind, and need to know what heading will get us there. Thinking back to the river illustration at the beginning of this chapter, if you want to arrive at the town, you'll have to row with the boat pointed somewhat to the west to cancel the current flowing to the east. This is typical: when the desired course is known, the boat must be headed slightly (or maybe not so slightly) into the current. Question is . . . how slightly? In other words, when we know the speed of the boat and the course that we want, and also know the set and drift of the current, what heading do we have to use? Also, what will be our speed made good?

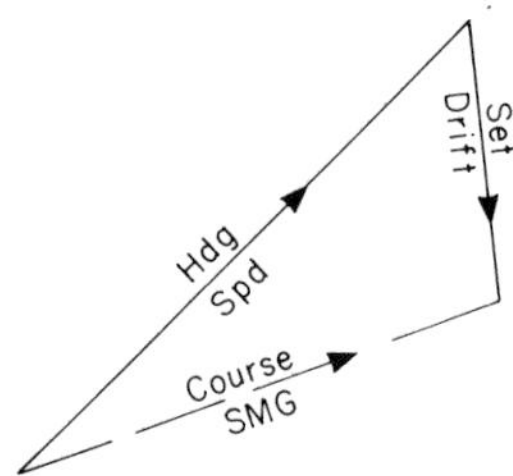

Figure 7-11 The basic current triangle. Its parts can be constructed in any order, depending on the problem to be solved.

Example 7-6

The current set and drift are 205° and 2.0 knots. The boat speed is 5.0 knots. We want a course of 101°. What heading should we use, and what will be the SMG?

First draw the current line, since its direction and length are both known (see Figure 7-12(A)). Next, remember that the heading line plus the current line equals the course line, so the point of the current line must meet the point of the course line. Check back to Figure 7-11. We know the course is 101°, so draw a line in this direction, meeting the point of the current line. Finally, though we don't know the direction of the heading line, we do know its length, and also that it must meet both the tail of the current line and the course line. Using the tail of the current line as a center, pivot a heading line of the correct length until it crosses the course line, as in Figure 7-12(B). This will establish the triangle. Measurement on Figure 7-12(C) shows that the heading must be 078°, and the SMG will be 4.1 knots. For a check, see that the boat is heading into the current, as it must be.

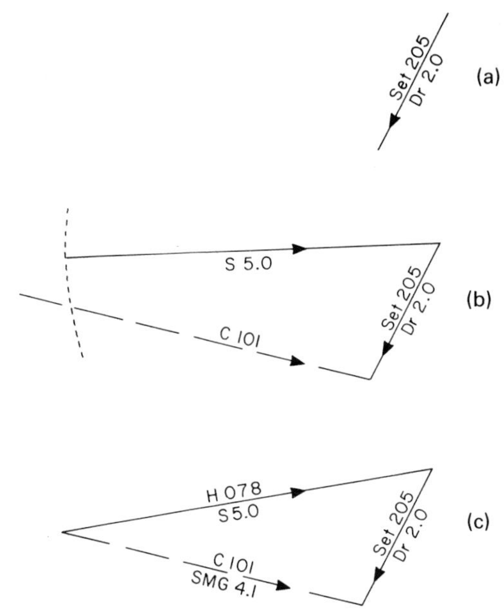

Figure 7-12 Constructing the current triangle to find the heading and SMG.

Example 7-7

Here, the current has a set of 230° and drift of 2.5 knots. The boat speed is 4.7 knots, and we want a course of 203°. Find the necessary heading, and the SMG.

Draw the current line in the 230° direction to a length of 2.5, as in Figure 7-13(A). Then draw the course line in the 203° direction, and pivot the heading line to cross the course line, as in Figure 7-13(B). The triangle is shown in Figure 7-13(C), with a heading of 189° and a SMG of 6.8 knots. In this case the current is helping the speed, although the boat is again (as always) pointed into the current.

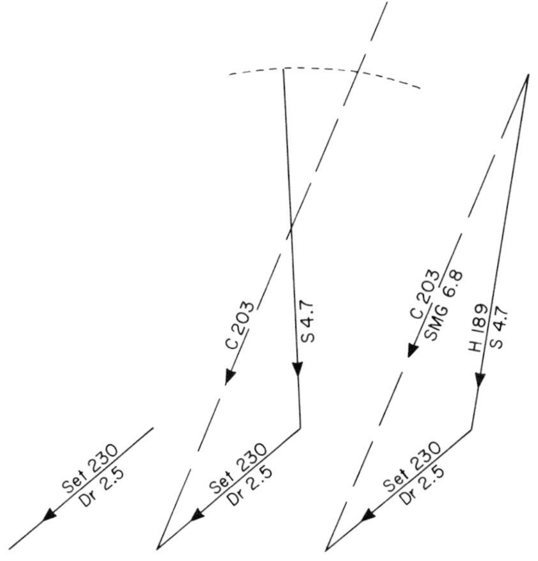

Figure 7-13 The current triangle for Example 7-7.

Example 7-8

The set is 060°, and the drift is 2.4 knots. Our speed is 5.3 knots, and the desired course is 107°. Figure 7-14 shows the solution. Measurement shows that the required heading is °126°, and the SMG is 6.6 knots.

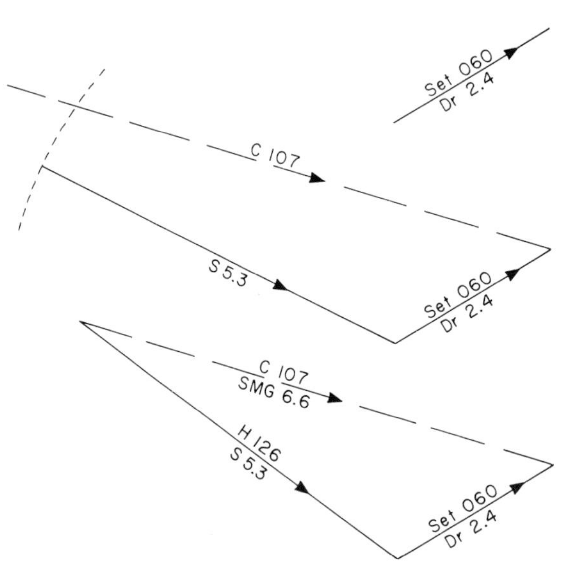

Fig 7-14 The current triangle for Example 7-8.

Determining the Current

Suppose you leave a certain point, with a known heading and speed. Later you reach another point, such as a buoy, which is not on your intended course. If you know the location of the buoy, you will know your actual course (track) and speed made good. From the four known quantities, you can work out the current's set and drift. These figures will be useful as you continue your cruise.

Example 7-9

Assume you leave a known point on a heading of 241°, with a speed of 7.3 knots. After 25 minutes, you pass a buoy which is 2.2 miles away from your starting point in a direction of 218°. From the known time and distance, your speed made good is 5.3 knots, and your course is 218°. What are the set and drift of the current?

From your starting point, draw the course line (218°) and the heading line (241°), both of the proper length (see Figure 7-15(A)). The missing side of the triangle is the current line. Figure 7-15(B) shows the current line, with a set of 102° and a drift of 3.2 knots.

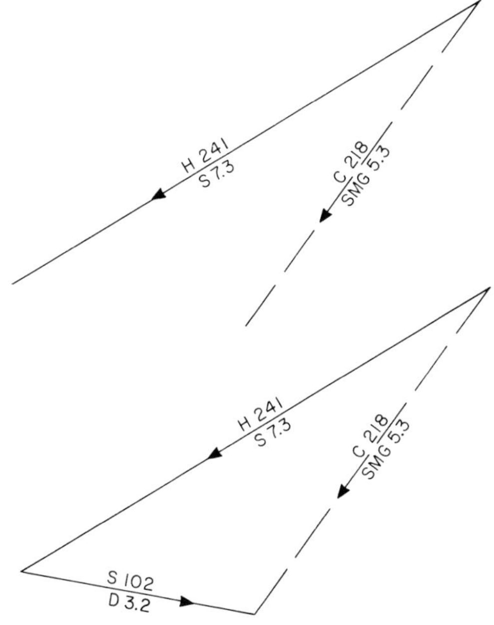

Figure 7-15 Constructing the current triangle to find the set and drift.

Problem 7-1

Find the missing two quantities in each of the following.

	Heading	Speed	Set	Drift	Course	Speed Made Good
1)	249	8.3	093	3.1	( )	( )
2)	093	4.6	160	2.7	( )	( )
3)	164	2.7	310	5.8	( )	( )
4)	019	2.7	064	4.6	( )	( )
5)	( )	3.3	286	2.8	255	( )
6)	( )	6.2	172	1.8	042	( )
7)	( )	5.0	350	5.7	117	( )
8)	( )	3.4	012	5.5	338	( )
9)	121	4.6	( )	( )	104	6.3
10)	217	6.0	( )	( )	254	3.3

CURRENT SOLUTIONS ON THE CR SLIDE RULE

The previous method of constructing the current triangle is very valuable, as it allows you to visualize the problem and relate cause to effect. It isn't always easy to use though, especially in rough and wet conditions. An extremely useful alternative is provided by the CR slide rule. Chapter 6 showed how to use the scales on the front for solving speed-time-distance problems. There is another set of scales on the back, which solves current problems quickly and easily. Designed for aircraft use, the scales have names like airspeed and wind, so we'll mentally transpose those to boat speed and current.

Have another look at the basic current triangle shown in Figure 7-16(A). We're going to confine our interest to just one part of the triangle, shown in Figure 7-16(B). The effect of the current can be separated into two parts; the part helping us along (in this case) is called a tail current, and the part pushing us sideways is called a crosscurrent. These are shown in Figure 7-16(C). The CR slide rule changes the set and drift figures into tail current and crosscurrent, and shows the effect these have on our heading and speed.

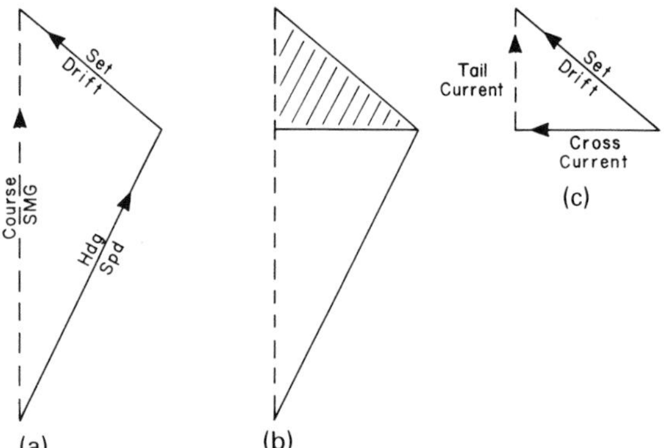

Figure 7-16 The current triangle on a CR slide rule.

Finding the Heading for a given Course with the CR

Figure 7-17 shows the current side of a CR1 slide rule. The outside scale is for our speed. The next scale gives the difference between our heading and the course. For now, we'll ignore the short black scale. The third scale is for the course, and the inner grid shows the current.

Example 7-10

Suppose the set and drift of the current are 240° and 2.0 knots. Our speed is 5.8 knots, and we want a course of 030°. (Again, all directions are in degrees true.) What heading must we use, and what will be the SMG?

The first step is to place the current dot on the blue grid, using a radial line for direction (set) and a ring for speed (drift). If we had a *wind* of 240° at 2.0 knots, the dot would be on the 240° line, 2 rings out from the center. However, a west wind blows *from* the west,

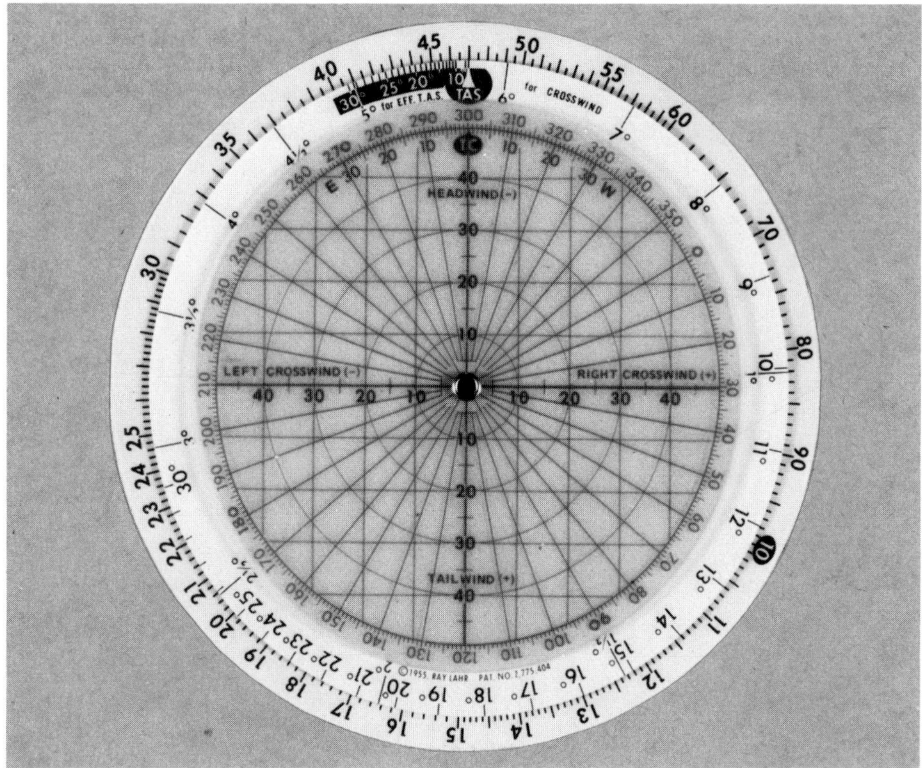

Figure 7-17 Current side of the CR slide rule

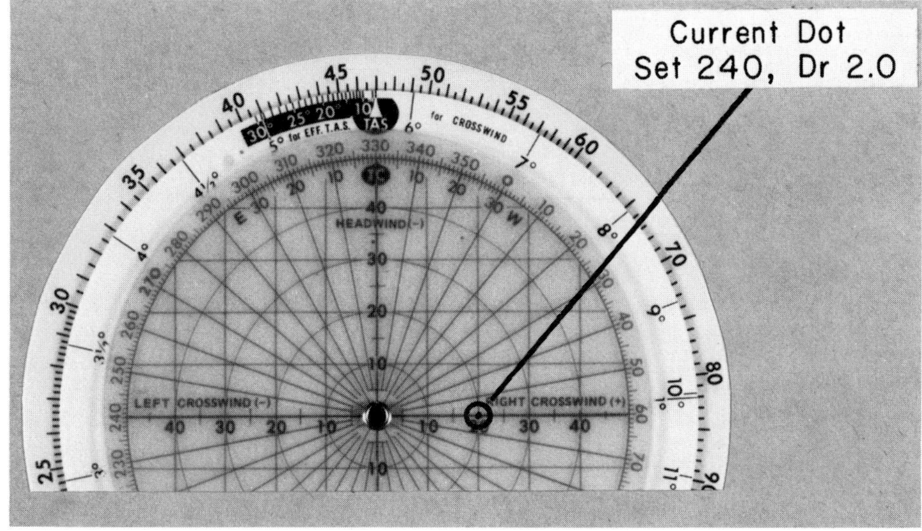

Figure 7-18 Placing the current dot.

while a west current flows *to* the west. So we must place the current dot on the line opposite to 240°. This is easily done by setting 240° on the left, and marking the current dot with a pencil on the right, at the second ring. Make a small dot for accuracy, with a circle around so it's easy to find. See Figure 7-18.

Now set the speed index (TAS stands for true air speed) to 5.8, and the course index (TC stands for true course) to 30°, as in Figure 7-19. The position of the current dot immediately shows that we have a right cross-current of 1.0 knot, and a head current of 1.8 knots.

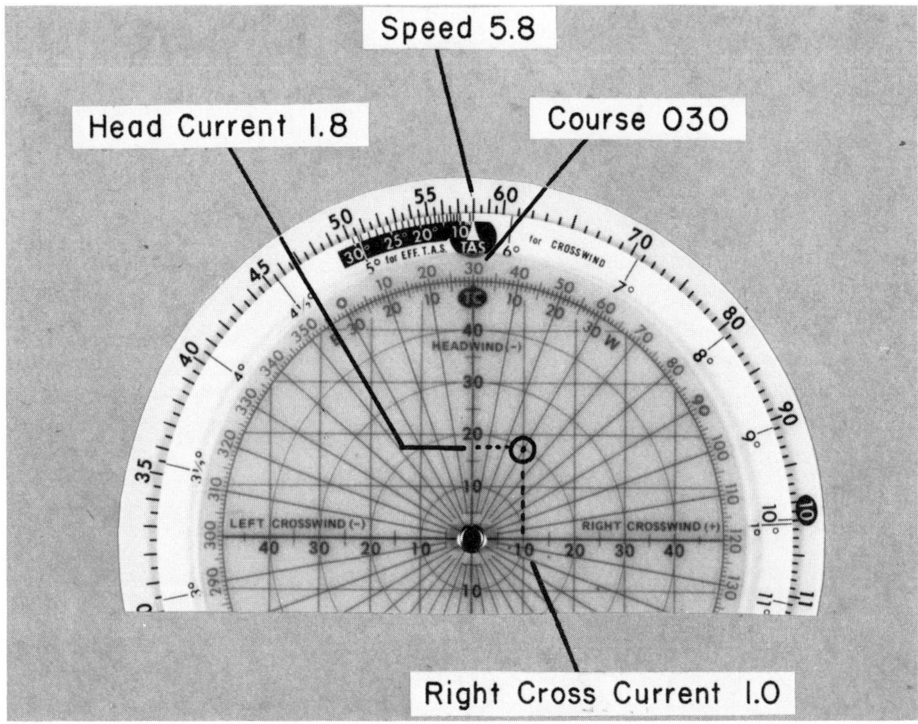

Figure 7-19 The current components.

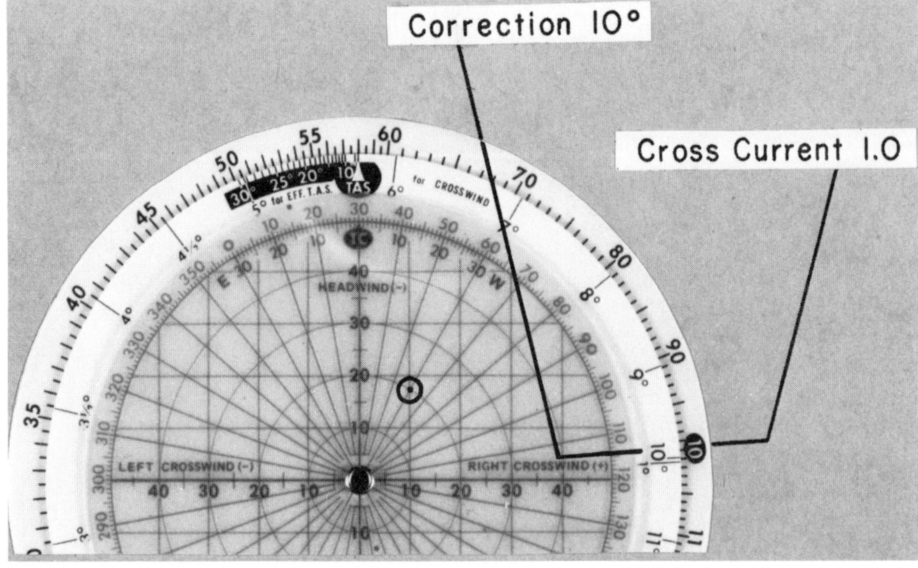

Figure 7-20 Finding the course correction.

How much do we have to change our heading to allow for the cross current? Refer to Figure 7-20. The speed of the crosscurrent is 1.0 knot, so find that value on the outside scale. Read the correction next to it on the second scale (10°). Since the current is from our right, we must head more to the right—into the current—to correct for it. The 10 degree correction must be added to the course to obtain the heading (040°). In case of doubt whether to add or subtract the correction, the (+) sign on the right cross current scale will remind you. Now, what about the speed made good? Our speed is 5.8, but we have a head current of 1.8 knots. Subtracting that figure gives the speed made good : 4.0 knots.

Let us review briefly. First place the current dot. Then make the speed and course settings. Find the crosscurrent from the dot, and note the course correction on the outside scale. Combine the correction with the course to find the heading. Finally, find the head current (or tail current) from the dot, and combine this figure with the speed to find the SMG. As a check on the CR method, Figure 7-21 shows the current triangle for the same problem.

All this description sounds like a lot of complication, but, like most jobs, it takes longer to tell about than to do. Once you've tried a few of these, you'll find that using the CR takes about 15 seconds, and you'll wonder why you ever used pencil and paper.

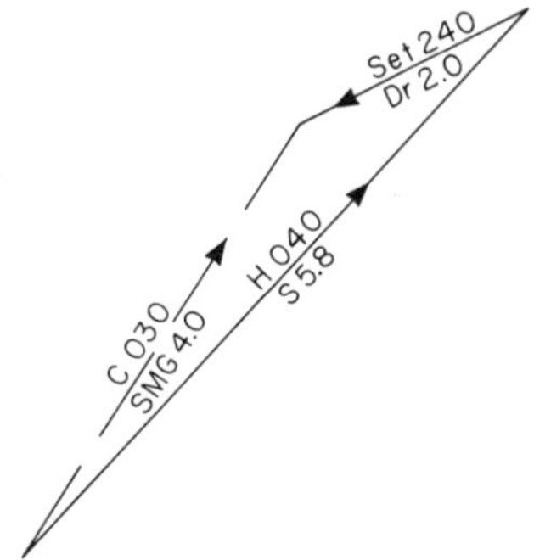

Figure 7-21 Current triangle for Example 7-10.

Example 7-11

The current is 130°, 1.0 knot. Our speed is 5.1 knots, and we want a course of 100°. Find the heading and SMG.

Place the current dot and set the speed and course, as shown in Figure 7-22. In this case we have a left crosscurrent of .5 knot, (the (−) shows that the correction must be subtracted from the course to find the heading). Locate .5 knot on the outer scale, and read the correction −6°. The heading is then 100° minus 6°, or 094°. The tail current amounts to .8 knot. Added to our speed of 5.1 knots, this gives a SMG of 5.9 knots. Compare the CR solution with the triangle in Figure 7-23.

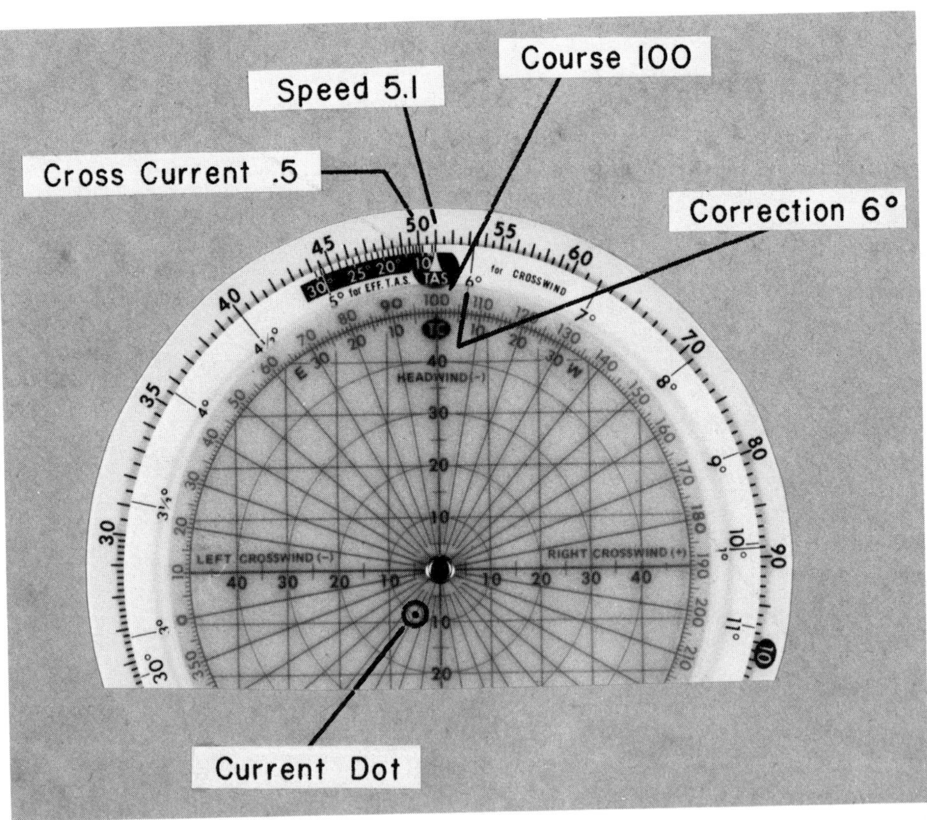

Figure 7-22 CR solution of Example 7-11.

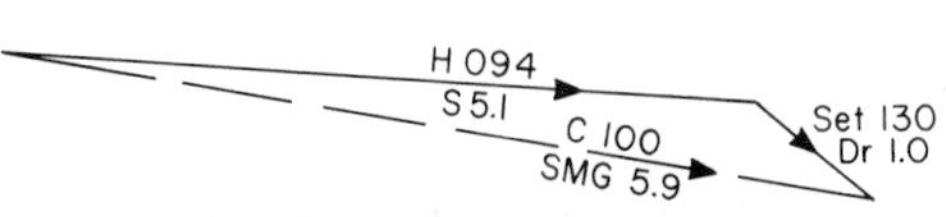

Figure 7-23 Current triangle for Example 7-11.

Example 7-12

In the previous examples, the course corrections have been 10 degrees or less. Often the correction is more than 10 degrees, and then an extra step is needed. Suppose the current's set and drift to be 140° and 2.0 knots, respectively. We want a course of 036°, and our speed is 5.0 knots. Find the heading and the SMG.

The current dot and scale settings are shown in Figure 7-24. Find the heading as before: the crosscurrent is almost 2.0 knots from the left, giving a (−) 23° correction, and a heading of 013°. Now comes the new step. The correction of 23° is quite large, and means that our *effective* speed is substantially less than 5.0 knots. Locate 23° on the short black scale and read the effective speed −4.6 knots—opposite it (see Figure 7-25). Now subtract the head current (.5 knot) to find the SMG −4.1 knots. Figure 7-26 shows the triangle for comparison.

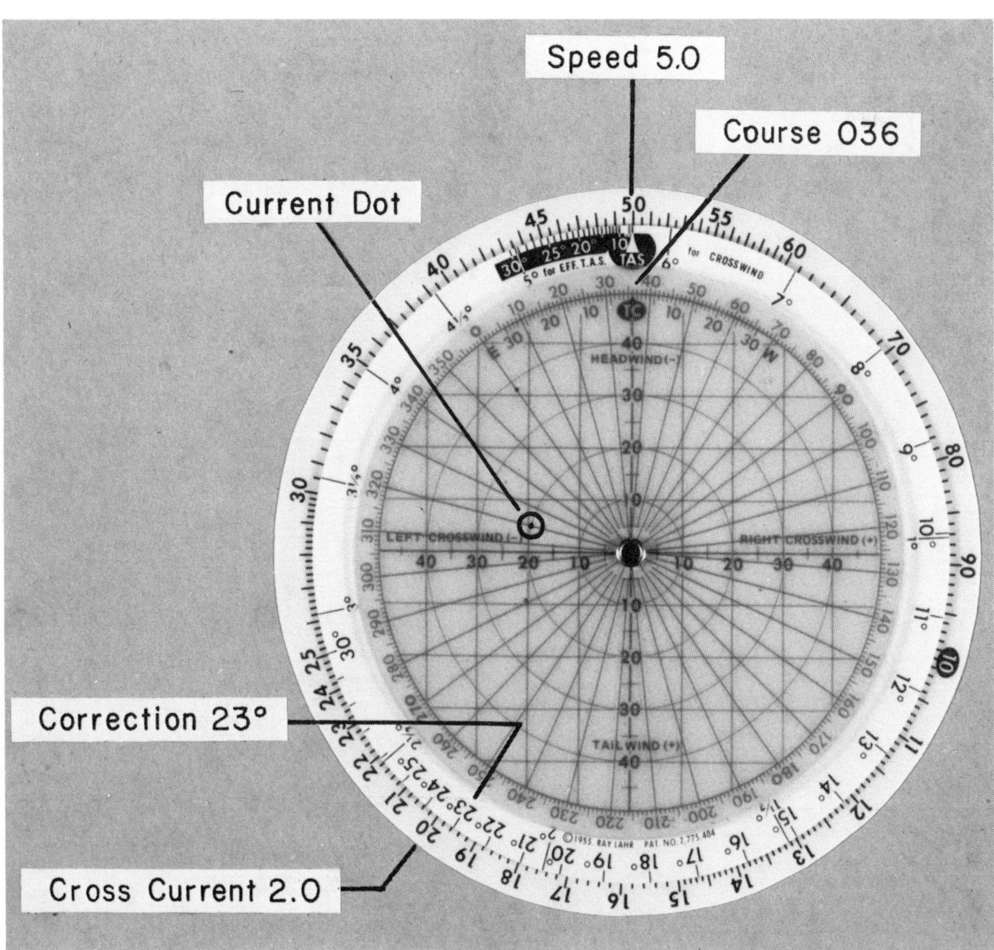

Figure 7-24 Finding the heading.

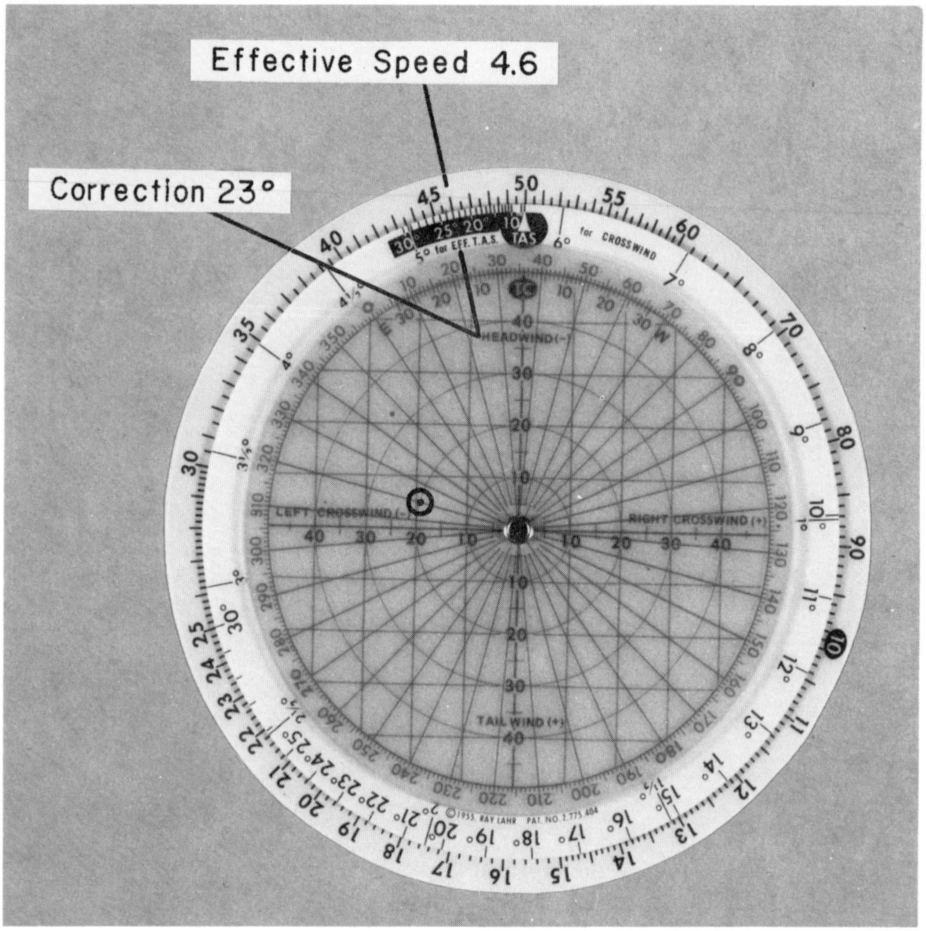

Figure 7-25 Finding the SMG.

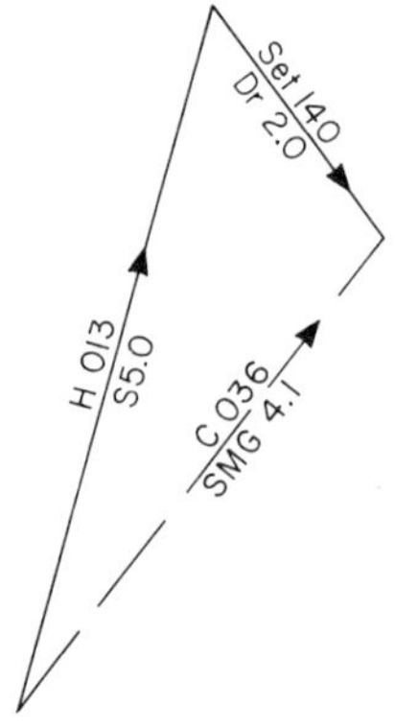

Figure 7-26 The current triangle.

Example 7-13

Here's another example of finding the required heading for a given course, with a correction larger than 10 degrees. Let the set and drift be 236° and 2.5 knots. Our speed is 4.3 knots, and we want a course of 282°.

Locate the current dot and set the speed and course scales in the usual way. The dot in Figure 7-27 shows that the current is from the right at 1.8 knots. Checking the outside scale, we find a required correction of 25°, which must be added to our course to find the heading—307°. Since the correction is greater than 10°, the first step in finding the SMG is to find the effective speed. The black scale gives us a figure of 3.9 knots, as shown in Figure 7-28. To this we add the tail current of 1.7 knots, for a SMG of 5.6 knots.

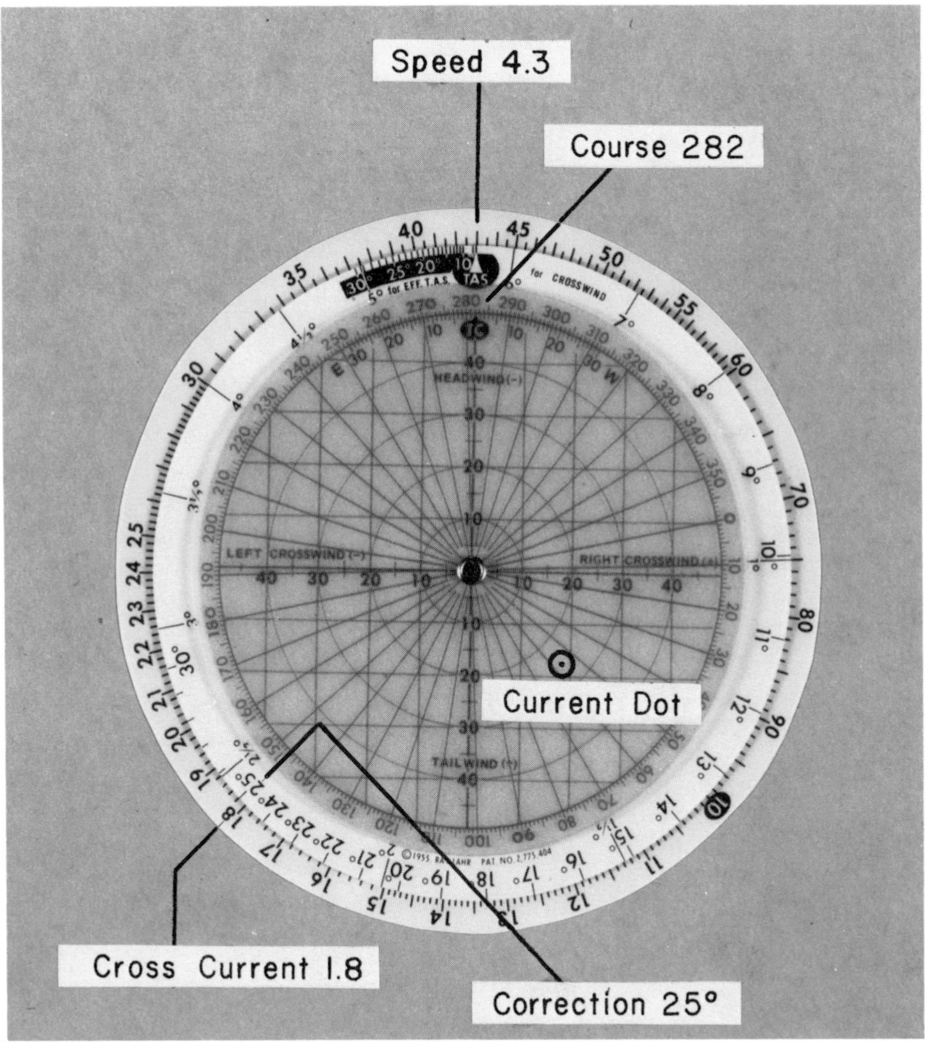

Figure 7-27 Finding the heading.

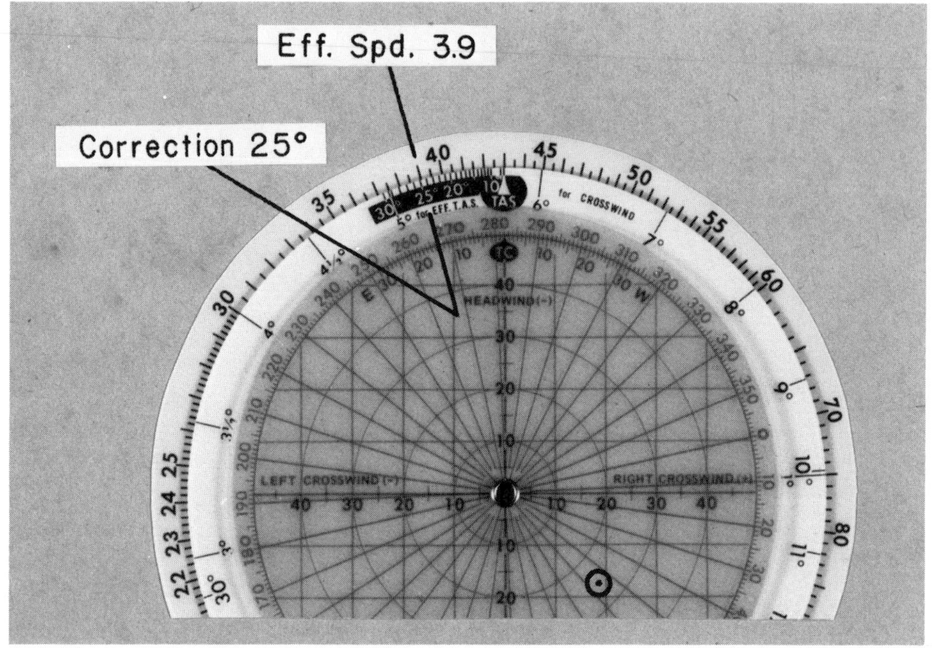

Figure 7-28 Finding the SMG.

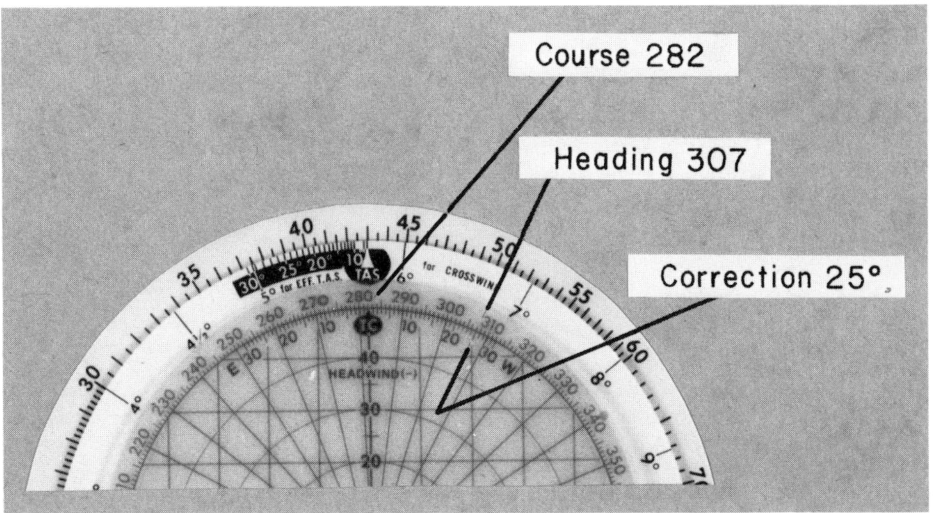

Figure 7-29 Correcting course to heading on the CR.

Here's a handy trick to save time. When you add the 25° correction to the course to find the heading, you can use pencil and paper (dumb-dumb!) or do it in your head (better). Best of all, use the CR! The course is already set at the TC index. On either side of the index there is an auxiliary black scale. Find 25° on the right side of this scale (since the current is from the right) and read the heading opposite: 307°. This is shown in Figure 7-29, and the current triangle is given in Figure 7-30 for comparison.

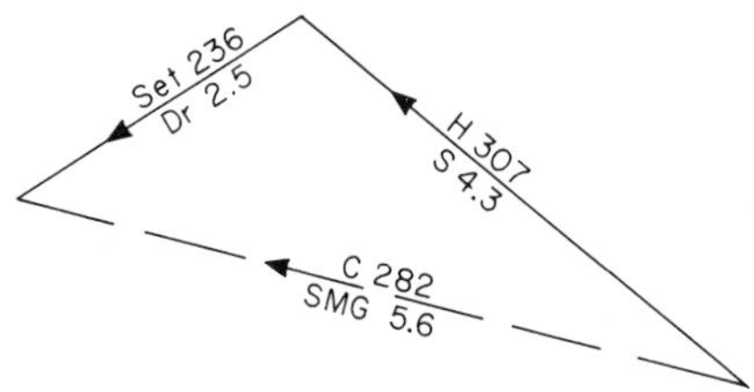

Figure 7-30 The current triangle for Example 7-13.

Finding the Course for a given Heading with the CR

In cases where we are steering a certain heading and want to find the resulting course, the CR can also be used. Since this isn't its intended application, the solution is not quite as direct.

Example 7-14

Let the heading and speed be 080° and 6.8 knots, and the set and drift be 210° and 2.5 knots. What are the course and SMG?

Place the current dot as usual. Set the speed index to 6.8 and the course index to 080°, as shown in Figure 7-31. We find a left current of 1.9 knots, and the outer scale gives a "correction" of 16°.

Careful, now. The current is from the left, but in this case we're not correcting for it. So the left current must be pushing us to the right. In other words, our course must be about 16° more than our heading, or 096°. But we cheated; the 080° we set earlier on the course index was the *heading*, not the course. Now we'd better set the *course*. When we change the setting on the course index to 096°, the current dot also moves; now it shows 2.3 knots left current (see Figure 7-32).

For this crosscurrent, the outer scale shows a "correction" of 20°, so our course must be more like 100°. When we set 100° on the course index, the current dot still shows 2.3 knots left current, so we have found the correct solution (see Figure 7-33).

The SMG is found as before. With a 20° course "correction", we have an effective speed of 6.4 knots. Subtracting the head current of .9 knot gives 5.5 knots for our SMG.

Figure 7-34 shows the current triangle. For more practice in using the CR, try solving the situations of Problem 7-1.

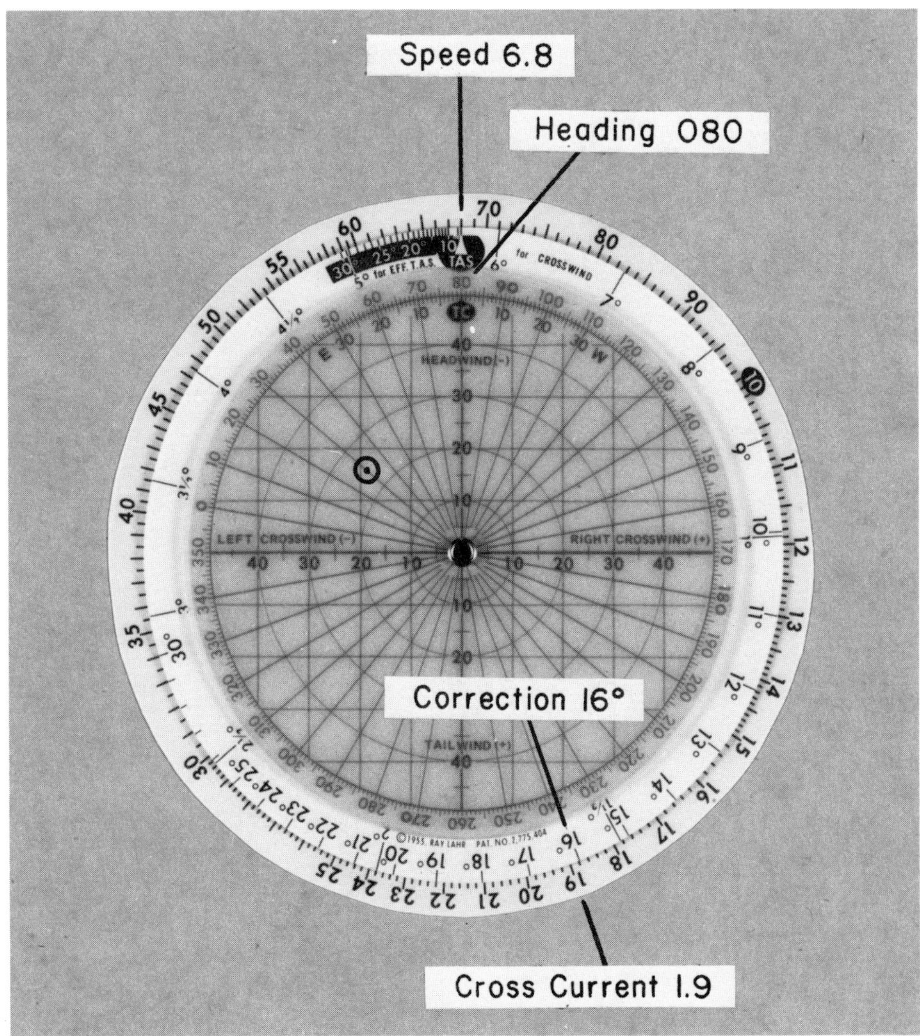

Figure 7-31 First step.

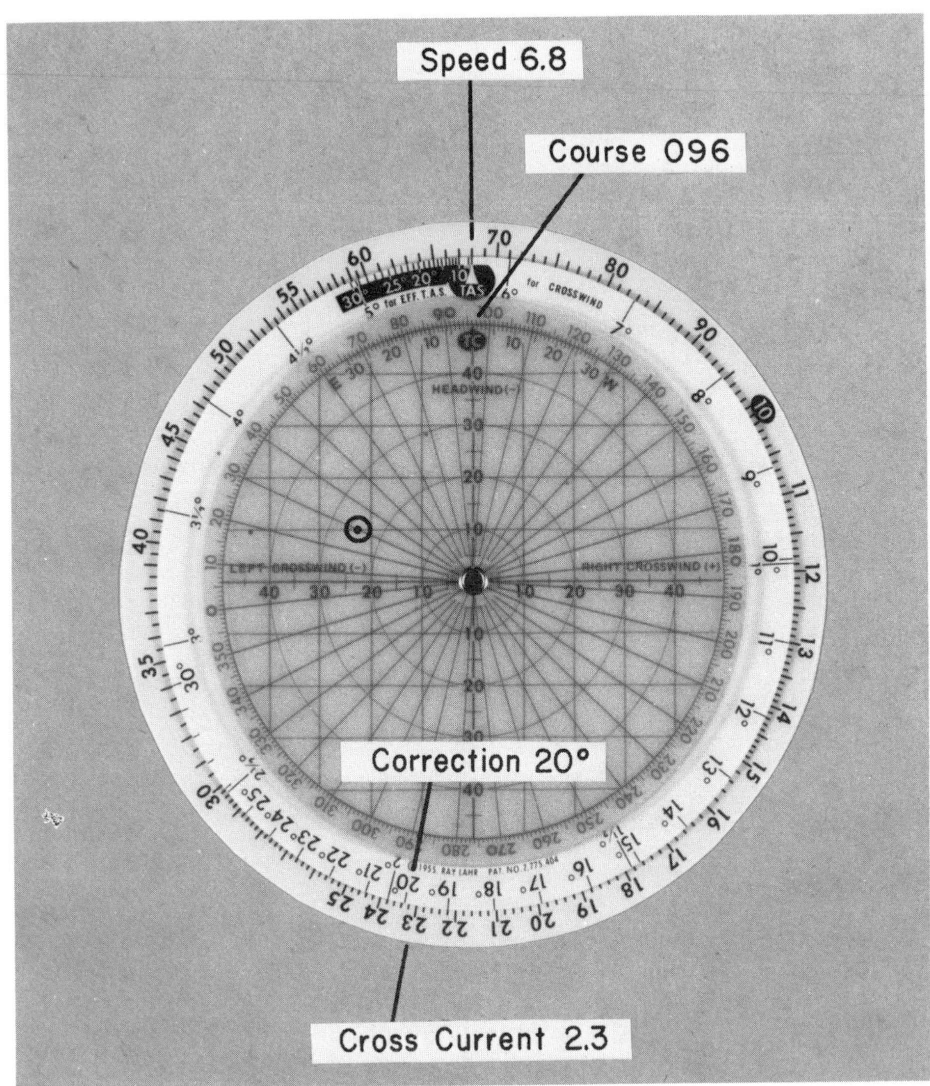

Figure 7-32 Second step.

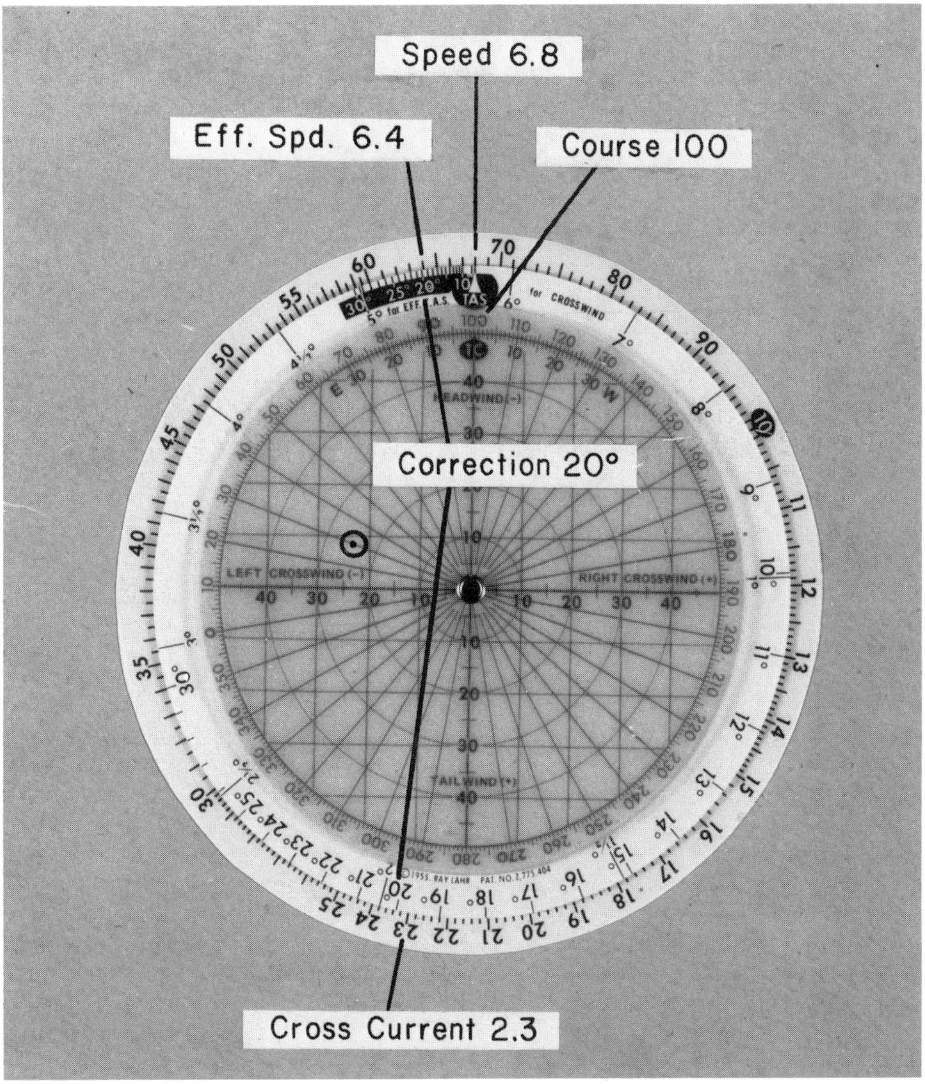

Figure 7-33 Third step.

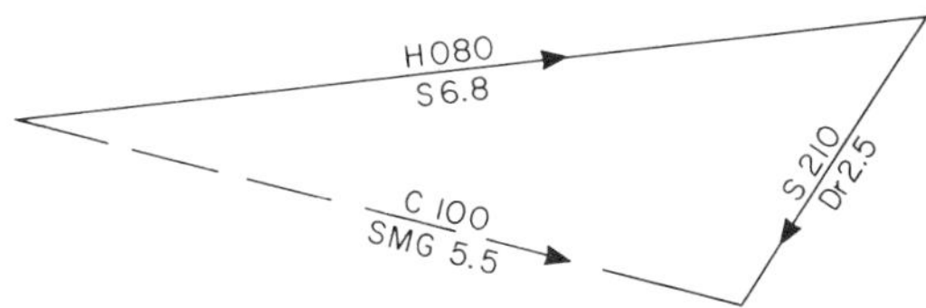

Figure 7-34 Current triangle for Example 7-14.

8: Dead Reckoning with Current

We streamed the patent log, something we only do when an accurate speed record is required, since the spinning rotator astern has a far greater attraction for predatory fish than any hook or lure I ever possessed. 'Speed through the water' is the key phrase here because the log takes no account of the tide or current set. Therefore, although according to the log we had covered 116 miles in the 23 hours since Nomuka and would still have ample sea room at daybreak, we might nevertheless be in the process of being swept more briskly towards the Laus than this indicated, so that evening as a precaution we took star sights.

David Lewis, Children of Three Oceans

When the dead reckoning process involves the question of current, the navigator can choose between two systems of allowing for current. One system says that, strictly speaking, a dead reckoning plot shows motion *through the water*. The DR plot is drawn from headings and speeds, and the effect of current is added afterwards. The result is called an *estimated position*, since the set and drift are not known with certainty. This system, while quite correct, works best if the set and drift are constant for hours or days. As such, it is used mostly for offshore navigation, and is covered later in this chapter.

When piloting near shore, the navigator is working with currents that change rapidly from hour to hour. In this case, it's far more practical to include the effect of current at each step of the dead reckoning process. The results are called estimated positions, since they are based on current figures that may not be correct. This method is illustrated here by several examples.

Cruise 5

We leave the south point of Wolf Island at 0700 on January 1, heading for the black can buoy at Friar Island. From the chart, it is determined that the required course is 153°. Our speed is a constant 4.0 knots, and there is no compass deviation. Variation in the area is 24° E. Checking the current table for 0700, we work out the set as 280° and the drift as 1.6 knots. Figure 8-1 shows one way of using the current curve. From that information, we can obtain the required heading (110 magnetic) and the SMG (2.8 knots). Accordingly, we set off at 0700 steering 110° by the compass.

At 0730 it's time for a new log entry. Calculate the distance as 30 minutes at 2.8 knots, or 1.4 miles. Plot the estimated position, using a square instead of a circle. Now refigure the current. The set is still 280°, but the drift has dropped to .9 knot. On this basis, we work out a heading of 142° true, or 118° magnetic, and a SMG of 3.4 knots. So, beginning at 0730, we steer 118° by the compass.

Every half hour we repeat the process: plot the present EP, calculate the present current, and work out a heading for the next half hour. The log is shown in Figure 8-2. There is an added column for the True Course; an extra column for the SMG might also be helpful if space permits. Notice that the current decreases, until it reaches zero at 0800. After 0800 it picks up again but in the 100° direction, so it is helping us along somewhat and our SMG becomes greater than our speed. Also notice that the heading changes regularly, from 134° at 0700 to 172° at 0900. The EP plot at 0900 shows that the buoy should be .9 mile ahead. At the present SMG of 4.8 knots, we should cover that distance in 11 minutes, for an estimated time of arrival (ETA) of 0911 (see Figure 8-3).

A word of caution. The EP plot shows that we pass half a mile from Bone Island. But, if our course is actually slightly to starboard of our calculation, we'll run aground on the island at 0900. A course error of 4 degrees is all that's required for this to happen, and such an error could easily occur if the current turns slightly later than the predicted 0800. On a clear day there's no problem, because you'll see the island and avoid it. But an night or in fog, you must remember the possibility of such an error. When you plot the 0830 EP, ask yourself this question: "If my course is not what I think, it is how soon might I meet land?" If the course is 4 degrees off, you'll be at Bone Island in 30 minutes. If it's 15 degrees off, you'll be at Green Island in *only 11 minutes*.

Cruise 6

This time we'll go the other way; from the Friar Island can buoy to the south point of wolf Island, leaving at 1000 on January 1. There is no deviation, variation is 24° E, and the boat speed varies from time to time, according to the wind.

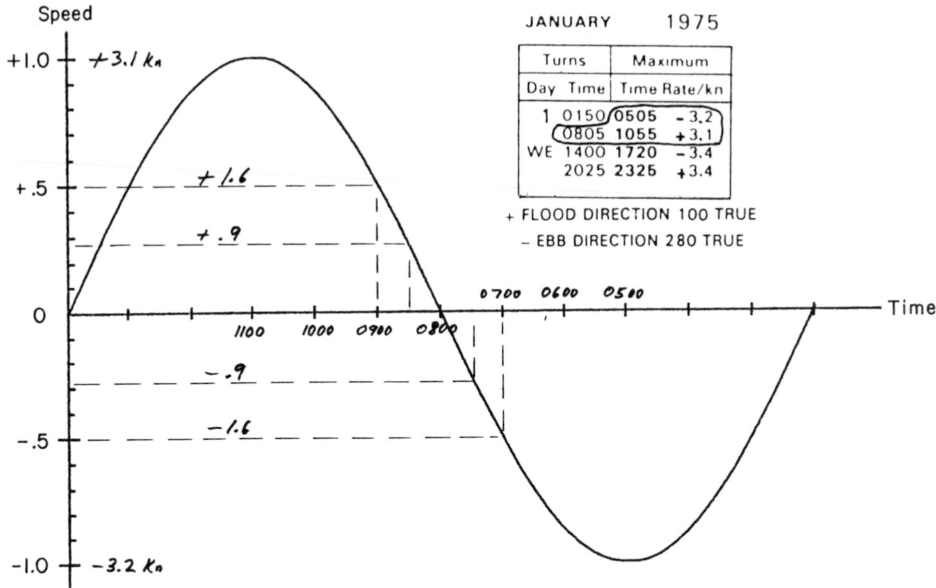

Figure 8-1 The current curve for Cruise 5.

The current curve is shown in Figure 8-4, and the log sheet in Figure 8-5. From 1100 to 1130, the speed picks up and the current drops off. Accordingly, we don't have to head into the current as much, and the heading changes from 309° to 312°. A similar change occurs between 1130 and 1200. At 1200, the plot in Figure 8-6 shows that the EP is 1.5 miles from the island. At the SMG of 4.5 knots, we should cover that distance

	HEADING						
Time	**Compass**	**Magnetic**	**True**	**Speed**	**True Course**	**Distance**	**Remarks**
0700	*110*		*134*	**4.0** *SMG 2.8*	**153**	—	Depart Wolf Island Variation 24° E Set 280, Dr 1.6
0730	*118*		*142*	**4.0** *SMG 3.4*	**153**	*1.4*	Set 280, Dr .9
0800	*129*		*153*	**4.0** *SMG 4.0*	**153**	*1.7*	Set nil, Dr nil
0830	*139*		*163*	**4.0** *SMG 4.4*	**153**	*2.0*	Set 100, Dr .9
0900	*148*		*172*	**4.0** *SMG 4.8*	**153**	*2.2*	Set 100, Dr 1.6

ETA0911

Figure 8-2 Log book for Cruise 5

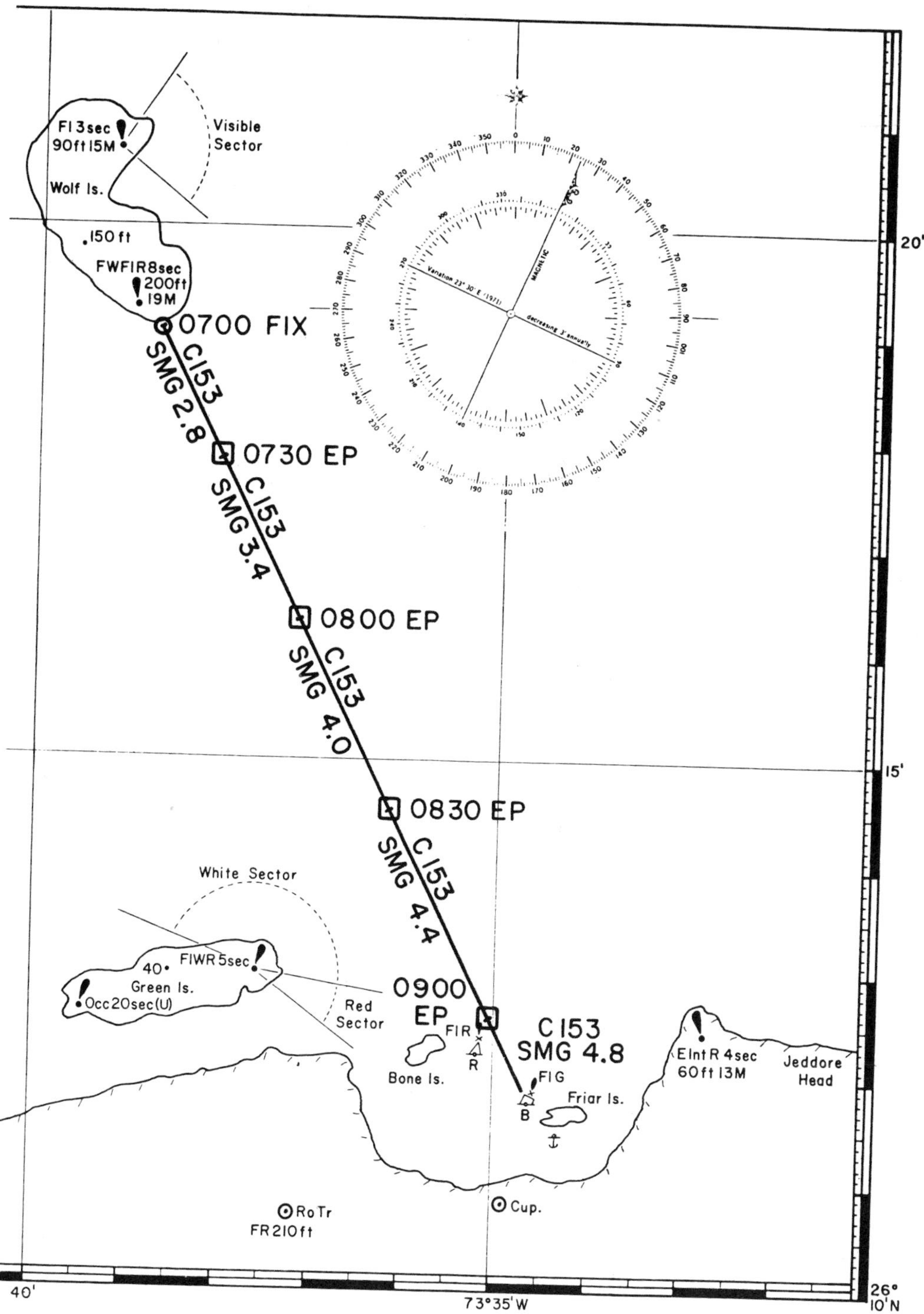

Figure 8-3 The plot of Cruise 5.

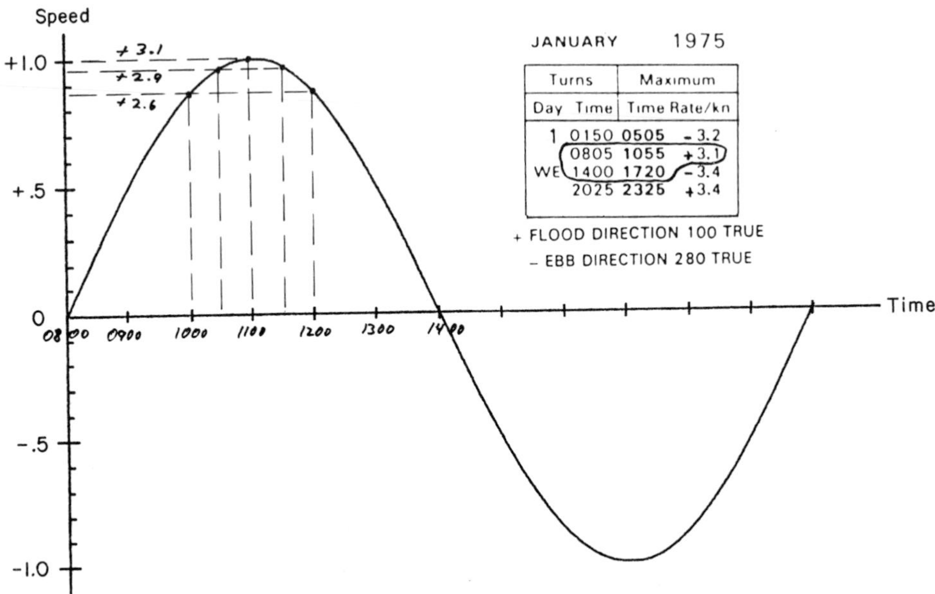

Figure 8-4 The current curve for Cruise 6.

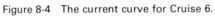

Time	HEADING Compass	Magnetic	True	Speed	True Course	Distance	Remarks
1000	*282*		*306*	**4.5** *SMG 2.6*	**333**	—	*Depart Friar I. Can* *Variation 24°E* *Set 100, Dr 2.6*
1030	*283*		*307*	**5.0** *SMG 2.8*	**333**	*1.3*	*Set 100, Dr 2.9*
1100	*285*		*309*	**6.0** *SMG 3.6*	**333**	*1.4*	*Set 100, Dr 3.1*
1130	*288*		*312*	**6.5** *SMG 4.3*	**333**	*1.8*	*Set 100, Dr 2.9*
1200	*290*		*314*	**6.5** *SMG 4.5*	**333**	*2.2*	*Set 100, Dr 2.6*

ETA 1220

Figure 8-5 Log book for Cruise 6.

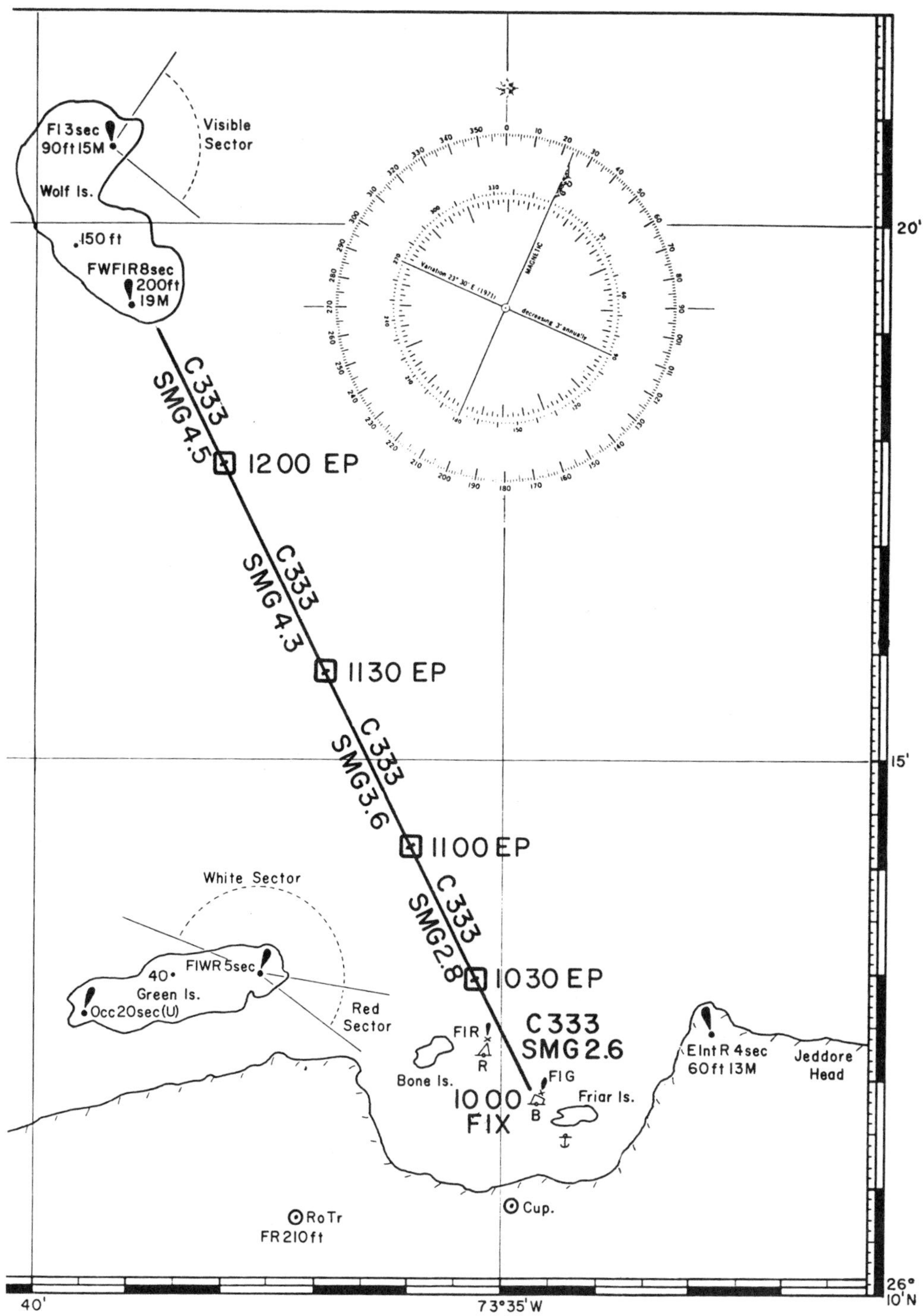

Figure 8-6 The plot for Cruise 6.

in 20 minutes, for an ETA of 1220. If the course is slightly in error, the remaining distance is greater, and the arrival time will be later.

Cruise 7

For this cruise, we depart the outer fairway buoy (HA) at 1530 on January 4, destined for the Brig Rock buoy. Our speed is a constant 2.5 knots, variation is 24° E, and there is compass deviation according to the table in Figure 8-7. the current curve is set up as shown in Figure 8-8; the time axis tick marks are shifted to the half hour to obtain the best match with the table.

The log and EP plot are shown in Figures 8-9 and 8-10. Several things can be observed. Initially, the current was partially behind us (set 100°), so it helped us along and the SMG was greater than the speed. As the current dropped to nothing, and then picked up from ahead of us (set 280°) the SMG dropped steadily. Also, our true heading changed from 173° (greater than the true course) to 128° (less than the true course) as the current changed. The magnetic heading changed by a corresponding amount, and so, the deviation found in the table changed from 3° E to 1° W.

It's also interesting to speculate on making this trip in a fog. The ETA for the buoy is 1746, but the uncertainties of current calculation are such that we must be prepared to miss it. If our actual course is slightly greater than planned (to starboard), we might run up on Brig Rock. If we manage to pass that safely, it becomes a certainty that we'll meet the shore west of Cape Entry, perhaps unavoidably. The logical alternative is to steer a heading slightly less than calculated (to port), which should take us east of the buoy, We'll probably locate it from the sound, since the whistle carries well. If not, we're almost sure to pick up one of the other bell

Deviation Table

Vessel *Deviant* **Adjuster** *JPB*
Compass *Steering* **Date** *15-8-75*

Ship's Head - Magnetic	Deviation
000	5° W
045	4° W
090	2° W
135	2° E
180	4° E
225	5° E
270	2° E
315	2° W

Figure 8-7 Deviation table for Cruise 7.

buoys shortly afterwards. Then we can 'buoy-hop' safely in the anchorage.

This is a good time to point out another good use for the CR slide rule. It converts true headings to magnetic headings, or magnetic to true, in short order. If the true heading is 173°, and variation is 22° E, what magnetic heading must we use? Refer to Figure 8-11. Set 173° on the TC index, and find 22° E on the inner black scale. The magnetic heading is opposite this (151°).

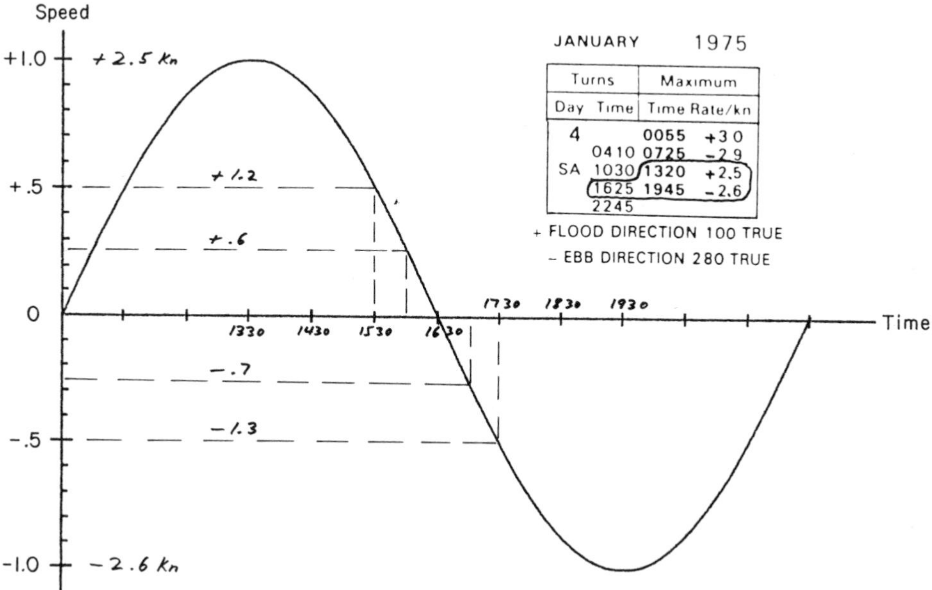

Figure 8-8 Current curve for Cruise 7.

Time	HEADING Compass	Magnetic	True	Speed	True Course	Distance	Remarks
1530	*146*	*149*	*173*	**2.5** *SMG 3.0*	**152**	—	*Depart buoy HA.* *Variation 24°E* *Deviation per table* *Set 100, Dr 1.2*
1600	*136*	*138*	*162*	**2.5** *SMG 2.8*	**152**	*1.5*	*Set 100, Dr .6*
1630	*126*	*128*	*152*	**2.5** *SMG 2.5*	**152**	*1.4*	*Set nil, Dr nil*
1700	*114*	*114*	*138*	**2.5** *SMG 2.0*	**152**	*1.2*	*Set 280, Dr .7*
1730	*105*	*104*	*128*	**2.5** *SMG 1.5*	**152**	*1.0*	*Set 280, Dr 1.3*

ETA 1746

Figure 8-9 Log book for Cruise 7

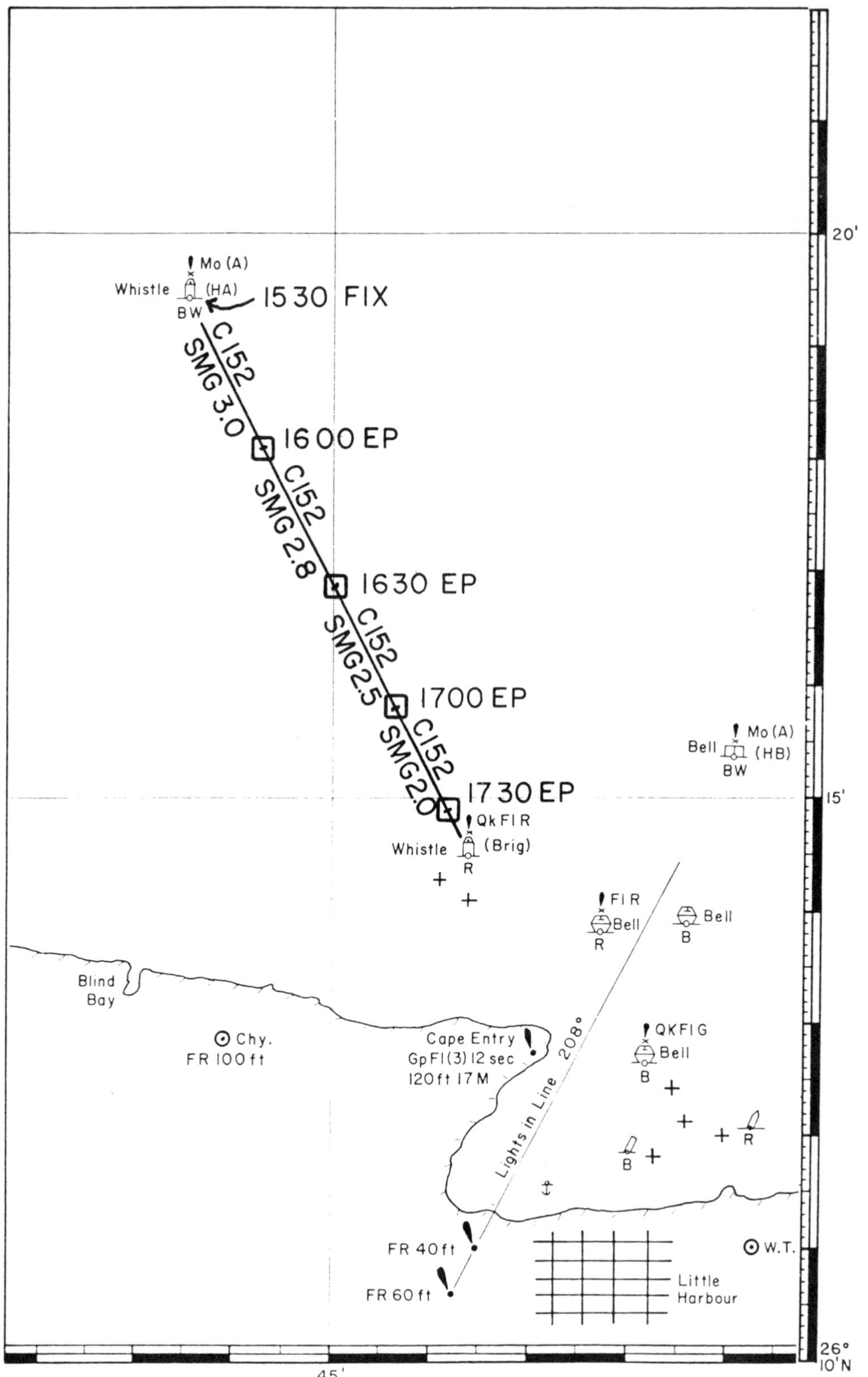

Figure 8-10 Plot of the EP's for Cruise 7.

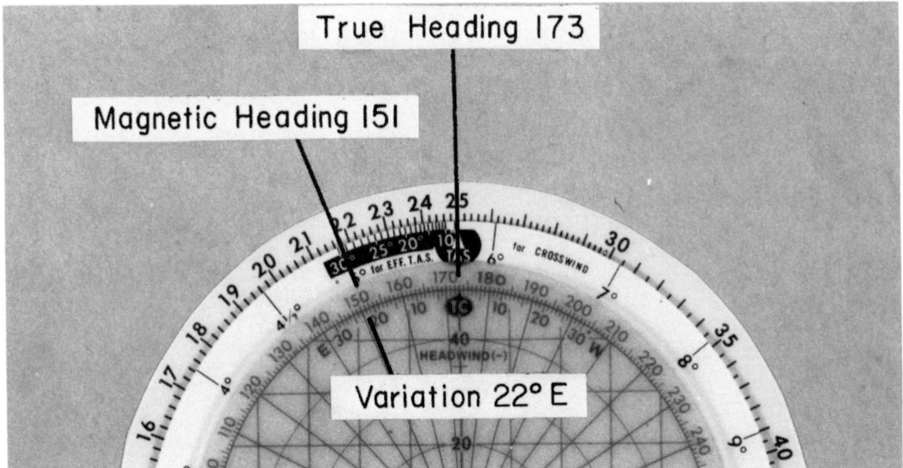

Figure 8-11 Converting true heading to magnetic on the CR slide rule.

Cruise 8

We depart from the Bone Island nun buoy (pointed red) on 2 January at 0730. We hold a compass heading of 324° and a speed of 3.0 knots, until 0900. Then, we hold a compass heading of 251° and a speed of 3.0 until 1000. At 1000 we decide to set a course directly for the Little Harbour red bell buoy, with a speed of 3.4 knots, using headings as necessary to offset the current. There is no deviation, and variation is 24° E. What headings are required, and what is the ETA at the buoy?

The current curve is shown in Figure 8-12. The time scale runs from right to left. The log is shown in Figure 8-13, and the plot in Figure 8-14.

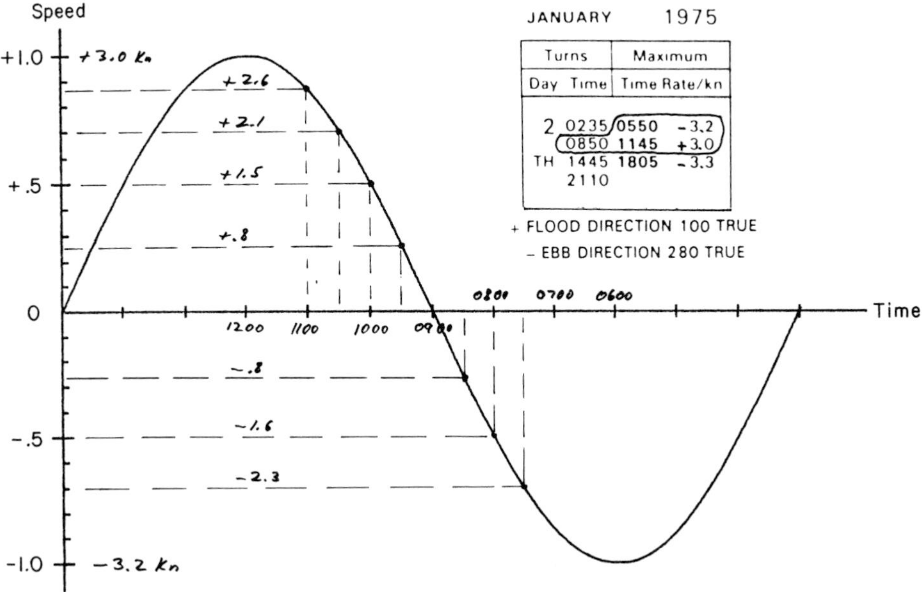

Figure 8-12 Current curve for Cruise 8.

	HEADING						
Time	Compass	Magnetic	True	Speed	True Course	Distance	Remarks
0730	324	324	348	3.0 SMG 4.4	319	—	Depart Bone I mun. Variation 24° E Set 280, Dr 2.3
0800	324	324	348	3.0 SMG 3.9	326	2.2	Set 280, Dr 1.6
0830	324	324	348	3.0 SMG 3.4	335	1.9	Set 280, Dr .8
0900	251	251	275	3.0 SMG 3.0	275	1.7	Set nil, Dr nil
0930	251	251	275	3.0 SMG 2.2	273	1.5	Set 100, Dr .8
1000	Find course and heading to Little Hr. red bell buoy, at speed of 3.4 knotts. 190	190	214	3.4 SMG 3.1	188	1.1	Set 100, Dr 1.5
1030	202	202	226	3.4 SMG 2.7	188	1.6	Set 100, Dr 2.1
1100	214	214	238	3.4 SMG 2.3	188	1.3	Set 100, Dr 2.6

ETA 1116

Figure 8-13 Log book for Cruise 8.

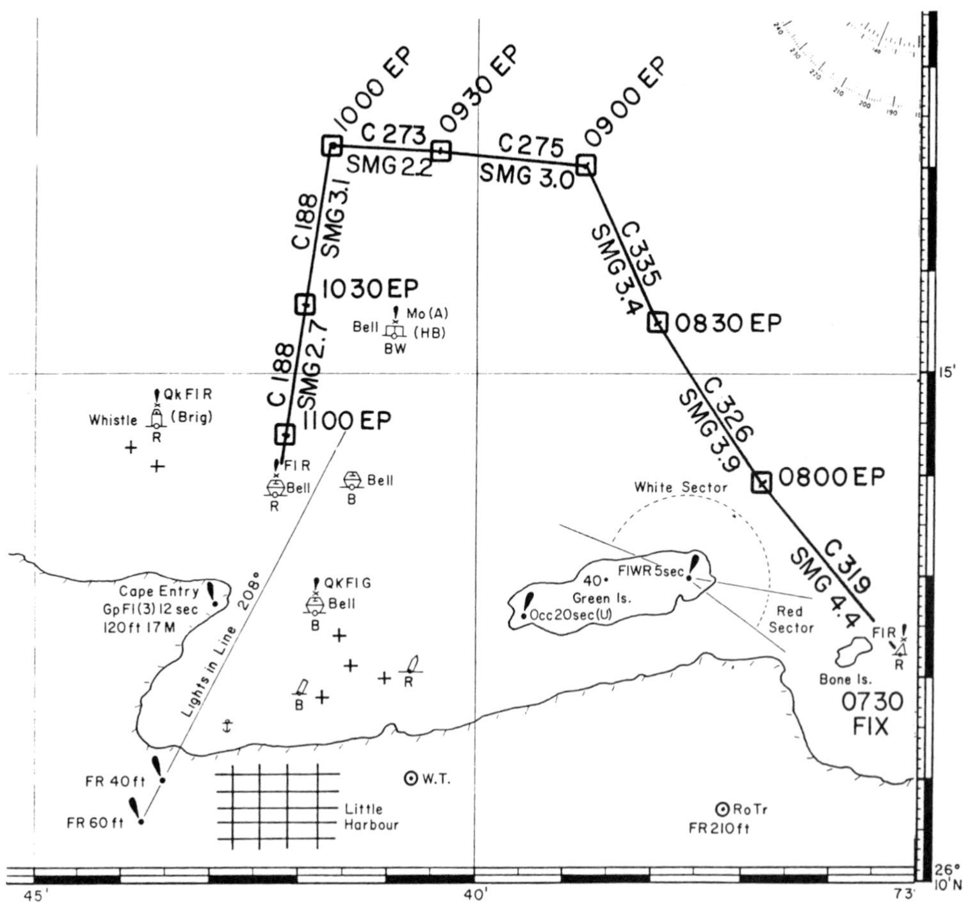

Figure 8-14 Plot of the EP's for Cruise 8.

From 0730 to 0900 the course changes as the current drops. After 0900, the current picks up in the other direction, but now is almost directly against the heading, so it affects the SMG considerably and the course only slightly. After 1000 the course is fixed, and the headings increase rapidly to offset the current, while the SMG drops. At 1100 the remaining distance to the buoy is .6 mile; at the SMG of 2.3 knots, this will take 16 minutes, for an ETA of 1116.

A DIFFERENT SYSTEM OF DEAD RECKONING WITH CURRENT

All the dead reckoning work so far has included the effect of current at each step, so the course and headings have always been different. If we temporarily ignore the current, the course will be the same as the heading. We can enter the heading in the log, and plot it as a course. Cruise 9 is worked on this basis; Figure 8-15 shows the log, and Figure 8-16 shows the plot. Each DR position, including 1700, is plotted as though there were no current. Then at 1700, we can think about the current this way: in this area, the current has a constant set of 110° and a constant drift of 1.2 knots. We have been under way for 2 hours and 25 minutes, so the current must have moved us 2.9 miles from our DR position, in a direction of 110°. Plot this point, and label it as an estimated position. If our dead reckoning has been correctly done, and *if our estimate of the current is also correct,* the EP should be our actual position.

I'm not totally in love with this system for coastal piloting. For one thing, we assumed the current was constant. That can be true with offshore ocean currents, but in coastal areas the current changes rapidly from hour to hour. For another thing, we don't believe, even for a minute, that the plotted "course" really represents our actual track. Moreover, the error gets larger as time goes on. That's usually all right for offshore navigation with time and room to spare, but I think it's foolish for coastal work. I'd much rather have a plot that at least resembles the truth. The important thing is to always remember that the plotted EP's are estimates, subject to the accuracy of the current predictions.

Time	HEADING Compass	Magnetic	True	Speed	Distance	Remarks
1435	**000**		*343*	**5.8**	—	Depart Light Ship
						Variation 17° W
1500	**000**		*343*	**5.8**	*2.4*	
1530	**277**		*260*	**4.4**	*2.9*	
1600	**337**		*320*	**6.2**	*2.2*	
1630	**083**		*066*	**6.0**	*3.1*	
1700	**083**		*066*	**6.0**	*3.0*	

Figure 8-15 Log book for Cruise 9.

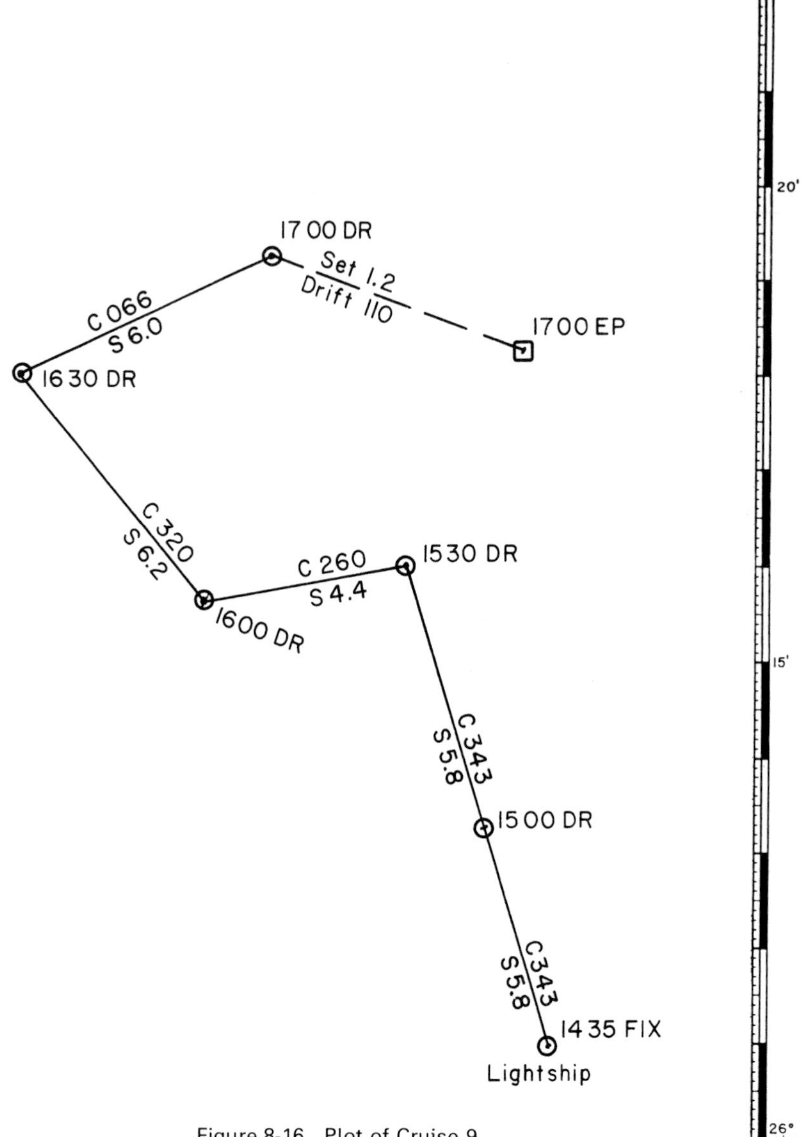

Figure 8-16 Plot of Cruise 9.

Problem 8-1

Work out the headings and plot the estimated positions for a cruise from the Little Harbour red spar to Wolf Island south point, departing at 1300 on January 1. Speed is 4.2 knots, variation is 24° E, and there is no deviation.

Problem 8-2

Depart the Little Harbour, inner, black bell-buoy on January 3 at 0200. Steer a constant compass heading of 350° from 0200 until 0400. The speeds are:

0200–3.2 knots
0230–3.5 knots
0300–3.2 knots
0330–2.8 knots.

There is no deviation. Plot the 0400 EP. Work out the course required to travel directly to the red bell-buoy. Calculate the necessary heading each half hour, with a constant speed of 3.2 knots. On the return leg, what check on the progress may be available? What is the ETA at the buoy?

9: Bearings

The wind, which as before had been allowing us just to lay the course, then backed, and all through the night we beat wetly to windward to round the apparently never-ending bulge of land, fixing our position now and then by bearings of the lights on Punta Estaca (25 miles visibility) and Punta Candelaria (22 miles).

Eric Hiscock, Atlantic Cruise in Wanderer III

The process of dead reckoning might be called the fundamental system of piloting, because it's the *only* system that is sure to be always available. Done with due care in the proper conditions, dead reckoning can give surprising accuracy. It can also give unpleasant surprises, so the prudent navigator will not only calculate his position by dead reckoning, but will frequently *measure* his position, using some other system. There are two basic systems available. The first one, based on bearings, is illustrated in this chapter. The second is covered in Chapter 10.

A bearing is a direction, measured from our own vessel to another object. Any measurement must have a starting point, so a bearing needs a reference direction. We can use true north as a reference, and call the bearing a *true bearing*, or we can use the bow of our boat as a reference, and call the bearing a *relative bearing*. Both types of bearings are useful.

RELATIVE BEARINGS

Relative bearings are frequently used in relationship to other boats. This subject is important in naval fleet maneuvers, and naval books and navigation manuals go into great detail on the subject. The relative bearings are measured accurately with a special accessory to the gyro compass, and a special "maneuvering board" plotting sheet (HO2665). When the small boat navigator reports a relative bearing, he may say, quite informally, that it's on the "port bow" or the "starboard quarter" and let it go at that. Or he may be more precise and report "22 degrees to port" or "55 degrees to starboard."

Here is a situation where relative bearings are really significant. Suppose you're cruising along, and sight another boat approaching. His bearing is 90 degrees to starboard (on the starboard beam). A little later, his bearing is more toward your bow, say 70 degrees. You would probably know, intuitively, that he will pass ahead of you; and you'd be correct. On the other hand, suppose his bearing changed from 90 to 120 degrees—more toward your stern. Your intuition would say that he will pass astern—correct again. But suppose his bearing doesn't change. He won't past ahead and he won't pass astern; you will collide. So, here we have a special case: *if the relative bearing to another boat doesn't change, you are on a collision course.* To avoid collision, you have to change course and/or speed.

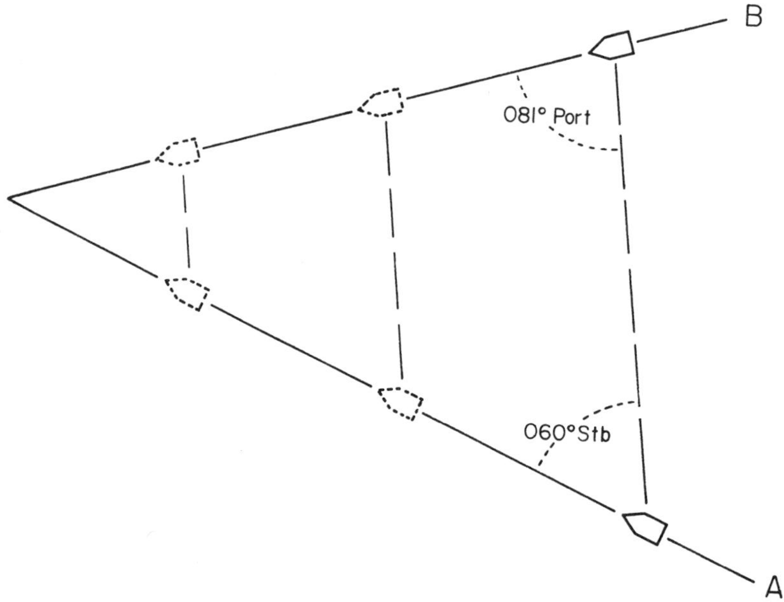

Figure 9-1 Two boats on a collision course.

Relative bearings to other boats are usually estimated. You're not so much interested in the exact bearing as in whether or not it changes, so, it's easy to check by sighting against an object on your own boat, such as a shroud. Figure 9-1 illustrates a situation where boats A and B approach each other on a collision course. The skipper of A has a relative bearing to B of 60 degrees to starboard, while B sees A 81 degrees to port. Either skipper would have a constant relative bearing on the other, so either skipper could detect the collision course and alter to avoid it.

Accurate relative bearings, for which two applications are given below, can be obtained quickly and easily with a sextant. Stand or sit with your eye on the centerline of the boat; in a sailboat this is easily checked by lining up the mast with the forestay. Turn the sextant on its side; mirrors down if the object is to port, up if it's to starboard. Aim the telescope or sight tube forward, and move the index arm until the object appears to line up with the mast (on a heeling sailboat, use the part of the mast level with your eye). The relative bearing is read directly on the sextant scale, and is usually rounded off to the nearest degree.

Such a relative bearing is often reported in a 360 degree system, measured clockwise from the bow. A relative bearing of 30 degrees to starboard would also be 030 degrees in the 360 degree system. A relative bearing of 70 degrees to port would be 290 degrees.

One important application of the relative bearing is its ability to check your steering compass. Chapter 5 gave the details of finding the deviation for a steering compass. It was usually assumed that we could sight across the compass card to find the compass bearing to a known object. With many compass installations, especially in bulkheads, sighting across the card isn't possible. A relative bearing will cure the problem. To obtain the compass bearing, you only have to add the relative bearing (in the 360 degree system) to the compass heading.

Let's say that your boat is on a compass heading of 205 degrees. You measure the relative bearing to a known object as 042 degrees. Then the compass bearing is 205° plus 042°, or 247°. However, the chart shows that the true bearing is actually 229°, and that variation is 15° W. Then the compass bearing *should* be 229° plus 15°, or 244°. Since you obtained a measured value of 247°, you can say that on a heading of 205°, the compass deviation is 3° W. Always remember that *deviation tables are entered with the heading of the boat,* not the bearing to the object. After all, the compass has no way of knowing where you're looking.

There's another important application for relative bearings: they can be converted to true bearings, which are extremely useful for finding position. This idea could go in the section on true bearings, but that section is long enough anyway, so the conversion idea is here.

Let's assume that the steering compass has no deviation, or that a correct deviation table is at hand. Then a compass heading can be converted to a true heading, as you already know how to do from Chapter 5. With the boat on a known heading, we measure the relative bearing to an object on shore. The true bearing is found by adding the relative bearing to the true heading. In equation form: True Bearing = True Heading + Relative Bearing; or TB = TH +RB.

Figure 9-2 illustrates a case where the boat is steering a compass heading of 070° magnetic with no deviation and a local variation of 10° E. The true heading is then 080°. With the sextant, a relative bearing of 65° to starboard is measured. The true bearing, then, is 080° plus 065°, or 145°.

Figure 9-3 illustrates another case. Here, the heading is 118° magnetic, with a deviation on that heading of 1° E, and a local variation of 9°W. The

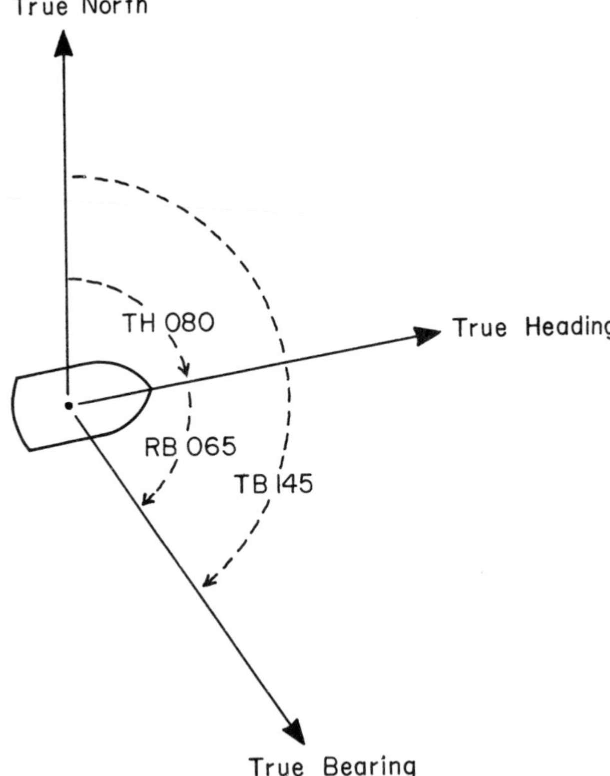

Figure 9-2 Converting a relative bearing to a true bearing.

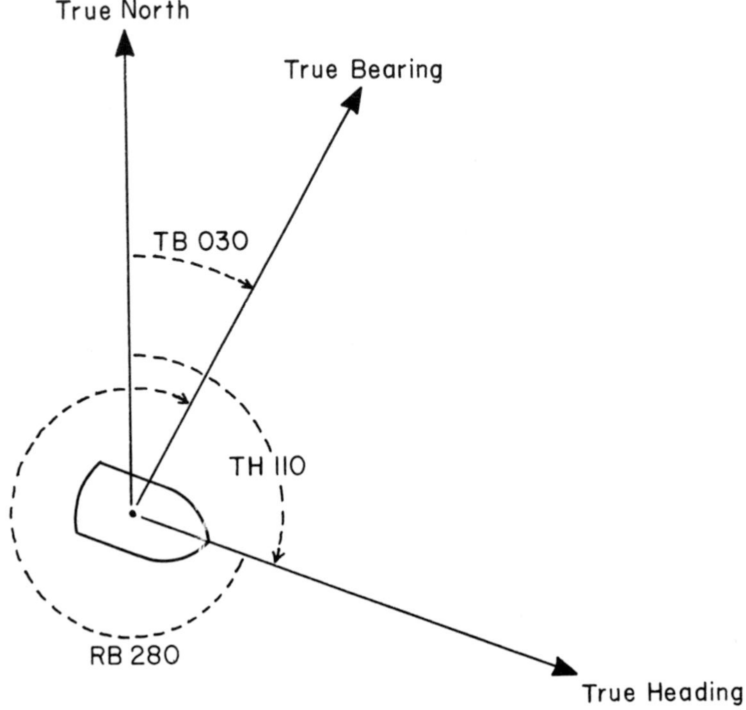

Figure 9-3 Converting a relative bearing to a true bearing.

true heading is then 110°. A relative bearing of 80° to starboard is measured, which becomes 280° relative. The true bearing is then 110° plus 280°, or 390°. In this case we subtract 360°, obtaining a true bearing of 030°.

TRUE BEARINGS

A true bearing is given with respect to true north. Since charts are also drawn based upon true north, the true bearing can be plotted on the chart. As we will soon see, this is extremely useful. It's a curious paradox, though, that although true bearings are given and plotted with respect to true north, the only way they can be *measured* with respect to true north is with a gyro compass. Most of us have to measure them as compass or magnetic bearings, and convert to true bearings.

One method of plotting the true bearing uses the steering compass and a relative bearing, as shown in the previous section. If you don't have a sextant, or aren't sure about the deviation of your steering compass, another solution is to use a hand-bearing compass. It has a small card, and either a set of sight vanes or a mirror, which it uses to line up on the object. Then, you read the compass bearing directly. It's usually possible to carry the hand-bearing compass to part of the boat where there is no magnetic disturbance from the engine or keel, so you only have variation to allow for. Figure 9-4 shows one type of hand-bearing compass.

Well, you learn something every day. I sailed in a race just after writing the above, and a fellow sailor discovered that his metal eyeglass frames upset the bearing compass readings by 10 degrees.

A true bearing is usually measured to a fixed object on shore that can be identified on the chart. A lighthouse, radio mast, church spire, large chimney, or natural feature such as a cliff or point of land, would be a useful object. You can also use a buoy or light vessel, keeping in mind that it may have moved from its charted position.

Once you have measured the true bearing, you can plot it to the object shown on the chart, obtaining a line of position. Position lines obtained by true bearings form an accurate and important method of finding your position. There are many ways that bearings can be used, and for each situation a certain method will be the most useful and accurate. The rest of this chapter covers the basic methods.

POSITION LINE FROM A BEARING ON ONE OBJECT

This is the basic method of finding a position line. Suppose you're sailing along at night, and at 2208 you see a light that is fixed white and flashing

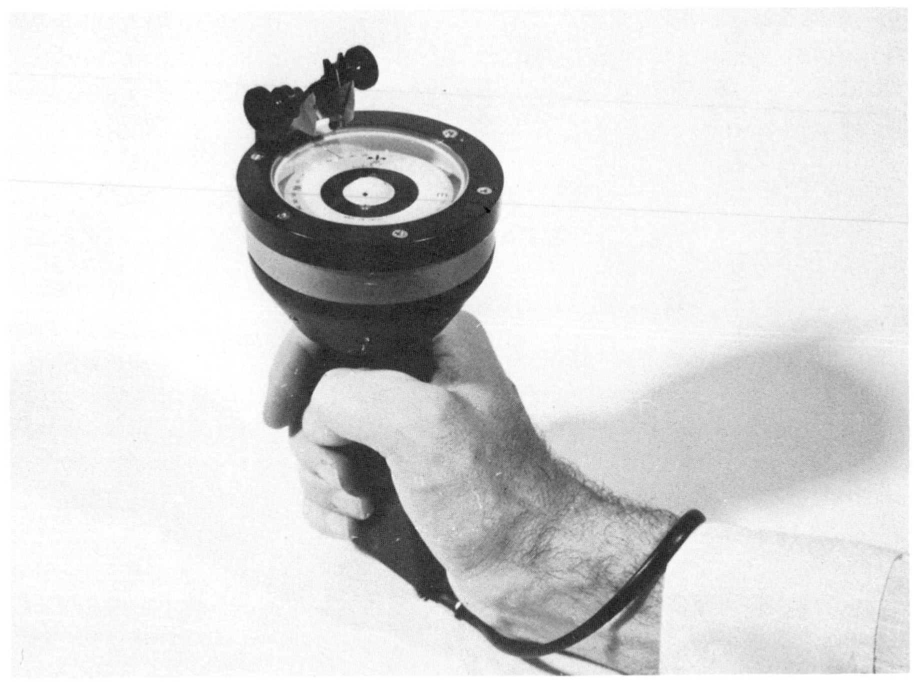

Figure 9-4 The hand-bearing compass is useful on any boat.

red. From the chart you identify it as the Wolf Island south light. The hand-bearing compass gives a bearing of 291° magnetic, which converts to 315° true, or northwest. Since you are looking northwest toward the light, it follows that the light-keeper would be looking southeast toward your boat. Draw a line from the light in a southeast direction. Numerically, you want the *reciprocal* of 315°, which is 315° minus 180°, or 135°. This is your line of position (LOP). You are located somewhere along it, though as yet you don't know where. Label the line with the time, and the true bearing to the light. As a matter of habit, *any* line you draw on the chart should be labeled so you can look at it later and know what it means. See Figure 9-5.

Another example. At 2235 you take a sight on the Green Island west light with a hand-bearing compass, obtaining a magnetic bearing of 166°. With a variation of 24° E, this converts to a bearing *to* the light of 190° true, and you plot your LOP *from* the light in a direction 010°. Label the line with the time and bearing. Again, you know that you're somewhere on this line, but you don't know exactly where. See Figure 9-5.

It's quite common to need a bearing during the day, when a light isn't visible. If the light structure is a tower of substantial size, you may be able to see it. Still, there are lots of light on skeleton towers which are quite impossible to pick out from any distance. Natural features can help. For example, at 1015 you see the "left end" of Bone Island, and take a bearing of 137° magnetic, or 161° true. To plot the line, the reciprocal is

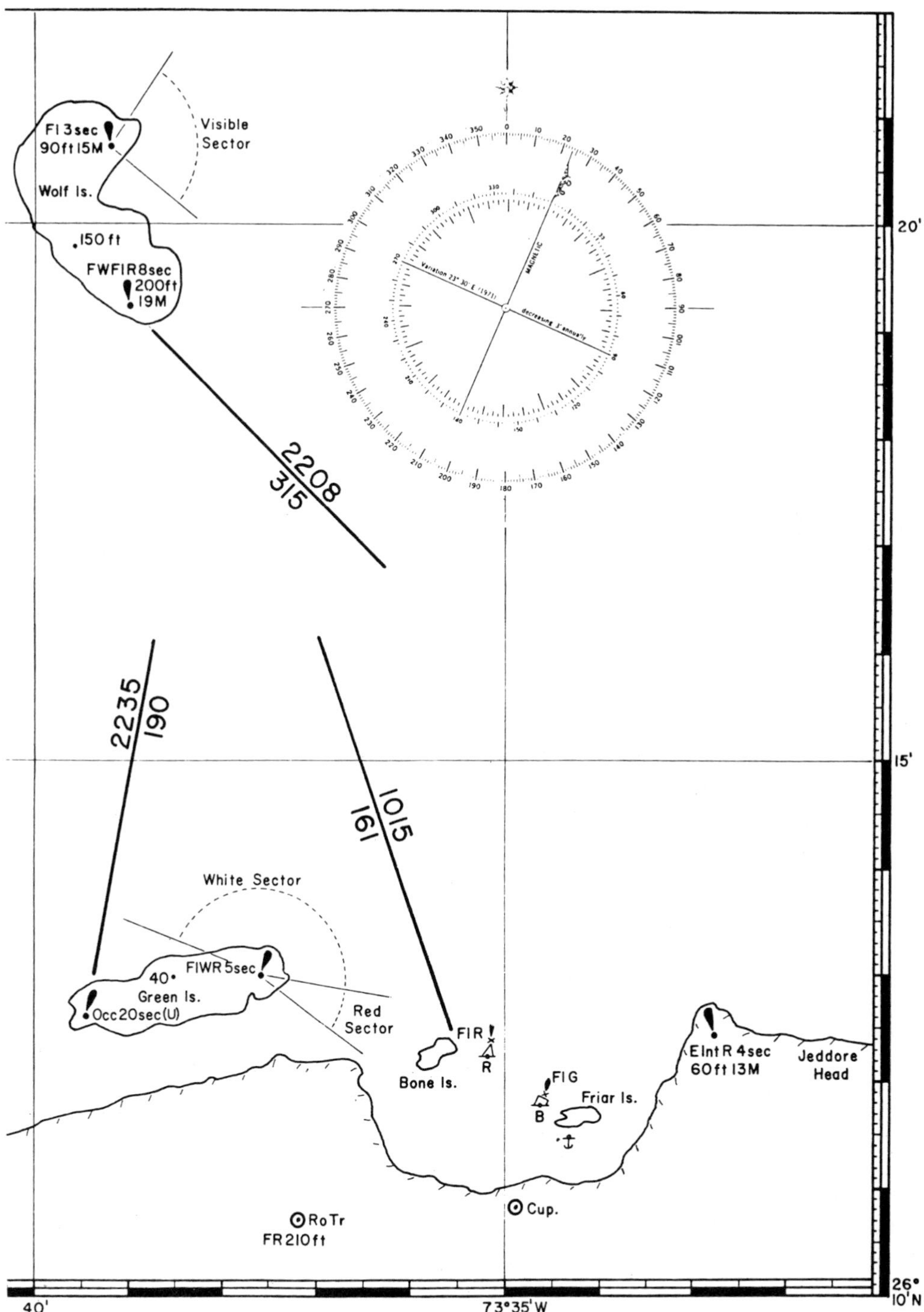

Figure 9-5 A single bearing gives a line of position.

341°. The "left end" of the island, as seen from seaward, is the east end on the chart. Plot the line from this point, as shown in Figure 9-5.

RANGES

Although most bearings used in piloting are measured, there is a special case that doesn't need to be. This is the range—an alignment of two objects. Pairs of lights or beacons are often established just for this purpose. Beacons will often carry lights for night use, and the rear one will always be higher than the front one, so it's a simple matter to know which side of the range you're on. If the lower beacon opens out to the left, you're to the right of the range. For example, the range lights at Little Harbour on the practice chart are 40 and 60 feet high, each being fixed red. The chart also shows the direction of the range as seen from seaward—208° true. This can be very handy for checking to see if you have lined up the right pair of lights. It's also useful as a known bearing for checking the compass.

Ranges are often used to excellent advantage for marking the approach to narrow channels and harbors. By keeping the beacons in line, you will stay in the center of the channel. This can be very exact; with many ranges it's no trick to stay within a few feet of the line. Figure 9-6 reproduces part of Canadian chart #4478 showing approach ranges to the government wharf. The pilot of a boat drawing less than 6 feet of water would follow the beacon range (approximately west) until the lights of the wharf range came into line; then he would turn and keep the lights in line to approach the wharf.

In our case, a vessel drawing more than 6 feet could not follow the beacon range all the way to the wharf light range; an earlier turn would be needed and buoys are placed for this purpose. Also, the range bearings are not given because the ranges are occasionally shifted to allow for changes in the channel.

Ranges with beacons are wonderful things, but a bit scarce. You can often take advantage of an "opportunity range," using natural objects or other charted features. Figure 9-7 shows some possibilities, as they would appear from seaward and as they would be charted. No bearing figures are shown, because these ranges were observed, not measured.

FIXING THE POSITION BY BEARINGS ON TWO OBJECTS

It's all very well to find your line of position with a bearing to an object. However, you could be anywhere along that line, from a yard to a mile from shore. Since you usually want to know your position along the line, you need a second piece of information.

The classical way of solving this problem is to take two bearings on two objects. Suppose that at 1410 you take magnetic bearings on the radio tower and on the Jeddore Head light, of 180° and 136°, respectively.

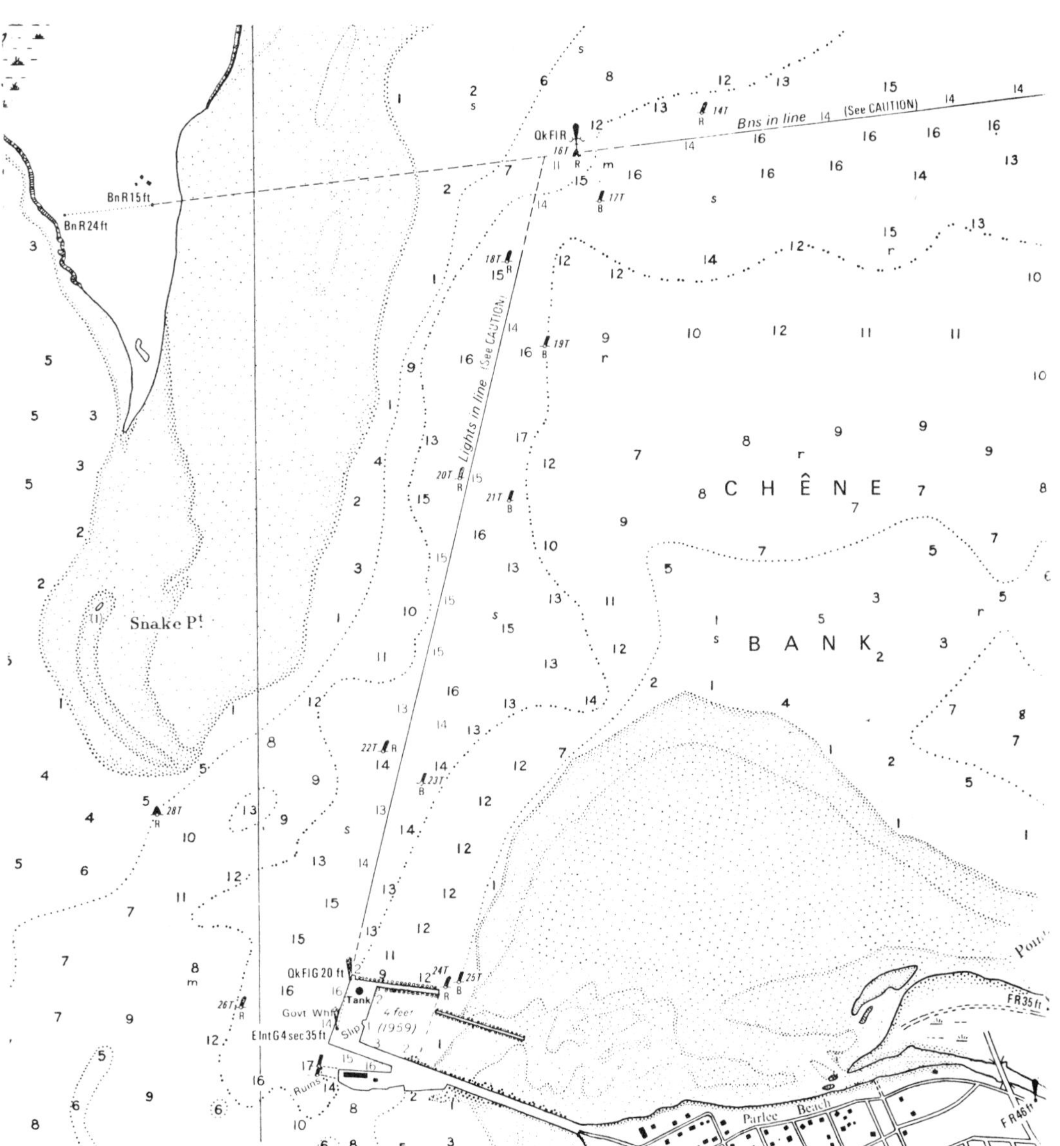

Figure 9-6 Two ranges provide a safe approach to this wharf.

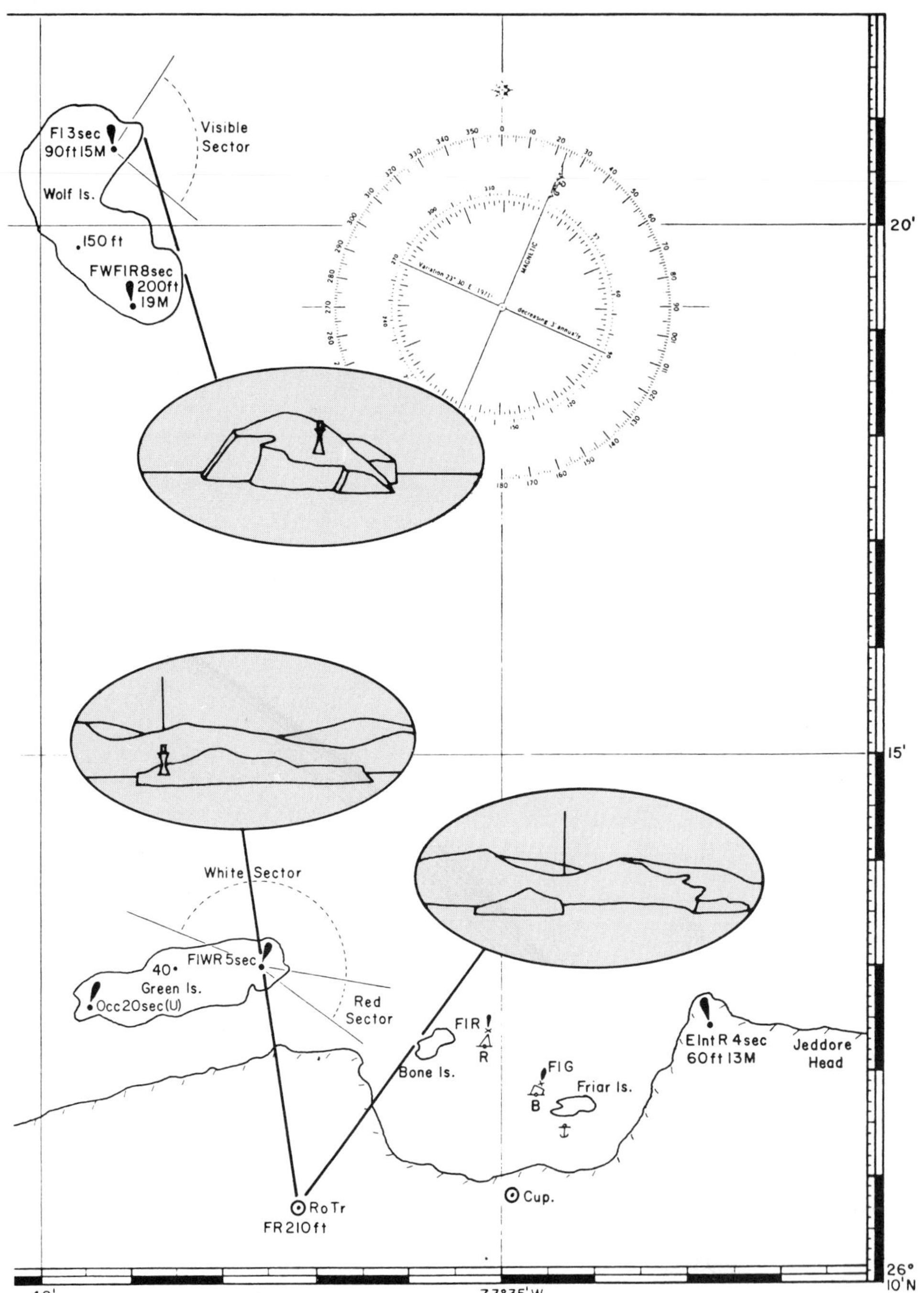

Figure 9-7 Ranges can be obtained by using charted features.

These convert to 204° and 160° true. They are plotted on the chart as shown in Figure 9-8, and their intersection gives a position fix at 26° 17′ N, 73° 34′ W.

Can anything that simple really work? Well, maybe not. The problem is this; just when you really want a position fix, you can bet your boots that all the towers and lights in the neighborhood will conspire to vanish. It never fails! You can greatly improve the prospects by using natural objects. For example, in the same general area at 1530, you might get magnetic bearings on the left side of Wolf Island and the right side of Green Island, of 293° and 201°, respectively. These convert to 317° and 225° true, and are plotted as shown in Figure 9-8, giving a position fix at 26° 16′ N, 73° 36′ W.

Problem 9-1

At 1230 you use a hand-bearing compass to take bearings on the Jeddore Head light and the Green Island east light, obtaining figures of 118° and 205° magnetic, respectively. What is your position?

Problem 9-2

At 1400 you take bearings by sighting across the steering compass. There is deviation according to Table 9-1 below, and variation is 24° E. The compass heading is 175°. The bearing to fairway buoy HB is 056°, and the bearing to buoy HA is 315°. What is your position?

Problem 9-3

At 1615 you are steering a compass heading of 005°. Variation is 24°E, and deviation is according to Table 9-1. with a sextant you obtain a relative bearing on the water tank of 165° to starboard, and on the Brig buoy of 123° to port. Find the position.

Deviation Table

Vessel Deviant Adjuster JPB
Compass Steering Date 15-8-75

Ship's Head - Magnetic	Deviation
000	5° W
045	4° W
090	2° W
135	2° E
180	4° E
225	5° E
270	2° E
315	2° W

Table 9-1 Deviation of the steering compass.

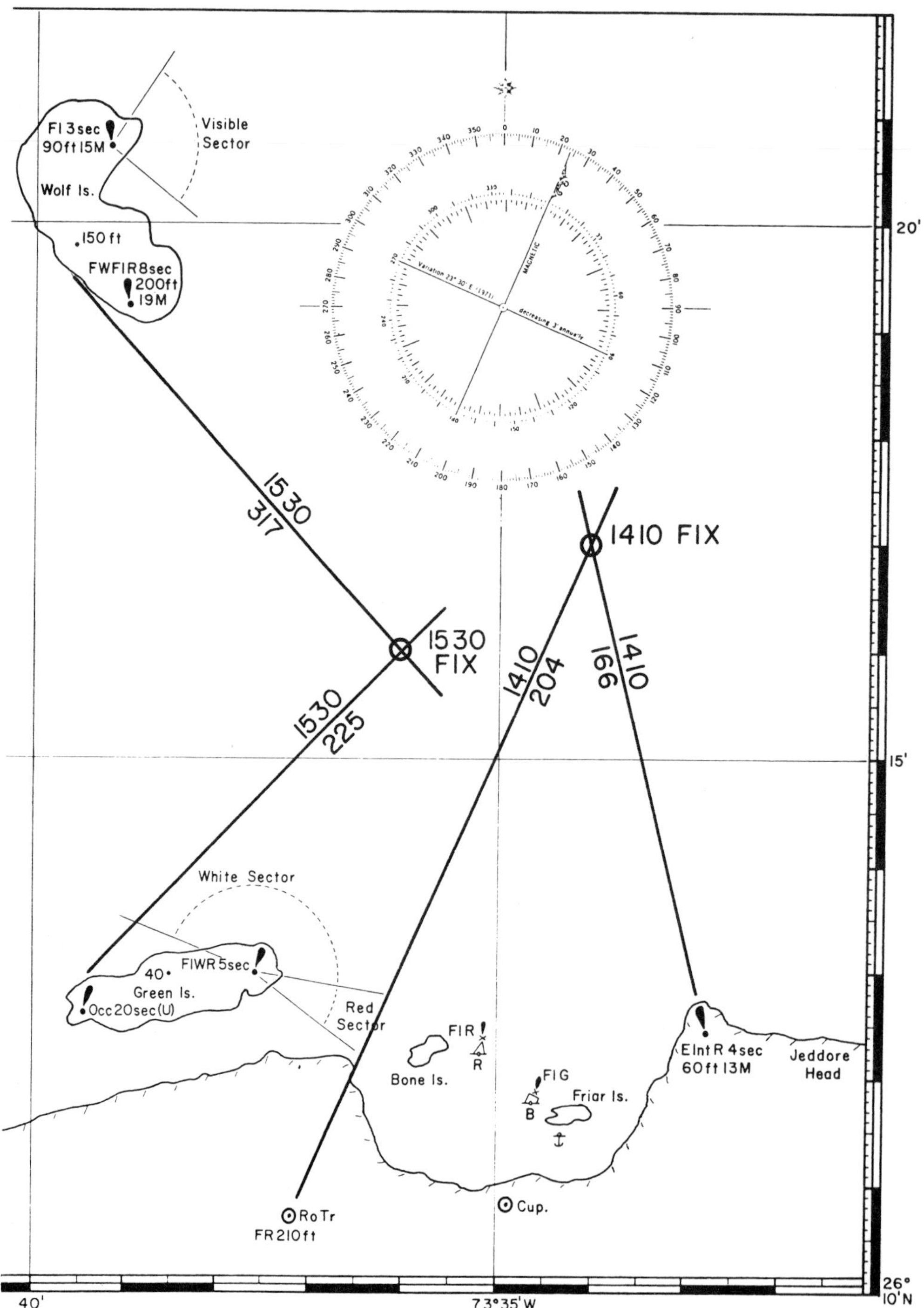

Figure 9-8 Bearings on two objects will fix the position.

ADVANCING THE LINE OF POSITION

Very often you can get a bearing line from one object, but have no other object in view for a second line to fix your position. Take the bearing anyway; it can be "saved" for later use by keeping a careful dead reckoning plot. Let's say that at 1300 you take a bearing on a beacon, and convert the magnetic bearing to 026° true. This line is plotted and labeled as in Figure 9-9. If you now sail due east at 4.0 knots, at 1400 you will have moved 4.0 miles east. If your first position has been at A, it would now be at B. If your position had been at C, it would now be at D. In the figure, each of the new points is 4.0 miles east of the corresponding first point. As you'll see, the new points form a straight line, parallel to the old one and 4.0 miles east of it. You have "advanced" the 1300 line, and at 1400 you are on the advanced line. It is identified by labeling with the first and advanced times, and the true bearing.

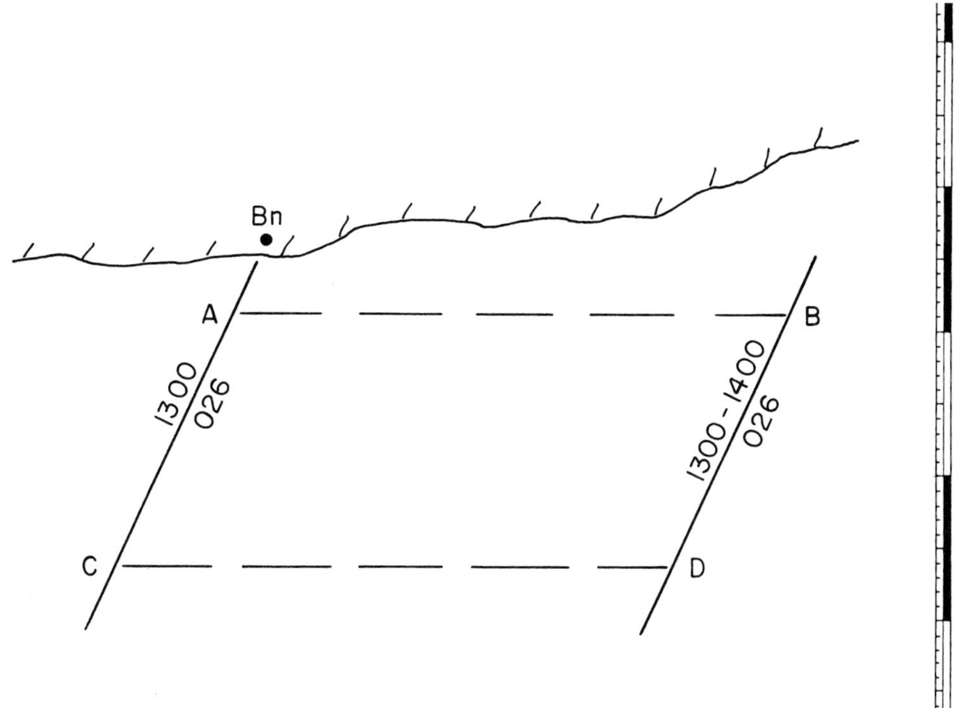

Figure 9-9 Advancing the line of position.

ADVANCING THE FIRST LOP TO A SECOND OBJECT

Figure 9-10 illustrates a classic situation. You are on a compass heading of 275°, with no deviation, and variation of 5° E. The speed is 6.0 knots. At 1040, with a DR position as shown, you obtain a magnetic bearing, on a light, of 155°. At 1120, a radio tower is seen on a magnetic bearing of 200°. Find the position at 1120.

The 1040 bearing is converted to 160° true and plotted. The DR position for 1040 is evidently wrong since it doesn't fall on the bearing line, but that's normal enough. After all, if we trusted the DR position completely, we wouldn't be bothering with bearings! The true course is 280°, and is plotted from the 1040 DR position. At 1120, the new bearing is converted to 205° true and plotted. The 1120 DR position is also plotted—4.0 miles (40 minutes at 6.0 knots) along the course line from the 1040 DR position. The direction and distance between the two DR positions shows how to advance the 1040 LOP.

The intersection of the advanced 1040 line with the 1120 line is called a running fix, because it is less accurate than a fix by two simultaneous bearings. A new DR plot is started from the running fix. The 1040 DR position and LOP are in the same relative position as the 1120 DR position and LOP. (This point, which may seem obvious, will prove very useful in the next example.)

ADVANCING THE LOP WITH COURSE CHANGES

The log in Figure 9-11, and the plot in Figure 9-12, illustrate another common situation. At 1310 we obtain a magnetic bearing of 147° to

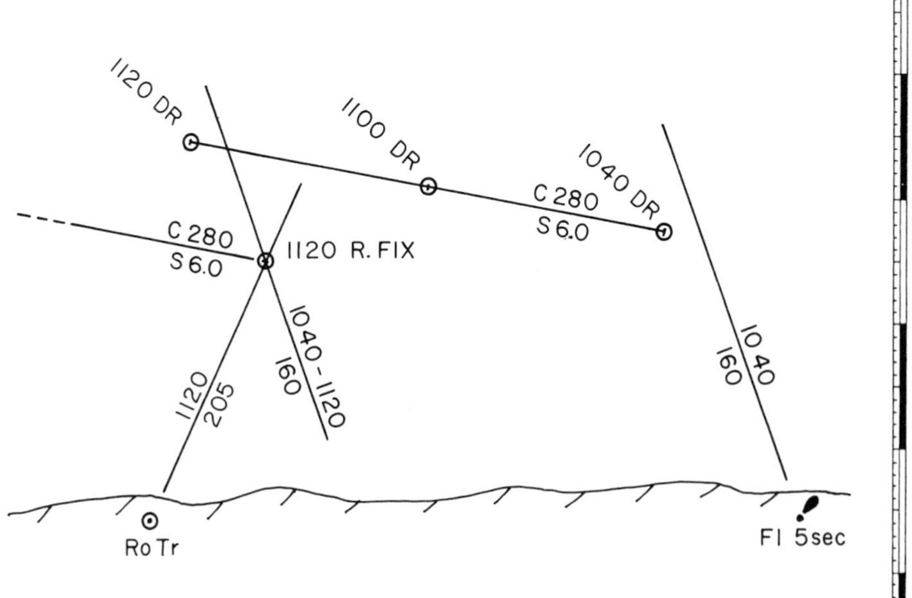

Figure 9-10 A bearing on one object can be advanced to a bearing on a second object to find your position.

Time	HEADING Compass	Magnetic	True	Speed	Distance	Remarks
1310	252	*252*	*246*	6.0	—	DR Position as shown Variation 6°W No Deviation Brg to "A" 147 M *140T*
1330	342	*342*	*366*	6.0	*2.0*	
1340	252	*252*	*246*	6.0	*1.0*	
1400	252	*252*	*246*	6.0	*2.0*	Brg to "B" 195 M *189T*

Figure 9-11.

beacon "A". At 1400, after a couple of course changes, we obtain another magnetic bearing of 195° to beacon "B".

Plot the 1300 LOP, and the DR positions as usual. Plot the 1400 LOP. The 1300 LOP is advanced by noting its position relative to the 1300 DR position.

Of course, there's a moral to all this: *when you have a chance to take an accurate bearing, do it.* You man not need it then, but later might be very glad of the chance to advance the first LOP to cross a second and fix your position.

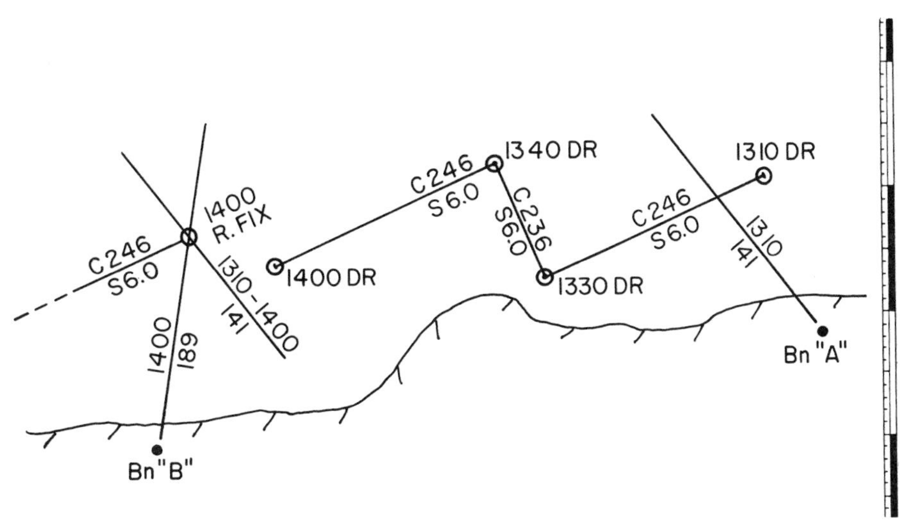

Figure 9-12 Advancing an LOP with course changes.

TWO BEARINGS ON ONE OBJECT

The previous method works fine, but here's an even better one. It's my favorite in the bearing-taking department; in fact, I'll even use it when I don't really need bearings at all, just for the fun. Now, what's so great about this method? You only need *one* object to find your position. Take a bearing, wait a while, and take another bearing. Then advance the first LOP to cross the second. Hey, presto—position fix.

Suppose you are on a magnetic heading of 250°, with variation of 20° E. At 2205, the magnetic bearing to the flashing light on a buoy is 300°. At 2250, the bearing to the same buoy is 015°. The speed is 4.0 knots. The course and bearings converted to true are 270°, 320°, and 035°. (Figure 9-13 shows the plot of these and the DR positions.) The 2205 LOP is advanced in the normal way; where it intersects the 2250 LOP we have the 2250 running fix. Again, don't be surprised that the running fix doesn't agree with the DR position, although the difference is exagerated in these illustrations for the sake of clarity.

If there are changes in course and/or speed between the times of the two bearings, there's no problem. Just plot the DR positions for the two times, and use these to advance the first LOP, as shown in the previous example.

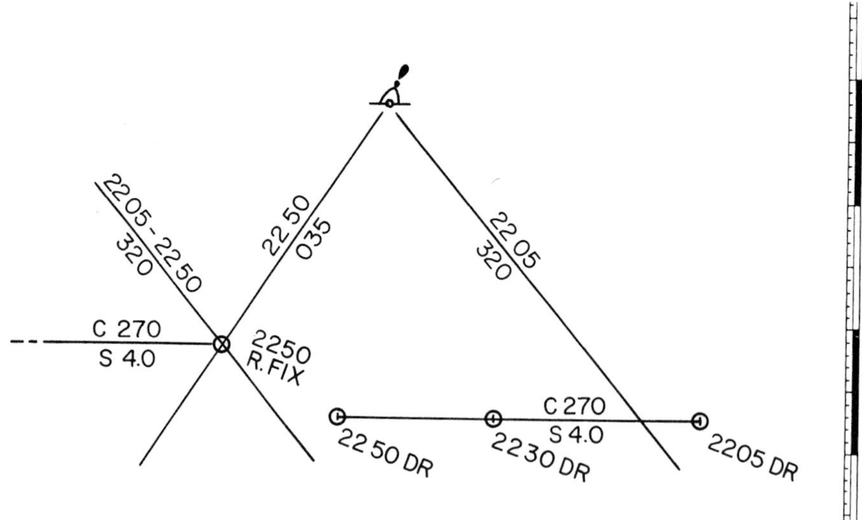

Figure 9-13 Finding the position by taking two bearings on one object.

TWO BEARINGS ON ONE OBJECT WITH THE CR SLIDE RULE

One of the reasons that taking two bearings on one object is a favorite method of mine, is that the plotting work can be done on the CR slide rule. This lets you find a position by bearings very quickly and easily. If you want just the distance to the object, you don't even need a chart!

Suppose you're on a magnetic heading of 315°, and the variation is 15° W. Your speed is 8.0 knots. At 1000 you sight a beacon on a bearing of 025°, and at 1030 the bearing to the same beacon is 085° magnetic. To find your position at 1030, set the true course (300°) on the TC index. Draw radial lines along the two true bearings, 010° and 070°. Now, you know that in 30 minutes you moved 4.0 miles. Find the place where the vertical distance between the two bearing lines is 4.0 units (one unit representing one mile); dividers or pencil marks on a scrap of paper are useful for this purpose. Mark the two points on the bearing lines. The lower point (second bearing) gives your position; you are 4.3 miles from the beacon, and the bearing is 070°. Figure 9-14 shows the settings. Again, the inner black scale is handy for converging magnetic headings and bearings to true.

You can also use another method that's basically the same, but does not

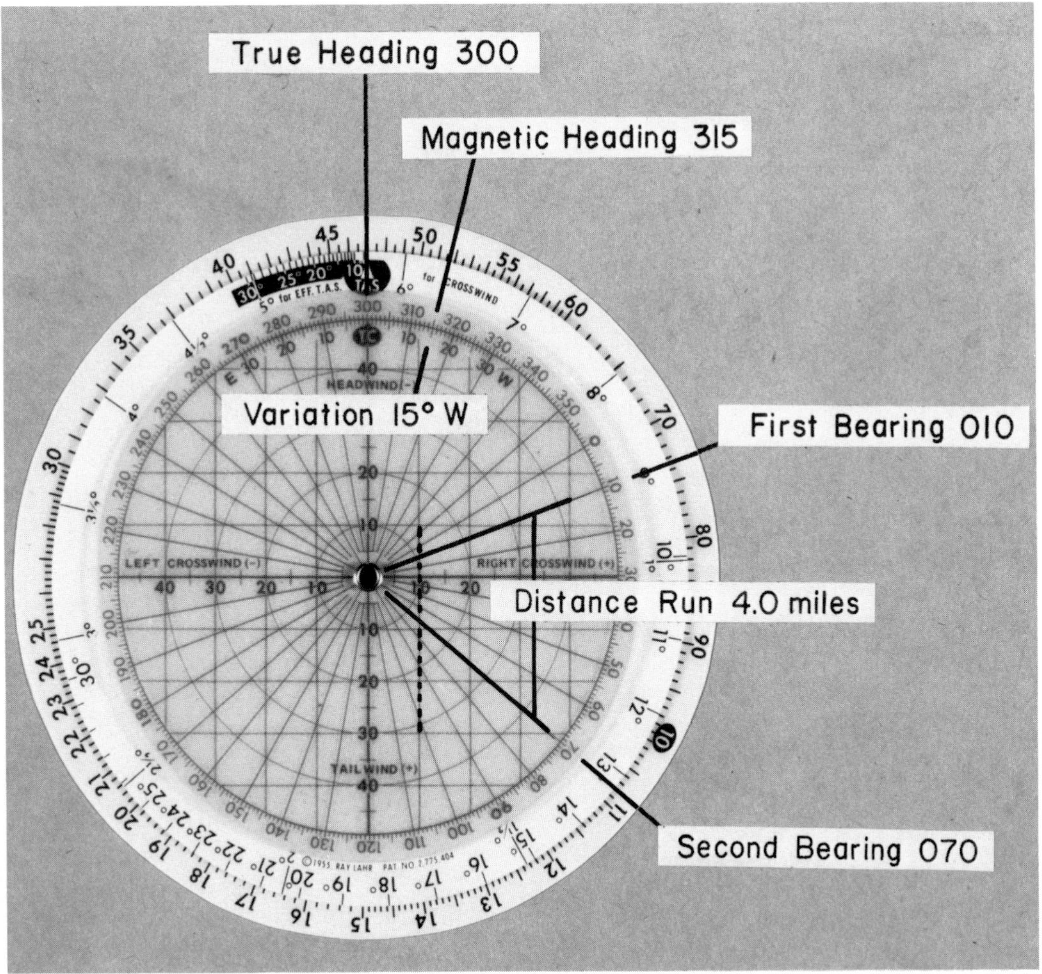

Figure 9-14 The CR slide rule will find the position from two bearings on the same object.

require a CR slide rule. Draw the two true bearings on the chart. Then draw a line on a piece of tracing paper, representing your course and distance traveled between the two bearings. Move it around until the ends of the course line meet the two bearing lines. The intersection of the course line with the second bearing line gives your position. Figure 9-15 illustrates this method. The results agree with the figures obtained on the CR slide rule.

The two bearing method, whether you use a slide rule or tracing paper, assumes that there is no current, or that you've allowed correctly for it, so the proper course is used. If there is an unknown current, the results will be incorrect, because the actual distance between bearings will be different from the calculated distance that you used.

The effect of current can be found by taking *three* bearings. Using your boat's speed, or any convenient figure, calculate the distance run between bearings. Mark these on tracing paper, and move the paper until all three points get the bearing lines. The intersections then give the course,

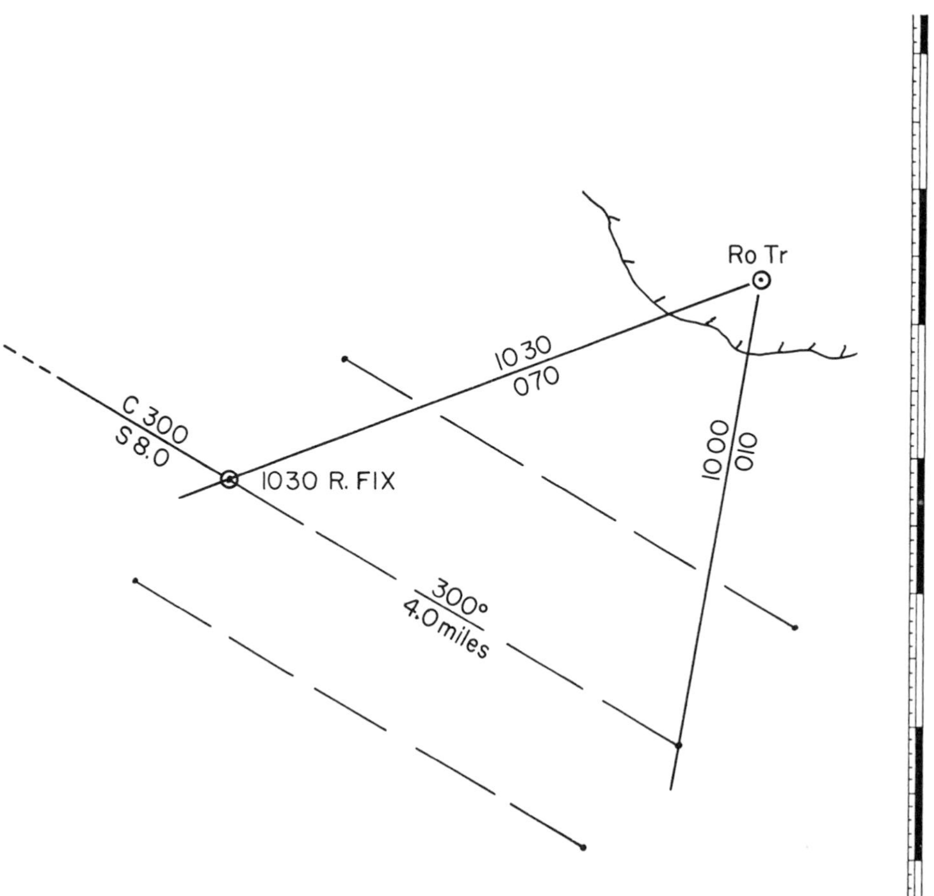

Figure 9-15 An easy chart-work method for finding the position from two bearings on one object.

which may be quite different from the heading. To find the actual track and speed made good, project this course from a previous accurate fix (not a running fix). You will have the actual track, and the SMG can be worked out from the distances between the bearing lines.

DOUBLING THE ANGLE ON THE BOW

This is a special case of the two bearing method. The advantage is that it uses *relative* bearings, which can be very accurately measured without variation or deviation, by using a sextant. If you take two relative bearings some time apart, and the second is twice as large as the first, *the distance to the object at the time of the second bearing is the same as the distance run between bearings.*

Let's illustrate this. Figure 9-16 gives the first relative bearing as 035°, and the second as 070°. The distance traveled between the two bearings, as well as the distance from the running fix to the object, is 3.0 miles. In practice, you take the first bearing which you have the chance, and note the bearing, time, and speed. Watch the bearing as it increases, and when it doubles its first value, note the time again. Work out the distance run, and you have the distance off. A small practical problem; I always manage to miss the second bearing by waiting too long. But, that's another matter.

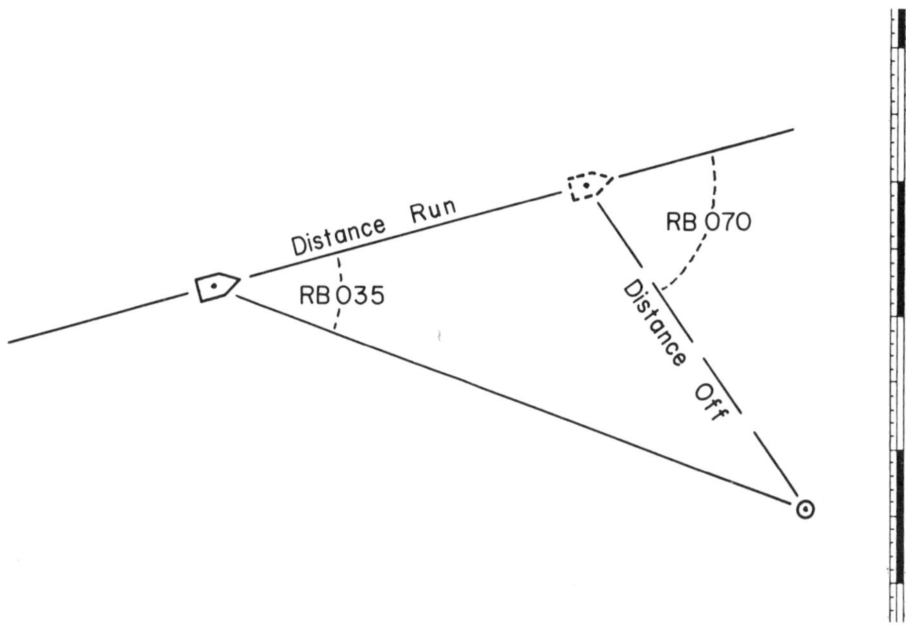

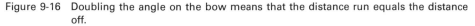

Figure 9-16 Doubling the angle on the bow means that the distance run equals the distance off.

DANGER BEARINGS

Where are you *not* located? If there's a hazard in the neighborhood, this question can be easily as important as where you are located. It can be answered with a single bearing. If you're proceeding generally eastward from the outer black bell-buoy, you'll want to avoid Green Island. (For this occasion, we'll assume that it isn't lit.) Draw a line past the island to the Jeddore Head light. This is the *danger bearing,* and measures 101° on the chart, as shown in Figure 9-17. Convert this to a magnetic bearing of 077°. As you sail along, you can check that you're clear of the island by taking a bearing on the Jeddore Head light. If the bearing is greater than 077° magnetic, you are clear of the island.

This is a useful check because it's quick and simple. To make it even more foolproof, I like to label the line with the magnetic as well as the true bearing, so it can be instantly compared with the compass reading. It can also be helpful to have the figures available for ready reference at the helm.

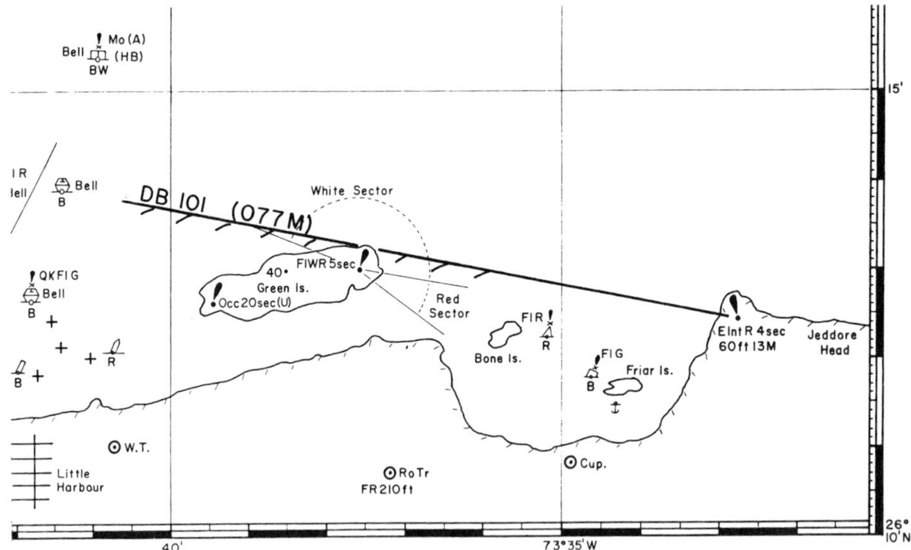

Figure 9-17 If you're bearing to the Jeddore Head light is greater than 077° magnetic, you will safely clear Green Island.

Problem 9-4

Time	HEADING Compass	Magnetic	True	Speed	Distance	Remarks
1000	253			5.2		Dr 26° 17.5 N 73° 32'.9W No current, no deviation Wolf I. south light 350 M
1030	253			5.2		Buoy (HA) 310 M
1100	253			5.2		Find the running fix

Problem 9-5

Time	HEADING Compass	Magnetic	True	Speed	Distance	Remarks
1400	056			7.0		Dr 26°15'.5 N 73°38'.0W Green I east light 136M
1430	056			7.0		
1447	056			7.0		Jeddore Hd. light 173M Find the running fix.

Problem 9-6

Time	HEADING Compass	Magnetic	True	Speed	Distance	Remarks
0800	281			4.4		Dr. 26°15'N 73°35'W Deviation per table 9-1 Jeddore Hd light 130M
0830	281			4.4		
0900	167			4.0		
0915	238			6.0		
0930	238			6.0		
1000	238			6.0		Brig buoy 176 M Find the running fix

Problem 9-7

Time	HEADING Compass	Magnetic	True	Speed	Distance	Remarks
1400	056			7.0		Dr 26°15'N, 73°40'W Green I. east light 117M
1428	056			7.0		Same light 193M Find the running fix

Problem 9-8

Time	HEADING Compass	Magnetic	True	Speed	True Course	Distance	Remarks
1000	285			3.6			Dr 26°15'N, 73°30'W Deviation per table 9-1 Set 200, Dr 1.2 Jeddore Hd. light 179M
1030	285			3.6			Set 200, Dr 1.2
1100	242			3.0			Set 200 Dr 1.2
1130	242			3.0			Set 200, Dr 1.2 Jeddore Hd light 098M Find the running fix

Solutions are in the Appendix.

10: The Sextant as Rangefinder

Then on along the lovely mountainous coast we plodded our slow way, our only excitements being those incidental to pilotage, for none of the many off-lying dangers are marked, except perhaps by breakers, and the only way of fixing one's position is by bearings or angles of distant mountain peaks . . .

***Eric Hiscock,** Atlantic Cruise in Wanderer III*

I'll have to confess that I've been saving the best for last. The methods in this chapter—some old, some new—are among the best available to the navigator. A good method must be fast, accurate, and available. By available, I mean that the method has to work when you need to use it, and not just when the circumstances happen to suit the method.

Any method of position finding used in piloting depends on measuring angles.* Angles measured by compass are called bearings (the previous chapter showed a number of ways of using bearings). Perhaps their main virtue is that almost every boat has at least one compass on board. But, remember that all bearings are limited by the accuracy of the compass. The compass itself is usually accurate within a few degrees; add to that the effects of reading uncertainty, deviation, and variation, and you have possible errors ranging from several degrees to many degrees.

A better angle-measuring machine than a sextant has yet to be invented. Light, portable, simple to use, and *accurate*, the sextant opens the door to several extremely valuable methods. Some of them have been known for a long time, but haven't achieved the popularity they deserve,

* Certain electronic systems such as Decca and Loran excepted.

because of the high price of brass sextants. Now that plastic sextants cost as little as $15, these methods are coming into their own.

Another factor has been the scarcity of tables. Bowditch (**HO9,** *The American Practical Navigator)* has one table which covers only a limited range, and requires several manual calculations. This chapter gives an expanded table, which needs no calculation and covers a wide range.

This chapter also presents a new method I've developed for finding distance with a sextant. It hasn't been published before, probably because *generating* the table is a reiterative process, and requires a large computer to do the enormous number of calculations. On the other hand, *using* the table is simplicity itself, and you'll find this method very valuable.

CHOOSING THE SEXTANT

At $15, the Davis Mark III, shown in Figure 10-1, is the cheapest sextant available. The accuracy is adequate, but it has a habit of changing its setting while you're reading it, and most people seem to prefer a better model. Figures 10-2 and 10-3 show Davis (American) and Ebbco (English) sextants that sell for about $65 and are very similar. They are widely available, and either would be an excellent choice.

I regretfully have to advise that you should not use the "Precision Small Craft Sextant," made by Francis Barker and Son in England. I say regretfully, because its miniature size would be very convenient, and their literature advertises its accuracy at 1 minute of arc, which is typical of many sextants. However, I've tested three of these sextants by

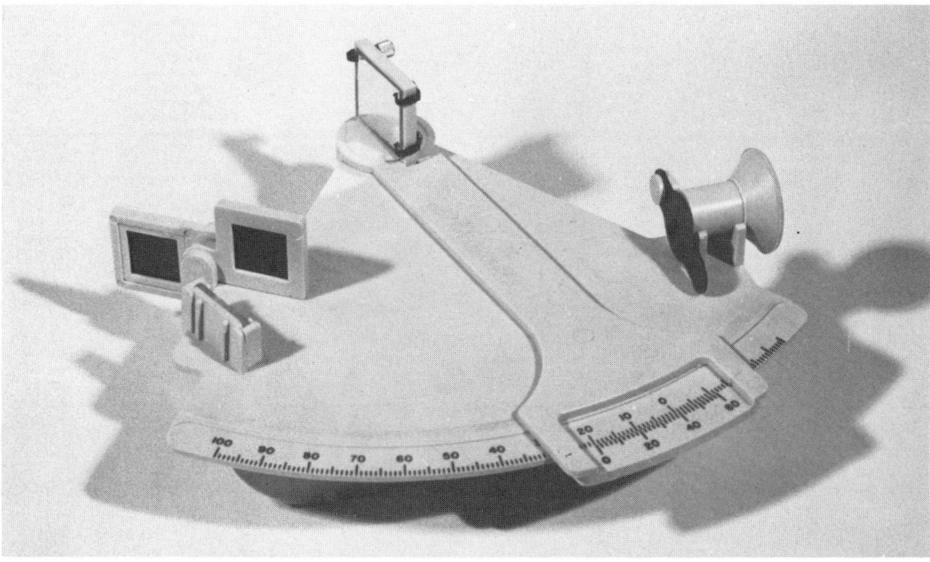

Figure 10-1 The Davis Mark III, an inexpensive sextant.

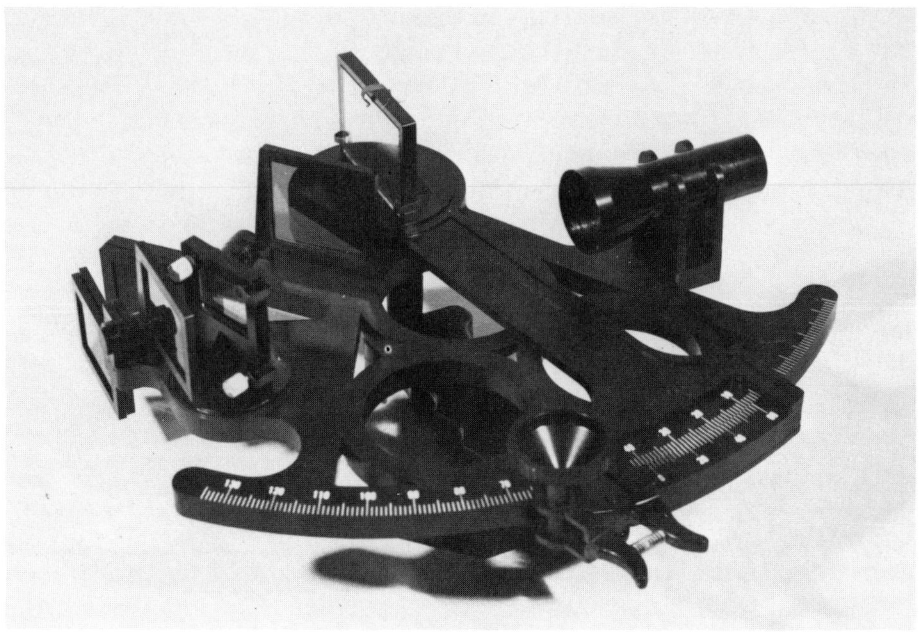

Figure 10-2 Davis Mark 12 Sextant.

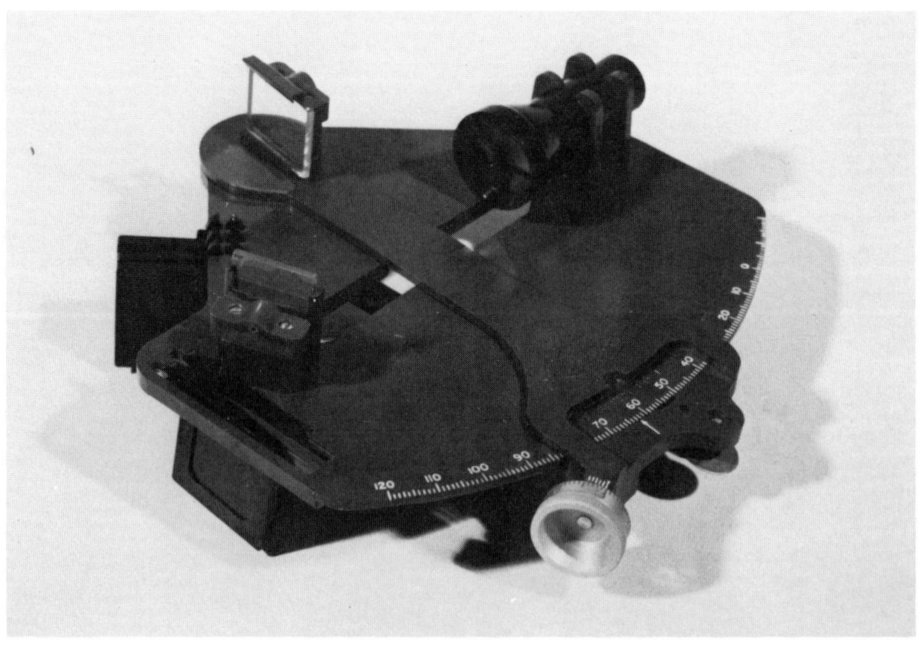

Figure 10-3 Ebbco sextant.

several independent methods, and all of them had errors far in excess of the advertised value. In one case the error was more than 1 *degree*. Admittedly, achieving 1 minute accuracy in a sextant only 3 inches in diameter would be extremely difficult.

Of course, any of the high grade brass sextants will serve admirably, and you may already have one for celestial navigation. I'm very fond of a compact model made by Toizaki, shown in Figure 10-4. Whatever sextant you use, make sure it's in good adjustment. The procedure for checking and/or adjusting sextants is easy, and is given in the Appendix.

Horizontal Angle

By turning the sextant on its side, you can measure the angle between two objects in a horizontal direction, and obtain a circle of position. This isn't a range *per se*, but it's a useful method, since any two charted objects can be used.

Suppose the horizontal angle between the Jeddore Head light and the radio tower is measured as 50 degrees. To plot the circle of position, first draw a baseline between the two points on the chart. Then subtract the measured horizontal angle from 90 degrees, obtaining 40 degrees. From each point, draw a line at an angle of 40 degrees from the baseline. The intersection of these lines is the center of the circle of position. Draw the appropriate part of the circle, with the ends at the two charted points, as in Figure 10-5. You are somewhere along the circle. Be careful! You are not at the intersection of the lines used to find the center, so it's a good idea to erase them.

Figure 10-4 A compact brass sextant by Toizaki.

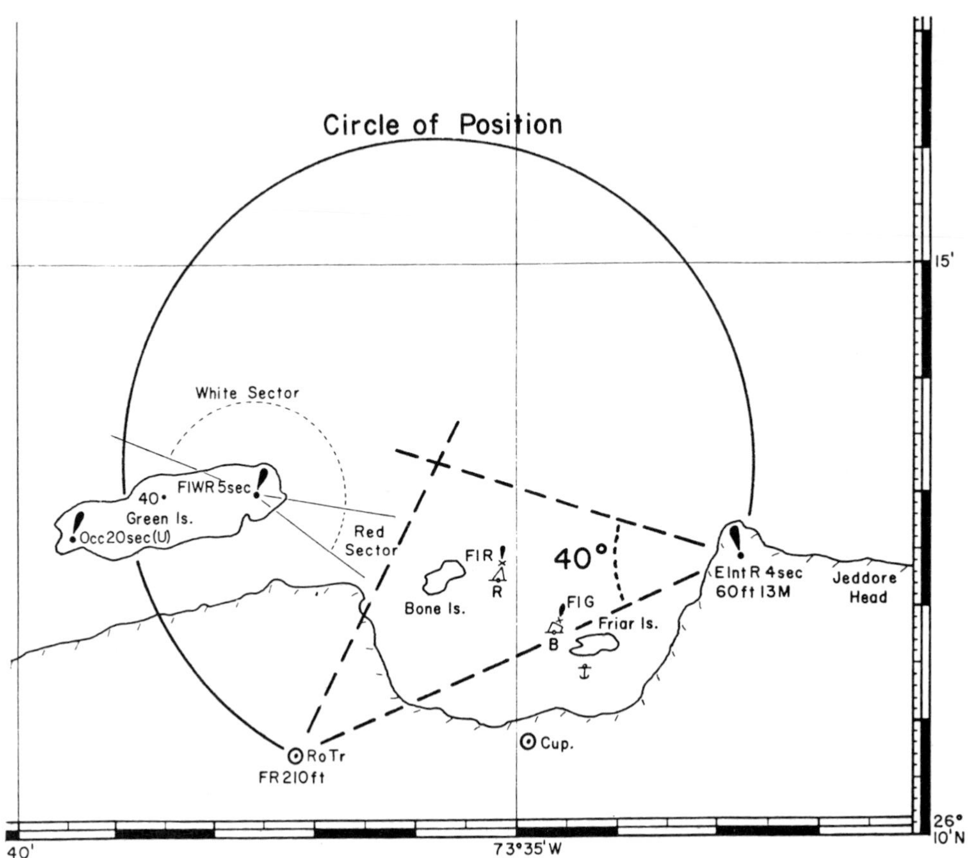

Figure 10-5 An accurate circle of position can be determined by measuring the horizontal angle with a sextant.

It's fun to prove that the circle is correct. Pick a point—any point—along the circle. Pretend it's your location, and draw lines to both charted points. The angle between the lines will be 50 degrees. Try it!

Now you'd like to know where you are along the line. A good method is to plot two circles. Their intersection gives the position. Of course two circles can have two intersections, but usually one can be eliminated by common sense. Suppose you measure the horizontal angle between Wolf Island south light and Green Island east light at 0750, obtaining 66 degrees. At the same time, the horizontal angle between the Jeddore Head light and the Green Island east light is 53 degrees. Plot both circles as shown in Figure 10-6. The 0750 position fix at the intersection is shown.

The beauty of this method is its *accuracy*. Just about any sextant will measure the angle with 1 or 2 minute accuracy. If you do the plotting work with reasonable care, the position fix in this example will be accurate within 1/10 mile. By contrast, if the position was found by bearings, one bearing could quite easily be 5 degrees off, and the position would be wrong by about half a mile.

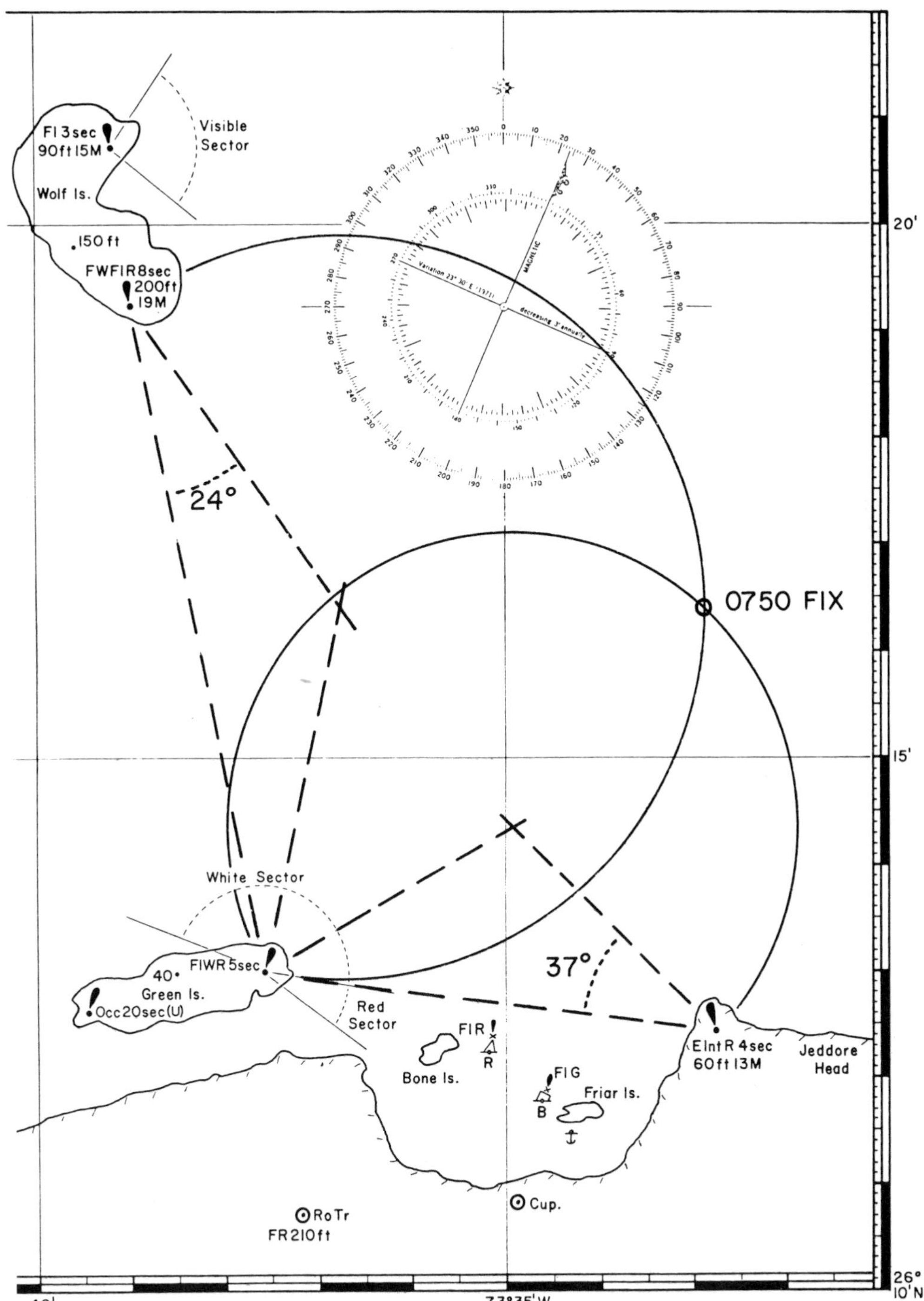

Figure 10-6 Fixing the position by two circles of position obtained from horizontal angles.

Very possibly, you won't have three objects in view. Then, one solution is to plot one circle, and a bearing on one of the objects. This isn't as good as the two circle method, but it's better than two bearings.

If you measure a horizontal angle of more than 90 degrees, the plotting work is almost the same. Let's say your DR position is 26° 15′ N, 73° 35′ W, and you measure the horizontal angle between the Wolf Island south light and the Green Island east light as 105 degrees. Subtracting this from 90 degrees gives −15 degrees. Then measure from the baseline 15 degrees *away* from the DR position to find the center of the circle. The left hand portion of the circle is not drawn in. You know you are not on that portion because, a) it's miles from your DR position, and b) the horizontal angle from any point on the left hand portion is not 105° degrees (see Figure 10-7).

Another application of the horizontal angle comes about when you're more interested in knowing where you're *not* located than where you *are* located, as often occurs in avoiding hazards. Suppose you're cruising in a generally westward direction from the inner fairway buoy HB, and you want to keep at least half a mile away from the Brig Rocks. The chimney with the fixed red light and the Cape Entry light will make useful markers. Using them as a baseline, draw a circle of position which gives the desired clearance, as shown in Figure 10-8. From any point on the circle, draw lines to both lights, and measure the angle between the lines. In this case it is 70 degrees. Then, as you sail along, check the horizontal angle periodically. So long as it's less than 70 degrees, you are outside the circle. If it becomes more than 70 degrees, look out.

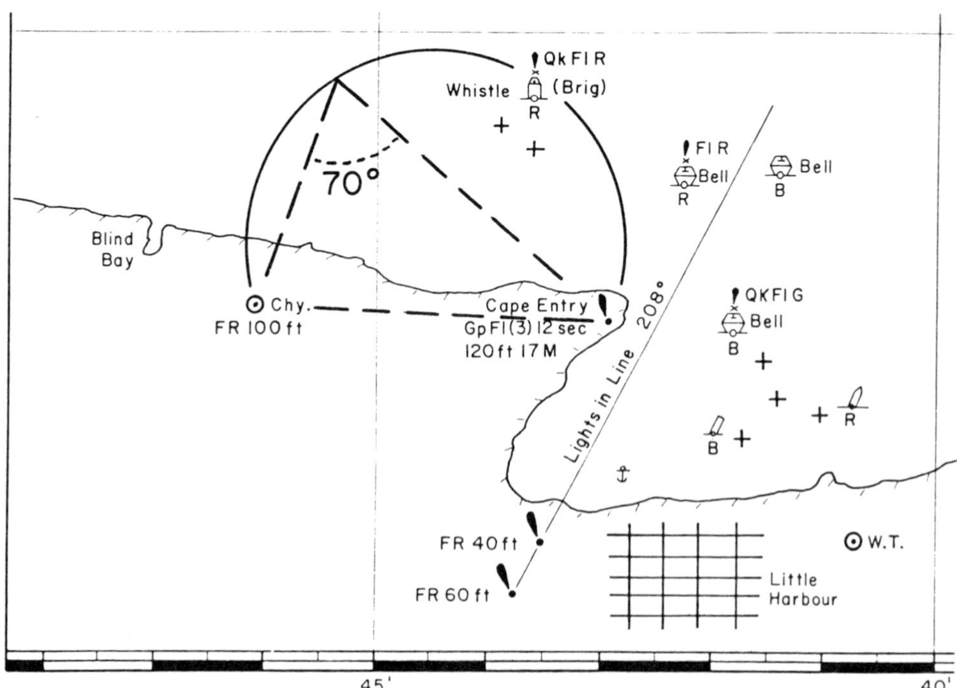

Figure 10-8 Using the horizontal angle as a check on clearing a hazard.

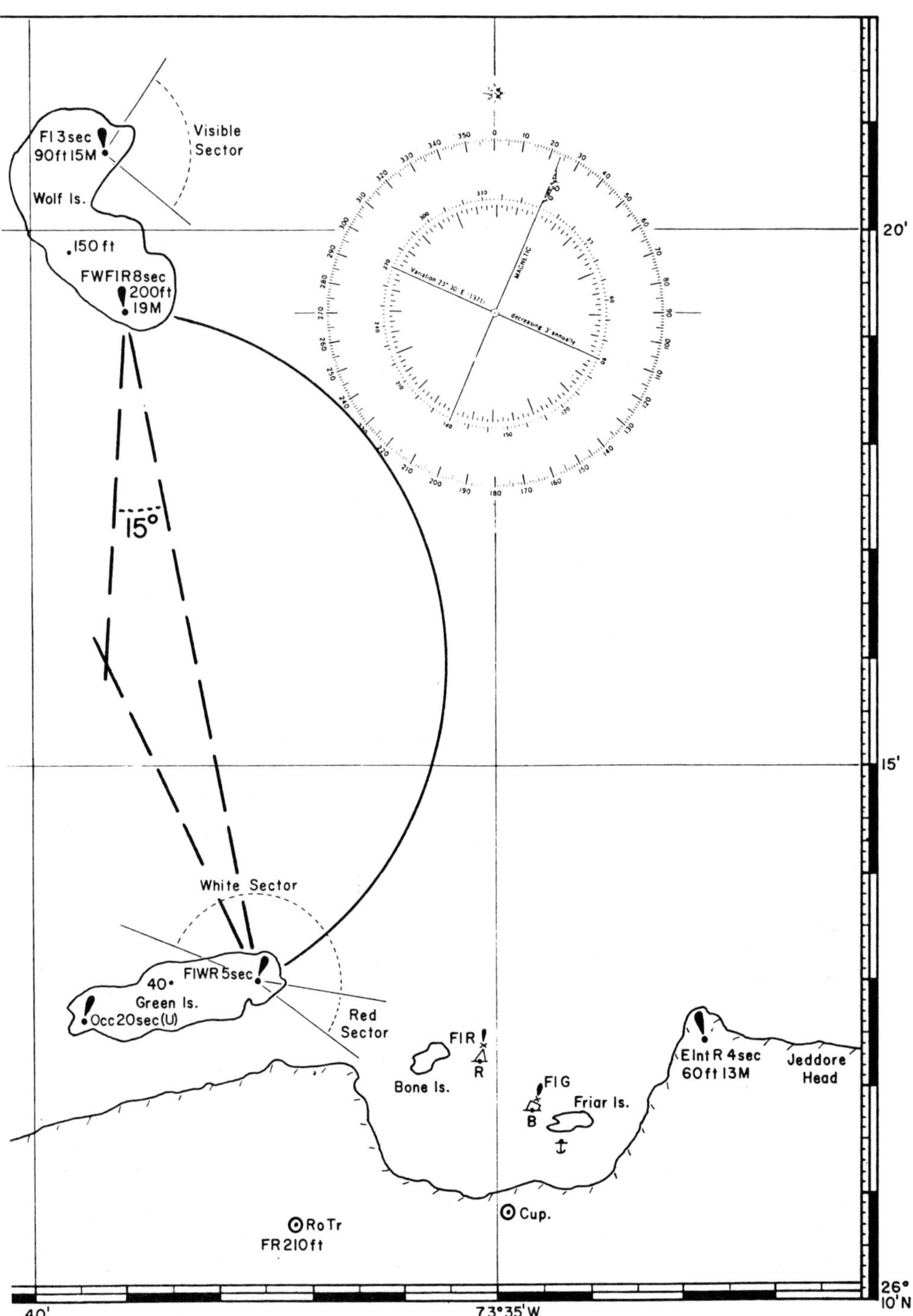

Figure 10-7 The circle of position for a horizontal angle of 105 degrees.

FINDING DISTANCE WITH THE SEXTANT

A given object looks smaller as you move away from it. If you know the size of the object, and measure its apparent angular height with a sextant, the distance can be found. This is an extremely useful concept, because charts show the height of many objects such as hills, lights, radio towers, bridges, and so on. With this information, and an inexpensive sextant, the navigator has an accurate rangefinder at his disposal—a pretty potent tool!

If the object is closer than your horizon, the distance can be found by the simple formula $D = .565 \times H/M$, where D is the distance in nautical miles, H is the height of the object in feet, and M is the sextant angle in minutes. For example, if you measure the sextant angle of a light as 12′, and the charted height is 110 feet, the distance is 5.2 nautical miles. However, the horizon is probably closer than you think. If your height of eye is 4 feet, the horizon distance is only 2.3 miles. If the object is farther away than that, part of it is lost below the horizon. The calculation has to allow for this effect of the earth's curvature, as well as for dip and refraction, and it gets a bit hairy. A prepared table is much simpler to use.

Table 10-1—Distance Off by Vertical Angle—gives the distance, according to the angle measured on the sextant and the height of the object above sea level. Distances are in nautical miles, sextant angles are in degrees and minutes, and heights are in feet. Corrections for curvature, dip, and refraction are included in the table, so the user only allows for the IC of his sextant, if any. The table works for any distance, either closer or farther than the horizon. If it's farther, measure the angle above the horizon. If it's closer, measure above sea level in the vicinity of the object, which will appear slightly below the horizon (see Figure 10-9).

As an example, suppose you measure the vertical angle of the Jeddore Head light, at 1945, as 9 minutes. The height of the light is 60 feet, and the table gives a distance of 3.8 miles. At the same time, the high point (40 feet) of Green Island measures 4 minutes, and the table gives a distance of 5.1 miles. You then have a 1945 position fix, as shown in Figure 10-10.

A few words of caution. First, the charted height of a light is the height of the lantern itself, not the structure. Second, heights are computed in reference to mean high water. At lower stages of tide, the actual height and the observed angle will be greater, giving a smaller distance. This is usually a safety factor, but should be remembered if you're passing on the inside of a hazard. Finally, the table is based on a 6 foot height of

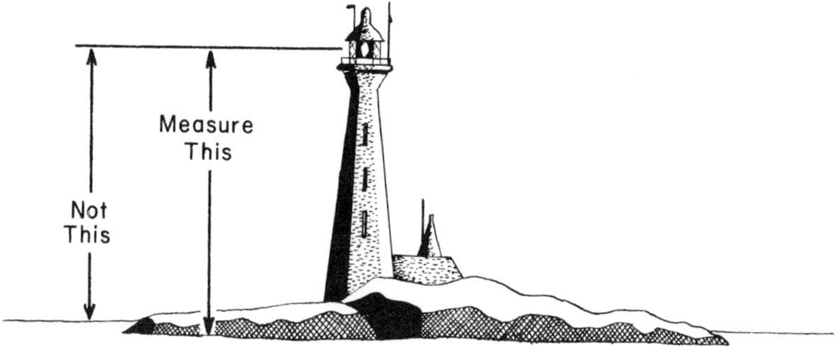

Figure 10-9 Measuring the vertical angle.

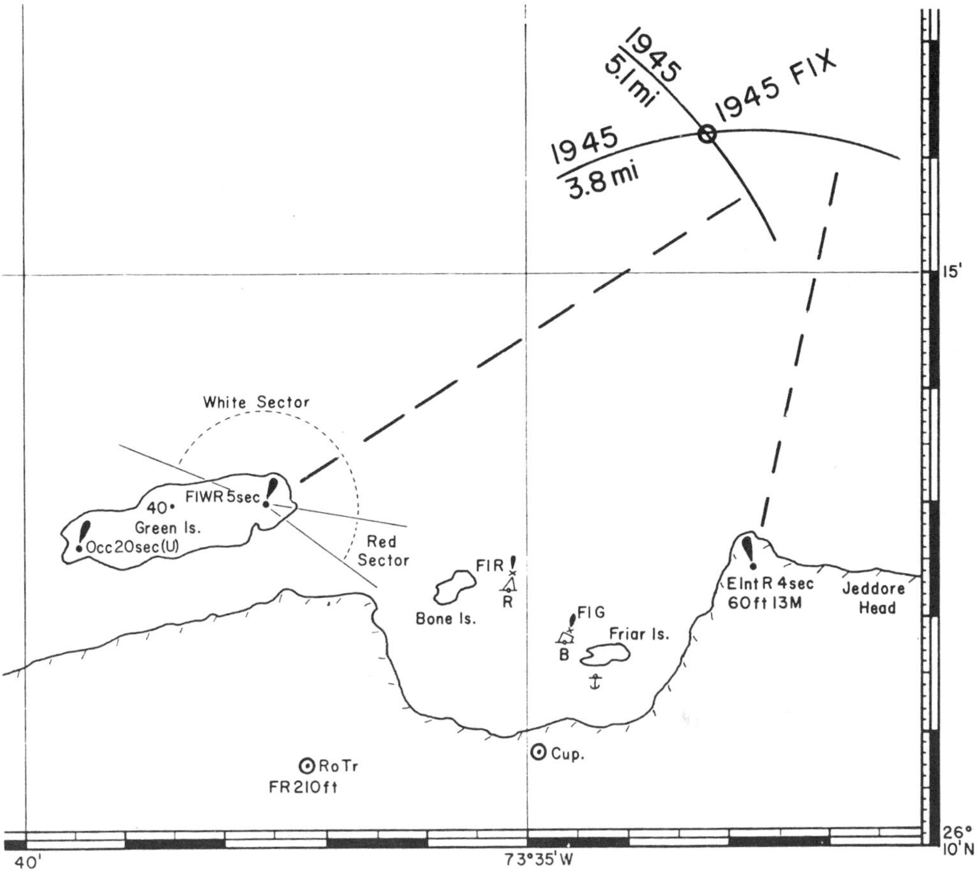

Figure 10-10 An accurate position fix is obtained from distances determined by vertical angles.

eye, which is typical of many boats. I have computed a complete set of tables for all heights of eye, which I hope to publish in the near future. In the meantime, an individual table for any given height of eye, from 4 feet to 60 feet, can be obtained by writing the publisher of this book.

Suppose there's only one object in view—what then? We've seen, in Chapter 9, how to get a running fix. But, it takes time, and the accuracy depends on how well you know your true course and speed made good. Here's a method that uses the one object to give an accurate position fix. It's such a useful method, that the Liar's Club president couldn't exagerate it. An ordinary member wouldn't even try. I use it in preference to anything else whenever possible, which is most of the time.

Measure the vertical angle to find the distance, and take a bearing. Draw the position circle for the distance, and cross it with the bearing LOP to find the position. That's it! The method is simple, accurate, fast, and—I can't resist repeating—you need only one object.

As an example, suppose you measure the vertical angle of the Cape Entry light as 18′, and the bearing as 165° magnetic at 2015. Then the distance is 3.8 miles, and the true bearing is 189°. Figure 10-11 shows the resulting position fix.

A tip for racers. Want to keep tabs on another boat? If you know their masthead height, either from the deck or from the waterline, you can find the distance by using the vertical angle table. Just tip the sextant to match the angle of heel of the other boat.

Distance by Base Angle

If an object like a boat, buoy, or island is between you and the horizon, the distance to the object can be found by measuring the angle from the horizon down to the waterline of the object, as shown in Figure 10-12. The distance calculation is very tedious, even with a programmable calculator, so I've worked out a set of tables with the help of a computer. They're given in this chapter as Table 10-2. This method hasn't been published before, so far as I know. One thing for sure; the angle involved has no standard name, so I had to invent one. "Dip" belongs to something else, "depression angle" sounds too pompous, and "horizon angle" would be too easily confused with horizontal angle. I finally settled on "base angle," but would be glad to accept suggestions for a better name.

To use the table, you need the measured base angle and your height of eye. Distances are given in nautical miles, or, if less than 1.0 mile, in feet. For example, suppose your height of eye is 10 feet. At 1430 you measure the base angle for the Brig Rocky buoy as 1′, and for the outer black bell as 3′. Table 10-2 gives distances of 1.7 and 1.0 miles, respectively. The position fix obtained is shown in Figure 10-13.

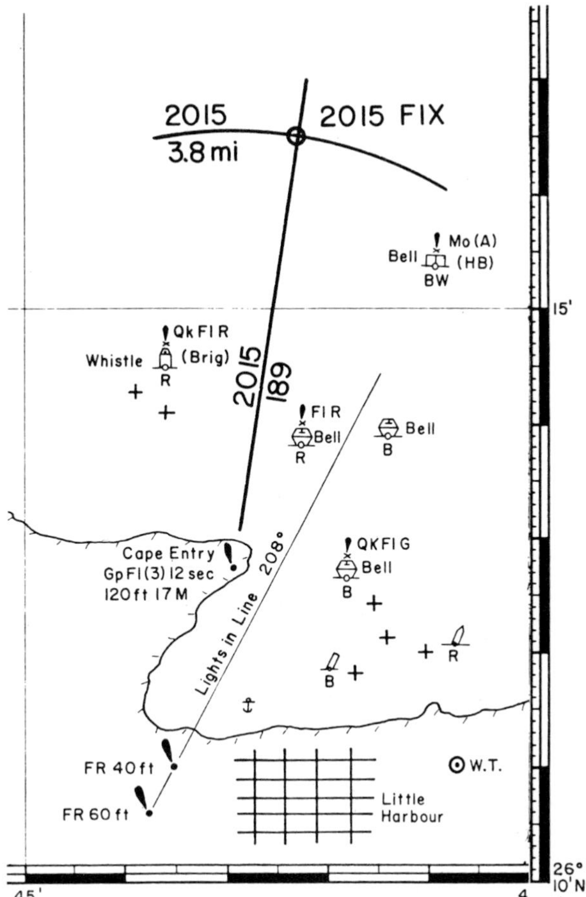

Figure 10-11 Fixing the position by a vertical angle and bearing on one object.

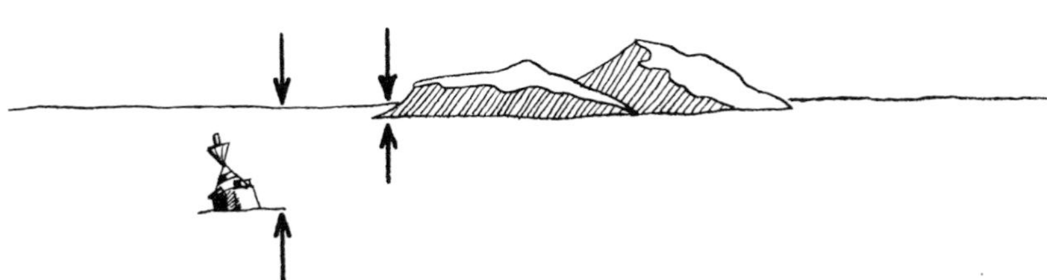

Figure 10-12 Distance can be found by measuring the angle from the horizon to the waterline of a nearby object. Two such angles are shown here.

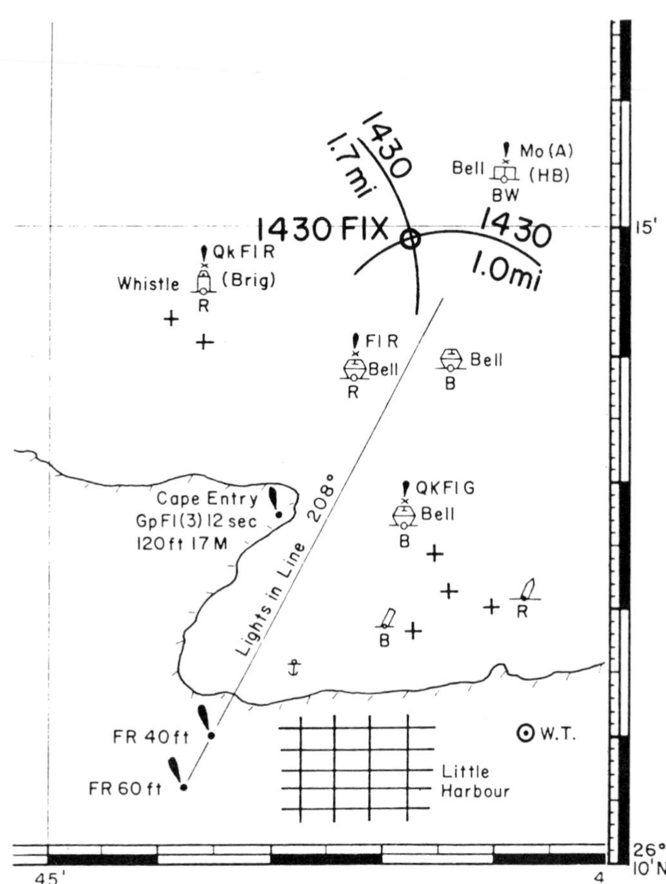

Figure 10-13 A position fix can be obtained from distances found by measuring base angles.

Table 10-1 Distance by Vertical Angle

Measure the angle from the horizon or waterline to the top of the object. Given the height of the object in feet or meters, the table gives the distance to the object in nautical miles. Corrections are included for dip (assuming a 6 foot (1.8 meter) height of eye), curvature of the earth, and refraction. Only the index correction (if any) for the individual sextant must be applied to the reading.

Height of eye—6 feet *(1.8 meters)* Horizon distance—2.8 nautical miles

Height of Object—feet *(meters)*

Vertical Angle	*1.5* 5	*3.0* 10	*4.6* 15	*6.1* 20	*7.6* 25	*9.1* 30	*11* 35	*12* 40	*14* 45	*15* 50
0	5.4	6.4	7.3	8.0	8.6	9.1	9.6	10.1	10.6	11.0
1	2.8	4.5	5.5	6.3	6.9	7.5	8.1	8.6	9.0	9.5
2	1.4	2.8	3.9	4.8	5.5	6.1	6.7	7.2	7.7	8.1
3	.9	1.9	2.8	3.7	4.4	5.0	5.5	6.0	6.5	7.0
4	.7	1.4	2.1	2.8	3.5	4.1	4.6	5.1	5.6	6.0
5	.6	1.1	1.7	2.3	2.8	3.4	3.9	4.4	4.8	5.3
6	.5	.9	1.4	1.9	2.4	2.8	3.3	3.7	4.2	4.6
7	.4	.8	1.2	1.6	2.0	2.4	2.8	3.2	3.6	4.0
8	.4	.7	1.1	1.4	1.8	2.1	2.5	2.8	3.2	3.5
9	.3	.6	.9	1.3	1.6	1.9	2.2	2.5	2.8	3.1
10	.3	.6	.8	1.1	1.4	1.7	2.0	2.3	2.5	2.8
11	.3	.5	.8	1.0	1.3	1.5	1.8	2.1	2.3	2.6
12	.2	.5	.7	.9	1.2	1.4	1.7	1.9	2.1	2.4
14	.2	.4	.6	.8	1.0	1.2	1.4	1.6	1.8	2.0
16	.2	.4	.5	.7	.9	1.1	1.2	1.4	1.6	1.8
18	.2	.3	.5	.6	.8	.9	1.1	1.3	1.4	1.6
20	.1	.3	.4	.6	.7	.8	1.0	1.1	1.3	1.4
22	.1	.3	.4	.5	.6	.8	.9	1.0	1.2	1.3
24	.1	.2	.4	.5	.6	.7	.8	.9	1.1	1.2
26	.1	.2	.3	.4	.5	.7	.8	.9	1.0	1.1
28	.1	.2	.3	.4	.5	.6	.7	.8	.9	1.0
30	.1	.2	.3	.4	.5	.6	.7	.8	.8	.9
32	.1	.2	.3	.4	.4	.5	.6	.7	.8	.9
34	.1	.2	.2	.3	.4	.5	.6	.7	.7	.8
36	.1	.2	.2	.3	.4	.5	.6	.6	.7	.8
38	.1	.1	.2	.3	.4	.4	.5	.6	.7	.7
40	.1	.1	.2	.3	.4	.4	.5	.6	.6	.7
45	.1	.1	.2	.3	.3	.4	.4	.5	.6	.6
50	.1	.1	.2	.2	.3	.3	.4	.5	.5	.6
55	.1	.1	.2	.2	.3	.3	.4	.4	.5	.5
1-00	.0	.1	.1	.2	.2	.3	.3	.4	.4	.5
1-05	.0	.1	.1	.2	.2	.3	.3	.3	.4	.4
1-10	.0	.1	.1	.2	.2	.2	.3	.3	.4	.4
1-15	.0	.1	.1	.2	.2	.2	.3	.3	.3	.4
1-20	.0	.1	.1	.1	.2	.2	.2	.3	.3	.4
1-30	.0	.1	.1	.1	.2	.2	.2	.3	.3	.3
1-40	.0	.1	.1	.1	.1	.2	.2	.2	.3	.3
1-50	.0	.1	.1	.1	.1	.2	.2	.2	.2	.3
2-00	.0	.0	.1	.1	.1	.1	.2	.2	.2	.2
2.10	.0	.0	.1	.1	.1	.1	.2	.2	.2	.2
2-20	.0	.0	.1	.1	.1	.1	.1	.2	.2	.2
2-30	.0	.0	.1	.1	.1	.1	.1	.2	.2	.2
2-40	.0	.0	.1	.1	.1	.1	.1	.1	.2	.2
3-00	.0	.0	.0	.1	.1	.1	.1	.1	.1	.2
3-20	.0	.0	.0	.1	.1	.1	.1	.1	.1	.1
3-40	.0	.0	.0	.1	.1	.1	.1	.1	.1	.1
4-00	.0	.0	.0	.0	.1	.1	.1	.1	.1	.1
4-20	.0	.0	.0	.0	.1	.1	.1	.1	.1	.1
4-40	.0	.0	.0	.0	.1	.1	.1	.1	.1	.1
5-00	.0	.0	.0	.0	.0	.1	.1	.1	.1	.1

Height of Object—feet *(meters)*

Vertical Angle	*17* 55	*18* 60	*20* 65	*21* 70	*23* 75	*24* 80	*26* 85	*27* 90	*29* 95	*30* 100
0	11.4	11.8	12.1	12.5	12.8	13.1	13.5	13.8	14.1	14.4
1	9.9	10.3	10.7	11.0	11.4	11.7	12.0	12.4	12.7	13.0
2	8.6	9.0	9.3	9.7	10.1	10.4	10.7	11.1	11.4	11.7
3	7.4	7.8	8.2	8.5	8.9	9.2	9.6	9.9	10.2	10.5
4	6.4	6.8	7.2	7.5	7.9	8.2	8.5	8.9	9.2	9.5
5	5.7	6.0	6.4	6.8	7.1	7.4	7.8	8.1	8.4	8.7
6	4.9	5.3	5.7	6.0	6.3	6.6	6.9	7.2	7.5	7.8
7	4.3	4.7	5.0	5.3	5.7	6.0	6.3	6.5	6.8	7.1
8	3.9	4.2	4.5	4.8	5.1	5.4	5.7	5.9	6.2	6.5
9	3.5	3.8	4.0	4.3	4.6	4.9	5.1	5.4	5.7	5.9
10	3.1	3.4	3.7	3.9	4.2	4.4	4.7	4.9	5.2	5.4
11	2.8	3.1	3.3	3.6	3.8	4.1	4.3	4.5	4.8	5.0
12	2.6	2.8	3.1	3.3	3.5	3.8	4.0	4.2	4.4	4.6
14	2.2	2.4	2.6	2.8	3.0	3.2	3.4	3.6	3.8	4.0
16	1.9	2.1	2.3	2.5	2.7	2.8	3.0	3.2	3.4	3.5
18	1.7	1.9	2.0	2.2	2.4	2.5	2.7	2.8	3.0	3.1
20	1.6	1.7	1.8	2.0	2.1	2.3	2.4	2.5	2.7	2.8
22	1.4	1.5	1.7	1.8	1.9	2.1	2.2	2.3	2.4	2.6
24	1.3	1.4	1.5	1.7	1.8	1.9	2.0	2.1	2.2	2.4
26	1.2	1.3	1.4	1.5	1.6	1.7	1.8	2.0	2.1	2.2
28	1.1	1.2	1.3	1.4	1.5	1.6	1.7	1.8	1.9	2.0
30	1.0	1.1	1.2	1.3	1.4	1.5	1.6	1.7	1.8	1.9
32	1.0	1.1	1.1	1.2	1.3	1.4	1.5	1.6	1.7	1.8
34	.9	1.0	1.1	1.2	1.2	1.3	1.4	1.5	1.6	1.7
36	.9	.9	1.0	1.1	1.2	1.3	1.3	1.4	1.5	1.6
38	.8	.9	1.0	1.0	1.1	1.2	1.3	1.3	1.4	1.5
40	.8	.8	.9	1.0	1.1	1.1	1.2	1.3	1.3	1.4
45	.7	.8	.8	.9	.9	1.0	1.1	1.1	1.2	1.3
50	.6	.7	.7	.8	.8	.9	1.0	1.0	1.1	1.1
55	.6	.6	.7	.7	.8	.8	.9	.9	1.0	1.0
1-00	.5	.6	.6	.7	.7	.8	.8	.8	.9	.9
1-05	.5	.5	.6	.6	.7	.7	.7	.8	.8	.9
1-10	.4	.5	.5	.6	.6	.6	.7	.7	.8	.8
1-15	.4	.5	.5	.5	.6	.6	.6	.7	.7	.8
1-20	.4	.4	.5	.5	.5	.6	.6	.6	.7	.7
1-30	.3	.4	.4	.4	.5	.5	.5	.6	.6	.6
1-40	.3	.3	.4	.4	.4	.5	.5	.5	.5	.6
1-50	.3	.3	.3	.4	.4	.4	.4	.5	.5	.5
2-00	.3	.3	.3	.3	.4	.4	.4	.4	.4	.5
2-10	.2	.3	.3	.3	.3	.3	.4	.4	.4	.4
2-20	.2	.2	.3	.3	.3	.3	.3	.4	.4	.4
2-30	.2	.2	.2	.3	.3	.3	.3	.3	.4	.4
2-40	.2	.2	.2	.2	.3	.3	.3	.3	.3	.4
3-00	.2	.2	.2	.2	.2	.3	.3	.3	.3	.3
3-20	.2	.2	.2	.2	.2	.2	.2	.3	.3	.3
3-40	.1	.2	.2	.2	.2	.2	.2	.2	.2	.3
4-00	.1	.1	.2	.2	.2	.2	.2	.2	.2	.2
4-20	.1	.1	.1	.2	.2	.2	.2	.2	.2	.2
4-40	.1	.1	.1	.1	.2	.2	.2	.2	.2	.2
5-00	.1	.1	.1	.1	.1	.2	.2	.2	.2	.2

Height of Object—feet *(meters)*

Vertical Angle	*30* 110	*36* 120	*40* 130	*43* 140	*46* 150	*49* 160	*52* 170	*55* 180	*58* 190	*61* 200
0	14.9	15.5	16.0	16.5	17.0	17.4	17.9	18.3	18.7	19.2
1	13.5	14.1	14.6	15.1	15.6	16.1	16.5	17.0	17.4	17.8
2	12.2	12.8	13.3	13.8	14.3	14.8	15.3	15.7	16.1	16.6
3	11.1	11.6	12.2	12.7	13.2	13.6	14.1	14.5	15.0	15.4
4	10.0	10.6	11.1	11.6	12.1	12.6	13.0	13.5	13.9	14.3
5	9.2	9.8	10.3	10.8	11.3	11.7	12.2	12.6	13.0	13.5
6	8.4	8.9	9.4	9.9	10.4	10.8	11.3	11.7	12.1	12.5
7	7.6	8.1	8.6	9.1	9.6	10.0	10.4	10.9	11.3	11.7
8	7.0	7.5	7.9	8.4	8.8	9.3	9.7	10.1	10.5	10.9
9	6.4	6.9	7.3	7.8	8.2	8.6	9.0	9.4	9.8	10.2
10	5.9	6.3	6.8	7.2	7.6	8.0	8.4	8.8	9.2	9.5
11	5.4	5.9	6.3	6.7	7.1	7.5	7.9	8.2	8.6	8.9
12	5.0	5.5	5.9	6.2	6.6	7.0	7.4	7.7	8.1	8.4
14	4.4	4.8	5.1	5.5	5.8	6.2	6.5	6.8	7.2	7.5
16	3.9	4.2	4.5	4.9	5.2	5.5	5.8	6.1	6.4	6.7
18	3.5	3.8	4.1	4.4	4.7	4.9	5.2	5.5	5.8	6.1
20	3.1	3.4	3.7	3.9	4.2	4.5	4.7	5.0	5.3	5.5
22	2.8	3.1	3.3	3.6	3.8	4.1	4.3	4.6	4.8	5.1
24	2.6	2.8	3.1	3.3	3.5	3.8	4.0	4.2	4.4	4.7
26	2.4	2.6	2.8	3.0	3.3	3.5	3.7	3.9	4.1	4.3
28	2.2	2.4	2.6	2.8	3.0	3.2	3.4	3.6	3.8	4.0
30	2.1	2.3	2.5	2.6	2.8	3.0	3.2	3.4	3.6	3.8
32	1.9	2.1	2.3	2.5	2.7	2.8	3.0	3.2	3.4	3.5
34	1.8	2.0	2.2	2.3	2.5	2.7	2.8	3.0	3.2	3.3
36	1.7	1.9	2.0	2.2	2.4	2.5	2.7	2.8	3.0	3.1
38	1.6	1.8	1.9	2.1	2.2	2.4	2.5	2.7	2.8	3.0
40	1.6	1.7	1.8	2.0	2.1	2.3	2.4	2.5	2.7	2.8
45	1.4	1.5	1.6	1.8	1.9	2.0	2.1	2.3	2.4	2.5
50	1.2	1.4	1.5	1.6	1.7	1.8	1.9	2.0	2.1	2.3
55	1.1	1.2	1.3	1.4	1.5	1.6	1.7	1.9	2.0	2.1
1-00	1.0	1.1	1.2	1.3	1.4	1.5	1.6	1.7	1.8	1.9
1-05	1.0	1.0	1.1	1.2	1.3	1.4	1.5	1.6	1.7	1.7
1-10	.9	1.0	1.1	1.1	1.2	1.3	1.4	1.5	1.5	1.6
1-15	.8	.9	1.0	1.1	1.1	1.2	1.3	1.4	1.4	1.5
1-20	.8	.8	.9	1.0	1.1	1.1	1.2	1.3	1.3	1.4
1-30	.7	.8	.8	.9	.9	1.0	1.1	1.1	1.2	1.3
1-40	.6	.7	.7	.8	.8	.9	1.0	1.0	1.1	1.1
1-50	.6	.6	.7	.7	.8	.8	.9	.9	1.0	1.0
2-00	.5	.6	.6	.7	.7	.8	.8	.8	.9	.9
2-10	.5	.5	.6	.6	.7	.7	.7	.8	.8	.9
2-20	.4	.5	.5	.6	.6	.6	.7	.7	.8	.8
2-30	.4	.5	.5	.5	.6	.6	.6	.7	.7	.8
2-40	.4	.4	.5	.5	.5	.6	.6	.6	.7	.7
3-00	.3	.4	.4	.4	.5	.5	.5	.6	.6	.6
3-20	.3	.3	.4	.4	.4	.5	.5	.5	.5	.6
3-40	.3	.3	.3	.4	.4	.4	.4	.5	.5	.5
4-00	.3	.3	.3	.3	.4	.4	.4	.4	.4	.5
4-20	.2	.3	.3	.3	.3	.3	.4	.4	.4	.4
4-40	.2	.2	.3	.3	.3	.3	.3	.4	.4	.4
5-00	.2	.2	.2	.3	.3	.3	.3	.3	.4	.4

Height of eye—6 feet *(1.8 meters)* | Horizon distance—2.8 nautical miles

Height of Object—feet *(meters)*

Angle	*37* 210	*67* 220	*70* 230	*73* 240	*76* 250	*79* 260	*82* 270	*85* 280	*88* 290	*91* 300
0	19.6	20.0	20.3	20.7	21.1	21.5	21.8	22.2	22.5	22.8
1	18.2	18.6	19.0	19.4	19.8	20.1	20.5	20.8	21.2	21.5
2	17.0	17.4	17.8	18.1	18.5	18.9	19.2	19.6	19.9	20.3
3	15.8	16.2	16.6	17.0	17.3	17.7	18.1	18.4	18.8	19.1
4	14.7	15.1	15.5	15.9	16.3	16.6	17.0	17.3	17.7	18.0
5	13.9	14.3	14.6	15.0	15.4	15.7	16.1	16.5	16.8	17.1
6	12.9	13.3	13.7	14.1	14.4	14.8	15.1	15.5	15.8	16.2
7	12.1	12.4	12.8	13.2	13.5	13.9	14.2	14.6	14.9	15.2
8	11.3	11.6	12.0	12.4	12.7	13.1	13.4	13.7	14.1	14.4
9	10.6	10.9	11.3	11.6	12.0	12.3	12.6	13.0	13.3	13.6
10	9.9	10.3	10.6	10.9	11.3	11.6	11.9	12.3	12.6	12.9
11	9.3	9.6	10.0	10.3	10.6	11.0	11.3	11.6	11.9	12.8
12	8.8	9.1	9.4	9.7	10.1	10.4	10.7	11.0	11.3	11.6
14	7.8	8.1	8.4	8.7	9.0	9.3	9.6	9.9	10.2	10.5
16	7.0	7.3	7.6	7.9	8.2	8.4	8.7	9.0	9.2	9.5
18	6.3	6.6	6.9	7.1	7.4	7.7	7.9	8.2	8.4	8.7
20	5.8	6.0	6.3	6.5	6.8	7.0	7.3	7.5	7.7	8.0
22	5.3	5.5	5.8	6.0	6.2	6.5	6.7	6.9	7.1	7.4
24	4.9	5.1	5.3	5.5	5.8	6.0	6.2	6.4	6.6	6.8
26	4.5	4.7	4.9	5.2	5.4	5.6	5.8	6.0	6.2	6.4
28	4.2	4.4	4.6	4.8	5.0	5.2	5.4	5.6	5.7	5.9
30	3.9	4.1	4.3	4.5	4.7	4.9	5.0	5.2	5.4	5.6
32	3.7	3.9	4.1	4.2	4.4	4.6	4.7	4.9	5.1	5.2
34	3.5	3.7	3.8	4.0	4.1	4.3	4.5	4.6	4.8	4.9
36	3.3	3.5	3.6	3.8	3.9	4.1	4.2	4.4	4.5	4.7
38	3.1	3.3	3.4	3.6	3.7	3.9	4.0	4.2	4.3	4.4
40	3.0	3.1	3.3	3.4	3.5	3.7	3.8	4.0	4.1	4.2
45	2.6	2.8	2.9	3.0	3.1	3.3	3.4	3.5	3.6	3.8
50	2.4	2.5	2.6	2.7	2.8	2.9	3.1	3.2	3.3	3.4
55	2.2	2.3	2.4	2.5	2.6	2.7	2.8	2.9	3.0	3.1
1-00	2.0	2.1	2.2	2.3	2.4	2.5	2.5	2.6	2.7	2.8
1-05	1.8	1.9	2.0	2.1	2.2	2.3	2.4	2.4	2.5	2.6
1-10	1.7	1.8	1.9	1.9	2.0	2.1	2.2	2.3	2.3	2.4
1-15	1.6	1.7	1.7	1.8	1.9	2.0	2.0	2.1	2.2	2.3
1-20	1.5	1.6	1.6	1.7	1.8	1.8	1.9	2.0	2.1	2.1
1-30	1.3	1.4	1.4	1.5	1.6	1.6	1.7	1.8	1.8	1.9
1-40	1.2	1.2	1.3	1.4	1.4	1.5	1.5	1.6	1.6	1.7
1-50	1.1	1.1	1.2	1.2	1.3	1.3	1.4	1.4	1.5	1.5
2-00	1.0	1.0	1.1	1.1	1.2	1.2	1.3	1.3	1.4	1.4
2-10	.9	1.0	1.0	1.0	1.1	1.1	1.2	1.2	1.3	1.3
2-20	.8	.9	.9	1.0	1.0	1.1	1.1	1.1	1.2	1.2
2-30	.8	.8	.9	.9	.9	1.0	1.0	1.1	1.1	1.1
2-40	.7	.8	.8	.8	.9	.9	1.0	1.0	1.0	1.1
3-00	.7	.7	.7.	.8	.8	.8	.8	.9	.9	.9
3-20	.6	.6	.7	.7	.7	.7	.8	.8	.8	.8
3-40	.5	.6	.6	.6	.6	.7	.7	.7	.7	.8
4-00	.5	.5	.5	.6	.6	.6	.6	.7	.7	.7
4-20	.5	.5	.5	.5	.5	.6	.6	.6	.6	.7
4-40	.4	.4	.5	.5	.5	.5	.5	.6	.6	.6
5-00	.4	.4	.4	.5	.5	.5	.5	.5	.5	.6

Height of eye—6 feet *(1.8 meters)* Horizon distance—2.8 nautical miles

Height of Object—feet *(meters)*

Vertical Angle	*97* 320	*103* 340	*110* 360	*116* 380	*122* 400	*128* 420	*134* 440	*140* 460	*146* 480	*152* 500
0	23.5	24.1	24.8	25.4	25.9	26.5	27.1	27.6	28.1	28.7
1	22.2	22.8	23.5	24.1	24.6	25.2	25.8	26.3	26.9	27.4
2	20.9	21.6	22.2	22.8	23.4	24.0	24.5	25.1	25.6	26.2
3	19.8	20.4	21.0	21.6	22.2	22.8	23.4	23.9	24.5	25.0
4	18.7	19.3	19.9	20.5	21.1	21.7	22.3	22.8	23.3	23.9
5	17.8	18.4	19.0	19.6	20.2	20.8	21.4	21.9	22.4	23.0
6	16.8	17.4	18.0	18.6	19.2	19.8	20.3	20.9	21.4	21.9
7	15.9	16.5	17.1	17.7	18.3	18.8	19.4	19.9	20.5	21.0
8	15.0	15.6	16.2	16.8	17.4	17.9	18.5	19.0	19.5	20.0
9	14.2	14.8	15.4	16.0	16.6	17.1	17.6	18.2	18.7	19.2
10	13.5	14.1	14.7	15.2	15.8	16.3	16.8	17.4	17.9	18.4
11	12.8	13.4	13.9	14.5	15.0	15.6	16.1	16.6	17.1	17.6
12	12.2	12.7	13.3	13.8	14.3	14.9	15.4	15.9	16.4	16.8
14	11.0	11.6	12.1	12.6	13.1	13.6	14.1	14.6	15.0	15.5
16	10.0	10.5	11.0	11.5	12.0	12.5	13.0	13.4	13.9	14.3
18	9.2	9.7	10.1	10.6	11.1	11.5	12.0	12.4	12.8	13.3
20	8.4	8.9	9.3	9.8	10.2	10.7	11.1	11.5	11.9	12.3
22	7.8	8.2	8.7	9.1	9.5	9.9	10.3	10.7	11.1	11.5
24	7.2	7.6	8.0	8.4	8.8	9.2	9.6	10.0	10.4	10.7
26	6.7	7.1	7.5	7.9	8.3	8.6	9.0	9.4	9.7	10.1
28	6.3	6.7	7.0	7.4	7.7	8.1	8.4	8.8	9.1	9.5
30	5.9	6.3	6.6	7.0	7.3	7.6	8.0	8.3	8.6	8.9
32	5.6	5.9	6.2	6.6	6.9	7.2	7.5	7.8	8.1	8.5
34	5.3	5.6	5.9	6.2	6.5	6.8	7.1	7.4	7.7	8.0
36	5.0	5.3	5.6	5.9	6.2	6.5	6.8	7.0	7.3	7.6
38	4.7	5.0	5.3	5.6	5.9	6.1	6.4	6.7	7.0	7.2
40	4.5	4.8	5.0	5.3	5.6	5.9	6.1	6.4	6.7	6.9
45	4.0	4.3	4.5	4.7	5.0	5.2	5.5	5.7	6.0	6.2
50	3.6	3.8	4.1	4.3	4.5	4.7	4.9	5.2	5.4	5.6
55	3.3	3.5	3.7	3.9	4.1	4.3	4.5	4.7	4.9	5.1
1-00	3.0	3.2	3.4	3.6	3.8	4.0	4.1	4.3	4.5	4.7
1-05	2.8	3.0	3.1	3.3	3.5	3.7	3.8	4.0	4.2	4.3
1-10	2.6	2.7	2.9	3.1	3.2	3.4	3.6	3.7	3.9	4.0
1-15	2.4	2.6	2.7	2.9	3.0	3.2	3.3	3.5	3.6	3.8
1-20	2.3	2.4	2.5	2.7	2.8	3.0	3.1	3.3	3.4	3.5
1-30	2.0	2.1	2.3	2.4	2.5	2.6	2.8	2.9	3.0	3.1
1-40	1.8	1.9	2.0	2.1	2.3	2.4	2.5	2.6	2.7	2.8
1-50	1.6	1.7	1.9	2.0	2.1	2.2	2.3	2.4	2.5	2.6
2-00	1.5	1.6	1.7	1.8	1.9	2.0	2.1	2.2	2.3	2.4
2-10	1.4	1.5	1.6	1.7	1.7	1.8	1.9	2.0	2.1	2.2
2-20	1.3	1.4	1.5	1.5	1.6	1.7	1.8	1.9	1.9	2.0
2-30	1.2	1.3	1.4	1.4	1.5	1.6	1.7	1.7	1.8	1.9
2-40	1.1	1.2	1.3	1.3	1.4	1.5	1.6	1.6	1.7	1.8
3-00	1.0	1.1	1.1	1.2	1.3	1.3	1.4	1.4	1.5	1.6
3-20	.9	1.0	1.0	1.1	1.1	1.2	1.2	1.3	1.4	1.4
3-40	.8	.9	.9	1.0	1.0	1.1	1.1	1.2	1.2	1.3
4-00	.8	.8	.8	.9	.9	1.0	1.0	1.1	1.1	1.2
4-20	.7	.7	.8	.8	.9	.9	1.0	1.0	1.0	1.1
4-40	.6	.7	.7	.8	.8	.8	.9	.9	1.0	1.0
5-00	.6	.6	.7	.7	.8	.8	.8	.9	.9	.9

Height of Object—feet *(meters)*

Vertical Angle	*168* 550	*183* 600	*198* 650	*213* 700	*229* 750	*244* 800	*259* 850	*274* 900	*280* 950	*305* 1000
0	29.9	31.1	32.3	33.4	34.5	35.5	36.5	37.5	38.5	39.4
1	28.7	29.9	31.0	32.1	33.2	34.3	35.3	36.3	37.2	38.1
2	27.4	28.6	29.8	30.9	32.0	33.0	34.1	35.0	36.0	36.9
3	26.3	27.5	28.6	29.7	30.8	31.9	32.9	33.9	34.8	35.7
4	25.1	26.3	27.5	28.6	29.7	30.7	31.7	32.7	33.7	34.6
5	24.2	25.4	26.6	27.7	28.8	29.8	30.8	31.8	32.7	33.7
6	23.2	24.4	25.5	26.6	27.7	28.8	29.8	30.7	31.7	32.6
7	22.2	23.4	24.5	25.6	26.7	27.7	28.7	29.7	30.6	31.6
8	21.3	22.5	23.6	24.7	25.7	26.8	27.8	28.7	29.7	30.6
9	20.4	21.6	22.7	23.8	24.8	25.8	26.8	27.8	28.7	29.6
10	19.6	20.7	21.8	22.9	23.9	24.9	25.9	26.9	27.8	28.7
11	18.8	19.9	21.0	22.1	23.1	24.1	25.1	26.0	26.9	27.8
12	18.0	19.1	20.2	21.3	22.3	23.3	24.2	25.2	26.1	27.0
14	16.6	17.7	18.8	19.8	20.8	21.7	22.7	23.6	24.5	25.4
16	15.4	16.5	17.5	18.5	19.4	20.4	21.3	22.2	23.0	23.9
18	14.3	15.3	16.3	17.3	18.2	19.1	20.0	20.8	21.7	22.5
20	13.3	14.3	15.2	16.2	17.1	17.9	18.8	19.6	20.5	21.3
22	12.4	13.4	14.3	15.2	16.0	16.9	17.7	18.5	19.3	20.1
24	11.7	12.6	13.4	14.3	15.1	15.9	16.7	17.5	18.3	19.1
26	11.0	11.8	12.6	13.5	14.3	15.1	15.8	16.6	17.3	18.1
28	10.3	11.1	11.9	12.7	13.5	14.3	15.0	15.7	16.5	17.2
30	9.7	10.5	11.3	12.1	12.8	13.5	14.3	15.0	15.7	16.4
32	9.2	10.0	10.7	11.4	12.2	12.9	13.6	14.3	14.9	15.6
34	8.7	9.5	10.2	10.9	11.6	12.3	12.9	13.6	14.2	14.9
36	8.3	9.0	9.7	10.4	11.0	11.7	12.3	13.0	13.6	14.2
38	7.9	8.6	9.2	9.9	10.5	11.2	11.8	12.4	13.0	13.6
40	7.6	8.2	8.8	9.5	10.1	10.7	11.3	11.9	12.5	13.1
45	6.8	7.4	7.9	8.5	9.1	9.6	10.2	10.8	11.3	11.8
50	6.1	6.7	7.2	7.7	8.3	8.8	9.3	9.8	10.3	10.8
55	5.6	6.1	6.6	7.1	7.6	8.0	8.5	9.0	9.5	9.9
1-00	5.2	5.6	6.1	6.5	7.0	7.4	7.9	8.3	8.7	9.2
1-05	4.8	5.2	5.6	6.0	6.5	6.9	7.3	7.7	8.1	8.5
1-10	4.4	4.8	5.2	5.6	6.0	6.4	6.8	7.2	7.6	7.9
1-15	4.1	4.5	4.9	5.3	5.6	6.0	6.3	6.7	7.1	7.4
1-20	3.9	4.2	4.6	4.9	5.3	5.6	6.0	6.3	6.6	7.0
1-30	3.5	3.8	4.1	4.4	4.7	5.0	5.3	5.6	5.9	6.2
1-40	3.1	3.4	3.7	4.0	4.2	4.5	4.8	5.1	5.3	5.6
1-50	2.8	3.1	3.3	3.6	3.9	4.1	4.4	4.6	4.9	5.1
2-00	2.6	2.8	3.1	3.3	3.5	3.8	4.0	4.2	4.5	4.7
2-10	2.4	2.6	2.8	3.0	3.3	3.5	3.7	3.9	4.1	4.3
2-20	2.2	2.4	2.6	2.8	3.0	3.2	3.4	3.6	3.8	4.0
2-30	2.1	2.3	2.5	2.6	2.8	3.0	3.2	3.4	3.6	3.8
2-40	1.9	2.1	2.3	2.5	2.7	2.8	3.0	3.2	3.4	3.5
3-00	1.7	1.9	2.0	2.2	2.4	2.5	2.7	2.8	3.0	3.1
3-20	1.6	1.7	1.8	2.0	2.1	2.3	2.4	2.5	2.7	2.8
3-40	1.4	1.5	1.7	1.8	1.9	2.1	2.2	2.3	2.4	2.6
4-00	1.3	1.4	1.5	1.7	1.8	1.9	2.0	2.1	2.2	2.4
4-20	1.2	1.3	1.4	1.5	1.6	1.7	1.8	2.0	2.1	2.2
4-40	1.1	1.2	1.3	1.4	1.5	1.6	1.7	1.8	1.9	2.0
5-00	1.0	1.1	1.2	1.3	1.4	1.5	1.6	1.7	1.8	1.9

Height of Object—feet *(meters)*

Vertical Angle	*335* 1100	*366* 1200	*396* 1300	*427* 1400	*457* 1500	*488* 1600	*518* 1700	*549* 1800	*579* 1900	*610* 2000
0	41.2	42.9	44.5	46.1	47.6	49.1	50.5	51.9	53.2	54.5
1	39.9	41.6	43.3	44.8	46.4	47.8	49.3	50.6	52.0	53.3
2	38.7	40.4	42.1	43.6	45.2	46.6	48.1	49.4	50.8	52.1
3	37.5	39.2	40.9	42.5	44.0	45.5	46.9	48.3	49.6	50.9
4	36.4	38.1	39.7	41.3	42.8	44.3	45.7	47.1	48.5	49.8
5	35.4	37.2	38.8	40.4	41.9	43.3	44.8	46.1	47.5	48.8
6	34.4	36.1	37.7	39.3	40.8	42.3	43.7	45.0	46.4	47.7
7	33.3	35.0	36.7	38.2	39.7	41.2	42.6	44.0	45.3	46.6
8	32.3	34.0	35.6	37.2	38.7	40.2	41.6	42.9	44.3	45.6
9	31.4	33.0	34.7	36.2	37.7	39.2	40.6	41.9	43.3	44.6
10	30.4	32.1	33.7	35.2	36.7	38.2	39.6	40.9	42.3	43.6
11	29.5	31.2	32.8	34.3	35.8	37.2	38.6	40.0	41.3	42.6
12	28.7	30.3	31.9	33.4	34.9	36.3	37.7	39.1	40.4	41.6
14	27.0	28.6	30.2	31.7	33.2	34.6	35.9	37.3	38.6	39.8
16	25.5	27.1	28.6	30.1	31.5	32.9	34.3	35.6	36.9	38.1
18	24.1	25.7	27.2	28.6	30.0	31.4	32.7	34.0	35.3	36.5
20	22.8	24.3	25.8	27.2	28.6	29.9	31.2	32.5	33.8	35.0
22	21.6	23.1	24.5	25.9	27.3	28.6	29.9	31.1	32.3	33.5
24	20.5	22.0	23.4	24.7	26.0	27.3	28.6	29.8	31.0	32.2
26	19.5	20.9	22.3	23.6	24.9	26.1	27.4	28.6	29.7	30.9
28	18.6	19.9	21.3	22.5	23.8	25.0	26.2	27.4	28.5	29.7
30	17.7	19.0	20.3	21.6	22.8	24.0	25.2	26.3	27.4	28.5
32	16.9	18.2	19.4	20.6	21.8	23.0	24.2	25.3	26.4	27.5
34	16.2	17.4	18.6	19.8	21.0	22.1	23.2	24.3	25.4	26.5
36	15.5	16.7	17.9	19.0	20.1	21.2	22.3	23.4	24.5	25.5
38	14.8	16.0	17.1	18.3	19.4	20.4	21.5	22.6	23.6	24.6
40	14.2	15.4	16.5	17.6	18.6	19.7	20.7	21.8	22.8	23.7
45	12.9	14.0	15.0	16.0	17.0	18.0	19.0	19.9	20.9	21.8
50	11.8	12.8	13.7	14.7	15.6	16.6	17.5	18.4	19.3	20.2
55	10.8	11.8	12.7	13.6	14.4	15.3	16.2	17.0	17.9	18.7
1-00	10.0	10.9	11.7	12.6	13.4	14.2	15.0	15.8	16.6	17.4
1-05	9.3	10.1	10.9	11.7	12.5	13.2	14.0	14.8	15.5	16.3
1-10	8.7	9.4	10.2	10.9	11.7	12.4	13.1	13.8	14.6	15.3
1-15	8.1	8.9	9.6	10.3	11.0	11.7	12.3	13.0	13.7	14.4
1-20	7.7	8.3	9.0	9.7	10.3	11.0	11.6	12.3	12.9	13.6
1-30	6.8	7.5	8.1	8.7	9.2	9.8	10.4	11.0	11.6	12.2
1-40	6.2	6.7	7.3	7.8	8.4	8.9	9.4	10.0	10.5	11.0
1-50	5.6	6.1	6.6	7.1	7.6	8.1	8.6	9.1	9.6	10.1
2-00	5.2	5.6	6.1	6.6	7.0	7.5	7.9	8.4	8.8	9.3
2-10	4.8	5.2	5.6	6.1	6.5	6.9	7.3	7.8	8.2	8.6
2-20	4.4	4.8	5.2	5.6	6.0	6.4	6.8	7.2	7.6	8.0
2-30	4.1	4.5	4.9	5.3	5.6	6.0	6.4	6.7	7.1	7.5
2-40	3.9	4.2	4.6	4.9	5.3	5.6	6.0	6.3	6.7	7.0
3-00	3.5	3.8	4.1	4.4	4.7	5.0	5.3	5.6	5.9	6.3
3-20	3.1	3.4	3.7	4.0	4.2	4.5	4.8	5.1	5.4	5.6
3-40	2.8	3.1	3.3	3.6	3.9	4.1	4.4	4.6	4.9	5.1
4-00	2.6	2.8	3.1	3.3	3.5	3.8	4.0	4.2	4.5	4.7
4-20	2.4	2.6	2.8	3.0	3.3	3.5	3.7	3.9	4.1	4.3
4-40	2.2	2.4	2.6	2.8	3.0	3.2	3.4	3.6	3.8	4.0
5-00	2.1	2.3	2.5	2.6	2.8	3.0	3.2	3.4	3.6	3.8

Height of eye—6 feet *(1.8 meters)* Horizon distance—2.8 nautical miles

Height of Object—feet *(meters)*

Vertical Angle	*762* 2500	*914* 3000	*1067* 3500	*1219* 4000	*1524* 5000	*1829* 6000	*2134* 7000	*2438* 8000	*2743* 9000	*3048* 10000
0	60.6	66.2	71.2	76.0	84.6	92.4	99.6	106.3	112.5	118.5
1	59.4	64.9	70.0	74.7	83.4	91.2	98.4	105.1	111.3	117.3
2	58.2	63.7	68.8	73.5	82.2	90.0	97.2	103.9	110.1	116.1
3	57.0	62.6	67.6	72.4	81.0	88.8	96.0	102.7	109.0	114.9
4	55.9	61.4	66.5	71.2	79.8	87.7	94.8	101.5	107.8	113.7
5	54.9	60.4	65.5	70.2	78.8	86.6	93.8	100.5	106.7	112.6
6	53.8	59.3	64.4	69.1	77.7	85.5	92.6	99.3	105.6	111.5
7	52.7	58.2	63.3	68.0	76.6	84.4	91.5	98.2	104.4	110.4
8	51.6	57.1	62.2	66.9	75.5	83.3	90.4	97.1	103.3	109.3
9	50.6	56.1	61.1	65.8	74.4	82.2	89.3	96.0	102.2	108.1
10	49.6	55.1	60.1	64.8	73.3	81.1	88.2	94.9	101.1	107.0
11	48.6	54.0	59.1	63.7	72.3	80.0	87.2	93.8	100.1	106.0
12	47.6	53.1	58.1	62.7	71.3	79.0	86.1	92.8	99.0	104.9
14	45.8	51.1	56.1	60.8	69.3	77.0	84.1	90.7	96.9	102.8
16	44.0	49.3	54.3	58.9	67.3	75.0	82.1	88.7	94.9	100.7
18	42.3	47.6	52.5	57.0	65.4	73.1	80.1	86.7	92.9	98.7
20	40.7	45.9	50.8	55.3	63.6	71.2	78.2	84.8	90.9	96.7
22	39.2	44.3	49.1	53.6	61.9	69.4	76.4	82.9	89.0	94.8
24	37.7	42.8	47.5	52.0	60.2	67.7	74.6	81.1	87.2	92.9
26	36.3	41.4	46.0	50.4	58.6	66.0	72.8	79.3	85.4	91.1
28	35.0	40.0	44.6	48.9	57.0	64.3	71.2	77.6	83.6	89.3
30	33.8	38.7	43.2	47.5	55.5	62.8	69.5	75.9	81.9	87.6
32	32.6	37.4	41.9	46.1	54.0	61.2	67.9	74.3	80.2	85.9
34	31.5	36.2	40.6	44.8	52.6	59.7	66.4	72.7	78.6	84.2
36	30.4	35.1	39.4	43.5	51.2	58.3	64.9	71.1	77.0	82.6
38	29.4	34.0	38.3	42.3	49.9	56.9	63.5	69.6	75.5	81.0
40	28.5	33.0	37.2	41.2	48.7	55.6	62.1	68.2	74.0	79.5
45	26.3	30.6	34.6	38.5	45.7	52.4	58.8	64.7	70.4	75.8
50	24.4	28.5	32.3	36.0	43.0	49.6	55.7	61.5	67.1	72.4
55	22.7	26.6	30.3	33.8	40.6	46.9	52.9	58.5	64.0	69.2
1-00	21.2	24.9	28.4	31.9	38.3	44.5	50.3	55.8	61.1	66.2
1-05	19.9	23.4	26.8	30.1	36.3	42.2	47.8	53.2	58.4	63.3
1-10	18.7	22.1	25.3	28.4	34.4	40.2	45.6	50.8	55.9	60.7
1-15	17.7	20.8	23.9	26.9	32.7	38.3	43.5	48.6	53.5	58.2
1-20	16.7	19.7	22.7	25.6	31.2	36.5	41.6	46.5	51.3	55.9
1-30	15.0	17.8	20.6	23.2	28.4	33.4	38.2	42.8	47.3	51.7
1-40	13.7	16.2	18.8	21.2	26.0	30.7	35.2	39.6	43.9	48.0
1-50	12.5	14.9	17.2	19.5	24.0	28.4	32.6	36.8	40.8	44.7
2-00	11.5	13.7	15.9	18.1	22.3	26.4	30.4	34.3	38.1	41.8
2-10	10.7	12.7	14.8	16.8	20.7	24.6	28.4	32.1	35.7	39.2
2-20	10.0	11.9	13.8	15.7	19.4	23.0	26.6	30.1	33.6	36.9
2-30	9.3	11.1	12.9	14.7	18.2	21.6	25.0	28.4	31.6	34.9
2-40	8.7	10.5	12.2	13.8	17.1	20.4	23.6	26.8	29.9	33.0
3-00	7.8	9.3	10.9	12.4	15.4	18.3	21.2	24.1	26.9	29.7
3-20	7.0	8.4	9.8	11.2	13.9	16.6	19.2	21.9	24.5	27.1
3-40	6.4	7.7	8.9	10.2	12.7	15.1	17.6	20.0	22.4	24.8
4-00	5.9	7.0	8.2	9.4	11.6	13.9	16.2	18.4	20.7	22.9
4-20	5.4	6.5	7.6	8.6	10.8	12.9	15.0	17.1	19.2	21.2
4-40	5.0	6.0	7.0	8.0	10.0	12.0	14.0	15.9	17.8	19.8
5-00	4.7	5.6	6.6	7.5	9.4	11.2	13.1	14.9	16.7	18.5

TABLE 10-2 DISTANCE BY BASE ANGLE

This table is used only with objects closer than the horizon. Measure the angle from the horizon down to the waterline of the object. With this angle and the height of eye, the table gives the distance in feet or nautical miles.

Height of Eye—feet *(meters)*

Base	*1.2*	*1.5*	*1.8*	*2.1*	*2.4*	*2.0*	*3.0*	*3.3*	*3.7*	*4.0*
Angle	4	5	6	7	8	9	10	11	12	13
0	2.3	2.6	2.8	3.0	3.2	3.4	3.6	3.8	4.0	4.1
1	5355	1.0	1.2	1.3	1.4	1.6	1.7	1.8	1.9	2.0
2	3729	4447	5126	1.0	1.1	1.1	1.2	1.3	1.4	1.5
3	2897	3487	4046	4586	5104	5603	1.0	1.1	1.2	1.2
4	2374	2879	3351	3814	4262	4693	5117	5532	1.0	1.0
5	2019	2453	2873	3273	3667	4053	4426	4793	5152	5505
6	1753	2143	2509	2875	3224	3567	3904	4236	4561	4875
7	1554	1900	2236	2562	2877	3192	3497	3798	4093	4383
8	1395	1707	2015	2308	2602	2887	3168	3443	3715	3981
9	1264	1553	1829	2106	2375	2635	2895	3148	3400	3648
10	1156	1423	1681	1933	2181	2425	2665	2902	3135	3368
11	1067	1311	1551	1789	2019	2247	2470	2694	2911	3128
12	991	1219	1441	1664	1880	2093	2305	2512	2719	2919
13	923	1138	1347	1554	1760	1960	2158	2353	2548	2739
14	864	1067	1265	1461	1653	1841	2030	2215	2397	2578
15	812	1003	1191	1375	1558	1738	1916	2092	2265	2438
16	767	949	1125	1301	1473	1645	1813	1981	2146	2309
17	727	898	1068	1233	1398	1561	1721	1882	2038	2196
18	691	853	1014	1172	1331	1485	1639	1791	1941	2091
19	656	813	967	1118	1268	1417	1563	1710	1854	1997
20	627	776	923	1068	1212	1355	1495	1635	1774	1911
22	574	711	846	981	1114	1245	1375	1504	1632	1760
24	530	657	783	906	1030	1152	1273	1393	1511	1630
26	492	609	726	843	958	1072	1184	1298	1408	1520
28	458	568	679	787	896	1001	1107	1213	1317	1421
30	429	534	637	739	841	941	1041	1140	1238	1337
32	404	502	600	697	792	886	981	1075	1168	1260
34	381	474	567	657	749	839	927	1016	1105	1193
35	361	449	536	623	710	794	880	964	1048	1133
38	343	427	510	593	674	756	837	917	998	1077
40	327	407	486	565	643	721	798	876	952	1028
42	312	388	464	539	614	688	763	837	909	983
44	298	371	444	515	588	659	730	800	871	941
46	286	355	426	494	564	632	700	768	835	902
48	274	342	408	476	542	607	673	738	803	867
50	263	329	393	457	521	584	648	710	773	835
52	254	317	378	440	501	563	624	684	745	805
54	245	305	365	425	484	543	602	661	718	777
56	237	294	353	410	467	525	581	638	695	751
58	229	285	341	397	452	508	562	617	671	726
1-00	221	276	329	384	438	491	545	597	650	704
1-05	204	255	305	355	405	455	505	554	603	652
1-10	190	237	284	331	377	424	469	516	562	607
1-15	177	222	265	310	353	397	439	483	526	569
1-20	167	208	249	290	332	372	413	454	494	534
1-25	157	196	235	274	313	351	389	428	466	504
1-30	149	186	222	259	296	332	369	405	441	477
1-35	140	176	211	246	280	315	350	384	419	452
1-40	134	167	201	234	266	300	333	365	398	431
1-45	128	159	191	223	254	285	317	349	380	411

Height of Eye—feet *(meters)*

Base Angle	*4.3* 14	*4.9* 16	*5.5* 18	*6.1* 20	*7.6* 25	*9.1* 30	*11* 35	*12* 40	*14* 45	*15* 50
0	4.3	4.6	4.9	5.1	5.7	6.3	6.8	7.2	7.7	8.1
1	2.1	2.3	2.5	2.7	3.1	3.5	3.9	4.2	4.6	4.9
2	1.6	1.8	1.9	2.1	2.4	2.8	3.1	3.4	3.7	3.9
3	1.3	1.4	1.6	1.7	2.0	2.3	2.6	2.9	3.1	3.4
4	1.1	1.2	1.3	1.5	1.7	2.0	2.3	2.5	2.7	2.9
5	1.0	1.1	1.2	1.3	1.5	1.8	2.0	2.2	2.4	2.6
6	5189	1.0	1.1	1.1	1.4	1.6	1.8	2.0	2.2	2.4
7	4667	5227	5771	1.0	1.2	1.5	1.6	1.8	2.0	2.2
8	4244	4759	5265	5758	1.1	1.3	1.5	1.7	1.9	2.0
9	3892	4373	4841	5300	1.1	1.2	1.4	1.6	1.7	1.9
10	3594	4042	4482	4911	1.0	1.1	1.3	1.5	1.6	1.8
11	3342	3762	4173	4576	5556	1.1	1.2	1.4	1.5	1.6
12	3122	3517	3905	4284	5210	1.0	1.1	1.3	1.4	1.6
13	2928	3300	3669	4030	4908	5756	1.1	1.2	1.3	1.5
14	2757	3113	3460	3802	4637	5446	1.0	1.2	1.3	1.4
15	2608	2944	3274	3600	4396	5166	1.0	1.1	1.2	1.3
16	2471	2792	3108	3419	4178	4918	5636	1.0	1.2	1.3
17	2350	2657	2958	3256	3982	4690	5379	1.0	1.1	1.2
18	2239	2532	2821	3106	3804	4483	5145	1.0	1.1	1.2
19	2139	2420	2697	2971	3641	4294	4931	5555	1.0	1.1
20	2047	2318	2584	2847	3491	4120	4735	5335	1.0	1.1
22	1885	2137	2383	2627	3226	3811	4384	4947	5500	1.0
24	1749	1982	2212	2440	2999	3546	4084	4611	5129	5641
26	1630	1847	2064	2278	2801	3317	3822	4319	4807	5289
28	1526	1731	1934	2134	2629	3114	3591	4061	4524	4979
30	1434	1628	1819	2010	2476	2936	3387	3833	4271	4703
32	1354	1536	1718	1898	2341	2776	3206	3628	4045	4458
34	1281	1455	1626	1798	2219	2635	3043	3446	3843	4237
36	1215	1381	1545	1708	2111	2506	2895	3279	3660	4036
38	1157	1315	1472	1626	2010	2389	2762	3129	3494	3854
40	1104	1255	1405	1553	1921	2283	2640	2993	3342	3687
42	1056	1199	1343	1485	1839	2186	2528	2868	3202	3534
44	1011	1149	1287	1424	1762	2096	2426	2752	3074	3395
46	969	1104	1235	1367	1692	2014	2331	2646	2956	3265
48	932	1060	1188	1315	1629	1938	2244	2547	2847	3145
50	897	1021	1144	1266	1569	1867	2163	2456	2746	3033
52	866	984	1103	1221	1513	1803	2088	2371	2652	2929
54	835	950	1065	1179	1462	1741	2017	2292	2562	2832
56	806	918	1030	1140	1414	1684	1952	2217	2480	2742
58	780	889	996	1103	1368	1631	1890	2147	2403	2656
1-00	756	860	965	1069	1326	1581	1833	2082	2330	2576
1-05	700	798	895	991	1230	1468	1702	1936	2166	2396
1-10	653	744	835	924	1149	1370	1590	1808	2024	2240
1-15	611	696	781	866	1076	1284	1491	1696	1899	2102
1-20	575	655	735	815	1013	1209	1404	1598	1789	1981
1-25	542	618	693	769	956	1142	1326	1509	1691	1872
1-30	513	585	657	728	905	1082	1257	1431	1603	1775
1-35	487	555	624	692	860	1027	1194	1360	1524	1688
1-40	463	529	594	658	819	979	1137	1295	1452	1609
1-45	442	504	566	628	782	934	1086	1237	1387	1537

Height of Eye—feet *(meters)*

Base Angle	*1.2* 4	*1.5* 5	*1.8* 6	*2.1* 7	*2.4* 8	*2.7* 9	*3.0* 10	*3.3* 11	*3.7* 12	*4.0* 13
1-50	122	152	182	213	243	273	303	333	363	393
1-55	116	146	175	204	233	261	290	319	348	376
2-00	112	139	168	195	223	251	278	306	334	361
2-05	107	135	161	187	214	241	267	294	321	347
2-10	103	129	155	180	206	232	257	283	308	334
2-15	99	125	149	174	199	223	248	273	297	322
2-20	96	120	144	168	192	215	240	263	287	310
2-25	93	116	139	162	185	208	231	254	277	300
2-30	89	112	134	157	179	201	224	246	268	290
2-35	86	108	130	152	173	195	217	238	259	281
2-40	84	105	126	147	168	189	210	230	252	272
2-50	79	99	118	139	158	178	198	218	237	256
3-00	75	93	112	131	149	168	187	206	224	242
3-10	71	89	106	124	141	159	177	195	213	230
3-20	67	84	101	118	135	152	168	185	202	219
3-30	64	80	96	112	128	145	161	177	193	208
3-40	61	77	92	107	122	138	153	168	184	199
3-50	58	73	88	103	117	132	146	161	176	191
4-00	56	70	84	98	112	126	141	155	168	182
4-10	54	67	81	94	108	121	135	148	162	175
4-20	52	65	78	91	104	117	130	143	155	169
4-30	50	62	75	87	100	113	125	137	150	162
4-40	48	60	72	84	96	108	121	132	145	157
4-50	46	58	69	82	93	105	116	128	139	151
5-00	45	56	67	79	90	101	112	124	135	146
5-10	43	54	65	76	87	98	109	120	131	141
5-20	42	52	63	74	84	95	105	116	126	137
5-30	41	51	61	72	81	92	102	112	123	133
5-40	39	50	59	69	79	89	99	109	119	129
5-50	38	48	58	67	77	87	96	106	116	125
6-00	37	46	56	65	75	84	94	103	113	122
6-20	35	44	53	62	71	80	88	97	106	115
6-40	33	42	50	59	67	76	84	93	101	109
7-00	32	40	48	56	64	72	80	88	96	104
7-20	30	38	46	53	61	68	77	84	92	100
7-40	29	36	44	51	58	66	73	80	88	95
8-00	28	35	42	49	56	63	70	77	84	91
8-20	26	33	40	47	54	60	67	74	80	87
8-40	26	32	38	45	52	58	64	71	77	84
9-00	24	31	37	43	50	56	62	68	75	81
9-20	24	30	36	42	48	54	60	66	72	78
9-40	23	29	34	40	46	52	57	64	69	75
10-00	22	28	33	39	45	50	56	61	67	73
10-20	21	27	32	38	43	48	54	59	65	70
10-40	21	26	31	36	42	47	52	57	63	68
11-00	20	25	30	33	40	45	50	55	61	66
11-20	19	24	29	34	39	44	49	54	59	64
11-40	19	24	28	33	38	43	48	52	57	62
12-00	18	23	27	32	37	41	46	51	55	60

Height of Eye—feet *(meters)*

Base Angle	*4.3* 14	*4.9* 16	*5.5* 18	*6.1* 20	*7.6* 25	*9.1* 30	*11* 35	*12* 40	*14* 45	*15* 50
1-50	423	482	541	601	747	893	1039	1184	1327	1471
1-55	405	461	519	575	717	857	996	1134	1273	1410
2-00	388	443	497	552	688	822	956	1089	1222	1355
2-05	373	425	478	531	661	790	920	1048	1176	1303
2-10	359	410	461	511	637	761	885	1010	1132	1255
2-15	346	395	444	492	614	734	854	973	1093	1211
2-20	334	382	428	475	592	709	824	940	1055	1170
2-25	323	369	414	459	572	685	797	909	1020	1131
2-30	312	356	400	445	554	663	771	880	987	1095
2-35	302	345	388	430	537	642	748	852	957	1061
2-40	293	335	376	417	520	623	725	827	928	1029
2-50	276	315	354	393	491	587	684	779	875	970
3-00	261	298	335	372	464	555	646	737	828	919
3-10	248	283	318	353	440	527	613	700	785	872
3-20	235	269	302	335	418	501	584	666	748	829
3-30	224	256	288	320	399	477	556	635	713	791
3-40	214	244	275	305	381	456	532	606	681	756
3-50	205	234	263	292	365	437	509	581	652	724
4-00	197	224	252	280	350	419	488	557	626	694
4-10	189	215	242	269	336	402	469	535	601	668
4-20	181	207	233	259	323	387	451	515	578	642
4-30	175	200	225	249	311	373	435	496	557	619
4-40	168	192	216	240	300	360	419	479	538	597
4-50	163	186	209	232	290	348	405	463	520	577
5-00	157	180	202	225	281	336	392	447	503	558
5-10	152	174	196	217	272	326	379	433	487	540
5-20	148	169	190	210	263	316	367	420	471	524
5-30	143	163	184	204	255	306	356	407	458	508
5-40	139	159	178	198	248	297	346	395	444	493
5-50	135	154	174	193	241	288	336	384	431	479
6-00	131	150	168	187	234	280	327	373	420	466
6-20	124	142	160	177	222	266	310	354	398	442
6-40	118	135	152	169	210	253	294	336	378	420
7-00	112	128	144	160	201	240	281	320	360	400
7-20	107	123	138	153	192	229	268	306	344	382
7-40	102	117	132	146	183	220	256	292	329	365
8-00	98	112	126	140	175	210	245	280	315	350
8-20	94	108	121	135	168	202	235	269	302	336
8-40	91	103	117	129	162	194	226	259	291	323
9-00	87	99	112	124	156	187	218	249	280	311
9-20	84	96	108	120	150	180	210	240	270	300
9-40	81	92	104	116	145	174	203	232	261	289
10.00	78	89	101	112	140	168	196	224	252	280
10-20	76	87	97	108	135	162	190	216	243	271
10-40	73	84	94	105	131	157	183	209	236	262
11-00	71	81	91	102	127	153	178	203	228	254
11-20	69	79	88	99	123	148	172	197	221	246
11-40	67	76	85	95	120	144	167	191	215	239
12-00	65	74	83	93	116	139	163	186	209	232

APPENDIX

ADJUSTING THE SEXTANT

The cheaper sextants will general need adjusting when first bought, and a sextant may need occasional adjustment. The idea of adjusting an instrument as "complicated" as a sextant seems to frighten people, but it shouldn't. It's a simple job, taking less than five minutes to do.

We are interested in three "adjustable errors". A recent article of mine in *Pacific Yachting* discusses these and other errors and the editor has kindly permitted parts of the article to be reproduced below.

Let's get the names out in the open first: perpendicularity, side error, and index error. They are individually adjustable, and all relate to the index mirror and horizon glass, which should be **parallel** to each other and **perpendicular** to the frame. The adjustments are normally "tuned up" about once a season, the process is very easy.

Different models of sextants have different arrangements of the adjusting screws, so I can't be specific here about which screw you have to turn for which adjustment. Instead, Figure 1 shows the **direction of motion** of the mirror needed for each adjustment. Common sense will tell you which screw to use. **Caution:** some older sextants have a pair of screws for each adjusting point. Loosen one before you tighten the other.

If the index mirror isn't perpendicular to the plane of the arc, perpendicularity error will be present. To check this, hold the sextant flat and swing the index arm until you can sight obliquely across the index mirror and see the arc reflected. If the reflection seems to line up with the arc seen directly, no adjustment is needed. If the images are offset, the index mirror must be adjusted. Figure 2 shows the two images, and Figure 1(A) shows the adjustment.

Side error will be present if the horizon glass isn't perpendicular to the plane of the arc. To check this, look at a horizontal line (rooftop, power line, or whatever) and adjust the index arm to get an unbroken line. Now tip the sextant on an angle. If the line stays unbroken, there is no side error. If the two parts shift relative to each other, adjustment is needed. See Figure 3 for the images. Figure 1(B) shows the necessary motion of the horizon glass.

Another way of detecting side error—perhaps more accurate—is to look at a star while moving the index arm past zero. If the two images of the star pass directly over each other, there is no side error. If they pass without touching, side error is present. See Figure 4.

Finally, check the index error. This means that when the images of a faraway object are lined up, the scale should read zero. Pick an object at

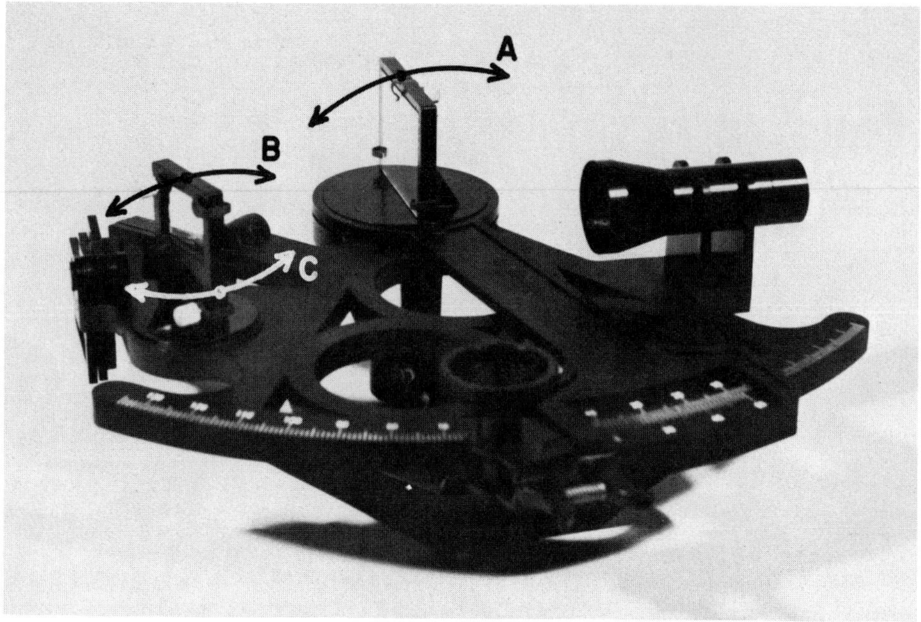

Figure 1 Three different motions of the two sextant mirrors are used in the adjustment process.

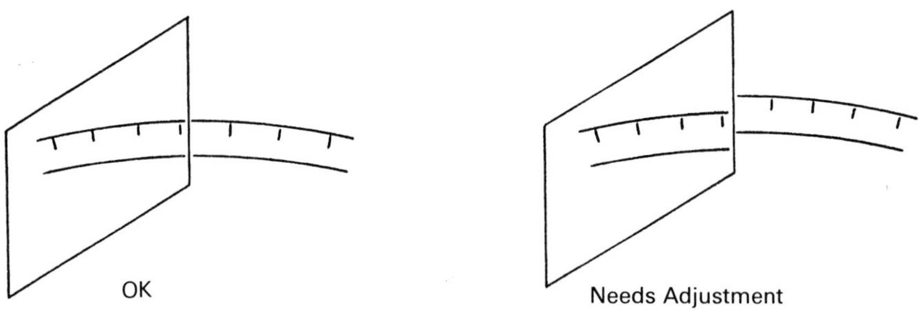

Figure 2 If the images are offset, the sextant needs adjustment.

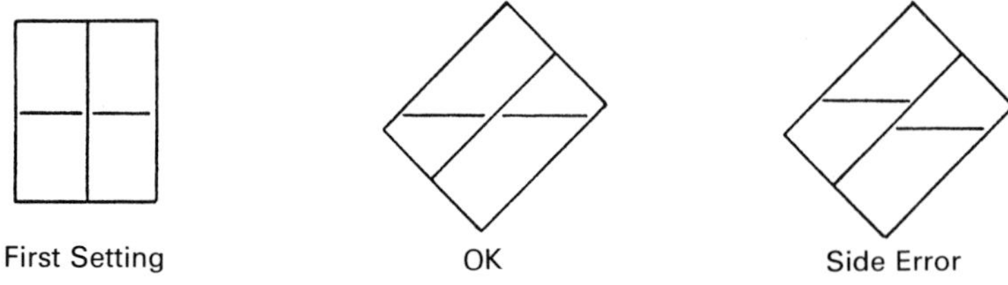

Figure 3 If a horizontal line remains unbroken when the sextant is tilted, there is no side error.

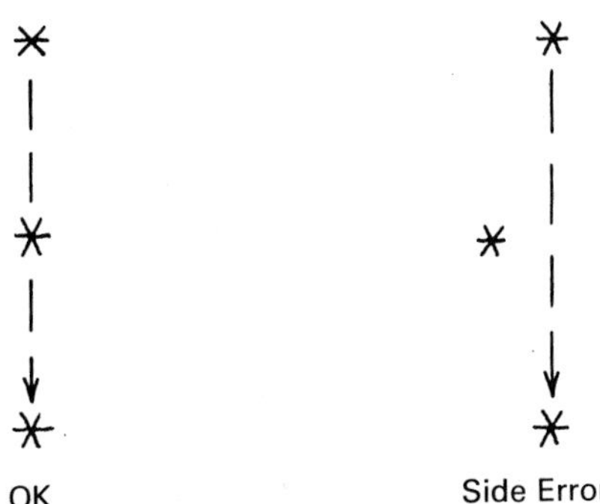

Figure 4 If the two images of a star pass directly over each other while the index arm moves past zero, there is no side error.

least half a mile away, and don't look though a glass window for this test. The horizon, a shoreline, or a rooftop can be used. If you hold the sextant on its side, the side of a building or a mast will also work. Set the index arm carefully to 0, and then look through the sextant. If the images are displaced, as in Figure 5(A) or (B), an index error is present. Adjust the horizon glass until you have an unbroken line as in 5(C). Figure 1(C) shows the mirror motion needed.

These adjustments don't change much and are generally left alone to avoid wearing the screw threads. As I mentioned before, one adjustment per season is about par. Each time you use a sextant, though, you should check the index error. It's about like taking a ruler out of the toolbox and looking at the end to make sure an inch hasn't been chopped off. Look at the horizon and adjust the index arm for an unbroken line, as in Figure 5(C), and then read the scale. If the reading is zero, there's nothing to do. If the reading is not zero, you must apply an **index correction** (IC) to the altitudes when you take sights. The correction is easy to remember: If **you're off you're on, but if you're on, you're off.** Which sounds like nonsense but means that if the index error is **off** the arc (less than zero), that amount must be added on the measured altitudes. If the index error is **on** the arc, it must be taken off the measured altitude.

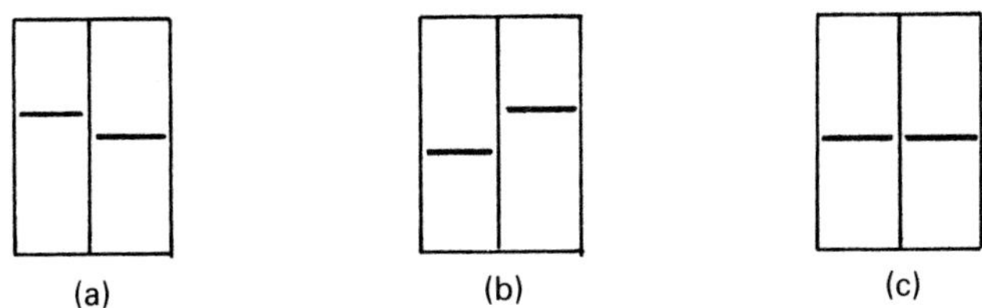

Figure 5 Index error can be checked against a distant object.

Problem 3-1 Solution

(1) 141°, 7.1 miles
(2) 041°, 6.2 miles
(3) 252°, 3.2 miles
(4) 292°, 7.9 miles

Problem 3-2 Solution

(1) 26° 20′.7 N, 73° 39′.2 W
(2) 26° 10′.9 N, 73° 40′.7 W
(3) 26° 19′.4 N, 73° 46′.5 W
(4) 26° 11′.8 N, 73° 34′.7 W

Problem 5-1 Solution

Magnetic Direction	Variation	True Direction
133	15 E	148
256	5 W	*251*
348	25 E	*013*
052	12 W	040

Problem 5-2 Solution

Compass Heading	Deviation	Variation	True Heading
220	*5 E*	25 W	*200*
315	*2 W*	8 W	*305*
079	*2 W*	10 E	087
273	*2 E*	14 W	*261*
147	*3 E*	5 E	155
024	*4 W*	20 E	040
130	*2 E*	12 W	*120*
210	*5 E*	15 E	230
015	*5 W*	22 W	*348*
012	*5 W*	17 W	350

Problem 5-3 Solution

Compass Heading	Compass Bearing	Deviation
000	316	*9 E*
045	322	*3 E*
090	330	*5 W*
135	335	*10 W*
180	334	*9 W*
225	328	*3 W*
270	320	*5 E*
315	315	*10 E*

Problem 6-1 Solution

Speed—Knots	Time	Distance—Nautical Miles
4.0	35 min	(2.3)
2.6	23 min	(1.0)
3.5	(36 min)	2.1
6.4	28 min	(3.0)
6.4	(45 min)	4.8
6.4	1 hr 15 min	(8.0)
5.0	9 min	(.7)
4.5	(3 hr 20 min)	15
4.5	2 hr 20 min	(10.5)
(7.2)	35 min	4.2

Problem 6-2 Solution

Time	HEADING Compass	Magnetic	True	Speed	Distance	Remarks
0930	047	*047*	*070*	6.0	—	Depart Little Hbr. inner bell (Qk Fl G) Current nil Deviation nil Variation 23°E
1000	067	*067*	*090*	4.8	*3.0*	
1030	147	*147*	*170*	5.5	*2.4*	When and where will we run aground? *1.3 miles remaining, at 5.5 knots takes 14 minutes. ETA 1044.*

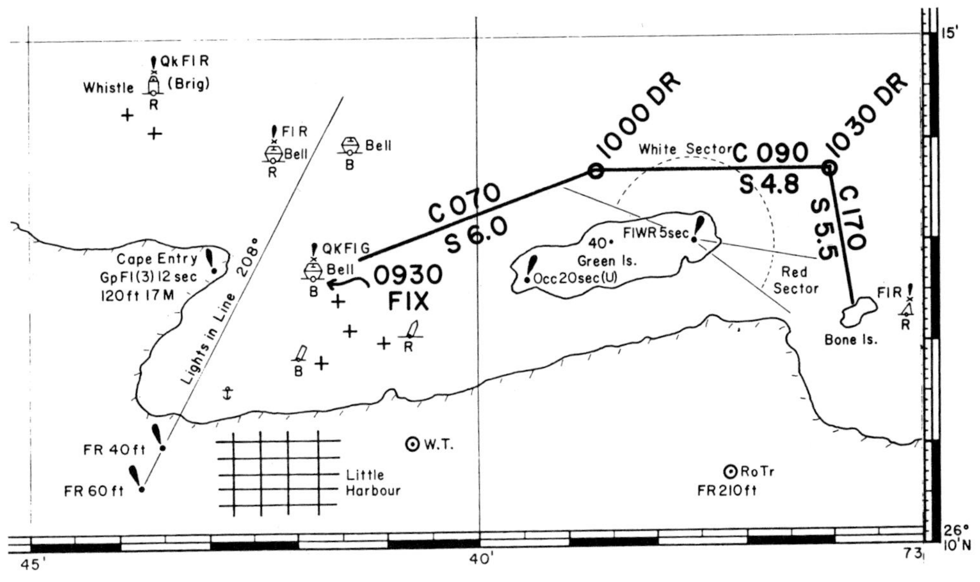

Problem 6-3 Solution

Time	HEADING Compass	Magnetic	True	Speed	Distance	Remarks
1810	307	*307*	*331*	7.0	—	Depart Brig Lucy Variation 24° E
1830	051	*051*	*075*	6.0	*2.3*	
1900	051	*051*	*075*	6.3	3.0	
1919	122	*122*	*146*	7.0	*2.0*	
1930	122	*122*	*146*	7.0	*1.3*	
2000	122	*122*	*146*	6.0	*3.5*	When will Green Is. east light change from white to red? *1.3 miles remaining.* *ETA 2013*

Problem 6-3 Solution Plot

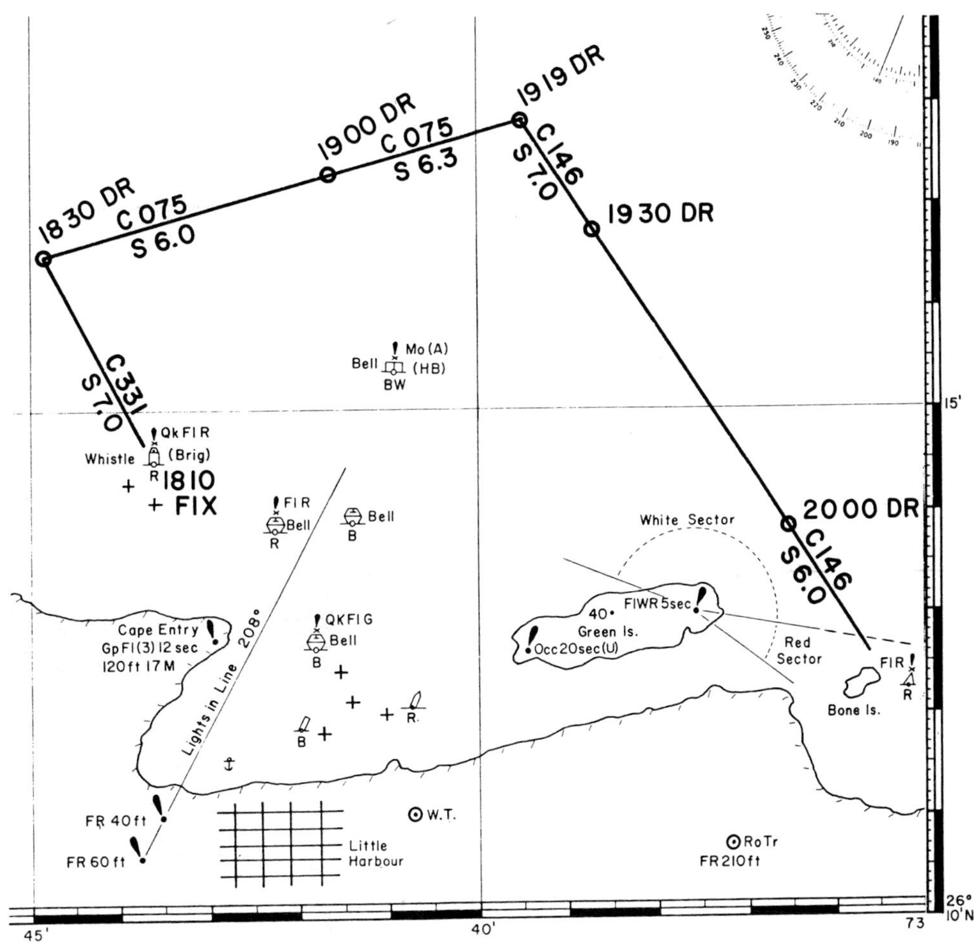

Problem 6-4 Solution Log

Time	HEADING Compass	Magnetic	True	Speed	Distance	Remarks
0900	288	*288*	*311*	7.5	—	Depart Little Hbr. Inner black bell.
0930	288	*288*	*311*	7.5	*3.2*	Variation 23° E
0942	025	*025*	*048*	6.8	*1.5*	
1000	025	*025*	*048*	6.8	*2.0*	
1014	025	*025*	*048*	7.8	*1.6*	
1030	025	*025*	*048*	7.8	*2.1*	
1037	245	*245*	*268*	5.1	*.9*	
1100	152	*152*	*175*	5.8	*2.0*	
1130	152	*152*	*175*	5.8	*2.9*	
1200	152	*152*	*175*	5.8	*2.9*	
1218	152	*152*	*175*	5.8	*1.7*	What is the 1218 DR position, relative to the 0900 fix? *We have returned to the departure point.*

Problem 6-4 Solution Plot

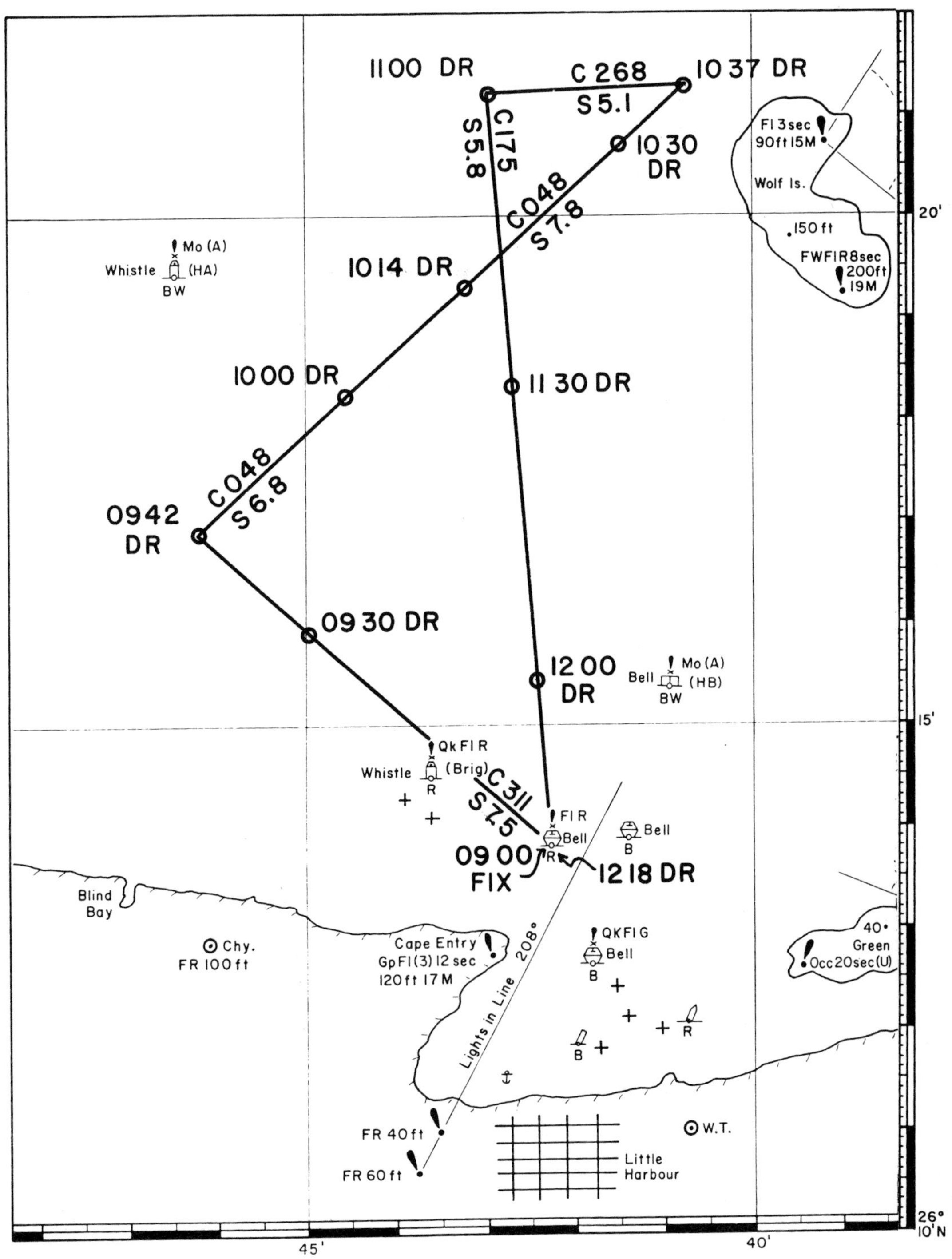

Problem 6-5 Solution Log

Time	HEADING Compass	Magnetic	True	Speed	Distance	Remarks
1000	311	*311*	*334*	4.0	—	Depart Friar Is. can
1030	311	*311*	*334*	4.0	2.0	Variation 23° E
1039	278	*278*	*301*	4.5	.6	
1100	278	*278*	*301*	4.5	1.6	
1130	278	*278*	*301*	4.5	2.2	
1143	326	*326*	*349*	5.2	1.0	
1200	326	*326*	*349*	5.2	1.5	
1209	075	*075*	*098*	4.8	.8	
1230	075	*075*	*098*	4.8	1.7	
1300	308	*308*	*331*	7.0	2.4	
1330	247	*247*	*270*	6.0	3.5	
1400	247	*247*	*270*	6.0	3.0	
1412	199	*199*	*222*	5.0	1.2	What is the 1430 DR
1430	199	*199*	*222*	5.0	1.5	position, relative to fairway buoy HA?
						068°
						2.2 miles

Problem 6-5 Solution Plot

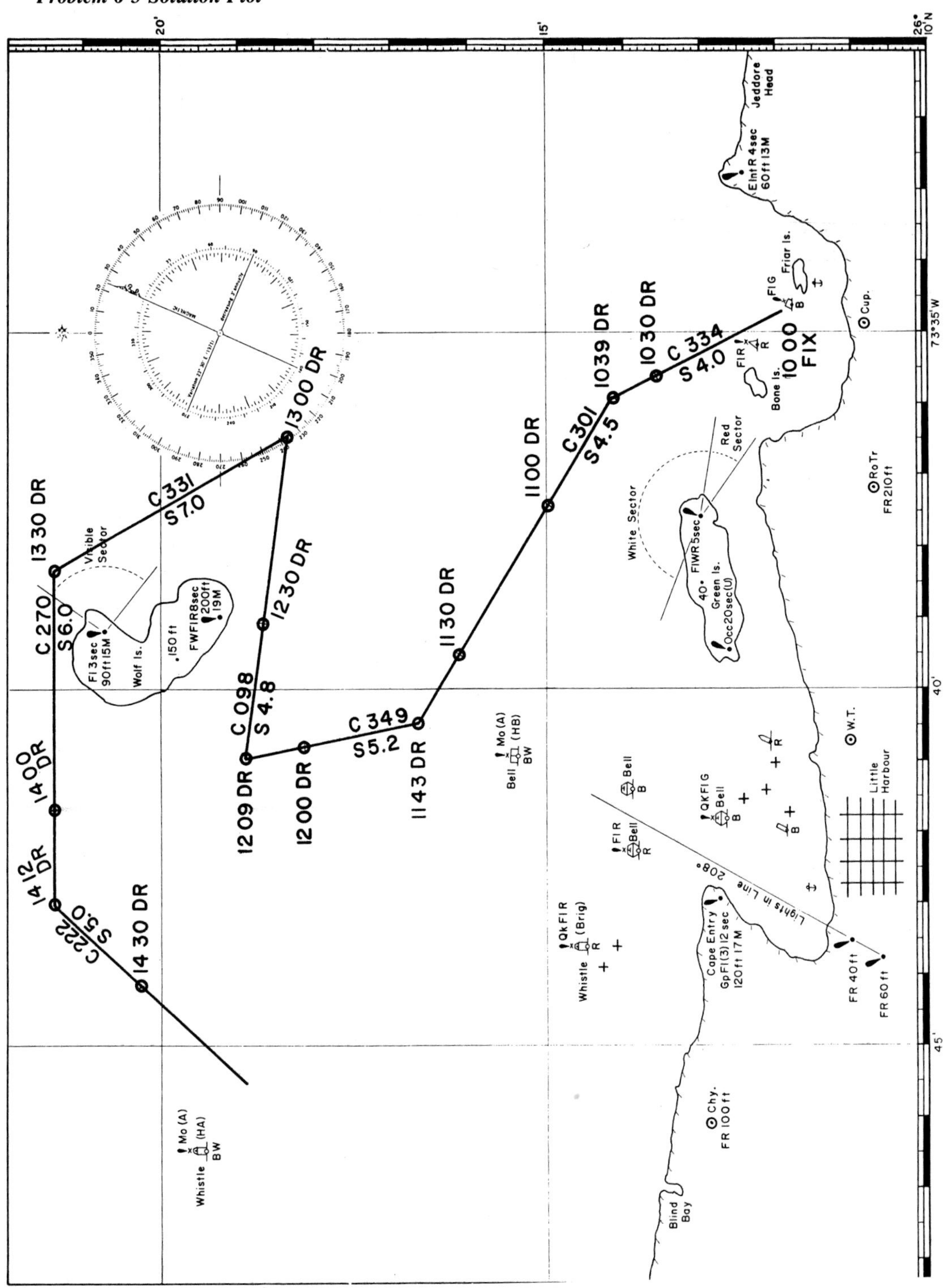

Problem 6-6 Solution Log

	HEADING					
Time	Compass	Magnetic	True	Speed	Distance	Remarks
0944	344	*340*	*004*	3.8	—	Depart Little Hbr. outer black bell Variation 24°E Deviation per table
1000	344	*340*	*004*	3.8	*1.0*	
1030	344	*340*	*004*	5.4	*1.9*	
1100	106	*105*	*129*	4.0	*2.7*	
1130	035	*031*	*055*	6.0	*2.0*	
1145	we're suddenly fogged in, Find the 1145 DR position. What is the compass heading to return to the starting point? At a speed of 4.0 knots, what is the ETA?					
					1.5	*DR position: 26°19′N 73°38′W* *Return course 211°* *Compass heading 182°*
1200	*182*	*186*	*211*	*4.0*	*1.0*	
1230	*182*	*186*	*211*	*4.0*	*2.0*	
1300	*182*	*186*	*211*	*4.0*	*2.0*	*1.1 miles remaining. ETA 1316.*

Problem 7-1 Solution

	Heading	Speed	Set	Drift	Course	Speed Made Good
1)	249	8.3	093	3.1	(236)	(5.6)
2)	093	4.6	160	2.7	(117)	(6.2)
3)	164	2.7	310	5.8	(287)	(3.9)
4)	019	2.7	064	4.6	(048)	(6.8)
5)	(229)	3.3	286	2.8	255	(5.4)
6)	(029)	6.2	172	1.8	042	(4.9)
7)	( )	5.0	350	5.7	117	( )
8)	(273)	3.4	012	5.5	338	(6.0)
9)	121	4.6	(068)	(2.3)	104	6.3
10)	217	6.0	(006)	(3.9)	254	3.3

Notes: There is no solution to number 7. With a speed of 5 knots, we simply can't cope with a current of 5.7 knots and make the desired course.

Number 8 has another possible solution: heading 222°, SMG 3.1 knots. This heading, with the much lower SMG, would not normally be used unless there is some other consideration.

Problem 6-6 Solution Plot

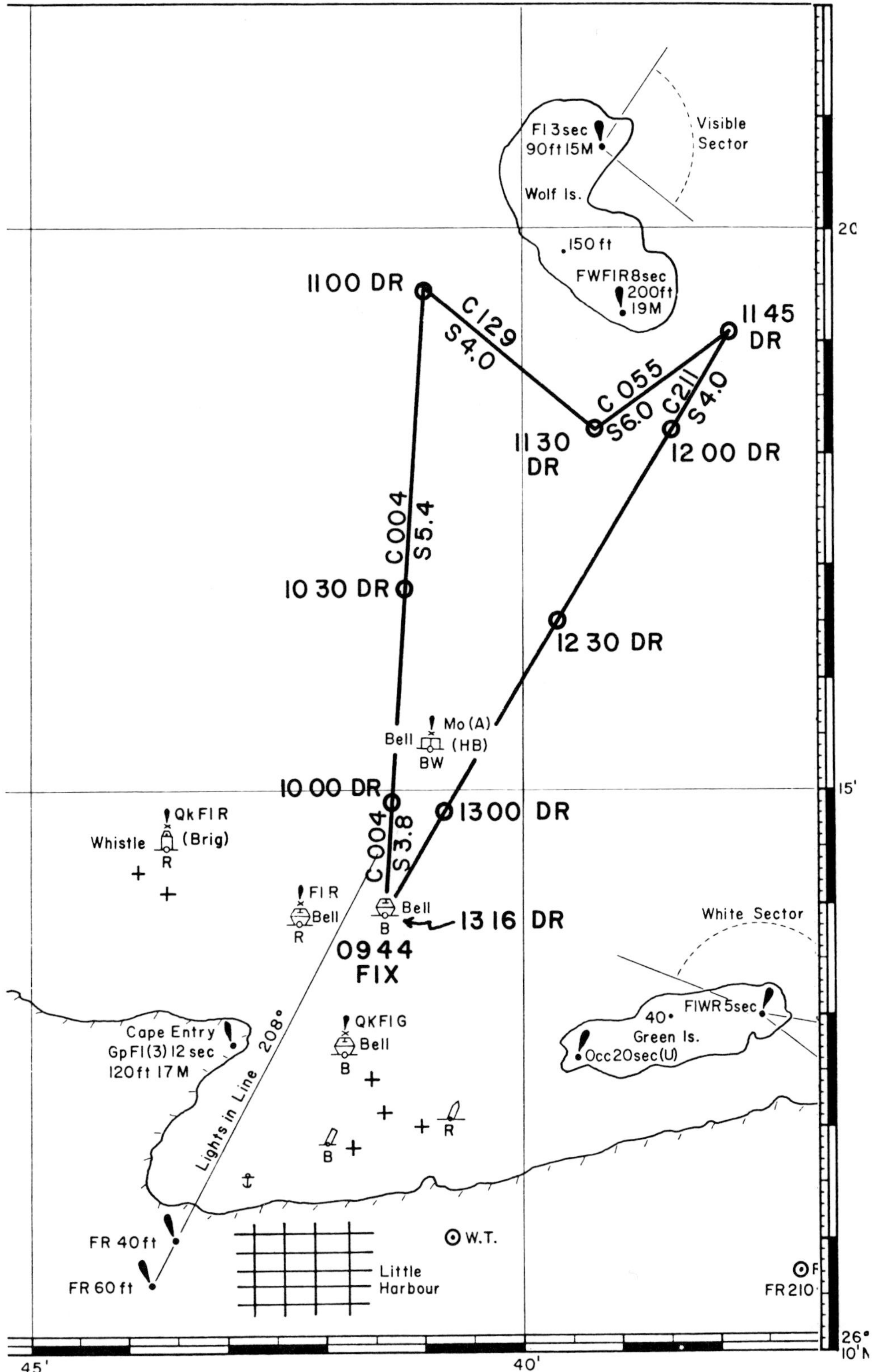

Problem 8-1 Solution; Log

Time	HEADING Compass	Magnetic	True	Speed	True Course	Distance	Remarks
1300				4.2	014		Depart Little Hbr. red spar Variation 24°E
	329		*353*	*SMG 4.0*		—	Set 100, Dr 1.5
1330				4.2	014		
	339		*003*	*SMG 4.2*		*2.0*	Set 100, Dr .8
1400				4.2	014		
	350		*014*	*MSG 4.2*		*2.1*	Set nil, Dr nil
1430				4.2	014		
	001		*025*	*SMG 4.0*		*2.1*	Set 280, Dr .8
							ETA 1445

In this problem, the current is at nearly right angles to our course, whether the set is 100° or 280°. Therefore, our SMG does not benefit in either case, but is less than our speed because we must head slightly into the current to maintain our course.

Problem 8-1 Solution; Current Curve

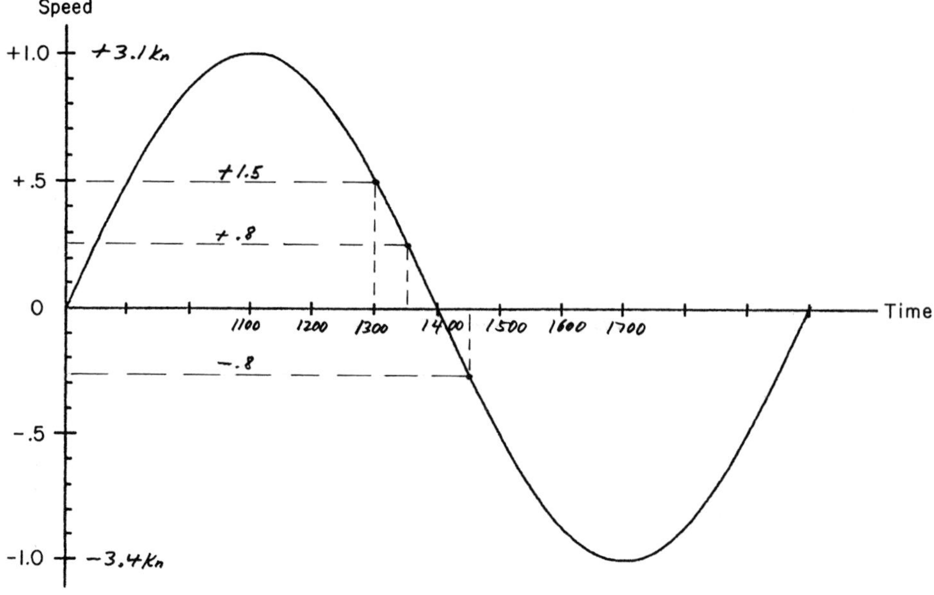

Problem 8-1 Solution; Plot (continued)

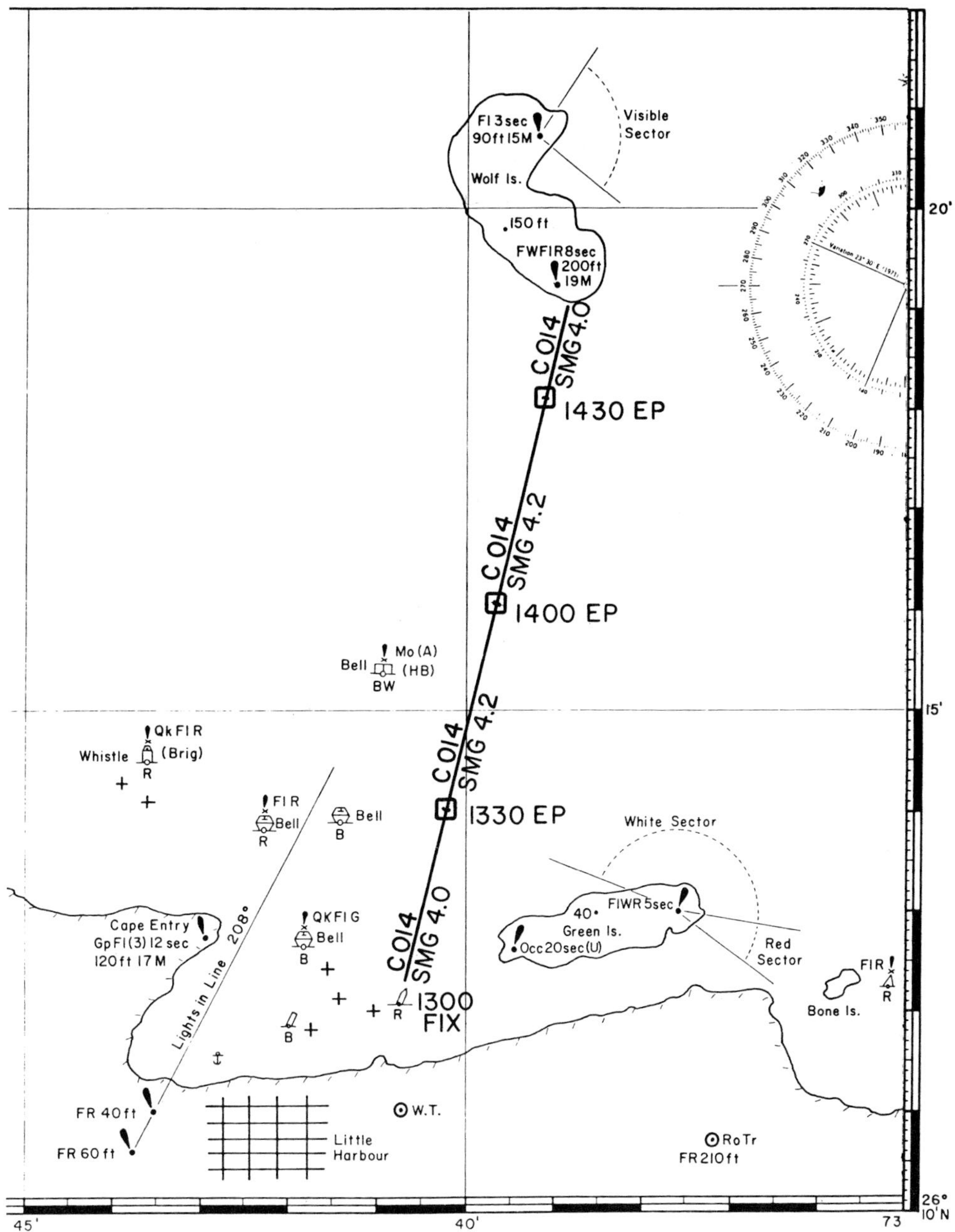

Problem 8-2 Solution

The outward leg clearly shows the result of holding a constant heading in a charging current. The 0400 EP is 26° 18′.6 N, 73° 39′.3 W. The return course is 210°; headings are shown in the log. If the actual track follows the plotted course, we should pass the outer fairway buoy HB at 0506, about .3 mile away.

At 0200 the compass heading is 50 degrees different from the true course. Wouldn't the results be interesting if a person just looked up the chart course and steered with that figure on the compass?!

	HEADING				True		
Time	Compass	Magnetic	True	Speed	Course	Distance	Remarks
0200	350	*350*	*014*	3.2 *SMG 3.7*	*040*	—	Depart inner black bell buoy. Deviation nil. Set 100 Dr. 1.6
0230	350	*350*	*014*	3.5 *SMG 3.6*	*027*	*1.8*	Set 100, Dr. .8
0300	350	*350*	*014*	3.2 *SMG 3.2*	*014*	*1.8*	Current nil
0330	350	*350*	*014*	2.8 *SMG 2.9*	*358*	*1.6*	Set 280, Dr. .8
0400	*160*	*160*	*184*	3.2 *MG 3.4*	*210*	*1.4*	*EP 26° 18′.6 N 73° 39′.3 W* *Return course 210°* Set 280, Dr 1.5
0430	*146*	*146*	*170*	3.2 *SMG 3.2*	*210*	*1.7*	Set 280, Dr 2.2
0500	*134*	*134*	*158*	3.2 *SMG 2.9*	*210*	*1.6*	Set 280, Dr 2.7
0530	*124*	*124*	*148*	3.2 *SMG 2.5*	*210*	*1.4*	Set 280, Dr 3.0
							ETA 0547

Problem 8-2 Solution: Current Curve and Plot

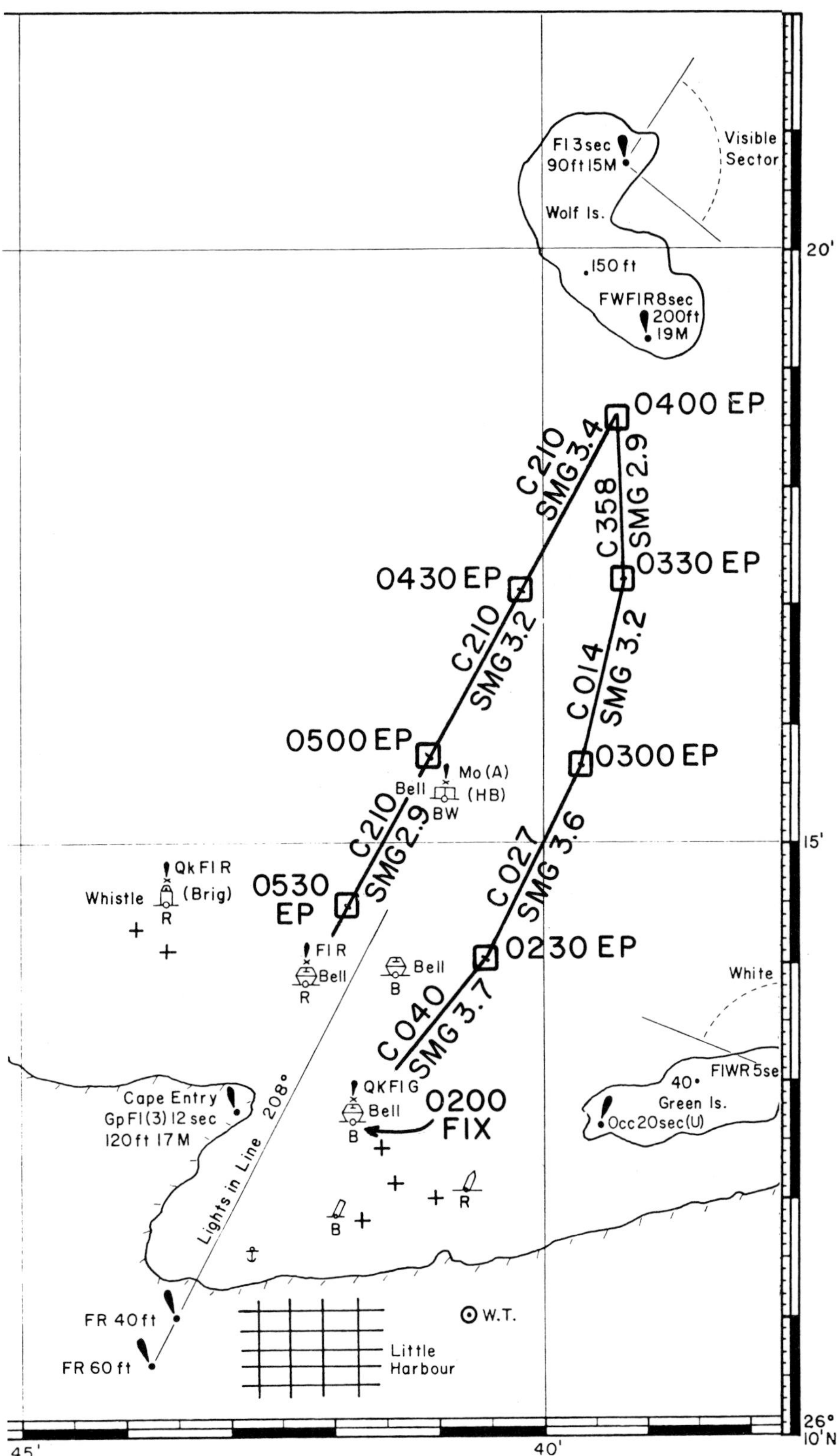

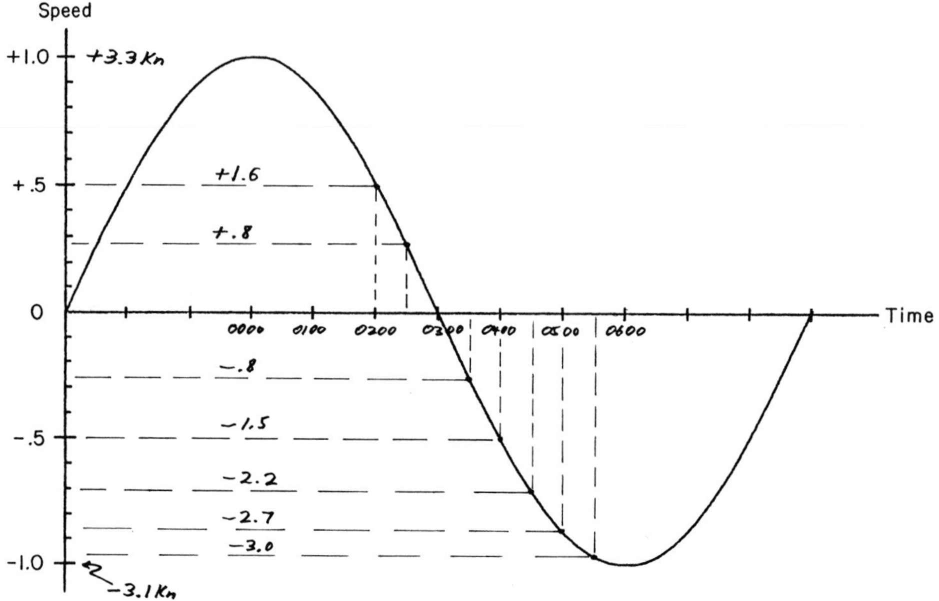

Problem 9-1 Solution

The magnetic bearings convert to 142° and 229° true. The 1230 FIX is at 26° 15′ N, 73° 35′ W.

Problem 9-2 Solution

On a compass heading of 175°, the deviation is 4° E, so the compass error is 28° E. The compass bearings convert to 084° and 343°, giving a 1400 FIX at 26° 15′ N, 73° 45′ W.

Problem 9-3 Solution

On a compass heading of 005°, the deviation is 5° W and the compass error is 19° E. The true heading is 024°. The relative bearings convert to true bearings of 189° and 261°, giving a 1615 FIX at 26° 15′ N, 73° 40′ W.

These three solutions are plotted on the next page.

Problem 9-1, 9-2, and 9-3 Solution Plots

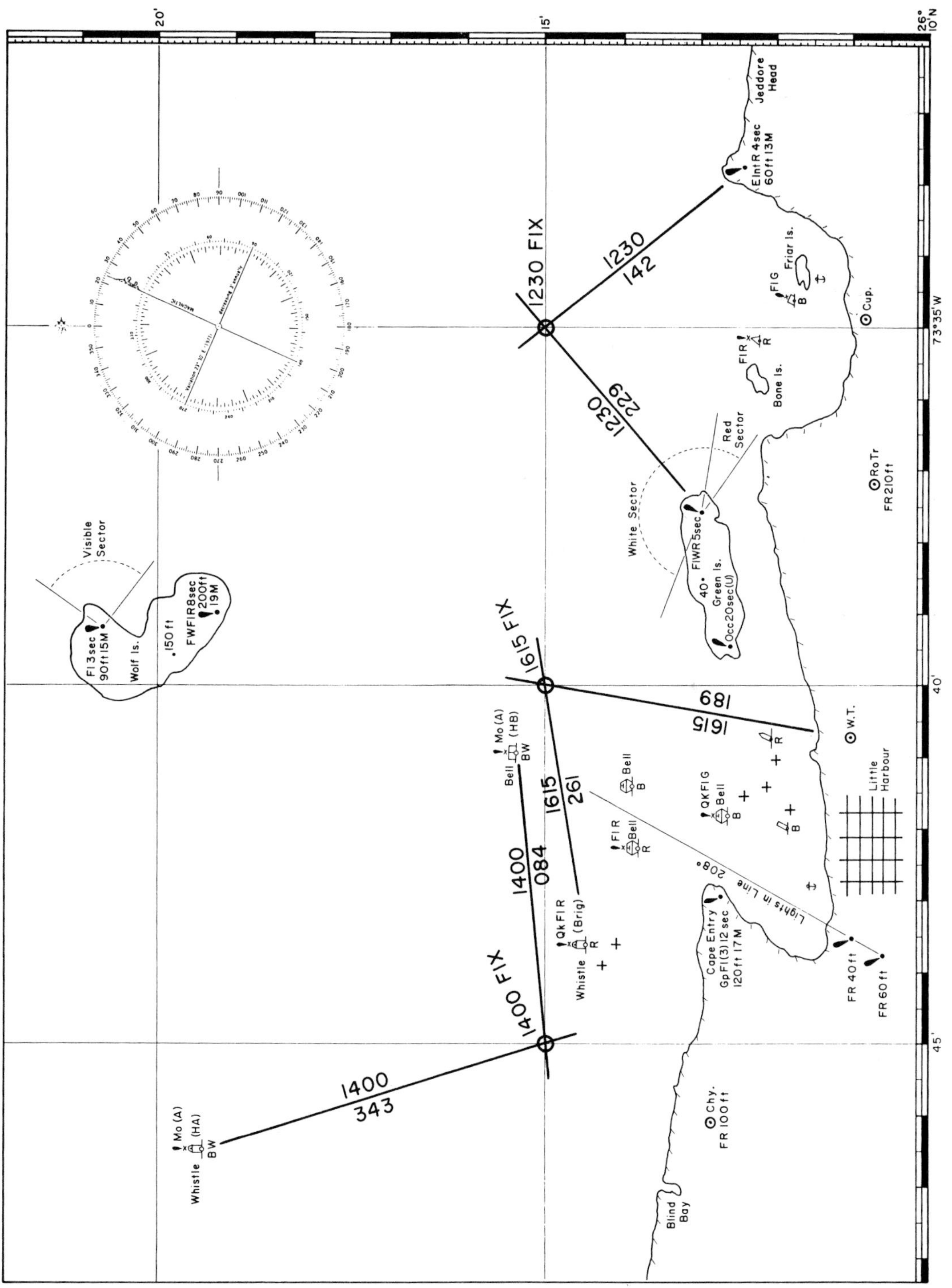

Problem 9-4 Solution Log

Time	HEADING Compass	Magnetic	True	Speed	Distance	Remarks
1000	253	*253*	*277*	5.2	—	Dr: 26° 17'.5 N 17° 39'.2 W Wolf I. south light 350 M *014 T*
1030	253	*253*	*277*	5.2	*2.6*	
1100	253	*253*	*277*	5.2	*2.6*	Buoy (HA) 310 M *334 T*
						R. Fix: 26° 17'.4 N *73° 45'.4 W*

Problem 9-5 Solution Log

Time	HEADING Compass	Magnetic	True	Speed	Distance	Remarks
1400	056	*056*	*080*	7.0	—	Dr 26° 15'.5 N 73° 38'.0 W Green I east light 136 M *160 T*
1430	056	*056*	*080*		*3.5*	
1447	056	*056*	*080*		*2.0*	Jeddore Hd. light 173 M *197 T*
						R. Fix: 26°14'.9 N *73° 31'.9 W*

Plots for these problems are on the next page.

Problem 9-4 and 9-5 Solution Plots

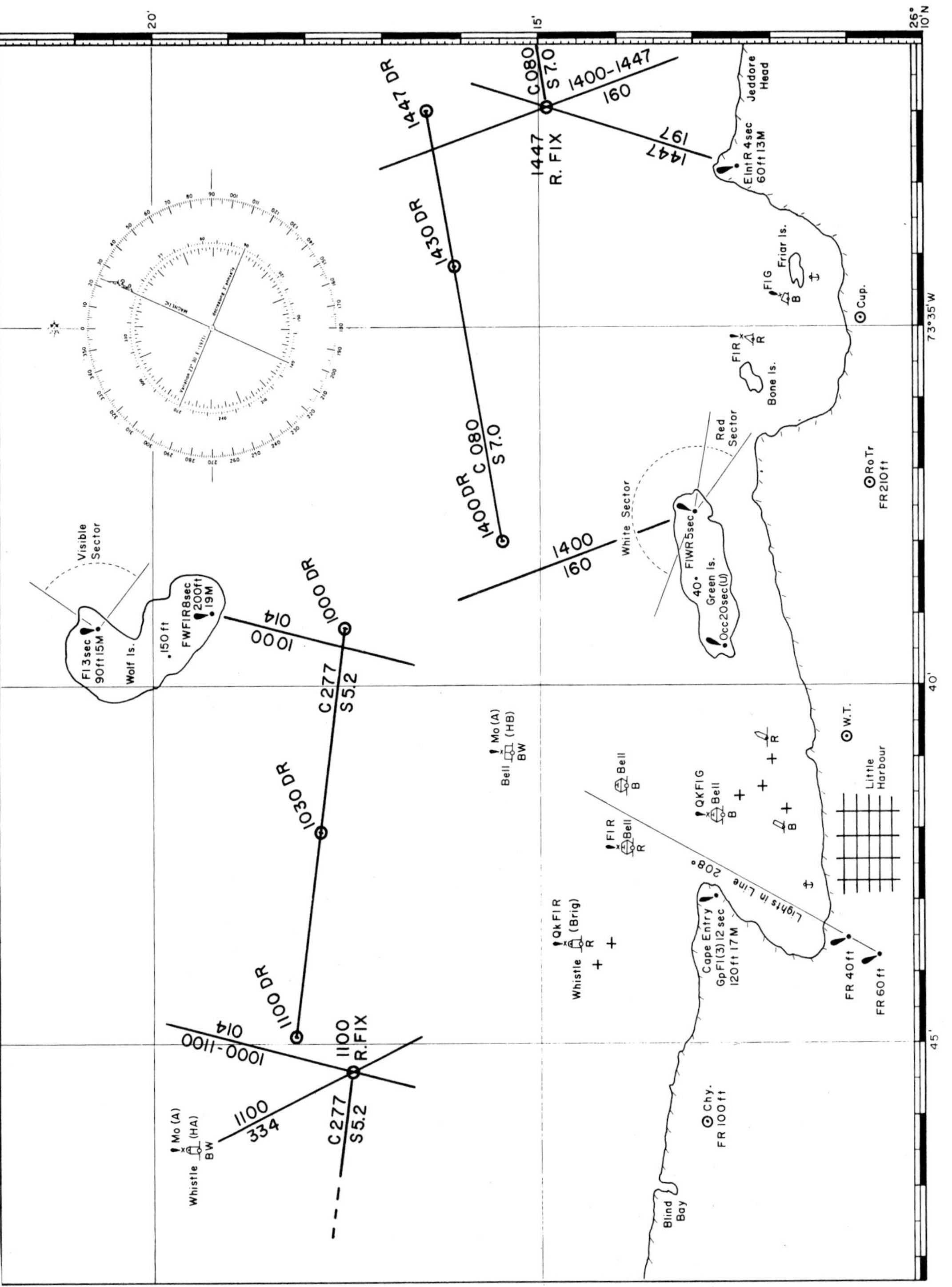

Problem 9-6 Solution

Time	HEADING Compass	Magnetic	True	Speed	Distance	Remarks
0800	281	*282*	*306*	4.4	—	DR 26°15'N 73°35'W Dev. per Table 9-1 Jeddore Hd. light 130 M *(154 T)*
0830	281	*282*	*300*	4.4	*2.2*	
0900	167	*171*	*195*	4.0	*2.2*	
0915	238	*242*	*266*	6.0	*1.0*	Big buoy 176 M
0930	238	*242*	*266*	6.0	*1.5*	
1000	238	*242*	*266*	6.0	*3.0*	*(200 T)*
						R. Fix: 26° 15'.8 N *73° 43'.1 W*

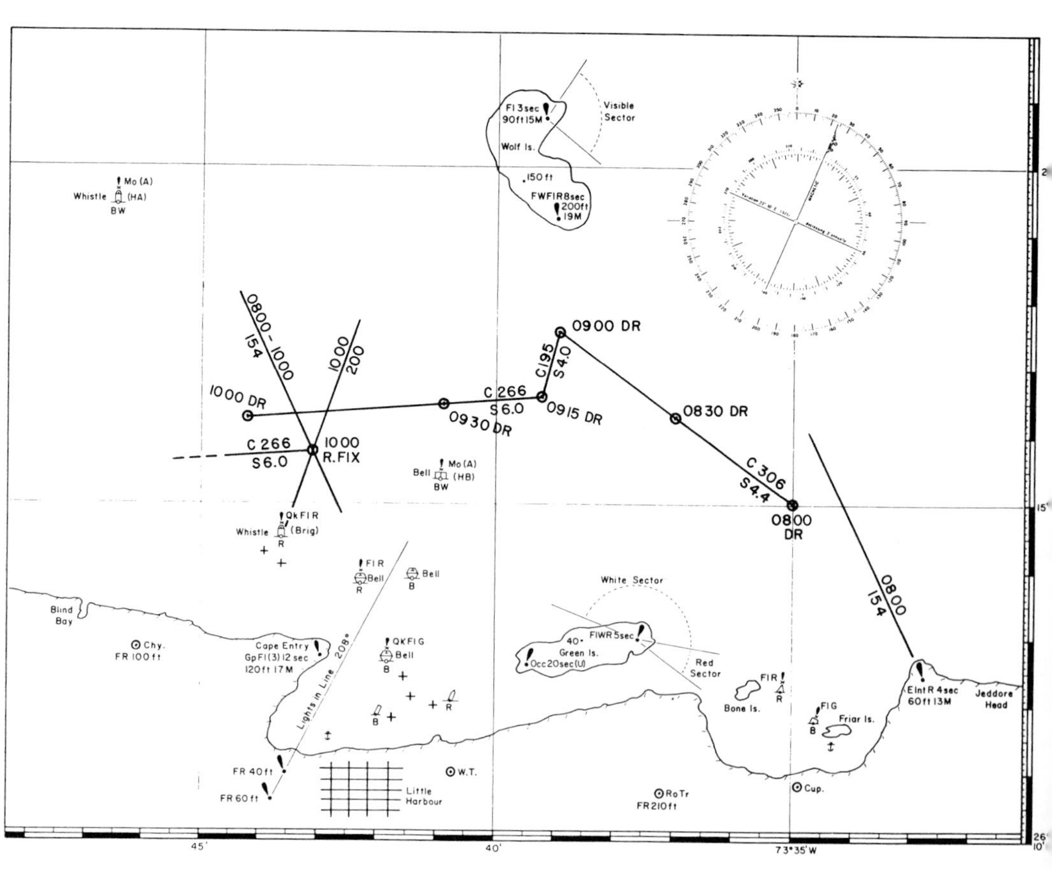

Problem 9-7 Solution

Time	HEADING Compass	Magnetic	True	Speed	Distance	Remarks
1400	056	*056*	*080*	7.0	—	Dr. 26°15'N, 73°40'W Green I. east light 117M
						Same light 193M *141 T*
1428	056	*056*	*080*	7.0	*3.3*	
						R. Fix: 26° 15'.4 N *217 T* *73° 35'.6 W*

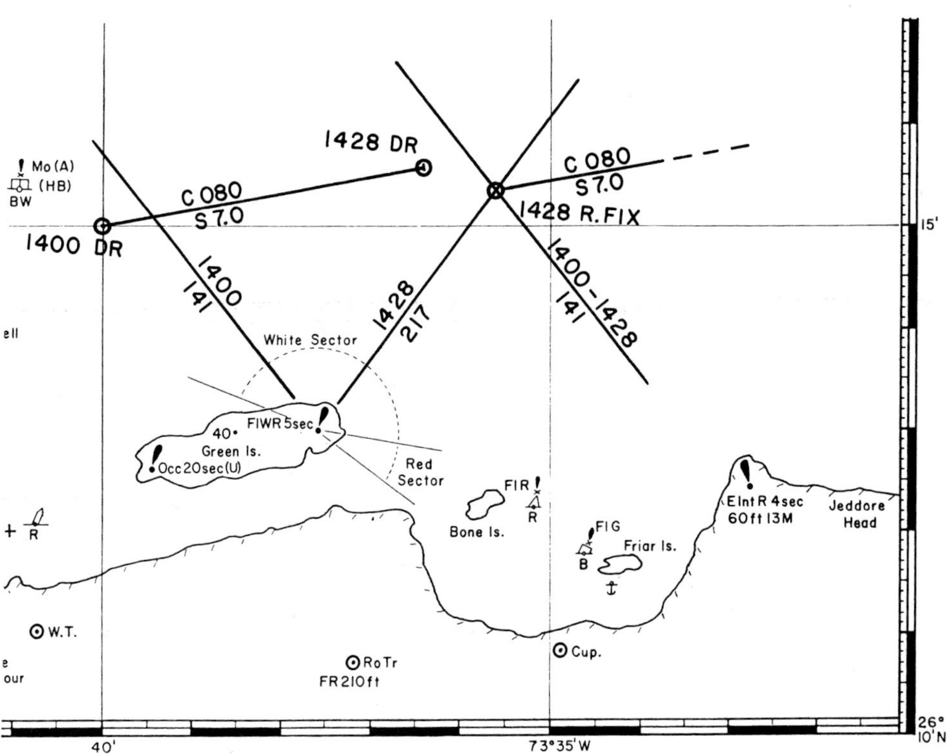

Problem 9-8 Solution

Time	HEADING Compass	Magnetic	True	Speed	True Course	Distance	Remarks
1000	285	*286*	*310*	*SMG 3.4*		—	DR: 26°15'N, 73°30'W Deviation per table 9-1 Set 200, Dr 2.1
				SMG 3.4	*290*		Jeddore Hd light 179 M *(203 T)*
1030	285	*286*	*310*	3.6 *SMG 3.4*	*290*	*1.7*	Set 200, Dr 2.1
1100	242	*246*	*270*	3.0 *SMG 3.6*	*252*	*1.7*	Set 200, Dr 2.1
1130	242	*246*	*270*	*SMG 3.6* *SMG 3.6*	*252*	*1.8*	Set 200, Dr 2.1 Jeddore Hd. light 098 M *(122 T)* *R. Fix 26° 15'.0 N* *73° 37'.3 W*

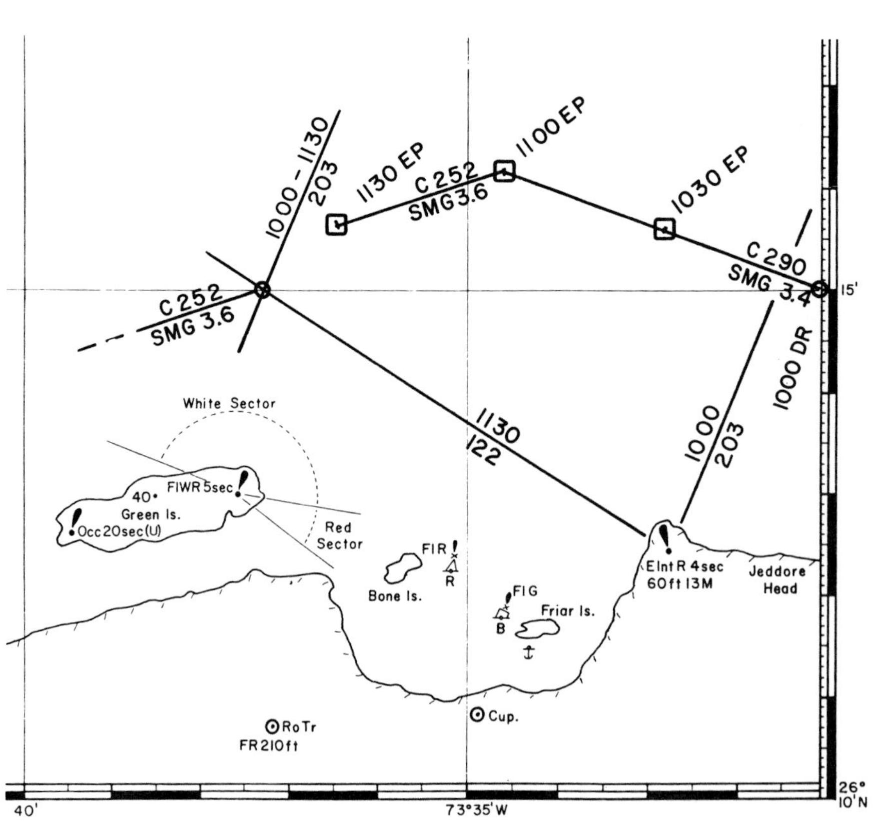

DEALERS FOR INSTRUMENTS AND EQUIPMENT

Obviously, this list cannot be complete. The dealers listed are intended to be a representative sample, with an indication of the selection available.

Canada

Gabriel Aero-Marine 1576 Hollis St. Halifax, Nova Scotia B3J 1V3 902-423-6627	General nautical instruments. Plath and Davis sextants.
Navigation World 5932 Thorncliffe Dr. N.W. Calgary, Alberta T2K 2Z7 403-274-4923	Toizaki sextants, CR slide rules, speed-time-distance templates. Sextant adjustment and calibration.
Boathouse Marine Supplies 566 Cardero St. Vancouver, B. C. V6G 2W6 604-685-4341	General nautical instruments, sextants.

United States

Weems and Plath Inc. P.O. Box 1991 Annapolis, Maryland 21404 301-263-6700	General line of high-grade instruments. Plath sextants, also Davis and Ebbco.
Sporty's Pilot Shop Clermont Coun Airport Batavia, Ohio 45103	Primarily aviation instruments, but has the CR slide rules.

INSTRUCTIONS FOR ORDERING CHARTS OR PUBLICATIONS DIRECT FROM THE CANADIAN HYDROGRAPHIC SERVICE

Payment for mail orders must be made in advance, by money order or bankable remittance (postage stamps will not be accepted) payable, in Canadian funds, to the Receiver General of Canada and sent to:

HYDROGRAPHIC CHART DISTRIBUTION OFFICE
DEPARTMENT OF THE ENVIRONMENT
1675 RUSSELL ROAD
P.O. BOX 8080
OTTAWA, ONTARIO, CANADA
K1G3H6

NAUTICAL PUBLICATIONS

These publications are of particular importance to Mariners and may be obtained from the Hydrographic Chart Distribution Office, authorized dealers, or Information Canada at the following addresses:

Information Canada, Publishing Division, Ottawa, Ontario, Canada, K1A0S9

Information Canada bookshops at:
1683 Barrington Street, Halifax, Nova Scotia
640 St. Catherine Street West, Montréal, Québec
171 Slater Street, Ottawa, Ontario
221 Yonge Street, Toronto, Ontario
393 Portage Avenue, Winnipeg, Manitoba
800 Granville Street, Vancouver, British Columbia

CHARTS AND PUBLICATIONS REGULATIONS (Published in the annual edition of Notices to Mariners)

Regulations, requiring ships to have on board, maintain and use appropriate charts, tide tables, lists of lights and other nautical publications.
The publications referred to in Regulations are included in the following listing:

Price

INFORMATION BULLETINS (Catalogues of charts and publications. Available only from the Hydrographic Chart Distribution Office and authorized dealers) ...... Free

I.B. 1 Great Lakes and Adjacent Waterways.
I.B. 4 Rainy Lake, Lake of the Woods, Lake Winnipeg, Lake Winnipegosis and Lac La Ronge.
I.B. 5 St. Lawrence River - Ile d'Anticosti to Lake Ontario.
(Formule Anglaise du Bulletin d'information 35)
I.B. 6 Northwestern Canada - Mackenzie River Basin.
I.B. 7 Island of Newfoundland and North Shore of the Gull of St. Lawrence.
I.B. 8 Nova Scotia, New Brunswick and Prince Edward Island.
I.B. 9 Labrador Coast.
I.B. 11 Hudson Bay and Hudson Strait.
I.B. 13 Southern British Columbia Coast including Vancouver Island.
I.B. 14 Northern British Columbia Coast including Queen Charlotte Islands.
I.B. 15 Canadian Arctic.
B.I. 35 Fleuve Saint-Laurent-de l'Ile d'Anticosti au Lac Ontario.
(French version of Information Bulletin 5)

SAILING DIRECTIONS

Newfoundland Pilot; 3rd, edition 1966 .... 5.00
Comprising Cape St. Francis to Cape Race, Cape Race to Cape Ray including St-Pierre and Miquelon, the Strait of Belle Isle to Cape Ray, and Cape St. Francis to Belle Isle.

Gulf and River St. Lawrence, First Edition 1973 .... 5.00
A description of the Gulf of St. Lawrence and the St. Lawrence River to Lake Ontario, including the coast of Cape Breton Island, Strait of Canso, Cabot Strait, Strait of Belle Isle, Saguenay, Richelieu and Ottawa Rivers.

Saint John River Pilot; 2nd edition 1965 .... 1.50
From Saint John Harbour to Fredericton with Grand Lake and Kennebecasis Bay.

Nova Scotia (S.E. Coast) and Bay of Fundy; 5th edition 1972 .... 5.00
Comprising the Grand Banks of Newfoundland, Sable Island, the Southeast Coast of Nova Scotia and the Bay of Fundy.

Supplements are published periodically and can be obtained without charge by purchasers of Sailing Directions.

WATER LEVEL REPORTS, ETC.

Canadian Tide & Current Tables (Bilingual)

	Price
Volume 1 — Atlantic Coast & Bay of Fundy	.50
2 — Gulf of St. Lawrence	.50
3 — St. Lawrence & Saguenay Rivers	.50
4 — Arctic & Hudson Bay	.50

These tables contain daily tide predictions for all Canadian reference ports along with tidal differences for secondary ports. Daily current predictions are also included for selected current stations except in Volume 4.

*Water Levels

	Price
Volume 1 — Inland	1.00
2 — Tidal	1.00
3 — Temporary Gauges	1.00

Annual publications which contain tabulated daily, monthly and yearly mean water levels, times and heights of observed high and low water, and other related information recorded throughout the year at permanent and temporary tide and water level gauges in the Great Lakes, the St. Lawrence and Saint John River Systems and Canadian Coastal Waters. Please specify the year required when ordering.

*Yearly Extreme Tide Levels 1.00

This booklet contains all available yearly extreme high and low tide levels at certain, past and present, tide gauging stations in Canadian Coastal Waters, prior to the commencement of their regular annual publication, in "Water Levels" 1962 or 1963, which includes all tide gauging stations.

*Monthly, Yearly and Average Mean Water Levels

	Price
Volume 1 — Inland	1.00
2 — Tidal	1.00

These tables are published annually and contain all available monthly and yearly mean levels along with 10-year and all-time average levels for most past and present permanent tide and water level gauges in the Great Lakes, the St. Lawrence River System and Canadian Coastal Waters.

*Daily Mean Water Levels

Individual Stations 1.00

These booklets contain all available daily mean levels and monthly extreme levels for most past and present tide and water level gauges in the Great Lakes, the St. Lawrence River System and Canadian Coastal Waters.

*Hydrograph No. 230 .... Free

Monthly and yearly mean tide levels for Halifax, N.S., Churchill, Man.; and Victoria, B.C.; from 1916 to date.

*Tides in Canadian Waters (English or French) .... .50

An information booklet containing an outline of the theory of tidal forces along with description and maps of the types of tides which are found in Canadian Waters.

*Tide and Water Level Bench Marks

	Price
Volume 1 — Atlantic Coast and Bay of Fundy	1.00
2 — Gulf of St. Lawrence	1.00
3 — St. Lawrence and Saguenay Rivers	1.00

These books provide the user with a comprehensive list of bench marks which are referred to the datum of Canadian Hydrographic Service charts. Elevations and descriptions of the bench marks are given along with sketches showing their location.

WATER SURVEY OF CANADA PUBLICATIONS

Surface Water Data .... Free

Contains information on stream flow and water levels (by province or region).

Surface Water Data Reference Index for Canada .... Free

Excludes Québec which publishes a separate reference index.

Sediment Data for Selected Canadian Rivers .... Free

These publications are available from Environment Canada, Enquiry Centre, Ottawa, K1A 0H3 or Information Canada.

LISTS OF LIGHTS, BUOYS AND FOG SIGNALS (Published annually)

	Price
Atlantic Coast and the Gulf and River St. Lawrence to Montréal	3.00
Inland waters (West of Montréal and East of British Columbia)	2.25
Newfoundland including the Coastal Waters of Labrador	.75

*indicates publication is available only from the Hydrographic Chart Distribution Office.

RADIO PUBLICATIONS

Radio Aids to Marine Navigation (Published quarterly)
Atlantic and Great Lakes (English or French) or Pacific
Single copy .... .75
**Yearly subscription for each section 2.00
Canadian Coastal Radiotelephone Service (Bilingual) .... Free

WEATHER PUBLICATIONS

Schedules and contents of Marine Weather Broadcasts are contained in the publication "Radio Aids to Marine Navigation" listed above under RADIO PUBLICATIONS.

*Weather Ways 2.00
An elementary textbook for the study of weather

"Using the Marine Forecast" (Form 62-9380) .... Free
A single-page leaflet delineating marine weather forecast areas in Eastern Canadian coastal waters and the St. Lawrence River with helpful hints on using the forecasts to best advantage. Available only from Regional Director, Atmospheric Environment Service at the following locations - Regional Administration Building, Montreal International Airport, Dorval, Quebec, or Box 42, Moncton, N.B.

MISCELLANEOUS

Navigation Canals (Bilingual) .... Free
Containing a description of all canals, mileages, lock dimensions, depths, etc.

Canal Regulations .... .35
Containing regulations for the guidance of those using the Ministry of Transport Navigation Canals

Small Vessel Regulations .... .60
Collision Regulations .... .60
Boating Safety Guide (English or French) .... Free
A publication which gives useful information for owners of pleasure and small commercial craft.

Ice Navigation in Canadian Waters. (Bilingual) 2.50
Code of Navigation Practices and Procedures .... .50

NOTICES TO MARINERS

Canadian "Notices to Mariners" published weekly, in English and French, contain important navigational information including amendments to Canadian Charts, Sailing Directions, Lists of Lights and Lists of Radio Aids. These "Notices" may be obtained free on request to the Chief, Marine Aids Division, Ministry of Transport, Ottawa. The collectors of Customs and Excise, the Marine Agents of the Ministry of Transport in Canada and the dealers for Canadian charts exhibit reference copies of "Notices to Mariners" in their offices.

CUSTOMS AND EXCISE REGULATIONS

Pleasure craft may enter Canada for a period of up to 12 months under a permit obtainable from Customs at the port of entry. For further information obtain a copy of "Border Crossing Information" from the Canadian Government Travel Bureau, Ottawa, Canada. Pleasure craft from Canada may enter the U.S.A. by obtaining a Cruising Permit from the Port Director at the port of entry.

**indicates publication is available only from Information Canada and Information Canada bookshops.

CHART DEALERS

ALBERTA	
Calgary	Carter Mapping Limited, 510 5th Street, S.W.
	Nickle Map Service, Ltd., 330 Ninth Avenue, S.W.
Edmonton	Technical Division, Department of Lands and Forests Natural Resources Building
BRITISH COLUMBIA	
Alert Bay	Alert Bay Shipyards Limited
Bamfield	Ostrum's Machine Shop
Bella Bella	B.C. Packers Limited
Bella Coola	Bella Coola Supply Co.
Big Bay	Big Bay Marina
Birds Eye Cove	Maple Bay Marina
Blind Channel	Blind Channel General Store
Bull Harbour	Canadian Fishing Co. Ltd.
Butedale	Canadian Fishing Co. Ltd.
Campbell River	Campbell River Sportsman Centre, 2115 Island Highway North
	Paper Clip, 994 Island Highway
	Tyee Marine, 880 Island Highway
	Marshall's Sporting Goods, 1120 Island Highway
Canoe Bay	Canoe Cove Store, 2300 Canoe Cove Road
Coal Harbour	Coal Harbour General Store
Courtenay	Peter's Sport Shop, 505 Duncan Avenue
	The Sports Centre, 433 - 5th Street
Cowichan Bay	Allen's Baystore Marina
	Anchor Marina
Crofton	Crofton Hardware
Dawson's Landing	Dawson's Landing General Store
Deep Cove	Deep Cove Marina, 10992 Madrona Drive
Delta	The Sportsman, 1183 B 56th Street
Duncan	Bucky's Sport Shop, 171 Craig Street
	Jim's Sporting Goods, 163 Station Street
East Thurlow Island	Shoal Bay Resort Ltd.
Egmont	Bathgate Egmont Enterprises
	Egmont Marina and Resort
Fisherman's Cove	Castle Industries Ltd., 5776 Marine Drive
Gabriola Island	Silva Bay Resort Ltd.
	Silva Bay Boatel
Galiano Island	El Sea Shop
	Montague Harbour Marina
Ganges	Driftwood Bookstore
	Ganges Boat Yard
Gibsons	Walt Nygren Sales
	Kruse Drug Stores Ltd., 1557 Gower Point Road
Hot Springs Cove	Canadian Fishing Co. Ltd.
Kitimat	K.T. Sporting Goods, 266 City Centre
Kyuquot	Kyuquot General Store
Ladysmith	Knights Limited, 521 - 1st Avenue
Lund	Lund Breakwater Inn Limited
Maple Bay	Richland Holdings
Masset	North Coast Supplies Co. Ltd.
Ministrel Island	Minstrel Island General Store
Namu	B.C. Packers Limited
Nanaimo	Bell Buoy Marina Ltd., 1340 Stewart Avenue
	Nanaimo News Stand, 8 Church Street
	Nanaimo Sportsman, 76 Commercial Street
	Newcastle Marina Ltd., 1300 Stewart Avenue
	Richardson's Marina, 1740 Stewart Avenue
Nanoose	Beachcomber Marina
Nelson	Nelson Marine Service, 524 Munro Street
New Westminster	Burr Office Supplies (Willsons), 554 Columbia Street
	Nixon's Book Store Limited, 635 Clarkson Street
North Pender Island	Puerto Lindo Marina, Port Browning
Oak Bay	Oak Bay Marine Sales, 1327 Beech Drive
	Samrend.200, Oak Bay Avenue
Port Alberni	Alberni Engineering and Shipyards, 104 Bird Street
	Alberni Hardware Company, 111 First Avenue North
	Port Alberni Marine Industries Ltd., 103 Bird Street
	Woodwards Stores
Port Albion	Canadian Fishing Co. Ltd.
Port Hardy	Port Hardy Hardware
	Seafood Products

Powell River	Bowes Hardware, 4555 Marine Avenue
Prince Rupert	Nelson Bros. Fisheries Ltd.
	Northern Marine Supply Ltd., 1st Avenue & McBride Street
	Prince Rupert Fishermens Supply Co. Ltd., Cow Bay
Quadra Island	April Point Resort Ltd., Quathiaski Cove
Queen Charlotte Island (Moresby)	Charlisle Clothiers Ltd., Queen Charlotte City
Queen Cove	Canadian Fishing Co. Ltd.
Refuge Cove	Refuge Cove General Store
Richmond	Nelson Bros. Fisheries Ltd., 1274 Trites Road
Rivers Inlet	J.B. Graham, Duncanby Landing
Salmon Arm	Mr. D. Marshall, The Observer Ltd.
Sechelt	Kruse Drug Stores Limited
	Tyee Products
Secret Cove	Secret Cove Marina
Sidney	Cornish's Book & Stationery Ltd., 2410 Beacon Avenue
Sointula	Sointula Co-operative Store Association
Sooke	G.E. Pallister, Foot of Maple Avenue
South Pender Island	Bedwell Harbour Resort
Steveston	Frederick Goertz Ltd., 398 Moncton Street
Stewart	Stewart Outdoor Ventures
Stuart Island	J.R. Howe's Resorts Limited
Surge Narrows	Dodman's Store
Thetis Island	Telegraph Harbour Marina
	Thetis Island Marina
Tofino	Canadian Fishing Co. Ltd.
	Walters Stores
Tsehum Harbour	Bosun's Charters Ltd., 10775 McDonald Park Road
	Van Isle Marina, 2306 Harbour Road
Ucluelet	Madden's General Store
	Ray Tec Services Ltd.
Vancouver	Adams Marine & Electronics, 1830 Ontario Street
	Aquacraft Marine Ltd., 1136 Boundary Road
	Boathouse Yacht Supplies Ltd., Foot of Cardero Street
	Bovey Marine (1952), 1117 West Pender Street
	Canadian Fishing Co. Ltd.
	Dominion Map Ltd., 626 Howe Street
	Frederick Goertz Ltd., 1328 West Pender Street
	Gundry Bilmac Ltd., 996 Powell Street
	Kelvin Hughes Division, 1790 West Georgia Street
	Kitsilano Marine & Lumber, 1500 West Second Avenue
	Small Craft of Canada, 112 East 6th Avenue
	Sounder Sales & Service Ltd., 683 West Hastings Street
	The Quarterdeck, 570 Seymour Street
	W.G. McWilliam Ltd., 1645 West 3rd Avenue
	Western Marine Supply Co. Ltd., 528 Powell Street
	Woodwards Stores, 101 West Hastings Street
Victoria	Bosun's Locker, 580 Johnson Street
	Frederick Goertz Ltd., 25 Dallas Road
	Island Marine Supplies, 1214 Wharf Street
	Ship Chandlers (McQuades), 1252 Wharf Street
	Spencer's Stores Ltd., 1110 Government Street
	The Island Blue Print, 1124 Blanshard Street
Wellington	Plaza News and Variety, Country Club Plaza
Westview	Marine Traders 6791 Wharf Street
Winter Harbour	Marpic Marine Sales
Zeballos	Canadian Fishing Co. Ltd.

MANITOBA

Churchill	Port Manager, National Harbours Board
Winnipeg	Surveys, Mapping & Lands Branch, Dept. of Mines, Resources & Environment Management, 1007 Century Street

NEWFOUNDLAND

Grand Falls	Baird Campbell Ltd.
St. John's	Campbell's Ships Supplies, 689 Water Street W.
	Kelvin Hughes Division, Smith Industries North America Ltd., 24½ Flavin Street

NEW BRUNSWICK

Castalia, Grand Manan	Herbert C. Macaulay
Fredericton	Department of Natural Resources
Saint John	Kelvin Hughes Division, Smith Industries North America Ltd., 72 Germain Street
	Vaughan Electronics Ltd., 1 Courtney Causeway

NORTHWEST TERRITORIES	
Fort Smith	Administrator of the Mackenzie, Department of Indian Affairs and Northern Development
Hay River	Area Administrator, Department of Indian Affairs and Northern Development
Inuvik	Sub-District Administrator, Department of Indian Affairs and Northern Development
Yellowknife	Resident Geologist, Department of Indian Affairs and Northern Development
NOVA SCOTIA	
Antigonish	Buckley's Marine Sales
Barrington Passage	Mar-Electra Co., Ltd.
Chester	Aubrey S. Evans
Digby	May's Stationery Ltd., 69 Water Street
Halifax	Gabriel Aero-Marine Instruments Ltd., 1576 Hollis Street
	Kelvin Hughes Division, Smith Industries North America Ltd., 5140 Prince Street
Liscomb Mills	Liscombe Lodge Marina
Lockeport	Swim Bros. Ltd.
Louisburg	Lewis & Company Limited
Lunenburg	Atlantic Shipbuilding Co., Ltd., 194 Montague Street
	Kinley Drug Co., Ltd., 264 Lincoln Street
North Sydney	Nickerson Outfitting Co. Ltd., Commercial Street
Shelburne	Robertson's Hardware
Sydney	Sydney Ship Supply Company, Dominion Street and Victoria Road
Western Shore	Scotia Yacht Marina Division Ltd., Mahone Bay Yacht Harbour
Yarmouth	Gateway Engineering Ltd., 83 Water Street
	R.H. Davis & Co., Ltd., Sherora Building, 361 Main Street
ONTARIO	
Barrie	The Port Hole, Bayfield Mall
Bay Ridges	The Aft Cabin, 595 Annland Street
Belleville	C. Keeble Sail Makers, 11 Water Street
Brighton	Salusbury Marina
Brockville	The St. Lawrence Engine Company Limited, St. Andrews Street
Burlington	Canada Centre for Inland Waters
	Robert O. Elstone Stationery, 3009 New Street, Roseland Plaza
Cobourg	Skeena Marina (July and August only)
Collingwood	Fisherman Point Marina, St. Lawrence Street
Cornwall	Kyte's, 217 Pitt Street
Desbarats	Langstaff Marine Ltd., Kensington Point
Espanola	Skipper Ed's Marine, 236 Station Road
Fairport Beach	East Shore Marina, 1295 Wharf Street
Fenelon Falls	King's Marina
Gananoque	Bennetts Hardware Ltd., 185 King Street
	Cuttle Marine, 129 South Street
	Donevan's Hardware Ltd., 135 King Street
Grand Bend	Manore Marine Ltd.
Gravenhurst	Gravenhurst Board of Trade, 140 John Street
Hamilton	Kelvin Hughes Division, Smith Industries North America Ltd., 103 Vine Street
Hawkesbury	Carillon-Marine, 945 Main Street E.
Ivy Lea	Holiday Afloat Marina
Kenora	Johnson's Pharmacy, 116 Main Street S. and 224 Second Street S.
	Pat's Stationery and Record Shop, 218 Second Street S.
	Strains Stationery Ltd., 213 First Street S.
Keswick	Ships Store
Killarney	A & R Marina
	Sportsman's Inn
Kincardine	Kincardine's Highland Cove Marina
Kingston	Kingston Yacht Club
	Knapp's Boats, Ontario Street E.
	Millan Bros., 53-55 Princess Street
	R.W. Alford & Company Ltd., 121 Princess Street
	Rideau Marina (Kingston) Limited
	The Port Hole, Kingston Shopping Centre, Princess Street
	Treasure Island Marina, R.R. 1
Kitchener	E. Ben Koenig Ltd., 200 Highland Road West
Lavigne	Lavigne Hotel, Highway 64
Little Current	Turners' of Little Current Limited
London	Oxford Book Shops Limited, 742 Richmond Street and Wellington Square
Long Sault	Long Sault Marina

Meldrum Bay	Arbour's General Store
Midland	Downer's Yacht Haven, King Street
	Rycroft Marina Limited, William Street at Waterfront
Morrisburg	Crysler Park Marina
Murray Canal	Bridgemaster's Office, Brighton Road Bridge
Niagara-on-the-Lake	The Gillingham Yacht Basin
Nobel	Killbear Marina and Shopping Centre, Pengallie Bay
North Bay	Baywood Marine Ltd., Government Dock
Oakville	Metro Marine Limited, Triller Street (Bronte)
Orillia	Crothers Twin Lakes Marina Limited, 674 Atherley Road
Oshawa	Oshawa Yachthaven Limited
Ottawa	The Port Hole, 396 Bank Street
Owen Sound	McGruer & Clark Ltd., The Georgian Marine, 2505 Third Avenue W.
Parry Sound	Information Bureau, The Parry Sound Chamber of Commerce, 2 Louisa Street
Penetanguishene	Bay Marine
Peterborough	Peterborough Chamber of Commerce, 116 Hunter Street W.
	Trent Canal Office, Dept. of Indian Affairs and Northern Development, Federal Building, Charlotte Street
Picton	Picton Bay Marina, 31 Bridge Street
Point Edward	Boston Sails Limited, 120 Michigan Avenue
	Bridgeview Marina
Port Carling	Duke Boats Limited
Port Colborne	Bell Marine & Mill Supply Ltd., West Pier
	Colonial Yacht Harbour Limited, Marina Drive
	Millen Marine & Mill Supply Ltd., 234 West Street
	Stan Kennedy Limited, 162 West Street
Port Dover	Strobridge Boat Works Limited
Port Elgin	Port Elgin Marina
Port Hope	Skeena Marina (July and August only)
Port Severn	Bush's Boat Livery and Marine
	Lockmaster, Port Severn Lock
Port Stanley	Port Stanley Marina Limited, Carlow Road
Rockport	Ed Huck Marine Ltd.
	W. E. Andress & Son
Rossport	Rossport Marina Ltd.
St. Catharines	The Port Hole, Pen Centre, Glendale Avenue
Sarnia	Manley's Limited, 142 Lochiel Street
Sault Ste. Marie	St. Lawrence Seaway Authority, Western Region, Sault Ste. Marie Canal
South Porcupine	Night Hawk Marina, Night Hawk Lake
Stoney Creek	The Port Hole, Eastgate Square, Store E2, Centennial Drive
Sudbury	Whiskey Jack Ltd., 2300 Maley Drive East
Thessalon	Bill's Marine, 56 Algoma Street, East Government Wharf
Thunder Bay	Lowerys Limited, Corner of Cumberland at Park
Tobermory	Big Tub Lodge
	Texaco Marine Service
Toronto	Boating Magazine, 5200 Dixie Road, Suite 204 (Mississauga)
	Davidson Sails & Marine Supplies Ltd., 107 King Street East
	Lackie's Marina, 4 South Kingsway
	Lakeview Marine, 857 Lakeshore Road E. (Port Credit)
	Mercator Marine Limited, 1088 Warden Avenue, Scarborough
	Tarling Map Mounting Co., 105 Church Street
	The Port Hole, 458 Eglinton Avenue W. and Sherway Gardens, G10, 25 The West Mall, Etobicoke
	The Rigging Shoppe, 1197 Ellesmere Road
	J.J. Taylor & Sons Ltd., 2 Stadium Road
	Tom Taylor Company Ltd., 136 Adelaide Street E.
	Willowdale Postal Station "C", Fairview Mall
Trenton	Darling's Stationery, 24 Dundas Street W.
	Lockmaster, Lock No. 1
Washago	Trent Canal Office
Waterloo	The Port Hole, Westmount Place
Wiarton	Fisherman's Wharf

PRINCE EDWARD ISLAND

Charlottetown	A. Kennedy & Co. Ltd., 32 Queen Street
Summerside	J. Lorne Driscoll Coal and Produce, Water Street

QUÉBEC

Cap-aux-Meules, Iles de la Madeleine	Les Agrès de Marine des Îles Ltée.
Grande-Rivière	Luc Imbeau, LPI Photo Enr.
Lachine	Boulanger Yacht Inc., 2225, boulevard St. Joseph

Lacolle	Association des fonctionnaires des Douanes et Accises, Bureau des Douanes
Montréal	Gabriel Aero-Marine Instruments Ltd., 351, rue St. Paul ouest
	Harrison Company, 1448, rue Ste-Catherine ouest
	Kelvin Hughes Division, Smith Industries North America Ltd., 401, rue McGill
	Marina Port Ste-Hélène
	The Binnacle, 1380, rue Sherbrooke ouest
Québec	T.J. Moore Ltée., 122, Côte de la Montagne
Ste-Anne-de-Bellevue	Ste. Annes Marine Service Ltd., 46, rue Ste-Anne
Sorel	Agent maritime du district, Ministere des Transports, 15, rue Prince

PUBLICATIONS RELATING TO NAUTICAL CHARTS PUBLISHED AND ISSUED BY THE NATIONAL OCEAN SURVEY

NATIONAL OCEAN SURVEY OFFICES

Information concerning publications and activities of the National Ocean Survey may be obtained by addressing the Director, National Ocean Survey, National Oceanic and Atmospheric Administration, Rockville, Maryland 20852, or from the following National Ocean Survey offices:

†NORFOLK	439 West York Street Norfolk, Virginia 23510	†DETROIT	Lake Survey Center 630 Federal Bldg. and U.S. Courthouse Detroit, Michigan 48226
SEATTLE	1801 Fairview Avenue East Seattle, Washington 98102	†ANCHORAGE	Chart Sales & Control Data Office Room 303, 632 6th Ave. Anchorage, Alaska 99501

†National Ocean Survey nautical charts may be purchased at sales counters in these offices.

UNITED STATES COAST PILOTS

A series of books that cover a wide variety of information important to navigators of United States coastal and intracoastal waters. Subjects include navigation regulations, outstanding landmarks, channel and anchorage peculiarities, dangers, weather, ice, freshets, routes, pilotage, and port facilities. New editions issued since 1970 are computerized and published annually. Free annual supplements are issued for older editions containing changes reported since issue dates.

Atlantic Coast:

- No. 1, Eastport to Cape Cod, 1973 .... $2.00
- No. 2, Cape Cod to Sandy Hook, 1974 .... 2.50
- No. 3, Sandy Hook to Cape Henry, 1974 .... 2.50
- No. 4, Cape Henry to Key West, 1974 .... 2.50
- No. 5, Gulf of Mexico, Puerto Rico and Virgin Islands, 1974 .... 2.50

Pacific Coast:

- No. 7, California, Oregon, Washington and Hawaii, 1968 .... 2.00

Alaska:

- No. 8, Dixon Entrance to Cape Spencer, 1969 .... 2.50
- No. 9, Cape Spencer to Beaufort Sea, 1964 .... 2.00

TIDE TABLES

Predictions of the times and heights of high and low waters for every day in the year for many of the more important harbors, and differences for obtaining predictions for numerous other places are given in annual tide tables.

- Tide Tables, East Coast, North & South America $2.00
- Tide Tables, West Coast, North & South America 2.00
- Tide Tables, Europe & West Coast of Africa 2.00
- Tide Tables, Central & Western Pacific & Indian Oceans 2.00

TIDAL CURRENT TABLES

Advance information relative to currents is made available in annual tidal current tables which include daily predictions of the times of slack water and the times and velocities of maximum flood and ebb currents for a number of waterways together with differences for obtaining predictions for numerous other places.

- Tidal Current Tables, Atlantic Coast of North America $2.00
- Tidal Current Tables, Pacific Coast of North America and Asia 2.00

TIDAL CURRENT CHARTS

These publications each consist of a set of 12 charts which depict, by means of arrows and figures, the direction and velocity of the tidal current for each hour of the tidal cycle. The charts, which may be used for any year present a comprehensive view of the tidal current movement in the respective waterways as a whole and also supply a means for readily determining for any time the direction and velocity of the current at various localities throughout the water areas covered.

- Tidal Current Charts, Boston Harbor, 3rd Edition $2.00
- Tidal Current Charts, Narragansett Bay to Nantucket Sound, 3rd Edition 2.00
- Tidal Current Charts, Narragansett Bay, 1st Edition (Reprint 1971) 2.00
- Tidal Current Charts, Block Island Sound and Eastern Long Island Sound, 1st Edition 2.00
- Tidal Current Charts, Long Island Sound and Block Island Sound, 4th Edition 2.00
- Tidal Current Charts, New York Harbor, 7th Edition 2.00
- Tidal Current Charts, Delaware Bay and River, 2nd Edition 2.00
- Tidal Current Charts, Upper Chesapeake Bay, 1st Edition 2.00
- Tidal Current Charts, Charleston Harbor, S.C., 1st Edition 2.00
- Tidal Current Charts, San Francisco Bay, 5th Edition (Reprint Sept. 1972) 2.00
- Tidal Current Charts, Puget Sound — Northern Part, 2nd Edition 2.00
- Tidal Current Charts, Puget Sound — Southern Part, 2nd Edition 2.00

The Narragansett Bay and New York Harbor tidal current charts are to be used with the annual tide tables. The other charts require the annual current tables.

TIDAL CURRENT DIAGRAMS

The Tidal Current Diagrams are a series of 12 monthly diagrams to be used with the Block Island sound and Eastern Long Island Sound Tidal Current Charts, and Long Island Sound and Black Island Sound Tidal Current Charts.

MISCELLANEOUS MAPS AND PUBLICATIONS

No.	Price	Title	Scale	Date
		NAUTICAL CHART CATALOGS		
1	Free	Atlantic and Gulf Coasts including Puerto Rico and the Virgin Islands		1974
2	Free	Pacific Coast including Hawaii, Guam, and Samoa Islands		1974
3	Free	Alaska		1974
4	Free	Great Lakes		1975
		CHART EDITIONS		
	Free	Dates of Latest Editions, Nautical Charts	Issued quarterly	
		SPECIAL MAPS		
1	$0.50	Nautical Chart Symbols and Abbreviations (pamphlet form)		1972
39Tr	.25	Nautical Training Chart (Great Lakes)	1:100,000	1972
116-SCTr	.25	Nautical Training Chart (Long Island Sound)	1:20,000-1:40,000	1970
1210Tr	.25	Nautical Training Chart (Narragansett Bay)	1:80,000	1963
		OUTLINE MAPS		
3045	2.00	United States and Adjacent Continental Shelf	1:5,000,000	1974
3060	.70	U.S. Outline Map, Lambert Conformal Conic Projection	1:5,000,000	1952
3068	.20	U.S. Outline Map, Lambert Zenithal Equal Area Projection	1:7,500,000	1952
3069	.40	Alaska Outline Map, Lambert Conformal Conic Projection (buff land tint)	1:5,000,000	1955
3074	.40	Great Circle, United States, Gnomonic Projection	1:5,094,000	1966
3078	.60	U.S. Outline Map (in two parts), Lambert Conformal Conic Projection	1:3,000,000	1952
3084	.10	Outline Map, United States	1:17,800,000	1951
3085	.25	U.S. Outline Map, Murdoch's projection on intersecting cone	1:7,000,000	1951
3090	.40	World, Mercator Projection	1:38,000,000	1966
		MISCELLANEOUS		
3008-3021	.25ea	Regional Seismicity Maps		
3060c	2.00	U.S. Base Map in gradient tints (two parts)	1:3,000,000	1956
	.25	Outline maps for construction of a model of the World; produces a "Lambert globe" 9 inches in diameter	1:55,803,788	1944
	.60	Distances Between United States Ports		1973
		PROJECTIONS		
3062	.25	Equatorial Gnomonic Projection	1:50,000,000	1942
3063	.25	Gnomonic Projection, Polar-Equatorial	1:50,000,000	
3065	.40	Equatorial Azimuthal Equidistant Projection	1:52,670,165	1944
3099	.40	Aitoff's Equal Area Projection of the Sphere		
		WORLD CHART ON AZIMUTHAL EQUIDISTANT PROJECTION		
3042	.40	Based on New York City	1:47,423,730	1951

UNITED STATES ISOMAGNETIC CHARTS

No.	Price	Title	Scale	Date
3077	.75	Isogonic chart including isoporic lines (Magnetic Declination)	Conterminous 48 states and Alaska ....1:5,000,000 (Hawaii inset) ....1:7,500,000 (each chart includes all 50 states)	1970
				1965
3077i	.50	Isoclinic chart including isoporic lines (Magnetic inclination)		1965
3077h	.50	Horizontal Intensity including isoporic lines		1965
3077z	.50	Vertical Intensity including isoporic lines		1965
3077f	.50	Total Intensity including isoporic lines		

GEOPHYSICAL MAPS

Price	Title	
2.00	Bathymetric	Free indexes showing available coverage may be obtained from the Distribution Division (C-44) National Ocean Survey, Riverdale, Maryland, 20840.
2.00	Sea Map Series (bathymetric)	
2.00	Overlaps (Gravity or Magnetic)	

PUBLISHED AND ISSUED BY OTHER FEDERAL AGENCIES

NOTICES TO MARINERS

The Weekly Notice to Mariners is published by the Defense Mapping Agency Hydrographic Center (DMAHC), to advise mariners of important matters affecting navigational safety, including new hydrographic discoveries, changes in channels and navigational aids, etc. These notices contain selected items from the Local Notices to Mariners and other reported marine information required by ocean-going vessels. The Notice to Mariners also provides information specifically useful for updating the latest editions of nautical charts and publications produced by the Defense Mapping Agency Hydrographic Center (DMAHC), the National Ocean Survey, and the U.S. Coast Guard.

Local Notice to Mariners are issued by each Coast Guard District to disseminate important information affecting navigational safety within the District. Since temporary information, known or expected to be of short duration, is not included in the Weekly Notice to Mariners, the appropriate Local Notice to Mariners may be the only source of such information. Small craft using the Intracoastal Waterway and other waterways and small harbors that are not normally used by ocean-going vessels will require the Local Notices to Mariners to keep charts and related publications up-to-date.

Local Notice to Mariners may be obtained free from the Commander of the Local Coast Guard District.

Authorized sales agents of the National Ocean Survey maintain reference files of notices to mariners for customer consultation.

THE AMERICAN NAUTICAL ALMANAC

Published by the U.S. Naval Observatory. For sale by the Superintendent of Documents, U.S. Government Printing Office, Washington, D.C. 20402.

UNITED STATES COAST GUARD LIGHT LIST

These lists are intended to furnish more complete information concerning aids to navigation than can be conveniently shown on charts. They are not intended to be used in navigation in the place of charts and coast pilots and should not be so used. The charts should be consulted for the location of all aids to navigation. It may be dangerous to use aids to navigation without reference to charts.

For sale by the Superintendent of Documents, U.S. Government Printing Office, Washington, D.C., 20402.

Light List, Vol. 1, Atlantic Coast from St. Croix River, Maine to Little River, South Carolina.... Price $4.75
Light List, Vol. II, Atlantic and Gulf Coasts from Little River, South Carolina to Rio Grande, Texas .... Price 4.60
Light List, Vol. III, Pacific Coast and Pacific Islands .... Price 3.15
Light List, Vol. IV, Great Lakes .... Price 2.50
Light List, Vol. V, Mississippi River System .... Price 4.25

UNITED STATES COAST GUARD DISTRICT OFFICES

FIRST	150 Causeway Street Boston, Mass. 02114	EIGHTH	Customhouse, New Orleans, La. 70130
THIRD	Governors Island, New York, N.Y. 10004	NINTH	Federal Office Building 1240 East 9th. St., Cleveland, Ohio 44199
FIFTH	Federal Building, 431 Crawford Street, Portsmouth, Virginia 23705	ELEVENTH	Heartwell Building 19 Pine Avenue Long Beach, Calif. 90802
SEVENTH	Room 1018, Federal Building 51 Southwest First Avenue, Miami, Fla. 33130	TWELFTH	Appraisers Building 630 Sansome St. San Francisco, Calif. 94126
		THIRTEENTH	Alaska Building 618 Second Avenue Seattle, Wash. 98104
		FOURTEENTH	677 Ala Moana Blvd. Honolulu, Hawaii 96813

Offices of the Defense Mapping Agency Hydrographic Center (Pilot Charts)

DMAHC OFFICES IN THE PACIFIC OCEAN AREA

San Diego, California, Building 654, U.S. Naval Air Station, North Island.
San Diego Detachment, San Pedro, California, Customs House (Terminal Island) 300 South Ferry Street.
Honolulu, Hawaii, Building 30, 3631 Nimitz Highway.
Atsugi, Japan, Building 181, U.S. Naval Air Station.
Cubi Point, Republic of the Philippines, Building 120—6, U.S. Naval Air Station.

DMAHC OFFICES IN THE ATLANTIC OCEAN AREA

Norfolk, Virginia, Building SP-238, U.S. Naval Air Station.
Jacksonville, Florida, Building 712, U.S. Naval Air Station.
Rodman, Canal Zone, Building 1501, near Pier 18 in Balboa, at the corner of Balboa Avenue and Pier Street.
Representative in Cristobal, Canal Zone, Customhouse.
Naples, Italy, Building 12, U.S. Naval Air Facility.

AUTHORIZED NAUTICAL CHART AGENTS FOR THE SALE OF NAUTICAL CHARTS AND RELATED PUBLICATIONS OF THE NATIONAL OCEAN SURVEY

ALABAMA—

Bayou La Batre: Coleman Marine & Hardware, Inc., 1 Burch Drive
Bon Secour: Coleman Marine & Hardware, Inc.
Dauphin Islands: Ship & Shore Sports Supplies, 401 Lemoyne Drive
Foley: Coleman Marine & Hardward, Inc., 119 So. McKenzie St.
Mobile: McLeod Marine, 1501 South Beltline Highway
†*Mobile Ship Chandlery Company, 256 Saint Louis Street
*Holmes and Company, 1205 Spring Hill Avenue
Orange Beach: Safe Harbor Marina, "On Cotton Bayou"

ALASKA—

Anchorage: Alaska Map Service, 723 W. Sixth Avenue 99501
Cordova: Hammersmith's Hardware, Maine Street 99574
Craig: J.T. Brown's Store, Main Street at Waterfront 99921
Gustavus: Alaska National Parks & Monuments Assn., Glacier Bay Branch, Glacier Bay National Monument 99326
Homer: The Sporter Arms Company, Airport Road 99603
Saling's, Sterling Highway 99603
Sportsman's Marine Supply, St. Rt. A Box 106 99603
Hoonah: Hoonah Seafoods
Juneau: Southeast Marine Center, Inc., 1415 Harbor Way 99801
Ketchikan: †*Service Electric Co., Inc., 744 Water Street 99901
Kodiak: Norman Sutliff & Son, Inc. 99615
Kodiak Outboard, Mill Bay Road 99615
Pelican: †Pelican Cold Storage Company 99832
Petersburg: Trading Union, Main Street North 99833
Port Protection: B. S. Trading Post, Port Protection, Ak. 99901
Sand Point: Aleutian Commercial Co. 99661
Seward: Durant's Hardware, 236 Fourth Avenue 99664
Sitka: Sitka Cold Storage Company, 201 Kathlean Street 99835
Tri-Ways Marina, 265 Katlean Street
Soldotna: C. L. Parker, RLS, Sterling Highway, 1/2 mile East of Soldotna Junction 99669
Tenakee Springs: Snyder Mercantile Company 99841
Unalaska: Carl's Commercial Company 99685
Valdez: Marine Ventures, Inc. 99686
Wrangell: Ottesen's, Inc., 91 Front Street 99929

ARIZONA—

Katherine: Katherine Ranger Station
Temple Bar: Temple Bar Ranger Station
Willow Beach: Willow Beach Ranger Station

CALIFORNIA—

Alameda: The Chandlery At Ballena Bay, 1136 Ballena Blvd.
Svendsen's Boat Works, Inc., 1851 Clement Avenue
John Beery Co., 2415 Mariner Square
Antioch: Antioch Marine Sales & Service, 625 W. Third St.
Bob's Bait Box, Foot of Antioch Bridge
Delta Marine Center, 111 Fulton Shipyard Rd.
Berkeley Brennan Supply Co., 805 University Avenue
Lucas College Book Co., Inc., 2430 Bancroft Way
John C. Beery Co., Aquatic Park
Bethel Island: Marine Emporium, 5993 Bethel Island Rd.
Delta Sportsman, 6131 Bethel Island Rd.
Bodega: McCaughey Brothers, General Merchandise, Corner of Main and Briard Streets
Bodega Bay: The Tides, On Highway #1
Carnelian Bay: Sierra Boat Company, 5146 North Lake Boulevard
Crescent City: Marion's Saw Shop, Marine & Sports Center, 1493 Northcrest Drive
Tex's Tackle & Bait, Crescent City Airport
Crockett: Dowrelio Boat Works, Foot of Port Street
Eureka: †Lincoln's, 615 Fifth Street
Seaman's Direct Buying Service, Inc., Foot of Commercial St.
Fort Bragg: Noyo Store, Noyo Fishing Village
Anchor Marine, Inc., South Harbor Drive
Fort Bragg Marine, North Harbor Drive
Fremont: Fremont Marine Sales, Inc., 4239 Peralta Boulevard
Half Moon Bay: Gardner's Fishing Trips, Pillar Pt. Harbor
Huntington Harbour: Huntington Harbour Marine Supply Co., 16865 Algonquin Street
Lodi: Tower Park Marina Resort, 14900 W. Hiway
Long Beach: Ace Blueprint Co., 2491 Long Beach Boulevard
B & B Supply Co., 1845 W. Anaheim Street
Bahia Marine Hardware, 6200 East Coast Pacific Highway
*Cantain's Locker, Long Beach, 251 Marina Drive
Los Angeles: Renie Map Service, Inc., 1101 W. 7th St.
Westside Maps Co., 114 West Third St.
Lynwood: Pacific Coast Map Service, 12021 Long Beach Boulevard
Marina Del Ray: Captain's Locker, 4766 Admiralty Way
Ships Store, 14025 Panay Way
Jeffries Del Rey, 4214 Lincoln Boulevard
Int'l Yacht Sales & Charter Agency, 4189 Admiralty Way
Tahiti Ship-Rite & Marine Supplies, 4039 Lincoln Blvd.
Monterey: Peninsula Boat Sales, 256 Figueroa Street
Morro Bay: Marine Service & Equipment, 1169 Market Avenue
Morro Bay Marina, 699 Embarcadero
Moss Landing: Moss Landing Marine Supply, 3 Clam Way
Napa: Napa Valley Marina, 1200 Milton Road
Newport Beach: Balboa Marine Hardware Co., 2612 West Coast Highway
*Newport Marine Supply Co., 2700 West Coast Highway
†*Phillips Marine Stores, 2825 Newport Boulevard
Fullerton Air Parts, 3928 Campus Dr.
North Hollywood: †*Pan-American Navigation Service, 12021 Ventura

Novato: The Boat Shop, 7000 Redwood Highway
Oakland: Johnson & Joseph Co., Retail Div. of C. J. Hendry Co., 76 Jack London Square
Steve's Marine, Inc., 1363 Embarcadero
C. E. Erickson & Associates, 337 17th St.
Marine Parts Company, 1937 Embarcadero
Oxnard: Oxnard Sporting Goods, 140 North "A" Street
Coast Chandlery and Yacht Sales, 3900 Bluefin Circle
Palo Alto: Glover Marine, 3705 El Camino Real
Pasadena: Crown Craft, 2385 E. Colorado
Pasadena Map Company, 148 East Colorado Boulevard
Pleasant Hill: Students' Bookstore-Book Center, Diablo Valley College, 321 Golf Club Road
Redondo Beach: Redondo Trading Post Co., 813 North Guadalupe
Captains Corner-King Harbor, 344 North Harbor Drive
Redwood City: SFO Marine, Inc., d/b/a The ship's Store of Redwood City, 690 Broadway
Al's Marine Store #1 Uccelli Blvd. Pete's Harbor
Rio Vista: Delta Marina Yacht Harbor, Inc., 100 Marina Drive
Sacramento: A-1 Map Center, 5511 - 33rd Avenue
Ogden Surveying Equipment Co., 5520 Elvas Avenue
M & N Service, 3333 Watt Ave. #101
San Bruno: Recreation World, 732 El Camino Real
San Diego: †*Arey-Jones Office Products, 1055 6th Ave.
Kettenburg, 2810 Carleton Street
†*Nuttall-Styris Company, 825 Columbia Street
Johnson & Joseph Co., 2727 Shelter Island Dr.
Map Centre, 2611 University Avenue
San Diego Marine Exchange, Inc., 2636 Shelter Island Dr.
San Francisco: †*George E. Butler, 356 California Street
Johnson & Joseph Co., 496 Jefferson Street
Nautical Charts, Inc., World Trade Center
San Jose: Maritime Electronics Co., 1539 Winchester Boulevard
San Pedro: †*Southwest Instrument Co., 235 W. 7th Street
GHA Company, Berth 84
Marine Hardware Company, Inc., 304 S. Beacon Street
San Rafael: Western Boat Shop, 101 Third Street
Loch Lomond Marine Supply, 100 Loch Lomond Dr.
Santa Barbara: *Coast Navigation School, 418 East Canon Perdido
Coast Chandlery, On the Breakwater
Santa Clara: Cope and McPhetres, Inc., 2931 El Camino
Santa Cruz: The Mariner, Santa Cruz Yacht Harbor, 413 Lake Avenue
Santa Cruz Boat Rentals, Municipal Wharf
Sausalito: †Bauman Bros. & Dick Miller Marine Supplies, Foot of Harbor Drive, Clipper Yacht Harbor
John Beery Company, 2650 Bridgeway
Maritime Electronics Co., Inc. of Sausalito, Harbor Dr., Clipper Yacht Harbor
Sherman Oaks: Map Service & Blueprint Co., 4419 Van Nuys Blvd.
South Gate: E. R. Jacobsen Suppliers
South Lake Tahoe: The Outdoorsman, Highway 50 (Main Street)
Stockton: Morris Bros., 630 North California Street
Harding Way News, 115 W. Harding Way
Stephens Marine Inc., 1048 W. Fremont St.
Tahoe City: Tahoe Boat Company, North Lake Boulevard, Highway 28
Terminal Island: California Commercial Fisherman's Assn., Inc., 745 South Seaside Avenue
Tiburon: Varney's Tiburon Hardware & Marine, 1650 Tiburon Boulevard
Vallejo: Vallejo Marine, 2430 Sonoma Boulevard
Ventura: County Stationers, Inc., 532 East Main
Walnut Creek: Stevenson Electronics, 1531 Locust Street
Boat Warehouse, 1559 — 3rd Avenue

CONNECTICUT—

Branford: Birbarie Marine Sales, 139 W. Main Street
Bruce & Johnson Marina, So. Montowese Street
Tafeen Yacht Sales, Inc., 61 N. Main St.
Bridgeport: Brainard Marine Sales, Post Road
Clinton Habor Marina, 131 Grove St.
Marine Sports Center, Inc., 2400 Fairfield Avenue
Orbit Marine Sports Center, 3273 Fairfield Avenue
Orbit Marine Sports Center, 264 Brewster Street
Clinton: The Ships Store, Cedar Island Marina, Riverside Drive
Cobalt: Cobalt Marina
Cos Cob: Port Chandler's, Inc., 67 River Road
Darien: The Tool Box, 21 Tokeneke Road
Devon: Flagship Marina, Inc., 40 Bridgeport Avenue
East Norwalk: The Tackle Box, 81 Seaview Ave.
Essex: †*Essex Paint & Marine Company, Norelty Lane
The Galleon and Galley, Ltd., Dauntless Shipyard Marina
Greenwich: *Landfall Navigation Ltd., 49 Greenwich Avenue
Groton: Court Colver, Inc., Long Hill Road
Spicer's Marinas, 916 Shennecossett Road
Guilford: W.E. Johnson Co., Old Whitfield St.
Madison: Madison Hardware, Inc., 30 Wall St.
Milford: Milford Harbor Marina, 2 High Street
Mystic: George W. Wilcox Co., Old Stonington Rd.
Seaport Marine, Inc., One Washington Street
New London: Burr's Yacht Haven, Inc., 244 Pequot Avenue
Gruskin Hardware Co., 208 Bank Street
MARSTERS, 262 Pequot Avenue
Niantic: Bayreuther Boat Yard, Inc., Smith Cove Boats, Inc., 133 East Main Street
Noank: Noank Shipyard, Pearl Street
Norwich: R.A. Thayer & Sons Marine Sales, 46 W. Main Street
Thames Hardware Co., 47 Franklin Street
Old Saybrook: Terra Mar Ship's Stores, Inc., 160 College St.
Connecticut Marine Center, Inc., 252 Main Street
Baldwin Bridge Yacht Basin, Inc., Riverside Avenue
Galleon & Galley Ltd., Black Swan Marina, Ferry Road
Ye Olde Fisherman, 2 Boston Post Rd.
Pawcatuck: Connors and O'Brien Marina, Inc., 197 Mechanic St.
Portland: Wm. J. Petzold, Inc., 37 Indian Hill Avenue
Portland Boat Works, Inc., 1 Grove St.
South Norwalk: Rex Marine Center, Inc., 144 Water Street
South Windsor: Mellen Marine, Inc., 1145 John Fitch Blvd., Rt. 5
Stamford: †Fairfield Marine North, Inc., 70 Main Street
†Stamford Bookstore, Inc., 127 Bedford Street
Hathaway Reiser & Raymond, Inc., 184 Selleck Street
Yacht Haven, Inc., Wallace St.
Ship's Store, Yacht Haven West, Washington Blvd.
Stonington: Dodson Boat Yard, Inc., 194 Water Street
Noank Marine Exchange, Front & High Streets

Stratford: Olsen Marine Co., Inc., 76 Ferry Boulevard
Stratford Marina, Inc., Foot of Broad Street
Waterford: Hillyer's Bait & Tackle Shop, 366 Rope Ferry Rd., Mago Point
West Hartford: †Clapp & Treat, Inc., 672 Farmington Avenue
West Haven: Kimberly Harbor, Inc., 13 Kimberly Avenue
Westbrook: Westbrook Boat & Engine Company, Boston Post Road
Pilot's Point Marina, Inc., Seaside Ave.
Tafeen Yacht Sales, Inc., Post Rd.
Wetmores Marina, Boston Post Rd.
Westport: Coastwise Marine Corp., 609 Riverside Avenue
The Boat Locker, 1375 Post Road

DELAWARE—

Frederica: Conley Hardware, RFD
Lewes: †Ellis Marine, Inc., 121-127 Front Street
Life of Riley Bait & Tackle, Kings Hwy.
Milford: Taylor Marine, Rehoboth Boulevard
Newark: Carlisle's, Churchman's Rd., R.D. 3
Rehoboth Beach: Rehobeth Bay Marina, Inc., Dewey Beach
Seaford: Holt's Marine, Inc., U.S. Hwy. 13 & Nanticoke River
Smyrna: Weatherly Yacht Co., N. DuPont Highway on U.S. 13
Wilmington: Hilton Marine Supply Co., Inc., 1900 Kirkwood Highway
Fort Christina Marina, Inc., 1126 E. 7th St.
Albatross Marine Supply, 5611 Old Capitol Trail

DISTRICT OF COLUMBIA—

The Map Store, Inc., 1636 Eye Street, N.W.
Buzzard Point Boat Yard Corp., Foot of First St., S.W.
The Washington Marina Company, 1800 Maine Avenue, S.W.

FLORIDA—

Anna Maria: Anna Maria Yacht Club, 902 South Bay Blvd.
Apalachicola: C.W. Randolph, Agent, 119 Water Street
Big Pine Key: The Sea Center, Inc., Overseas Highway
Boca Grande: Millers Marina, Harbor Drive
Boca Raton: Boca Marine Store, Inc., 253 North Federal Hwy.
Bradenton: †Turner Marine Supply, 826-13th Street West
Captiva Island: South Seas Plantation
Carrabelle: F.M. Lawhon, Distr., Marine Street
Charlotte Harbor: "Doc Potts Tackle Shop," 302 Bayshore Dr., S.E.
Chokoloskee: Chokoloskee Island Park
Clearwater: Edar Outsider, U.S. 19 & Ulmerton, Rt. 1
Marine Electronics & Controls, Inc., 504 N. Ft. Harrison Ave.
Clearwater Beach: †Clearwater Marine Sales, Mun. Marina Bldg.
Clewiston: Angler's Marina, 910 Okeechobee Boulevard
Cocoa: Simmons Sailing Corp., 104 Willard St.
Cocoa Beach Marine, Inc., 307 Orange Ave.
Coconut Grove: Blue Water Marine Supply, 3041 Grand Ave.
Ship's Store & Gear, Inc., 2550 So. Bayshore Dr.
Crystal River: Pete's Pier, Inc., 558 N.W. 3rd Ave.
Dania: Nautical Yacht Basin, Inc., 801 N.E. 3rd Street
Daytona Beach: Daytona Chris Craft, 3300 S. Peninsula Dr.
Hemisphere Yacht and Ship Brokerage, 302 South Beach St.
Delray Beach: *Marineway Corp., 777 Palm Trail
Del Raton Marine Center, Inc., 2600 S. Federal Highway
Englewood: Denny's Sports World, 1271 Beach Rd.
Everglades: Everglades National Park Boat Tours, Gulf Coast Rangers Headquarters on State Road 29
Fernandina Beach: Fernandina Beach Marina, Atlantic Ave. at River
Fort Lauderdale:
*Bahia Mar Marine, Inc., Bahia Mar Yachting Center
*Herold Boat Co., 1112 E. Las Olas Boulevard
*Lauderdale Marina, Inc., 1900 S.E. 15th Street
*Pier 66 Marina, 2301 S.E. 17th St. Causeway
Sportsman's Paradise, Inc., 5730 N. Federal Highway
†Vogel's Marine Supply Co., 601 S. Andrews Avenue
Boatarama, Inc., 4301 S. State Road 7
Charlie's Locker, Inc., 1445 S.E. 17th St.
Seven Seas Sailing Supplies, 802 S.E. 17th St.
Ship's Store & Gear, Inc., 1861 S.E. 17th Causeway
Striker Yachts, Inc., 1681 S.E. 17th St. Causeway
Fisherman's Paradise, Inc., 1184 N.W. 40th Ave.
Fort Myers: *Fort Myers Yacht Basin
Parker's Book Store, 1508 Hendry Avenue
Port Comfort Marina, Inc., McGregor Boulevard
Reception Harbor Marina, McGregor Boulevard
Coastal Marine Mart, Inc., 5605 Palm Beach Blvd.
Fort Myers Beach: San Carlos Marina, Inc., 703 San Carlos Dr.
Cooks Marine Service, 1011 San Carlos Blvd.
Fish-Tale Marina, 7105 Estero Blvd.
Fort Pierce: Horton's, Inc., 122 North 2nd Street
Fort Walton Beach: Gulf Marine Center, 36 Eglin Pkwy.
Hudson Marina, Inc., 9 Marina Drive
Safety Service Co., Inc., 8 Walter Martin Road
Standard Marine, Inc., 106 Chestnut Avenue
Gainesville: Florida Book Store, Inc., 1614 W. University Ave.
Goodland: Coon Key Pass Marina, East Palm Avenue
Kelmar Shells Coral & Gifts, Royal Palm Hammock
Hollywood: Van's Marine Service, Inc., 2451 Pembroke Road
Boats Unlimited, 220 N. State Road 7
Holmes Beach: Gateway Marina, Inc., 503-56th Street
Homestead: Don's Bait & Tackle, 30711 S. Federal Hwy.
Everglades Natural History Assoc., Inc., State Rd. 27 S.W.
South Florida Marine, Inc., 1460 N. Federal Highway
Hudson: Gulf View Marina, 241 Clark Avenue
Islamorada: Bud M' Mary's Marina, U.S. Highway 1 at Teatable Bridge
The Four Winds, Overseas Highway at Ocean Lane
Venetian Shores Fishing Center, 5101 Overseas Highway, Plantation Key
Jacksonville: †*Nautical Supply Company, 113 East Bay St.
Outboard, Inc., 6424 Arlington Expressway
Pier 17, Marina, Inc., 4669 Roosevelt Blvd.
Herb White's Marine, 2652 Blanding Blvd.
St. Johns River Park & Marina, 901 Gulf Life Dr.
A.R. Cogswell Blue Print & Supply Co., 738-800 N. Myrtle Ave.

Jacksonville Beach: Beach Marine, 2315 Beach Blvd.
Isle of Palms Marina, Inc., 14603 Beach Boulevard
Jensen Beach: Anchorage Marina, Rt. 707, On St. Lucie River
Jupiter: Conch Cove, Inc. Marina, 18781 SE Federal Hwy.
Dodge Marine of Jupiter, U.S. Highway #1
Key Largo: Gilbert's Fishing Camp & Marina, Inc., U.S. Rt. 1 & Intracoastal Waterway at Jewfish Creek
Key West: Angler's Service, 3318 N. Roosevelt Blvd.
Angler's Boat Rentals, U.S. 1, Stock Island
Canas Marine Electronics, Inc., Lt. #61, Pearle Trailer Ct., Stock Island, Highway #1
Kings Point Yacht Club & Marina, Inc., Stock Island
Key West Seaside Marina, U.S. 1 & SR 941, Big Copitt Key
Key West Pro Dive Shop, 1990 Roosevelt Blvd.
Reef Raiders Dive Shop, U.S. Hwy 1, Stock Island
Lake Park: Wood's Marine Supplies, Inc., 1432-10th St.
Lake Worth: Tuppen's Inc., 1002 N. Dixie Hwy.
Lakeland: Edwards-Panter Surveying & Engineering, Inc., 1520 Commercial Park Drive
Largo: Fore and Aft Marine, 904 West Bay Drive
Lighthouse Point: Hildebrand Marine, Inc., 1841 N.E. 25th St.
Maitland: Maitland Marine, 2032 North Highway 17-92
Marathon: Miller's Tackle Shop, 1901 Overseas Highway
Ye Old Feshin Hole, 1717 Overseas Highway
Nick's Sporting Goods, 11833 Overseas Highway
Bonefish Harbor Marina, On Grassy Key
Faro Blanco Marine Resort, 1996 Overseas Highway
Hall's Bait & Tackle, 1666 Overseas Highway
Marco Island: Marco River Marina, 951 State Road
Matlacha: Wooten's Bait & Tackle Shop, St. Rd. 78 E. of New Matlacha Bridge
Melbourne: Art's Bait & Tackle & Ships Store, 96 East Eau Gallie Blvd.
Dickerson Marine Center, Eau Gallie Branch
Eau Gallie Yacht Basin, Inc., 587 Young Street
Indian River Marine Basin, Inc., 2222 Front St.
Merritt Island: Banana River Marine Service, 1360 Banana River Dr. S.
Brevard Marine Service, Inc., 150 East Merritt Island
Missleland Marina, Inc., 582 S. Banana River Dr.
Mexico Beach: Capt. Joe's Marina, Highway 98
Miami: Bird Marine, 7100 Bird Road
Crook & Crook Marine Supplies, 2804 Bird Avenue
Discount Marine Supplies, Inc., 9900 N.W. 7th Ave.
Everglades Park Co., Inc. 18494 S. Federal Highway
Fisherman's Paradise, Inc., 18430 South Dixie Hwy.
Fisherman's Paradise, Inc., 3800 N.W. 27th Avenue
*Florida Precision Instrument Corp., 800 N.W. 7th Avenue
*L.B. Harvey, 252 S.W. 6th Street
†*Hopkins-Carter Hardware Co., 3701 N.W. 21st Street
†Phillips Hardware Co., 490 N.W. South River Drive
Southern Marine Supply Co., 12952 S.W. 89th Avenue
Portable Power Products, 4031 S.W. 110 Court
Miami Beach: Junior's Tackle Shop & Marine, 1310-5th St.
Naples: Boat Haven Naples, Inc., 1485-5th Avenue
Hansen Chris Craft Sales, Inc., 1146-6th Ave. So.
Marine Center, Inc., 893 Tenth Street South
Naples Yacht & Ship Chandlers, 840 12th Ave. South
Tamiami Marina, 1312-5th Avenue South
New Smyrna Beach: Dan's Boathouse, Inc., 111 N. Riverside Drive
North Palm Beach: Sea Chest of Old Port Cove, 1290 U.S. Hwy. 1
Sea Chest of the Palm Beaches, Inc., Old Port Cove
Orlando: Florida Marine & Equipment Co., 1104-06 N. Mills St.
Ransom Downes Outboard Service, 1101 S. Orange Avenue
Palatka: Boathouse Marina, 329 River Street
Oliver & Garrett Co., 227 Reid Street
Palm Beach Gardens: Waterway Marina, Inc., 2361 PGA Blvd.
Panama City: Harby Marina, 1055 E. Highway 98
Pier 98 Marina, 5904 East Highway 98
Guy-Rogers Marine, Inc./Grand Lagoon Marina, 5323 North Lagoon Drive
The Good Life Ship Chandlery & Mfg. Co., 5128 W. Hwy. 98
Treasure Island Marina, 3605 South Thomas Drive
Panama City Marina Service, Inc., L Harrison Ave.
Panama City Beach: Bay Point Marina, Bay Point Road
Pensacola: Gulf Marine Supply Co., 619 S. Palafox Street
Merritt Marina & Marine Supplies, Route 6
Runyan's Boats & Motors, Inc., 523 So. Baylen St.
Marine Unlimited, Inc., 530 E. Fairfield Drive
Perrine: South Date Bait & Tackle, Inc., 18014 S. Fed. Hgwy.
Pompano: Capt. Jack's, 2521 N. Dixie Hwy.
Pompano Beach: Rodi Chris-Craft Sales, Inc., 1500 N. Federal Highway
Chris Aquatics, 222 No. Pompano Beach Blvd.
Port Canaveral: Canaveral Fishermans Supply, 520 Avenue A
Port Charlotte: Harbor Marine, 400 South Tamiami Drive
Port Richey: Joe Kearns; Boathouse, 1123 Highway 19 South
Punto Gorda: Paradise Sportsman Shop, 1152 E. Marion Ave.
Riviera Beach: Lee's Marine Supplies, 2215 Broadway
Ruskin: Classic Boat Works, Shell Point Rd., Bahia Beach Marina
Sanford: Robson Sporting Goods, P.O. Box 1509
Monroe Harbour, Inc., 531 N. Palmetto Ave.
Sanibel: MacIntosh Bookshop, Periwinkle Way
St. Petersburg: Gary Sales Co., 2588-28th Ave., North
Hansen Chris Craft Sales, Inc., 3701-50th Ave. South
Marina Point, 500 1st Ave., N.E.
St. Petersburg Shipbuilding & Supply Co., 200 7th Ave. South
Stowaway Marina, 9333 Blind Pass Roa
The Lazarette, 20 Beach Dr., N.E.
Ship's Store & Gear, Inc., 12030 Gandy Blvd.
Suncoast Marine, Inc., 1477 Pasadena Ave. S.
American News Geographics Company's Map World, Suite 110, Fla. Bldg., 337-22nd Ave., North
Sarasota: Helmsmen Marina, 1139-10th Street, West
Hansen Chris Craft Sales, Inc., 1201 N. Tamiami Trail
Marina Operations, #2 Marina Plaza
Ship's Locker, 15 S. Blvd. of Presidents, St. Armands Key
Beach's Siesta Key Marine, Inc., 1265 Stickney Point Road

†Tucker's Sporting Goods, 1400 State St.
Helmsmen Sarasota Marina, 1550 Stickney Point Road
Design Products, Inc., 1127 Goodrich Ave.
Sebastian: Inlet Marina of Sebastian, Inc.
South Miami: Johnson-Kirby, Inc., 5966 S. Dixie Highway
Stuart: Ideal Sport Shop, Stuart Shopping Ctr., S. Federal Hwy.
Sailfish Marina, 2675 S. St. Lucie Boulevard
St. Lucie Marine, Inc., Alice Ave. near Radio Tower
Valentine's Bookshop, 329 East Ocean Boulevard
Sugar Loaf Key: Sugar Loaf Lodge, Inc.
Sunshine Key: Sunshine Key Aqua-Center, Inc., Holiday Inn Trav-L Park
Tallahassee: Blue Waters Marine, Inc., 1940-30 Northwood Mall
Photogrammetric Engineers, 515 N. Adams Street
Tampa: Marine & Outdoor World, Inc., 3616 Gandy Blvd.
Poston Marine Supply Co., Inc., 1012 East Cass Street
Tampa Marine Supply Co., Inc., 202 N. 13th Street
Windward Marine Sales, Inc., Imperial Yacht Basin, 5000A Gandy Boulevard
Tarpon Springs: Port Tarpon Marina, Inc., Anclote Road
Tavernier: Perdue-Dean, Inc., U.S. Route #1
Tavernier Creek Marina, Inc., U.S. 1 at Tavernier Creek
Titusville: Westland Marine, 419 North Washington
Rogers Outboard Sales and Service, 1103 Garden St.
Upper Key Largo: Coral Reef Park Co., Inc., John Pennekamp State Park
Venice: Tarpon Center Marine, Inc., 968 Tarpon Center Drive
Venice Marine Center, Inc., 1485 S. Tamiami Trail
Pelican Cove Marina, Inc., 996 Laguna Drive
Vero Beach: Seafari Marine, Inc., 3599 Rio Vista
†Vero Marine Center, 12 Royal Palm Boulevard
Cocoa-Canaveral Air Service, Inc., d/b/a Sparks Fly, Municipal Airport
Vero Beach Mun. Marina, 3611 Rio Vista Blvd.
West Palm Beach: †*Hopkins Marine Hardware Co., 207-6th St.
Spencer Boat Company, Inc., 4000 North Dixie Highway
Winter Haven: Marine Supply of Winter Haven, Inc., 717 6th St., S.W.
Winter Haven Marine, Inc., 701 Sixth St., S.W.

GEORGIA—

Atlanta: Jenkins Marine Sales, 6855 Peachtree Industrial Blvd.
Brunswick: Georgia Hardware & Marine Supply, 205 Monk St.
H & H Service Store, Inc., 1503 Gloucester Street
St. Simons Island: Golden Isles Marina, Inc., St. Simons Island Causeway
Savannah: Chatham Laminating Company, 3135 Bull Street
John D. Robinson Co., Inc., 17 West Bay Street
Savannah Marina, Inc., Tybee Road
†*Southern Marine Supply Co., Inc., 647 W. River Street
Baker Yachts, Inc., Baker Yachts Sailboard Marina
Thunderbolt: Thunderbolt Marina, River Drive
Townsend: Kip's Marina, Shellman Bluff

HAWAII—

Hilo: Petroglyph Press Ltd., 211 Kinoole Street
Honolulu: †McWayne Marine Supply Ltd., 1125 Ala Moana Blvd.
*Trans-Pacific Instrument Co., 1406 Colburn Street
Yacht Systems Hawaii, Inc., 1700 Ala Moana Blvd.
Kahului, Maui: Sue's Stationery, Inc., Kahului Shipping Ct.
Lahaina, Maui: Lahaina Book Shoppe, Dickenson & Chapel Streets

IDAHO—

Bayview: Bayview Mercantile Co., Main Street
Sandpoint: Pend Oreille Sport Shop, 312 N. First Avenue

ILLINOIS—

Chicago: Land's End Yacht Stores, Inc., 2241 N. Elston Ave.
†*Navigation Equipment Co., 228 W. Chicago Ave.
Rand McNally and Co., 39 So. LaSalle St.
The Adler Planetarium, 1300 S. Lake Shore Dr.
U.S. Army Engineer District, 219 S. Dearborn St.
Downers: Thede Marina LTD, 639 Ogden Avenue
Gurnee: The Boat Show and Camping Center, 4437 Grand Avenue
Oak Park: Sailboats, Inc., 639 W. Madison St.
Sailing Center of Chicago, Div. of High Performance
Waukegan: Larsen Marine Service, Inc., 625 Sea Horse Dr.
Waukegan Marine Co., Inc., 1208 Grand Ave.

INDIANA—

Michigan City: B. & E. Marine, Inc., 500 Center St.
Port Authority of Mich. City, Washington Park Marina
Valpacaiso: Erwin Marina and Travel Center, Rt. 9

LOUISIANA—

Abbeville: The Sportsman (David Russo Corp. d/b/a,) 1915 S. State St.
Baton Rouge: Steinberg's Sports Center, 832 St. Philip St.
Baton Rouge Blue Print & Supply Co., 207 St. Ferdinand
Red's Boat Store, River Road (Downtown)
Cameron: Gulf Coast Supply Co., Marshall St.
Covington: Carol's Corner Bookstore, 328 E. Lockwood St.
Galliano: Vidrine Office Supply, Inc., Highway 1
Hammond: The News Mart, 103 North Oak Street
Harvey: Duvic's, Inc., 3650 West Bank Expressway
Houma: Houma Reproduction & Map Co., 550 S. Van Avenue
Marine Education Associates, Inc., 317 Fifth St.
Lafayette: Bell's Marina, Inc., 200 New Flanders Road
Lake Charles: Boat Town Marine Supply, 4727 Common Street
Fenley's Sporting Goods, 213 Gill Street
Metairie: Soroe's Boat Exchange, Inc., 850 Veterans Blvd.
Morgan City: American Supply Co. of Morgan City, Highway 90 East
Shannon Hardware Co., Ltd., 606 Front Street

New Orleans: Aviation & Marine, Inc., New Orleans Lakefront Airport
†*Baker, Lyman Co., 308 Magazine Street
New Orleans Map Co., 110 Exchange Place
Trade Winds, Inc., 8650 Pontchartrain Boulevard
Slidell: Sportsman's Paradise, Inc., 3320 Pontchartrain Drive

MAINE—

Augusta: Merrill's, Div. of Loring, Short, & Harmon, 221 Water St.
Bailey Island: Dockside Marine, Mackerel Cove Road
Bar Harbor: Sherman's Book Store, 56 Main Street
Bass Harbor: Bass Harbor Marine
Bath: John E. Cotter, d/b/a Shaws Bookstore, 49 Front Street
Blue Hill: Candage Hardware & Supply, Main Street
Boothbay Harbor: Blakes Marine, Gulf Wharf
Pierce's Marine Service, Inc.
Brunswick: Macbeans of Brunswick, Inc., 134 Maine Street
Calais: Johnson Company, 96 Main Street
Camden: The Owl and The Turtle, 8 Bay View
The Smiling Cow, 41 Main Street
†Village Shop, 25-27 Main Street
Wayfarer Marine Corp., Sea Street
Damariscotta: Damariscotta Appliance and Outboard Co., & Chasse's Marina, 1 Foye St.
The Old Maine Shop, Maine Street
Eastport: *S.L. Wadsworth & Son, 5-8 Central Wharf
Ellsworth: H. F. Wescott Hardware Co., 120 Main Street
Shepard Hardware, West Main St.
Falmouth: Handy Boat Service, Inc., 215 Foreside Road
Kennebunkport: The Sea Crafters, Ocean Drive
Chick's Marina, Ocean Avenue
Kennebunk Book Port, 10 Dock Square
Kittery: Jackson's U.S. Bypass No. 1 (Southbound)
Sea Cabin, Pepperell Road, Kittery Point Bridge
The Bosun's Locker, 48 Bowen Rd.
North Haven: J.O. Brown & Son, Inc.
Northeast Harbor: F. T. Brown, Main Street
Port Clyde: Port Clyde Gen. Store, Inc., Box 138
Portland: *Chase, Leavitt & Co., Ten Dana Street
Robinhood: Robinhood Marina, Inc.
Rockland: †Huston-Tuttle, Inc., 18 School Street
South Brooksville: American Practical Navigators, Inc., Box 205
South Freeport: Harraseeket Marine Service, Main Street
Ring's Marine Service, Inc., On Harraseeket River
South Harpswell: Dolphin Marine Service, Inc., Basin Point
South Portland: Marineast at Mill Cove, 38 Ocean Street
Southwest Harbor: H.R. Beal & Sons, Inc., Clark Point Road
Southwest Boat Corp., Clark Point Road
Stonington: †Atlantic Ave. Hardware, Inc., Atlantic Ave.
Tenants Harbor: Spindrift Cruises, Inc., Next to Town Landing
Thomaston: Snow Harbor Corporation, Water Street
West Southport: Brewer's Boatyard, Inc., Ebenecook Harbor
York: York Harbor Marine Service, Inc., Route 103

MARYLAND—

Annapolis: †Fawcett Boat Supplies, Inc., 110 Compromise Street
Viking Boat Supplies, 320 Sixth Street, Eastport
Electronic Marine, Inc., 418 Fourth St.
Fairwinds Marina, Inc., Rt. 6, 1001 Lake Claire Dr.
Weems and Plath, Inc., 48 Maryland Avenue
Waterway Guide, Inc., 238 West Street
Baltimore: Bosun's Locker, In 2 Charles Center Plaza
Dotties Duffle Bag, Div. of Baltimore Chris-Craft Sales, Inc., 5816 Ritchie Highway
*Maryland Nautical Sales, Inc., 406 Water Street
†*The R. J. Taylor Co., 3200 Annetta Avenue
The Wm. H. Whiting Co., 6701 Moravia Park Drive
Cambridge: Cambridge Office Supply Co., 414 Race Street
Cambridge Shipyard, Inc., Hayward St.
Camp Springs: Bos'n Locker, Inc., 6516 Old Branch Avenue
Chesapeake City: Schaefer's Market & Marina
Cottage City: Sears, Roebuck & Co., Marine Center, 3554 Bladensburg Rd.
Crisfield: J. P. Tawes & Bros, 1100 West Main Street
Deale: Berlitz Marine Anchorage, Rockhold Creek near Deale Post Office
Easton: Easton Point Marina, Box 185
Rowens Stationery, Inc., 12 North Washington St.
Elkton: Bay Head Hardware and Marine, 207 South Bridge Street
Essex: Marine Basin, Inc., 1900 Block Old Eastern Avenue
Galesville: Up Your Anchor, Inc., West River Marina
Georgetown: Skipjack Cove Marina, Inc., On Sassafras River
Sailing Associates, Inc., At the Granary
Havre de Grace: Tidewater Marina, Foot of Bourbon St.
Hollywood: Blackstone Marina, Blackstone Road
Laurel: Key Marine, 1608 Washington Blvd.
Lexington Park: Loffler Enterprises, Inc., Esperanza Shpg Ctr.
North East: Bay Boat Works, Inc., Hances Point
McDaniel Yacht Basin, Inc., Off Md. Rt. 272 South
Ocean City: Boulden's Marina, Inc., 5305 Coastal Highway
Oxford: †Oxford Yacht Agency, "The Strand"
Oxon Hill: Oxon Hill Marine, Inc., 6212 Livingston Road
Pasadena: Stammer's Sport & Marine Center, 1175 Ft. Smallwood Rd.
Riverdale: National Ocean Survey, 6501 Lafayette Avenue, Bldg. #1
Rockville: National Ocean Survey, 6001 Executive Avenue, Building #1, Room 709
St. Mary's County: Clayton Marina, Smith Creek-Potomac River
St. Michaels: St. Michaels Hardware & Gift Shop, 234 Talbot St.
Salisbury: Hickman Boat Supplies, Inc., 1307 Ocean City Rd.
White Marine Supplies, 202 Newton Street
Silver Spring: Cap'n Stan's Boat Center, Inc., 8236 Georgia Ave.
Solomons: A. W. Zahniser & Son, Marina & Boatyard
Calvert Marina, Solomons Harbor
Harbor Island Marina, Md. Routes 2 and 4
Stevensville: Pier One Marina
Taylors Island: Taylors Island Marina
Trappe: Bay Country Shop, Rt. #1

MASSACHUSETTS—

Barnstable: Barnstable Marine Service, Inc., Barnstable Hbr.
Millway Marine, Inc., Barnstable Harbor

Boston: Berry Hardware Co., 395 Neponset Avenue
Broad Marine Supply Co., 102 Broad St.
James Bliss Co., Inc., 82 Summer Street
Klausen-Gestby Company, 241 Northern Avenue
†Marine Hardware & Supply Co., 390 Atlantic Avenue
*Nautilus Ship Supply Corp., 332 Congress Street
Braintree: Bra-Wey Sport Shop, Inc., 178 Quincy Ave., Rt. 53
Brant Rock: Bud's Inc., of Marshfield, Mass., 21 Dyke Road
Buzzards Bay: †Bosnengo Hardware, Inc., 45-47 Main Street
Cambridge: Cambridge Camera & Marine, 37 Brattle Street
Canton: James Bliss & Co., Inc., Shawmut Road
Cataumet: Kingman Marine, Shipyard Lane
Chatham: Mayflower Shop, 469 Main Street
Stage Harbor Marine, Bridge Street
Cohasset: Fieldbrook Boat Sales, Inc., 40 Border Street
Mill River Marine Corp., 160 Cushing Highway
Cotuit: Cape Marine, Inc., Rt. 28
Dedham: †*James Bliss & Co., Inc., 100 Rt. 128 (Exit 61)
Dorchester: Norwood Marine Inc., R 24 Ericsson St.
Freeport Engine Co., d/b/a/ The Dinghy Shop, 272 Adams St.
Dracut: Roussel Marine, Inc., 1543 Bridge St., Rt. 38
Duxberry: Duxberry Marina Corp., 31 Mattakeeset Court
East Boston: West Products Corporation, 161 Prescott Street
East Dennis: Sesuit Marine, Inc., Sesuit Harbor
Edgartown: Robin Hood's Barn, Inc., Main Street
Norton & Easterbrooks, Inc., Morse Street
Essex: Book Barn, Old Essex Village
Fairhaven: Grey Lady of the Sea (Ship Chandlery), Fairhaven Marine, Inc., 50 Fort Street
Fall River: Capt. Joseph J. O'Connell Co., Inc., 180 River St.
Falmouth: †Falmouth Marine Railways, Inc.
The Boatyard, Inc., 53 Falmouth Heights Rd.
Gloucester: Building Center Stores, 1 Harbor Loop
Parisi Plastic Fishing Gear, Inc., 27 Commercial St.
Cape Ann Marina Corp., 75 Essex Avenue
Green Harbor: Green Harbor Marina, Rt. 139
Hanover: Marine Stores, Inc., 1775 Washington Street
Harwich Port: Allen Harbor Marine Service, Inc., 335 Lower County Road
Hingham: The Boat House, 14 North Street
Hyannis: Anchor Outboard Co., Inc., 135 South Street
Bradbury Marine, Inc., 157 Pleasant St.
Hyannis Marina, Inc., Arlington St.
Lawrence: Marine Publications, 130 Shepard St.
Lynn: Lynn Hardware Co., Inc., 34-38 Munroe Street
Manchester: Manchester Marine Corp., Ashland Ave.
Marblehead: †*Fred L. Woods, Jr., 76 Washington Street
Marblehead Transportation Company, Ferry Lane
Port of Call, Inc., 26 Atlantic Avenue
Marion: Barden's Board Yard, Inc., 2 Island Wharf Road
Burr Bros. Boats, Inc., Route No. 6
Nantucket: Hardys, Inc., 5 South Water Street
Natick: Natick Marine, Inc., 158 E. Central St., Rt. 135
New Bedford: †*C.E. Beckman Co., 11-35 Commercial Street
Newbury: Parker River Marine, Inc., Rt. 1A at Parker River
Newburyport: Merri-Mar Yacht Basin, Inc., 364 Merrimac St.
Jack Hart's Marine Supply, Tournament Wharf
North Quincy: Boston Harbor Marina, Inc., 542 E. Squantum Street
North Weymouth: Tern Harbor Marina, 275 River Street
Orleans: Compass Rose Book Shop, Main Street
Goose Hummock Shop, Inc., Route 6A
Osterville: Crosby Yacht, Inc., 72 Crosby Circle
Plymouth: Plymouth Marine Railways, Inc., 14 Union Street
Provincetown: Lands End Marine Supply Co., Inc., 337 Commercial Street
Marine Specialties, Inc., 235 Commercial St.
Richmond: J. Harry Martin, View Drive
Rockport: Building Center, Inc., Rockport, 18 Railroad Ave.
Salem: †Jaynes Marine Supplies Inc., 77 Bridge Street
Sandwich: E.T. Moffitt Corp., Sandwich Cape Cod Canal Marina, East Boat Basin
Scituate: The Ship's Locker, 124 Front Street
South Dartmouth: The Packet, Inc., 250 Elm Street
Sudbury: Havencraft of New England, Inc., 55 Union Ave.
Vineyard Haven: Martha's Vineyard Shipyard, Inc., Beach Rd.
Wareham: Warr's Marine, Inc., Lower Main St.
Wellfleet: Bay Sails Marine, Inc., Rt. 6
West Bridgewater: Tight Lines, Inc., 220 South Main St.
West Dennis: Bass River Marina, Inc., 140 Main Street
Weymouth: Monahan's Marine, 396 Washington Street
Winchester: Card Marine, Inc., 632 Main St.
Woburn: James Bliss & Co., Inc., 406 Washington Street
Worcester: "Doc" Chauvin, Inc., 63 Lake Ave.

MICHIGAN—

Algonac: Colony Marine Sales & Service, Inc., 6509 M-29 Hwy.
Alpena: Krueger's Marina, Inc., 400 E. Chisholm St.
Auburn Heights: Great Lakes Map Company, 2901 Auburn Road
Au Gres: Bob's Marina, 3712 E. Michigan Ave.
The Leisure Center, 353 N. Huron Drive (U.S. 23)
Barbeau: Channel View Sport Shop, Scenic Dr.
Bay City: Brennan Marine Sales, 1809 S. Water St.
Museum of the Great Lakes, 1700 Center Ave.
Sailing Center, Inc.
Stover's Sports Outfitters, Inc., 901 Saginaw St.
Benton Harbor: Gardner's Inc., 741 Riverview Dr.
Calumet: Granter's Marine, Inc., 432 Fifth St.
Caseville: Huron Marine Equipment, 6967 Main St.
Saginaw Bay Marina, Inc., 6591 Harbor St.
Cedar Springs: Sail Place, Inc., 142 Cherry St.
Cedarville: Texaco Service
Viking Boat Harbor, Rte. #1
Charlevoix: Captain's Corner, 110 Mason Street
Fairport of Charlevoix, Inc., 307 Belvedere Ave.
Irish Boat Shop on Lake Charlevoix at Stover Rd.
Cheboygan: Anchor In Marina, 220 Water St.
Cheboygan Harbor Marina, 101 E. Elm
Detour Village: Martin's Sportsman
Detroit: Detroit Marine Supply Co., 8717 W. Jefferson
Fairlane Boats & Motors, 1650 Plymouth Rd.
Great Lakes Maritime Institute, Dossin Museum-Belle Isle
Gregory Marine Supply Co., Clairpointe at the River
J.D. Lumley Ltd., 758 Atkinson
K & M Boat Co., 14950 Telegraph Rd.

Keans Detroit Yacht Harbor, 100 Meadowbrook Ave.
Lake Survey Center, 630 Federal Bldg. & U.S. Courthouse
Odin Enterprises, Inc., 4485 W. Jefferson
Silverstines, Inc., 6532 E. McNichols Rd.
Sinbads Marina, 11200 Freud
Douglas: "The Cargo Deck" Gift Shops, aboard the S.S. Keewatin moored at lower Marine
Drummond Island: Drummond Island Yacht Haven
East Tawas: Jerry's Marine, Inc., Tawas Point
Sail-Fish Marine, 110 S. Alice
Elk Rapids: Chain-O-Lakes Marine, Inc., 118 N. Bridge St.
Fair Haven: Dickie Dee Marina, 8709 Dixie Hwy.
The Piers Dining, Cocktail Lounge & Marina, 7479 Dyke Road
Ferndale: Acme Boat Co., 23520 Woodward Ave.
Flint: Doc Wise Boats and Motors, G-4219 Miller Road
Frankfort: Nelson's Marine Service, 324 Main St.
Gibraltar: Humbug Marina, Inc., 13400 M. Gibraltar Rd.
Goetzville: Le-Ja's Resort, Raber Route
Grand Haven: North Shore Marina, Inc., 18275 Berwyck
The Wharf Marina, Inc., 500 N. Second St.
Grand Rapids: Samson Marine of West Mich., 1524 28th St., S.W.
The Sailboat Center, 22 44th St., S.E.
Grandville: Dry Land Marina, Inc., 2705 Sanford Dr., S.W.
Grosse Ile: The Yardarm, 24149 Lyons
Grosse Pte.: The Ship's Wheel, Inc., 19605 Mack Ave.
Grosse Pte. Farms: Thomas Hardware Co., 18680 Mack Ave.
Hancock: Sam's Office & School Supply, 209 Quincy St.
Harbor Beach: Dickinson Marina, 5 Lytle Ave.
Harbor Springs: Irish Boat Shop, Inc., 400 Bay St.
Walstrom Marine, Inc., 105 Bay St.
Harsens Island: Minnich's Boats & Motors, Inc., 7858 Middle Channel Dr.
Haslett: Capitol City Sails, Inc., 1483 Haslett Rd.
Hessel: E.J. Mertaugh Boat Works
Highland Park: American Supply Co., 15 Ferris St.
Holland: Bay Haven Marina, Inc., 1862 Ottawa Beach Rd.
Easter Marine Service, 2081 Lakeway Dr.
Honor: Bud's Texaco & Bait Shop, 10791 Main St.
Houghton: Griffin's Sales & Service, 604 Bridge Street
Isle Royale Natural History Association, Isle Royale National Park
Indian River: Burt Lake Marina, 6831 Barbara St.
Howe Interlakes Marine, Inc.
Indian River Marina, Inc., 3019 Apple Blossom
Kewadin: The Sail Shop, Inc., 13589 Cairn Hwy.
Lasalle: North Shores Investment Co., Toledo Beach Marina, Rt. #1, South Otter Creek Rd.
Rainbow Marina, 5800 S. Otter Creek Rd.
Leland: The Fish Hook, 110 W. River St.
Livonia: Friendship Card Shop/Sea Chest, Inc., 27512 Schoolcraft Rd.
Ludington: Tamarac Harbor Enterprises, Inc., 2875 N. Lakeshore Dr.
Tamarac Sportfishing Dock, 105 Water St.
Macatawa: Jesiek Bros. Shipyard, Inc.
Mackinaw City: Shepler's, Inc.
Marine City: Marine City Marina, Inc., 1115 S. Belle River
Marquette: Marquette Yacht Club, 418 W. Ridge St.
The Adventure Center, 1175 W. Washington St.
Menominee: Nautical Chart Service, 3213-Tenth Street
Midland: Sailing Unlimited, 705 Townsend
Monroe: Harbor Marine, 13950 Bridge Dr.
Trout's Yacht Basin, 7970 Harbor Rd.
Montague: Skippers Landing, 4464 Dowling St.
Mt. Clemens: Anchor Yacht Sales, Inc., 39763 Jefferson Ave.
Boston Yacht Sail Co., 38807 Harper
D. B. Snider, Inc., 41001 Production Dr.
Gasow Marine, Inc., 32825 S. River Rd.
Romick's Boats, 32081 N. River Rd.
Ruddy's Landing, 32489 S. River Rd.
Tom's Marine Hardware, Inc., 30060 S. River Rd.
Wolf's Marine Sales, 24424 Crocker Boulevard
Zimmer's Boats, 32895 S. River Rd.
Munising: Forest Glen Marina, Inc.
Muskegon: G. Torresen Marine, 3181 Edgewater St.
Seaway Sports Center, Inc., 3126 Lakeshore Dr.
Naubinway: Naubinway Boat & Motor Co., US #2
New Baltimore: Michigan Marine Sport Center, 38572 M29
Schmid Marina, Inc., 50725 Taylor St.
New Buffalo: Oselka's Snug Harbor Marina, 514 W. Water St.
Newport: Bellino's Marine, 4088 Brest Rd.
Northport: Northport Bay Boat Yard, Inc., North Shore Road
Nunico: Bar's Marina, 15078-120th Ave.
Ogden: The Windjammer, Inc., U.S. 31
Pentwater: Snug Harbor Marine Center, Inc., 616 S. Hancock St.
Petoskey: Volume 1, 307 Howard St.
Port Austin: Eagles Marina, 119 E. Spring St.
Port Huron: Black River Marina, Inc., 1253 Water St.
City of Port Huron, 619 River St.
Ed's Shell Dock, 315 Water St.
Hardy Marine Sales, 3620 Military St.
Steven's Marina, Inc., 207 Water St.
Port Sanilac: Sanilac Marina, 7365 Cedar Street
Roseville: Macomb Dive Shop, 29950 Little Mack
St. Clair Shores: Jefferson Beach Marina, Inc., 24400 E. Jefferson Ave.
Michigan Owens, Inc., 24530 Jefferson Ave.
Shore's Marine, Inc., 24910 Jefferson Ave.
St. Clair Marine, 25835 E. Jefferson
Wholesale Charts, 33904 E. Jefferson
St. James: Beaver Haven, Beaver Island
Saugatuck: The Nautical Shop, 322 Water St.
Sault Ste. Marie: Dept. of the Army, Detroit District, Corps of Engineers, Soo Area Office
Lookout Point Resort, Sugar Island
South Haven: Black River Boat Shop, 280 Dyckman Ave.
South Haven Terminal Co., 234 Black River St.
Spring Lake: Barrett Boats, 821 W. Savidge
Traverse City: Murray's Boats & Motors, Inc., 507 E. Front St.
Northwestern Michigan College-Student, Center Bookstore
Trenton: Hicarts Bait Tackle & Things, 2751 Riverside Dr.
Wyandotte: Hidden Boat Harbor, Inc., 693 Biddle Ave.
The Chandlery, 940 Biddle Ave.

MINNESOTA—

Duluth: A & E Supply Co., 210 W. Michigan St.
Drill's Marina, Inc., Spring St. at Waterfront
E A R Marine Enterprise, 600 Board of Trade Building
Lakehead Boat Basin, 1000 Minn. Ave.
Ely: Waters, Inc., 111 E. Sheridan St.
Wilderness Outfitters, Inc., 1 East Camp Street
Grant Marais: Beaver House, Wisconsin & Broadway

International Falls: Sportsmen's Service, 424-3rd Ave.
Minneapolis: Who Cares, Inc., 7331 Wayzata Blvd.
Orr: Minnesota Voyageur Houseboats, Ash River Trail
Rainer: Bohman Airways, Inc., Island View Route
Silver Bay: Voyageurs Marina, 23 Floyd Circle
Wayzata: Reed's Quiet World, 15906 Wayzata Blvd.
Quiet World Sports Corporation, 15906 Wayzata Blvd.

MISSISSIPPI—

Bay St. Louis: Breath's Boats & Motors, Inc., Highway 90
Biloxi: Broadwater Beach Marina
Bel-Bru Marine Mart, 621 East Howard Avenue
Pitalo Hardware & Boat Supply, 200 Cedar Street
Gulfport:Jim True & Huntoon, Inc., 3220 Hewes Avenue
Mississippi Coast Marine, Inc., East Pier Drive
Mississippi Marine, Small Craft Harbor
Handsboro: Kremer Motor Company, 1408 Cowan Road
Pascagoula: Lewis Sporting Goods Co., 2817 Front Street

NEW HAMPSHIRE—

Newington: Great Bay Marine, Inc., Fox Point Road
Portsmouth: Taylor Marine and Boat Supply Co., 159 Deer St.

NEVADA—

Boulder City: Lake Mead Marina, Lakeshore Road on Lake Mead
Natl. Park Service Hqtrs., 601 Nevada Hwy.
Callville Bay: Callville Bay Ranger Station
Cottonwood Cove: Cottonwood Cove Ranger Station
Echo Bay: Echo Bay Ranger Station
Henderson: Las Vegas Boat Harbor, Lake Mead at Vegas Wash
Lake Mead: Boulder Beach Visitor Center
L. M. Enterprises, Callville Bay Marina
Las Vegas: Mercury Blueprint & Supply Co., 1600 S. Commerce St.
Las Vegas Bay: Las Vegas Bay Ranger Station

NEW JERSEY—

Atlantic City: Jack Blades Tackle Shop, 1331 Brigantine Blvd.
†Marine Mart, Inc., Melrose & Mass Avenues
Atlantic Highlands: Flagship Marine, Municipal Marine Basin
The Skipper's Shop, 46 First Avenue
Avon: H. Pollak & Sons, Inc., 526 Main St.
Barnegat Light: Andy's At-the-Light, Broadway at Bay
Beach Haven: Shelter Harbor Marina, 317-11th St.
Koseff's, Inc., Third and Bay Avenue
Beachwood: Barnegat Bay Sailing Center, 523 Atlantic City Blvd.
Belmar: Midlantic Yacht Sales, Belmare Marine Basin
Bridgeton: Husteds Landing
Brielle: Brielle Marine Basin, Inc., 608 Green Avenue
The Yachtman's Store, 410 Higgins Ave.
Brigantine: The Boat Shop, 3218 Brigantine Boulevard
Camden: †M & E Supply Co., Rt. 130 at Collingswood Overpass
Cape May: Cape Island Marina, West Basin, Rt. 9 & Cape Island Creek
Cape Island Marina, E. Basin, Ocean Drive and Harbor
Cherry Hill: Fletcher Marine, Rt. 70 and Greentree Rd.
Dorchester: Dorchester Industries, Inc., Shipyard Div., Front St.
Eatontown: Van Winkle Marine, 115 Highway 35
Edgewater: Richmond Chris Craft Sales, Inc., 989 River Road
Egg Harbor City: General Marine Supply, Inc., 339 Boston Avenue
Forked River: Ted French Marine Supplies, Main Street
Fort Lee: †Wilson's Marineland, Inc., 2295 Route #4
Kendall Park: Franklin Park Marine Supply, Inc., 3610 Hwy. 27
Koseff's Inc., 3rd and Bay Avenue
Manahawkin: Ed Tonnesen (Tony's) Bait & Tackle, 1347 E. Bay Avenue
Mantoloking: Winter Yacht Basin, Inc., Hwy. 528 at Mantoloking Bridge
Maple Shade: Shannon Outboard Motor Sales, Inc., Rt. 73
Metuchen: Prospect Marine, Inc., Hwy. #27 & Prospect St.
Normandy Beach: Book Wharf, 549 Rte. 35 N.
Ocean City: Boyer's Marina, 242 Bay Avenue
Old Bridge: The Crow's Nest, Fairway Plaza Shopping Center Rt. 9
Pennsville: Riverview Marina, Foot of Ferry Road
Perth Amboy: Levins Sporting Goods Co., 192 Smith Street
Point Pleasant: Johnson Bros. Boat Works, Foot of Bay Ave.
Point Pleasant Beach: †Point Pleasant Hardware Co., 528 Arnold Avenue
†The Ship Chandlers, Inc., 601 Bay Avenue
Port Republic: Chestnut Neck Boat Yard Co., Rt. 9 off Garden State Parkway-Exit #48
Rahway: B & D Motorcycles, Route U.S. 1 & Scott Avenue
Red Bank: †*Jersey Marine Co., Inc., 24 Wharf Avenue
Ridgefield: International Map Company, 595 Broad Avenue
Riverside: Dredge Harbor Yacht Basin, St. Mihiel Drive
P. Evanson Boat Co., Inc., Reserve Avenue
Riverside Marina, Inc., Norman Avenue
Rutherford: Paul's Hobby Sport Marine Center, 540 Patterson Avenue
Sea Bright: Nauvoo Marina, Inc., 1410 Ocean Avenue
Boat House, 1132 Ocean Avenue, Sea Bright
Sea Isle City: Edward H. Dever & Sons, Inc., 44th & Venicean Road
The Anchorage, 319-44th Street
Seaside Heights: Time Out, Inc., Rt. 37 East
Ship Bottom: Long Beach Marine, 236 W. 8th Street
Silverton: Mathews & Stevens, T/A Sportsmans Trading Post, 1830 Hooper Avenue
Somers Point: Somers Point Yacht Harbor Inc., 520 Bay Avenue
South Amboy: Vinces Marine Supplies, 117 South Pine Avenue
South Toms River: L.J.'s Marine Paint & Supply Co., 324 Atlantic City Blvd., Rt. 166
Stone Harbor: Kennedy's Sport Store, 320-96th Street
Stone Harbor Marina, Inc., Inland Waterway at Stone Harbor Boulevard
Toms River: Silver Bay Marine, Inc., 1235 Fischer Blvd.

Trenton: B & K Motors, Inc.; 1641 North Olden Avenue
Union: Dan-Jeff Corp., Sportsman's Trading Posts of America, 2268 Route 22
Wildwood: Bradshaw's Marine Supplies, 401 W. Rio Grande Ave.

NEW YORK—

Alexandria Bay: Bonnie Castle Yacht Basin
Hutchinson's Boat Works, Inc., Holland St.
O'Brien's Boats, 51 Walton St.
Rogers Texaco Marina, 14 Bethune St.
Van's Motor Marine, 5 Sisson St.
Amityville: Sportackular Corp., 183 Merrick Road
Aquebogue: C & L Marina, Inc., Lighthouse Marina, Meetinghouse Creek Road
Babylon, L.I.: Babylon Yacht Marina, Inc., 415 Fire Island Avenue
Baldwinsville: Cooper's Marina, Inc., W. Genesee St.
Bay Shore, L.I.: Bay Shore Marine Basin, Inc., 121 Maple Avenue
Brewster's Shipyard, Inc., 87 Ocean Avenue
Bayside: Capt. Cutter's Discount Harbor, 220-34 Northern Blvd.
Bayville: Geraghty's Marine, Inc., 14 Bayville Avenue
Bellmore: Island Marine Base, Inc., 2832 Merrick Road
Binghamton: Dick's Clothing & Sporting Goods, Inc., 345 Court St.
Gagne Associates, Inc., 1080 Chenango Street
Brewerton: Del Bliss Boat Shop, Inc.
Ess-Kay Yards, Inc., Young Rd.
Trade-A-Yacht, Inc., Big Bay Road
Bronx: Bronx Johnson Motors, 3395 E. Tremont Avenue
City Island Surf 'n Sail, 278 City Island Ave.
Tivoli Radio & Marine Co., Inc., 414 City Island Ave.
Brooklyn: Bernie's Fishing Tackle, 3128 Emmons Avenue
H.P. Brown, Inc., 5300 Kings Plaza
Stella Maris Fishing Station, 2702 Emmons Ave.
Buffalo: George W. Collins, Inc., 1700 Niagara St.
SEL Yacht International, Inc., 1570 South Park Avenue
Tamco Marine-Jafco Marina, 2192 Niagara St.
U.S. Army Corps of Engineers, 1776 Niagara St.
Cape Vincent: Cape Vincent Marina, Inc., Point St.
Marine Craft Services, Inc., Anchor Marina, 400 Broadway
Marlow's Variety Store, 562 Broadway
Tallett Rod Co., 500 Broadway
Catskill: Hop-O-Nose, Marina, Inc., West Main Street
Centereach: The Suffolk Boat Locker, Inc., 2384 Middle Country Rd.
Chaumont: Crescent Marine, Washington St.
City Island: J. J. Burck, 526 City Island Avenue
Clayton: Calumet Island Marina, Corner James & Jane St.
Fishermen's Pier, 654 Riverside Drive
Kennedy Pharmacy, 203 James St.
Reinman News Stand, 439 Riverside Dr.
Tri-Pow, Inc., DBA/Clayton Marina, Rte. 12
Cleveland: Stoney Shores Marine, Inc., ST RT 49, at Jewell, N.Y.
Coeymans: Gerry Finke's Marine Corp., Westerlo Street
Cold Spring: Salmagundi House, Inc., Bookworks, 66 Main Street
Connelly: Republic Marine, Inc., First & Center Street
Copiague, L.I.: Boatland, Inc., 720 Merrick Road
Sportsman's Trading Posts of America Copiague, Inc., 720 Merrick Road
Croton-on-Hudson: Croton Food Center, 163 Grand St.
East Hampton: Three Mile Harbor Boat Yard, Three Mile Harbor Rd.
East Islip: Starfish Marine Co., 369 E. Main Street
East Moriches: Hi-Way Marina & Fishing Station, Inc., Foot of Atlantic Avenue
East Northport: North Shore Outdoor Recreation Center, 58 Larfield Rd.
East Patchogue: Dockside 500 Marina, Inc., 90 Colonial Dr.
Essex: The Shop on the Shore, on Lake Champlain
Fair Haven: Hadcock Motors, Inc., Main St.
Far Rockaway: Eddie's Marine Service Corp., Beach 2nd Street
Fishers Island: Pirate's Cover Marine, Inc.
Fisher's Landing: Bill & Jack's Marina
H. Chalk & Son, Inc.
Flushing, L.I.: Marinas of the Future, Inc., World's Fair Marina, Northern Boulevard
Svend Kent, 161-24 Northern Blvd.
Freeport, L.I.: Chatfield Marine, Foot of Gordon Place
†Freeport Marine Supply Co., 47 W. Merrick Road
Geneva: Seneca Marine Mart, Inc.
Glen Cove, L.I.: Glen Cove Marina, Inc., 76 Shore Road
Greenport, L.I.: Mitchell's Marina, 115 Front Street
S. T. Preston & Son, 102 Main Street
Hammond: Schermerhorn Boat Sales, Inc., RFD 2
Hampton Bays: Corrigan's Yacht Yard & Marine Sales, Inc., Newtown Rd.
Hobby Land Marine, Inc., 262 Montauk Hwy.
Henderson: Harbor Marina, R.D. #1
Hicksville: Sportsman's Trading Post of America-Hicksville, 13 West Marie Street
Howard Beach: Noehren's Fishing Station, Inc., 163-31 Crossbay Blvd.
Huntington, L.I.: Knutson Marine Center, Inc., Mill Dam Road
The Ship Shop, Inc., 294 New York Avenue
Island Park: Shane's Marine & Hardware Corp., 4365 Austin Blvd.
Islip: Coastal Yachting Center, 214 Main Street
Islip Marine Center, Inc., 259 Main Street
Ithaca: Inlet Park Marine, Inc., 435 Taughannock Blvd.
McPherson Sailing Products, Inc., 1001 W. Seneca St.
Pierce Cleveland, Inc., DBA/Johnson Boat Yard & Marina, 708 Willow Ave.
Kent: McMurray's Marine
Lansing: Finger Lakes Marine Service, Inc., 44 Marina Road
Larchmont: Ship's Store, 2031 Boston Post Road
Lindenhurst: Charlie's Bait & Tackle, 175 E. Montauk Hwy.
The Anchorage, Lindenhurst Channel Marina, Inc., 401 East Shore Road
Triton Yacht Sales, Inc., 189 W. Montauk Hwy.
Liverpool: A. C. Lamb & Sons, Vine St. Rd.
Long Island: Moorings at North Fork Shipyard, New Suffolk
Mamaroneck: †R.G. Brewer, Inc., 161 E. Boston Post Road
Manhasset, L.I.: Alwis Corp., 1215 Northern Blvd.
Maspath: Ripley Marine Supplies, 66-45 Grand Avenue
Massena: Westcott's Stationery Store, 61 Main St.
Mattituck: Phillips Dept. Store, Parking Square
Village Marine of Mattituck, Bay Avenue
Mechanicville: Riverside Marina, R.F.D. #2, Box 412

Merrick: Nick's Marina, Bayberry Avenue
Montauk: Montauk Marine Basin, Inc., West Lake Drive
Morristown: Wright's Sporting Goods & Marine, Inc., 511 Main St.
Nanuet: Durland Boat Company, 44 West Route 59
Newburgh: Hanaford's, 174 Rt. 9W South
New Rochelle: Defender Industries, Inc., 255 Main Street
J. J. McGuire's Sail & Trail, Inc., 7 Huguenot St.
New York: American Map Co., Inc., 1926 Broadway
Commodore Uniform Co., Inc., 396 Broadway
Goldberg's Marine Distributor's, Inc., 3 West 46th St.
†*Hammond Map Store, 10 East 41st Street
Manhattan Marine & Electric Co., Inc., 116 Chambers Street
*M. Low, Inc., 110 Hudson Street
†*New York Nautical Instrument & Service Corp., 140 W. Broadway
Rand McNally & Company, 10 East 53 St.
†*South Street Seaport Museum Book Store, 25 Fulton Street
Sportsman's Map Co., Ltd., 127 East 59th St.
†The Crow's Nest, 45th & Madison Street
Unz & Company, 24 Beaver Street
North Troy: Trojan Marine, 391-2nd Avenue
Northport: Northport Marine Center, Inc., Route 25A
Seawind Sail, Inc., 325 Route 25A
North Tonawanda: Hi-Skipper Marine of Buffalo, Inc., 377 Sweeney St.
Oakdale: Oakdale Yacht Service, Inc., Shore Drive
Oakdale Trading Post, 1384 Montauk Highway
Oceanside, L.I.: The mooring, 3280 Brower Avenue
Ossining: Westerly Marina, Inc., Westerly Road
Oswego: Oswego Marina, Inc., East First Street
Oyster Bay: Nobman's, Clock Tower Bldg., Corner of South & East Main
Patchogue: Patchogue Marine, 161 River Avenue
The Bargain Bilge, Div. of Patchogue Plating Works, 159 W. Main St.
Peekskill: J.W. Moretti, Crompond Road
Plattsburgh: Book House, Plattsburgh Plaza
Clinton Aero Corp., Clinton County Airport
Day Brothers, Inc., RFD 3
Dock & Coal Co., Inc., 1 Dock St.
Janco's Marine Center, Lake Shore Rd.
Point Lookout, L.I.: Pt. Lookout Hardware & Marine Co., 26 Lido Blvd.
Port Jefferson: Port Jefferson Marine Inc., 125 W. Broadway
True North Sail Shop, Inc., 27 East Broadway
Port Washington: †A.&R. Marshall Sales, Ltd., 403 Main Street
Riverhead: Edwards Discount Center, East Main St., & Route 58
Rochester: Anchor Marine of Rochester, Inc., 560 River St.
Inland Marine, Inc., 185 Norris Drive
Riverview Yacht Basin, DBA/Genesee Marina, Inc., 18 Petten St. Ext.
Seiler Marine Service, 344 Eaton Rd.
Shumway Marine, 70 Pattonwood Dr.
The Yacht Center, 5395 St. Paul Blvd.
Rockville Centre: Sportsman's Trading Posts, South Shore, Inc., 243 Merrick Road
Rocky Point, L.I.: Milne's Outboard Center, Route 25A
Rouses Point: Barcomb's Marina, 42 Montgomery St.
Sackets Harbor: Navy Point Corporation Marina
Sag Harbor: Peerless Marine Center, Inc., Bay Street
Springer & LoMonaco, Inc., d/b/a Mill Creek Marina, 313 Noyac Road
The Emporium Hardware, Inc., Main Street
Sayville: Lands End Apts. & Marina, 70 Browns River Road
Seaford, L.I.: Seaford Marine Corp., 3748 Merrick Road
Selden: Thrift Mart Marine, 456 Middle Country Road
Shelter Island: Coecles Harbor Marina & Boatyard, Inc., Hudson Avenue
Smithtown: Jericho Boats of Smithtown, Inc., 865 W. Jericho Turnpike
Sodus Point: Anchor Yacht Brokerage & Sales, Clover St.
Southold, L.I.: Ulrich Marine, Main Road
Staatsburg: Norrie Yacht Basin, Inc.
Staten Island: Great Kills Board Yard & Marina, Inc., 183 Mansion Ave.
Fred's Tackle Shop, 6276 Amboy Rd., Pleasant Point
Mijoa, Inc., All Points Adventure Center, 7423 Amboy Rd.
Syracuse: Economy Book & Stationery Store, Inc., 317 S. Salina St.
Harbors End, Inc.
Tarrytown: Sleepy Hollow Marine, Inc., c/o Tarrytown Marina, Inc., Ft. White Street
Union Springs: Hibiscus Harbor, Inc., Harbor Dr.
Upper Nyack: Julius Petersen, Inc., 1 Van Houten Street
Waterloo: Iroquois Marina, Inc., RD 1, West River Rd.
Watertown: Robinson's Book Store, Inc., 138 Court St.
West Hempstead: State Channel Marina, Inc., 284 Grand Avenue
West Monroe: Del Bliss Boat Shop, Inc., Rte. 49
Westville: Marine Equipment & Supply Co., Rt. 47 Harvard Ave.
Whitehall: Lock 12 Marina, 84 No. Williams St.
White Plains: The Book and Card Center, 215 E. Post Road
Willsboro: Willsboro Bay Campsite-Marina, Inc., 283A Willsboro Point Road
Yonkers: Intercounty Builders Supply Co., Inc., Marine Supply Division, 711 Saw Mill River Rd.
Youngstown: Pierce Marine Corp., 555 Water St.
Youngstown Boat Co., Inc., Water St.

NORTH CAROLINA—

Atlantic Beach: Anchorage Marina, Inc., Fort Macon Road
Crows Nest Marina, P.O. Box 95
Beaufort: Chadwick Brothers Service Station, Route 2
Belhaven: River Forest Manor, 600 Main St.
Buxton: Eastern National Park & Monument Association, Cape Hatteras National Seashore
Charleston: Houseboat Association of America, 4251 Spruill Avenue
Charlotte: Cap'n Ed's Boathouse, Inc., 6432 E. Independence Blvd.
Clinton: O-Boy-Wil Marine Sales, Inc., 824 Southeast Blvd.
Coinjock: Coinjock Esso Marine, Inc., Canal Rd.
Columbia: Prichett's Marina, U.S. 64 East
Durham: London Marina, Inc., 4125 Chapel Hill Boulevard
Show Boat's Marine Sales & Service, 1300 S. Miami Boulevard
Elizabeth City: Elizabeth City Yacht Yard & Marina, Inc., 722 Riverside Ave.
Fayetteville: A. K. McCallum Co., 715 Ramsey Street
Greenville: Greenville Marine & Sport Center, Inc., RFD #5
Grimesland: Gaskins Marina, Hwy. 17, South

Harkers Island: Cape Lookout Marina, Shell Point
Hatteras: Teach's Lair Marina, Inc., Rt. 12
Hatteras Village: Hatteras Marine & Trading Co., d/b/a Fishin' Stuff
Tackle Shop, State Rt. #12 at Hatteras Marina
Hobucken: Gladys I. Sadler Store
Jacksonville: Carolina Office Supply Co., 624 New Bridge St.
Kinston: Neuse Sport Shop, 225 New Bern Road
Kure Beach: New Hanover Resources Center
Manteo: Dare Marine Resources Center, Airport Road
Times Printing Co., Inc., 501 Budleigh St.
Morehead City: Carteret Marine Resources Center, Route #1
Cheek's Hardware & Antiques, Eighth & Arendell Str.
†Dee Gee's Gift Shop, 509 Evans Street
E.J.W. Bicycle & Sport Shop, 2204 Arendell Street
70 West Marina, Highway 70 West
Spooners Creek Yacht Harbor, Inc., Rt. 1
Nags Head: Nags Head Ice & Cold Storage, Highway 158
New Bern: Barbour Boat Works, Inc., 535 Tryon Palace Dr.
Trent Marine Service, Highway 70 East
Ocracoke: Harborside Motel & Gift Shop, N. Side of Ocracoke Harbor Near Coast Guard Station
Vista Associates, Ltd., Whittaker Creek
Oriental: Sailcraft Engineering, Tosto Circle-Oriental
Raleigh: Raleigh Blue Printers, 126 W. Martin Street
Southport: K & M Marine Sales & Service, Inc., Southport Boat Harbor
Swan Quarter: Oyster Creek Marina, Oyster Creek, Swan Quarter Bay
Swan Quarter Crab Company
Wanchese: Wanchese Marina
Washington: Pamlico Marine Co., 223 E. Water Street
J. D. McCotter, Inc., Rt. 2, Broad Creek
Whichard's Marina, Whichard's Beach Road
Wilmington: Bradley Creek "66" Marina, Inc., 6338 Oleaner Drive
Carolina Chandlers Corp., Carolina Beach Road
Cape Fear Chandlers, 1224 South 2nd Street
†O. E. Durant, Inc., 520 N. 3rd Street
Wilson: W. W. Furniture & Appliance Co., 230 S. Tarboro St.
Wrightsville Beach: Seapath Marina, Inc., The Causeway
Wrightsville Marina

OHIO—

Ashtabula: Anchor Point Boat Sales, 5401 N. Marginal Dr.
Jack's Automarine, 610 E. 6th St.
Sutherland Marine Co., 970 W. 5th St.
The Whale's Tale, Inc., 13214 Shaker Sq.
Canton: The Sail Place, Inc., 1506 Cleveland Avenue, N.W.
Chagrin Falls: Zucker Marine, Inc., 860 Washington St.
Cincinnati: Sailboat Sales Inc., 8540 E. Kemper Rd.
Cleveland: Anchor Point Boat Sales, 5401 N. Marginal Dr.
Cleveland Yacht & Supply Co., 3027 Detroit Avenue
The Whale's Tale, Inc., 13214 Shaker Square
Thomas Sailmakers, 19106 Detroit Road
Fremont: Happy Days Boating Co., E. State St.
Huron: Art Hayes Marina, 4319 E. Cleveland Rd.
Holiday Harbor Marina, Inc., South Main St.
Huron Lagoons Marina, Inc., End of Laguna Dr.
The Boat Harbor Co., 400 Huron St.
Lakeside: Channel Grove Marina, 389 Channel Grove Rd.
Lakevue Marina, Inc., 8549 N. Shore Dr.
The Gravel Bar Yacht Harbor, Inc., d/b/a Bar Harbor Marina, 8100 E. Gravel Bar Blvd.
Lakewood: Chuck Marine Supply, Inc., 18123 Sloane Avenue
Lorain: Lorain Marine Sales, 353 Broadway
Marblehead: Bass Haven, 6657 E. Harbor Rd.
Limpert's Marina, 424 Miley Drive
Marine City, 7401 E. Harbor Rd.
Oak Harbor: Northland Sporting Supplies, Inc., 715 N. Locust Street
Oregon: Sherman Marine, Inc., 6601 Corduroy Rd.
Peninsula: Hubbard Marine, 4575 Akron-Cleveland Rd.
Port Clinton: Catawaba Island Marine, 4236 E. Moore's Dock Rd.
Catawba Midway Marina, Inc., 1871 N.E. Catawba Rd.
Clinton Reef Marine Sales, Lakeshore Dr., West
Fisherman's Wharf, 1 Madison St.
Foxhaven Marina, 2737 N.E. Catawba Rd.
Gem Boat Service, Inc., 3000 N. Carolina St.
H.J. Marina, 451 Lakeshore Dr.
Lake Erie Sports, Inc., 124 W. Second
Rickard's Bait & Tackle Store, 17 N.E. Catawba Rd.
Sugar Rock Harbor & Marina, 4325 E. Barnum Rd.
Put-In-Bay: Lake Erie Patrol, Inc.
Sandusky: Battery Park Marine, 703 E. Water St.
Bob Clemens Boats, 8009 Barrett Rd.
Cedar Point, Inc., Marina Div.
Herb's Sportsman's Supplies, Inc., 215 Neigs St.
Vacationland Marina, 2013 First St.
Toledo: Bodette Marine Supply Co., No. 1 S. Summit St.
Brenner Marine, Inc., No. 1 Main St.
Counterman Marine Service, 5903 Edgewater Dr.
Harrison Marina, Inc., 3840 Summit St.
Marineland, Inc. 6755 W. Central Avenue
Mastercraft Marine & Sports, Inc., 2800 Tremainsville Rd.
The Tackle Box, Inc., 1120 Sylvania Avenue
Vermilion: Romp's Water Port, Inc., 5055 Liberty Avenue
Ryser's Boat Livery, 636 Sandusky St.
Vickery: Bay Harbor Marina, RD #1, Bay Blvd.

OREGON—

Astoria: †Englund Marine Supply Co., Foot of 15th Street
Brookings: Lorings Lighthouse Sporting Goods, 554 Chetco Ave.
Charleston: Hanson's Landing (Off Coos Bay Bar)
Coos Bay: Independent Stevedore Co., Inc., 275 North Bayshore
Garibaldi: D & D Charters Marine Supplies and Tackle, Garibaldi Boat Basin
Newport: Oregon State University, Marine Science Center, Public Wing
Schiewe Marine Supply, 663 S.W. Bay Blvd.
North Bend: Oregon-Pacific Company, Inc., 1760 Sheridan Street
Portland: Columbia Marine Electronics, 2901 N.E. Marine Drive
82nd Marine, 2815 S.E. 82nd Avenue
*Northwest Instrument Company, 1130 N. Jantzen Avenue
†Portland Precision Instrument & Repair Company, 3508 S.E. Hawthorne
Progress Electronics Co. of Oregon, 5160 N. Lagoon Ave.

Rodgers Marine Electronics, 3445 N.E. Marine Drive
The Crow's Nest, 521 S.W. Tenth
Springfield: Emerald Stationery & Office Supply, 1401 Market St.
*Agents handle certain Defense Mapping Agency Hydrographic Center Publications.
†Agents handle U.S. Coast Guard Publications.

PENNSYLVANIA—

Doylestown: Alfred B. Patton, Inc., 29-31 East Swamp Road
Erie: English & Whipple Sailyard, Ltd., 27 W. Public Dock
Erie Marine Supply, 17 W. Public St.
R.D. McAllister & Son, Ltd., East Bay Front
The Erie Book Store, 717 French St.
Essington: Governor Printz Maring, 2nd & Wanamaker Ave.
Lancaster: Darmastaetter's Inc., 37 N. Queen Street
Malvern: Clews Boat & Auto Centre, 310 Lancaster Pike
Philadelphia: †*Mr. Victor Auguste Gustin, 105 S. 2nd St.
John Wright Boats, Inc., 328 West Queen Lane
Goldberg's Marine Dist., Inc., 202 Market Street
Elisha Webb & Son Co., 136 S. Front St.

PUERTO RICO—

Ponce: Bonnin & Co., Inc., Ferreteria Bonnin-Hostos esq. Campeche
San Juan:
Fred Imbert, Inc., Pier 13, Stop 6, Fernandez Juncos Ave.
Nauticenter, Inc., 50 Covadonga Avenue
Padro-Campos Marine Hardware, 250 Ponce de Leon Avenue, Puerta de Tierra
Santurce: Nautirama, Inc., McLeary 1966
Miramar Marine Inc., #619 Fernandez Juncos Ave. Stop 10, Miramar

RHODE ISLAND—

Barrington: Cove Haven Corp., 101 Narragansett Avenue
†Ships Store, 32 Barton Avenue
Stanley's Boat Yard, 25 Barton Avenue
Block Island: Block Island Marina, Inc., Job's Hill, New Harbor
Esta's Copper Handcraft, Water Street
Payne's New Harbor Dock, New Harbor Dock
Bristol: Hawkins & Fales, Inc., 11 Hope St.
East Greenwich: Yacht Hardware, Inc., 247 Main Street
Edgewood: Port Edgewood, Inc., 1128 Narragansett Blvd.
Galilee: N. P. Marine Supply, Sand Hill Cove Road
Newport: J. T. O'Connell, Inc., 364 Thames Street
J. T. O'Connell, Inc., 89 Long Wharf
The Chandlery, Inc., 18 Bowen's Wharf
Goat Island Marinaa, Inc., Goat Island
North Kingstown: Wickford Cove Marina, Inc., Comer Reynolds & Cove
Providence: Champlin's Marina, Inc., 60 Pine Street
Goff & Page Co., 54 Custom House Street
Marine Sporting Center, 1076 North Main Street
R.I. Divers Supply, 209 Elmwood Avenue
Tiverton: Standish Boat Yard, Inc., 1697 Main Road
Wakefield: Ram Point Marina, Inc., Salt Pond Road
Salt Pond Marine Railway, 406 Sherman Road
Snug Harbor Marina, Gooseberry Road
Stone Cove Marina, Inc., Salt Pond Road
Warwick: Dickerson Bros.-Apponaug Harbor, 17-21 Arnold's Neck Dr.
Norton's Ship Yard & Marina, Ft. of Division St.
Watch Hill: Frank Hall Boat Yard, Inc., Bay St.
Westerly: Frank Hall Boat Yard, Inc., Avondale
Lotteryville Marina, 25 Avondale Rd.
Wickford: *Wickford Shipyard, 125 Steamboat Avenue

SOUTH CAROLINA—

Beaufort: Beaufort Book Shop, 808 Bay Street
Beaufort Marina, Inc., Star Route 1
Bucksport Boat Sales, Inc., Bucksport Marina
Charleston: †Coleman Supply Co., Inc., 211 East Bay Street
†*Heyward Supply Co., 212 Huger Street
Hi Way Marine, Inc., 47 Folly Road
J. J. W. Luden & Co., Concord at Charlotte Sts.
John Huguley Co., Inc., 263 King Street
The Marine Supply Store, Rice Mill Building, Charleston Municipal Marina
Charleston Heights: Marine Center, 4711 Rivers Avenue
Georgetown: Belle Isle Marina, Belle Isle Gardens
Exxon Marina, 18 St. James Street
Nautical Marine Center, 615 Front Street
Hilton Head Island: Harbour Town Marina Store, Harbour Town
Palmetto Bay Marina, Palmetto Bay Road
South Beach Marina, Sea Pines Plantation
The Hilton Head Harbor, Jenkins Island
Murrell's Inlet: Capt. Dick's Marina, Waterfront
Wacca Wache Marina, Wachesaw Landing
Myrtle Beach: Hague Marina, Inc., Pine Island Road at Intracoastal Waterway
N. Myrtle Beach: North Myrtle Beach Esso Marina, Inland Waterway & Coquina Dr., Cherry Grove
Walterboro: Low Country Marina, Inc., Rt. 1

TEXAS—

Aransas Pass: Aransas Shrimp Cooperative, 405 Bigelow, Conn Brown Harbor
Garrett's Marine Service, 269 South Bay
Baytown: Carroll's Bay Grocery, 9436 Tri-City Beach Road
Corpus Christi: Boat Shop, 1321 N. Water Street
*Figurehead General Store 309 Shoreline Dr.
Gunderland Marine Supply, Inc., 1221 Cantwell Lane
Dallas: Jack Sails, Inc., 5838 Live Oak
Freeport: Girouards, 626 West Second Street
Galveston: *R. H. John Chart Agency, 515-21st Street
Houston: *Baker, Lyman & Co., Inc., Cotton Exchange Building
*Figurehead General Store, 1401 Travis Street
*Navigation Associates, Inc., World Trade Bldg., 1520 Texas Avenue, Room 1-D
Power-Tran of America, Boatbuilding & Marine Supply Div. 9320 E. Avenue S.
Ship Shops, 6104 Windswept
League City: The Spinnaker Shop, 1500 FM 2094, Watergate Yachting Cntr.
Port Aransas: South Jetty Publishing Co., 103 N. Alister St.
Port Arthur: †Nielsen's Stationery & Gift Shop, 532-5th Avenue
Port O'Connor: Port O'Connor Fishing Center, 14th and Water St.

Rockport: Key Allegro Isle Marina, Inc., Key Allegro Isle
Marineland of Rockport, Inc., Hwy 35 North
San Antonio: Neptune Publications, Inc., 106 Broadway, Rm. 337
Seabrook: Gulf States Yachts, 3005 Nasa Road 1
Yach Equipment Specialties, 1105 Bayport Boulevard
Texas City: Boyd's One Stop, 227 Dike Rd.

VERMONT—

Burlington: Chiott's, Inc., 87 King St.
Everyman Sailboat Co., 26 Balsam St.
Halsted-Porter Co., Inc.
McAuliffe, Inc., McAuliffe Office Products Center, Burlington Square North
North Hero: North Hero Marine, Inc., Tudhope Marine Co., U.S. Route #2
Orwell: Buoy 39 Marina on Lake Champlain
Chipman Point Marina, Chipman Point
Shelburne: Garfield Langworthy Sail Charter, R.R. #1 Bay Rd.
Shelburne Shipyard, Harbor Road
Vergennes: LeVoyageur Marina, R.F.D. #3

VIRGINIA—

Alexandria: Backyard Boats, Inc., 100 Franklin Street
Burt Marine Center, Inc., 6231 Richmond Highway
John R. McLane & Co., 605 Franklin St.
Annandale: Annandale Marine & Sports Center, Inc., 4313 Markham St.
Arlington: William J. Little, Inc., 4032 So. 28th Street
Cape Charles: Kings Creek Marina, State Highway 1105
Watsons Hardware Co., 225 Mason Ave.
Chincóteague: Marine Railway, Inc., 434 Rear South Main St.
Colonial Beach: Colonial Yacht Club, 1787 Castlewood Drive
Deltaville: Deltaville Marina, Inc., on Jackson's Creek
The Harbour Loft
Fairfax: Nine Associates, Inc., 10680 Main Street
Northern Virginia Marine Sales, Inc., 8304 Merrifield Avenue
Fredericksburg: Pipeline Diving Company, 915 Lafayette Boulevard
Glen Allen: Brown Marine Sales, 8501 Washington Highway
Gloucester: The Ship's Chandler, Gloucester Court House
Gloucester Point: Seaboard Business Systems, Inc., Edgehill Shopping Center
York River Yacht Haven, Inc.
Grimstead: Davidson Marine Services
Hampton: Bluewater Yacht Sales, Inc., 529 Bridge St.
Hampton Roads Marina Corp., Marina Road
Irvington: Irvington Marina, Inc.
Kilmarnock: †Chesapeake Boat Basin, End of Waverly Ave.
Kinsale: Kinsale Marina
Lanexa: Chickahominy Haven Marina, Route 1
Lilian: Jett's Marine & Hardware, Rt. 360 East
Manassas: Manassas Marine, Inc., 7565 Gary Road
McLean: Marine Services, 1313 Forestwood Drive
Newport News: *E. Smala Co., Inc., 4514 Warwick Blvd. at 46th Street
Sports Inc., 775 J. Clyde Morris Blvd.
Norfolk: Cobb's Marina, 4524 Dunning Rd.
†*Henry Eagleton, 430 Boush Street
†M. Lee Hudgins & Son, 511 Front Street
Shore Drive Marina, 8180 Shore Drive
The Batten Pocket, 217D East Little Creek Road
†*W. T. Brownley, 118 West Plume Street
Willoughby Bay Marina, 1651 Bayville Street
Oak Hall: Highway Service, Inc., Route #13
Occoquan: Lynn's Store, Inc., 313 Mill St.
Prince William Marine Sales, Inc., 207 Mill Street
Onley: Shipmate, Road 785, 2½ Miles from Onley
Perrin: Buoy 22 Marina, Perrin River
Portsmouth: Holiday Harbor Marina, 10 Crawford Parkway
Reedville: Smith Point Marina, Route 1
Richmond: Pinnell's, Inc., 701 West Broad Street
Richmond Marine & Boat Co., Inc., 2906 Williamsburg Road
Tidewater Yacht Agency, Inc., 5016 Williamsburg Rd.
Trail 'N' Sail, 7401 Brook Road
Virginia Reproduction & Supply Co., Inc., 5 West Cary St.
Springfield: Boat Owners Association of the U.S., 5261 Port Royal Rd.
Harbin Marine Center, Inc., 8494 Terminal Road
Stafford: Virginia Marine, Inc., Rt. 1
Tabb: Peninsula Sailing Center, Inc., 1279 Route 17
Tappahannock: Rappahannock Products, Inc., 852 Church Lane
Urbanna: Urbanna Boat & Motor Sales, Foot of Waling Street
Vienna: Hapco Marine Inc., 134 West Maple St.
Virginia Beach: Trafton Marine Ltd., 3716 Shore Drive
Viking Marine, 3762 Shore Drive
Wachapreague: West Wind Corp., Wachapreague Marina, Main St.
Warsaw: Ed. Lewis Marine, Rt. 1, Hwy. 360 West
Williamsburg: Larry's Marine Sales, Inc., Rt. 1
Windmill Point: Windmill Point Marina
Woodbridge: E-Z Cruz, Inc., 15713 Jefferson Davis Highway
Occoquan Marina, Inc., 1214 Swan Point Road
Tyme N' Tyde, Inc., 14603 Featherstone Rd.
Yorktown: Wormley Creek Marina Corp., 110 Waterview Rd.

VIRGIN ISLANDS—

Christiansted: Sea Shop, Inc., 39 Strand Street
Cruz Bay, St. John: Eastern Nat'l Park & Monument Assoc.
St. Croix: St. Croix Marine & Dev. Co., Inc., Gallows Bay, Christiansted
Ship's Specialties, #2 Strand St.
St. Thomas: Antilles Yachting Services, Antilles Harbor Marina, Lagoon
Paperbook Gallery, Palm Passage
Peninsula Sailing Center, Inc., 16 House Street
Sunset Marina, Ltd. 25 Marina Road

WASHINGTON—

Anacortes: †Marine Supply & Hardware, 202 Commercial Avenue
Bryant's Marina, Cap Sante Waterway
San Juan Marine Service, 1302 Commercial Ave.
Bellingham: †Griggs, 120 East Holly Street
Eddystone Light, Inc., 2584 Harbor Loop Road
Redden Net Co., Inc., 2626 Harbor Loop
Bremerton: Buddy's Marina, Inc., 1515 Charleston Beach Road
Coulee Dam: Coulee Dam Agency, Mount Rainier Natural History Association

Des Moines: City of Des Moines Small Boat Harbor, 22307 Dock St.
Block & Tackle, 705 South 220th
Cascade Marine, 22634 6th Avenue South
Edmonds: Anderson Marine & Service, 100 Railroad Avenue — next to ferry
Everett: Everett Boat House & Marina, 1001 14th St.
The J. K. Gill Co., Ltd., Everett Store #14, 2944 Colby Ave.
Friday Harbor: †Friday Harbor Drug Co., Cor. Spring and 2nd Sts.
San Juan Marina, Inc., Spring and Front Streets
Hoquiam: Industrial & Marine Supply Co., 701 Levee Street
Ilwaco: Englund Marine Supply, Howerton & Williams Street
Kennewick: Metz Marina, Inc., Clover Island
LaConner: Otis Motor Service & Marina, First & Morris
Neah Bay: Norwest Fish Co., Bay Fish Company Dock
Oak Harbor: Chuck Dann's Sporting Goods, Inc., 1150 W. Pioneer Way
Mike's Sport Shop, 9026-900 Avenue West
Olympia: Olympia Marina, Foot of Washington St.
Lon and Pat Hogue d/b/a Chadwick's Marina, 611 North Columbia St.
Orcas Island: Darvill's Rare Print Shop, Main Street — Eastsound
Pasco: Beacon Marine, Pasco Port Dock
Port Angeles: Swain's General Store, Inc., 602 E. First Street
Straits Marine Supply, 826 Boathaven Dr.
Port Townsend: Exum Navigation-Art-Writing, 110 Taylor St.
Syd's Sports Shop, 311 Kearney Street
Point Hudson Company, At Point Hudson Harbor
Poulsbo: A to Z stationers, 121½ Main Street
Redondo: The Hatch Cover, 28212 Beach Drive South
Richland: Richland Yacht Club, Riverpoint Rd.
Columbia Park Marina, W 7500 Columbia Avenue
Seattle: †*Captain's, Salmon Bay Fishing Terminal
†*Captain's, 1324 Second Avenue
Windward Mark, 6317 Seaview Avenue, N.W.
†*Metsker Maps, 1222 Third Avenue
†*Northwest Instrument Co., 2525 W. Commodore Way
†*Carlsen & Larsen, 716-4th Avenue
Carlsen & Larsen (2), Pier 55 Seattle
Automobile Club of Washington, 330-6th Avenue, N.
Marine Center (Div. of Kaye/Smith Ent.) 2130 Westlake Ave. N.
Carlsen & Larsen, 6010 Seaview, N.W.
Tacoma: †*Metsker Maps, 111 South Tenth Street
Pacific Yacht Basin, 1009 Port of Tecoma Road
Howard's Landing, Point Defiance Park
Westport: Pacific Charters, Westhaven Drive opposite Float #12

WISCONSIN—

Ashland: Bodin's Seaway Marina, Lake Shore Drive, Hwy. 2
Baileys Harbor: Nelson Shopping Center
Bayfield: Apostle Islands Marina, 116 S. 1st St.
Eastern National & Monument Assoc., Apostle Islands National Lakeshore 1972 Centennial Dr., R.R.
Port Superior Village Marina, Rt. 1
Cornucopia: The Good Earth Shop, Inc.
Egg Harbor: Stagecoach Junction, Inc., Egg Harbor Rd.
Fond du Lac: Perry's Marine, Inc., 1706 Winnebago Drive
Green Bay: Al Zeller & Sons, 1310 S. Monroe
Quigley Marine, Inc., 830 Potts Avenue
Kaukauna: Clarkson Map Co., 724 Desnoyer St.
Kenosha: Gatti Boat Sales & Service, Inc., 443-50th St.
Madison: Petrie Sports, Inc., 1406 Emil St.
Marinette: 54143 Reimer's Marina, 300 Wells St.
Menasha: Valley Marine Mart, Inc., 100 Water St.
High Cliff Harbor, Rt. 1
Mequon: The Sailing Center, 10406 N. Cedarburg Road
Milwaukee: Harbor Marine, 700 South Water Street
Ken Olson Marine, Inc., 1971 S. First St.
Milwaukee Map Service, Inc., 4519 W. North Avenue
Reinke Brothers, 3144 W. Greenfield Avenue
Ship Repair and Supply Co., 1929 North Buffum St.
Oshkosh: Fox River Marina, Inc., 501 South Main at Bridge Pioneer Dr.
Sheboygan: Merlin Marine Inc., 517 North Commerce St.
Sister Bay: Anchor Marine, Inc.
Sherwood: High Cliff Marine, Inc.
Sturgeon Bay: Baudhuin Hacht Habor, Nautical Drive
Mac's Sport Shop, Inc., 27 S. Madison Avenue
Two Rivers: Gil's Sporting Goods, 1916 Washington St.
Suettinger Hardware, Inc., 1407 16th St.

*Agents handle certain Defense Mapping Agency Hydrographic Center Publications.
†Agents handle U.S. Coast Guard Publications.

INDEX